Lecture Notes in Artificial Intelligence 2443

Subseries of Lecture Notes in Computer Science
Edited by J. G. Carbonell and J. Siekmann

Lecture Notes in Computer Science

Edited by G. Goos, J. Hartmanis, and J. van Leeuwen

Springer
Berlin
Heidelberg
New York
Barcelona
Hong Kong
London
Milan
Paris
Tokyo

Donia Scott (Ed.)

Artificial Intelligence: Methodology, Systems, and Applications

10th International Conference, AIMSA 2002
Varna, Bulgaria, September 4-6, 2002
Proceedings

 Springer

Series Editors

Jaime G. Carbonell, Carnegie Mellon University, Pittsburgh, PA, USA
Jörg Siekmann, University of Saarland, Saarbrücken, Germany

Volume Editor

Donia Scott
University of Brighton, ITRI
Lewes Road, Brighton BN2 4GJ, UK
E-mail: donia.scott@itri.bton.ac.uk

Cataloging-in-Publication Data applied for

Die Deutsche Bibliothek - CIP-Einheitsaufnahme

Artificial intelligence: methodology, systems, and applications : 10th
international conference ; proceedings / AIMSA 2002, Varna, Bulgaria,
September 4 - 6, 2002. Donia Scott (ed.). - Berlin ; Heidelberg ; New York ;
Barcelona ; Hong Kong ; London ; Milan ; Paris ; Tokyo : Springer, 2002
  (Lecture notes in computer science ; Vol. 2443 : Lecture notes in
  artificial intelligence)
  ISBN 3-540-44127-1

CR Subject Classification (1998): I.2

ISSN 0302-9743
ISBN 3-540-44127-1 Springer-Verlag Berlin Heidelberg New York

Springer-Verlag Berlin Heidelberg New York
a member of BertelsmannSpringer Science+Business Media GmbH

http://www.springer.de

© Springer-Verlag Berlin Heidelberg 2002
Printed in Germany

Typesetting: Camera-ready by author, data conversion by PTP-Berlin, Stefan Sossna e.K.
Printed on acid-free paper   SPIN: 10871013   06/3142   5 4 3 2 1 0

Preface

The AIMSA conference series was first conceived in 1984 as a gathering of AI researchers and students from Eastern and Central Europe. Since then the conference has followed a biennial schedule of meetings in Bulgaria, attracting participants from a wider geographical area. Today, 20 years on, AIMSA is a thoroughly international conference, with contributions from most European countries and some from as far afield as the United States, Mexico and Brazil.

The AIMSA organizers are delighted to present you with another exciting program, covering most areas of Artificial Intelligence. In keeping with its mission to inform the research community and excite the commercial sector, AIMSA presents this year two invited contributions from world-leading European researchers working on cutting-edge AI research: Prof. Carole Goble, on the Semantic Web, and Prof. David House, on integrated speech and gestural synthesis. In addition, we present 26 contributions on topics covering almost all aspects of AI and bringing together basic and applied research. One of these, by Milos Kovačević and his colleagues on "Recognition of Common Areas in a Web Page Using a Visualisation Approach" was judged by reviewers to be the best submitted paper, and duly received the accolade of "Best Paper" of the Conference, with a special slot devoted to it in the program.

As Chair of the Program Committee, I am extremely grateful to those who so generously agreed to apply their expertise and valuable time to reviewing papers for the conference, and for their dedication in getting the best possible job done in what turned out to be a very short period of time.

Special thanks go to the local organizers, Danail Dochev and Gennady Agre, for their dedication and willingness to cooperate in solving problems each time it was necessary, and to Anja Wedberg and Jon Herring for their wonderful efficiency in administering the work of the Program Committee. I also gratefully acknowledge the role played by the team at Springer-Verlag in the production of these proceedings, and I thank the European Coordinating Committee for Artificial Intelligence (ECCAI), for their continued support of the conference.

September 2002   Donia Scott

Table of Contents

Multimodal Speech Synthesis: Improving Information Flow in Dialogue Systems Using 3D Talking Heads

David House and Björn Granström

Centre for Speech Technology, Department of Speech, Music and Hearing, KTH
Drottning Kristinas väg 31, 10044 Stockholm, Sweden
{davidh, bjorn}@speech.kth.se

Abstract. This paper describes activities at CTT, Centre for Speech Technology, using the potential of animated talking agents to improve information flow in dialogue systems. Our motivation for moving into audiovisual output is to investigate the advantages of multimodality in human-system communication. While the mainstream character animation area has focused on the naturalness and realism of the animated agents, our primary concern has been the possible increase of intelligibility and efficiency of interaction, resulting from the addition of a talking face.

1   Introduction

Spoken dialogue systems, which strive to take advantage of the effective communication potential of human conversation, need in some way to embody the conversational partner. A talking animated agent provides the user with an interactive partner whose goal is to take the role of the optimal human agent. This is the agent who is ready and eager to supply the user with a wealth of information, can smoothly navigate through varying and complex sources of data and can ultimately assist the user in a decision making process through the give and take of conversation. One way to achieve believability is through the use of a talking head which transforms information through text into speech, articulator movements, speech related gestures and conversational gestures.

The talking head developed at KTH is based on text-to-speech synthesis. Audio speech synthesis is generated from a text representation in synchrony with visual articulator movements of the lips, tongue and jaw. Linguistic information in the text is used to generate visual cues for relevant prosodic categories such as prominence, phrasing and emphasis. These cues generally take the form of eyebrow and head movements which we have termed "visual prosody". These types of visual cues with the addition of a smiling or frowning face are also used as conversational gestures to signal such things as positive or negative feedback, turntaking regulation, and the system's internal state. In addition, the head can visually signal attitudes and emotions.

In the context of this paper, the talking head is primarily discussed in terms of applications in spoken dialogue systems which enable the user to access information and

D. Scott (Ed.): AIMSA 2002, LNAI 2443, pp. 1-10, 2002.

reach a decision through a conversational interface. Other useful applications include aids for the hearing impaired, educational software, stimuli for audiovisual human perception experiments, entertainment, and high-quality audio-visual text-to-speech synthesis for applications such as news reading. In this paper we will focus on two aspects of effective interaction: presentation of information and the flow of interactive dialogue.

Effectiveness in the presentation of information is crucial to the success of an interactive system. Information must be presented rapidly, succinctly and with high intelligibility. The use of the talking head aims at improving the intelligibility of speech synthesis by the addition of visual articulation and also by providing a focus for the user's attention. This focus can be the agent's face or a common object of discussion. Important information is highlighted by prosodic enhancement and by the use of the agent's gaze and visual prosody.

The second issue of effective interaction focuses on facilitating the interactive nature of dialogue. In this area, the use of the talking head aims at increasing effectiveness by building on the user's social skills to improve the flow of the dialogue and engage the user interactively. Visual cues to feedback, turntaking regulation and signaling the system's internal state by visual facial gestures are key aspects of effective interaction.

This paper presents a brief overview and technical description of the KTH talking head explaining what the head can do and how. Examples of experimental applications in which the head is used are then described, and finally, the two issues of intelligibility and communication interaction are discussed and exemplified by results from applications and perceptual evaluation experiments.

2   Development and Technical Description of the Talking Head

Animated synthetic talking faces and characters have been developed using a number of different techniques and for a variety of purposes during the past two decades. Our approach is based on parameterized, deformable 3D facial models, controlled by rules within a text-to-speech framework [1]. The rules generate the parameter tracks for the face from a representation of the text, taking coarticulation into account [2]. We employ a generalized parameterization technique to adapt a static 3D-wireframe of a face for visual speech animation [3]. Based on concepts first introduced by Parke [4], we define a set of parameters that will deform the wireframe by applying weighted transformations to its vertices. One critical difference from Parke's system, however, is that we have de-coupled the model definitions from the animation engine, thereby greatly increasing flexibility.

The models are made up of polygon surfaces that are rendered in 3D using standard computer graphics techniques. The surfaces can be articulated and deformed under the control of a number of parameters. The parameters are designed to allow for intuitive interactive or rule-based control. For the purposes of animation, parameters can be roughly divided into two (overlapping) categories: those controlling speech articulation and those used for non-articulatory cues and emotions. The articulatory parameters include jaw rotation, lip rounding, bilabial occlusion, labiodental occlusion and tongue tip elevation. The non-articulatory category includes eyebrow raising, eyebrow shape, smile, gaze direction and head orientation. Furthermore, some of the articulatory parameters such as jaw rotation can be useful in signaling non-verbal elements such as certain emotions. The display can be chosen to show only the surfaces or the polygons for the different components of the face. The surfaces can be made (semi)transparent to display the internal parts of the model. The model presently contains a relatively crude tongue model primarily intended to provide realism as seen from the outside, through the mouth opening. A full 3D model of the internal speech organs is presently being developed for integration in the talking head [5]. This capability of the model is especially useful in explaining non-visible articulations in the language learning situation [6]. In Fig. 1 some of the display options are illustrated.

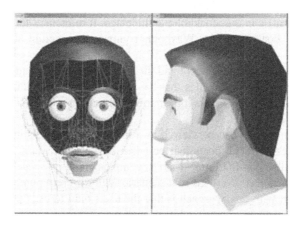

Fig. 1. Different display possibilities for the talking head model. Different parts of the model can be displayed as polygons or smooth (semi)transparent surfaces to emphasize different parts of the model

For stimuli preparation and explorative investigations, we have developed a control interface that allows fine-grained control over the trajectories for acoustic as well as visual parameters. The interface is implemented as an extension to the WaveSurfer application [7] which is a tool for recording, playing, editing, viewing, printing, and labeling audio data.

The parametric manipulation tool is used to experiment with and define different gestures. A gesture library is under construction, containing procedures with general emotion settings and non-speech specific gestures as well as some procedures with linguistic cues. We are at present developing an XML-based representation of visual cues that facilitates description of the visual cues at a higher level.

3 Experimental Applications

During the past decade a number of experimental applications using the talking head have been developed at KTH. Four examples which will be discussed here are the Waxholm demonstrator system designed to provide tourist information on the Stockholm archipelago, the Synface/Teleface project which is a visual hearing aid, the August project which was a dialogue system in public use, and the Adapt multimodal real-estate agent.

3.1 The Waxholm Demonstrator

The first KTH demonstrator application, which we named WAXHOLM, gives information on boat traffic in the Stockholm archipelago. It references timetables for a fleet of some twenty boats from the Waxholm company connecting about two hundred ports [8].

Besides the dialogue management and the speech recognition and synthesis components, the system contains modules that handle graphic information such as pictures, maps, charts, and timetables. This information can be presented as a result of the user-initiated dialogue.

The Waxholm system can be viewed as a micro-world, consisting of harbors with different facilities and with boats that be taken between the many harbors. The user gets graphic feedback in the form of tables complemented by speech synthesis. In the initial experiments, users were given a scenario with different numbers of subtasks to solve. A problem with this approach is that the users tend to use the same vocabulary as the text in the given scenario. We also observed that the user often did not get enough feedback to be able to decide if the system had the same interpretation of the dialogue as the user.

To deal with these problems a graphical representation that visualizes the Waxholm micro-world was implemented. An example is shown in Fig. 2. One purpose of this was to give the subject an idea of what can be done with the system, without expressing it in words. The interface continuously feeds back the information that the system has obtained from the parsing of the subject's utterance, such as time, departure port and so on. The interface is also meant to give a graphical view of the knowledge the subject has secured thus far, in the form of listings of hotels and so on.

The visual animated talking agent is an integral part of the system. This aims at raising the intelligibility of the system's responses and questions. Furthermore, the addition of the face into the dialogue system has many other exciting implications. Facial non-verbal signals can be used to support turntaking in the dialogue, and to direct the user's attention in certain ways, e.g. by letting the head turn towards time tables, charts, etc. that appear on the screen during the dialogue. The dialogue system also provides an ideal framework for experiments with non-verbal communication and facial actions at the prosodic level, as discussed above, since the system has a much better knowledge of the discourse context than is the case in plain text-to-speech synthesis.

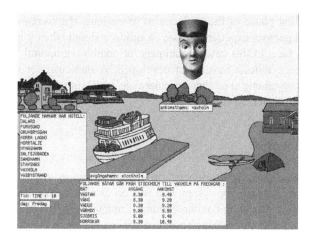

Fig. 2. The graphical model of the WAXHOLM micro-world

To make the face more alive, one does not necessarily have to synthesize meaningful non-verbal facial actions. By introducing semi-random eye blinks and very faint eye and head movements, the face looks much more active and becomes more pleasant to watch. This is especially important when the face is not talking.

3.2 The Synface/Teleface Project

The speech intelligibility of talking animated agents, as the ones described above, has been tested within the Teleface project at KTH [9], [10]. The project has recently been continued/expanded in a European project, Synface [11]. The project focuses on the usage of multimodal speech technology for hearing-impaired persons.

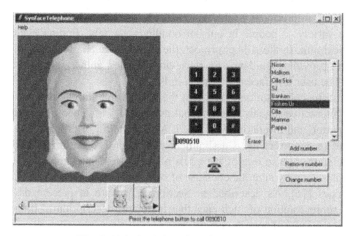

Fig. 3. Telephone interface for SYNFACE

The aim of the first phase of the project was to evaluate the increased intelligibility hearing-impaired persons experience from an auditory signal when it is complemented by a synthesized face. In this case, techniques for combining natural speech with lip-synchronized face synthesis have been developed. A demonstrator of a system for telephony with a synthetic face that articulates in synchrony with a natural voice is currently being implemented (see Fig. 3).

3.3 The August System

The Swedish author, August Strindberg, provided inspiration to create the animated talking agent used in a dialogue system that was on display during 1998 as part of the activities celebrating Stockholm as the Cultural Capital of Europe [12]. This dialogue system made it possible to combine several domains, thanks to the modular function-ality of the architecture. Each domain has its own dialogue manager, and an example based topic spotter is used to relay the user utterances to the appropriate dialog man-ager. In this system, the animated agent "August" presents different tasks such as taking the visitors on a trip through the Department of Speech, Music and Hearing, giving street directions, and also presenting short excerpts from the works of August Strindberg when waiting for someone to talk to.

August was placed, unattended, in a public area of Kulturhuset in the center of Stockholm. One challenge is this very open situation with no explicit instructions being given to the visitor. A simple visual "visitor detector" makes August start talk-ing about one of his knowledge domains.

3.4 The Adapt Multimodal Real-Estate Agent

The practical goal of the AdApt project is to build a system in which a user can col-laborate with an animated agent to solve complicated tasks [13]. We have chosen a domain in which multimodal interaction is highly useful, and which is known to en-gage a wide variety of people in our surroundings, namely, finding available apart-ments in Stockholm. In the AdApt project, the agent has been given the role of asking questions and providing guidance by retrieving detailed authentic information about apartments. The user interface can be seen in Fig. 4.

Because of the conversational nature of the AdApt domain, the demand is great for appropriate interactive signals (both verbal and visual) for encouragement, affirma-tion, confirmation and turntaking [14], [15]. As generation of prosodically grammati-cal utterances (e.g. correct focus assignment with regard to the information structure and dialogue state) is also one of the goals of the system it is important to maintain modality consistency by simultaneous use of both visual and verbal prosodic and con-versational cues [16]. As described in Section 2, we are at present developing an XML-based representation of such cues that facilitates description of both verbal and visual cues at the level of speech generation.

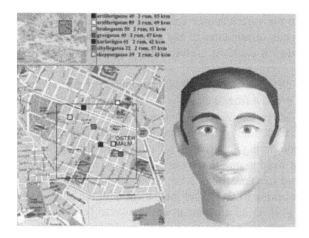

Fig. 4. The agent Urban in the AdApt apartment domain

These cues can be of varying range covering attitudinal settings appropriate for an entire sentence or conversational turn or be of a shorter nature like a qualifying comment to something just said. Cues relating to turntaking or feedback need not be associated with speech acts but can occur during breaks in the conversation. Also in this case, it is important that there is a one-to-many relation between the symbols and the actual gesture implementation to avoid stereotypic agent behaviour. Currently a weighted random selection between different realizations is used.

4   Improving Intelligibility and Information Presentation

One of the more striking examples of improvement and effectiveness in speech intelligibility is taken from the Synface project which aims at improving telephone communication for the hearing impaired [10]. The results of a series of tests using VCV words and hearing impaired subjects showed a significant gain in intelligibility when the talking head was added to a natural voice. With the synthetic face, consonant identification improved from 29% to 54% correct responses. This compares to the 57% correct response result obtained by using the natural face. In certain cases, notably the consonants consisting of lip movement (i.e. the bilabial and labiodental consonants), the response results were in fact better for the synthetic face than for the natural face. This points to the possibility of using overarticulation strategies for the talking face in these kinds of applications. Recent results indicate that a certain degree of overarticulation can be advantageous in improving intelligibility [17].

Similar intelligibility tests have been run using normal hearing subjects where the audio signal was degraded by adding white noise [10]. Similar results were obtained. For example, for a synthetic male voice, consonant identification improved from 31% without the face to 45% with the face. While the visual articulation is most probably the key factor contributing to this increase, we can speculate that the presence of visual information of the speech source can also contribute to increased intelligibility by sharpening the focus of attention of the subjects. Although this hypothesis has not been formally tested, it could be useful to test it generally in many different applications.

Another quite different example of the contribution of the talking head to information presentation is taken from the results of perception studies in which the percept of emphasis and syllable prominence is enhanced by eyebrow and head movements. In an early study restricted to eyebrows and prominence [18] it was shown that raising the eyebrows alone during a particular syllable resulted in an increase in prominence judgments for the word in question by nearly 30%. In a later study, it was shown that eyebrows and head movement can serve as independent visual cues for prominence, and that synchronization of the visual movement with the audio speech syllable is an important factor [19]. Head movement was shown to be somewhat more salient for signaling prominence as eyebrow movement could be potentially misinterpreted as supplying non-linguistic information such as irony.

A third example of information enhancement by the visual modality is to be found in the Waxholm demonstrator and the Adapt system. In both these systems, the agent uses gaze to point to areas and objects on the screen, thereby strengthening the common focus of attention between the agent and the user. Although this type of information enhancement has not yet been formally evaluated in the context of these systems, it must be seen as an important potential for improving information presentation.

Finally, an important example of the addition of information through the visual modality is to be found in the August system. This involved adding mood, emotion and attitude to the agent. To enable display of the agent's different moods, six basic emotions similar to the six universal emotions defined by Ekman [20] were implemented in a way similar to that described by Pelachaud, Badler & Steedman [15]. Appropriate emotional cues were assigned to a number of utterances in the system, often paired with other gestures.

5 Improving Interaction

The use of a believable talking head can trigger the user's social skills such as using greetings, addressing the agent by name, and generally socially chatting with the agent. This was clearly shown by the results of the public use of the August system during a period of six months [21]. These striking results have led to more specific studies on visual cues for feedback [22]. In one experiment the response of the agent was to be judged as affirmative or negative/questioning. Both acoustic cues, intonation (F0 contour) and the agent's delay in responding, and a variety of visual cues were combined. In Fig. 5 the results of this experiment can be seen along with the most negative and the most affirmative combination. It is interesting to note that smile was found to be the strongest cue for affirmative feedback. The fact that the brow frown functions as a negative cue is not surprising as the frown can signal confusion or disconcernment. Brow rise as an affirmative cue is more surprising in that a question or surprise can also be accompanied by raised eyebrows. In this experiment, however, the brow rise was quite subtle, as can be seen in the figure. A larger raising movement is likely to be interpreted as surprise.

Further detailed work on visual cues for turntaking regulation, for seeking and giving feedback and for the signaling of the system's internal state will enable us to improve the gesture library available for the animated talking head and help us continue to improve the effectiveness of multimodal dialogue systems.

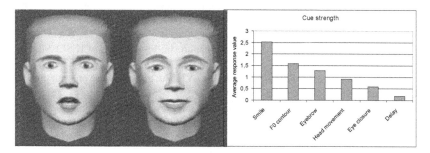

Fig. 5. The all-negative and all-affirmative faces sampled in the end of the first syllable of the test word, Linköping, (left). The relative cue strength, i.e. the average response value difference for stimuli with the indicated cues set to their affirmative and negative value (right)

Acknowledgements. The research reported here represents work by several former and present members of the KTH speech group, especially Jonas Beskow, who created the CTT talking head. The work was carried out at the Centre for Speech Technology, a competence center at KTH, supported by VINNOVA (The Swedish Agency for Innovation Systems), KTH and participating Swedish companies and organizations.

References

1. Carlson, R. and Granström, B.: Speech Synthesis. In: Hardcastle, W. and Laver, J. (eds.): The Handbook of Phonetic Sciences, Oxford: Blackwell Publishers Ltd. (1997) 768-788
2. Beskow, J.: Rule-based Visual Speech Synthesis. In: Proceedings of Eurospeech '95, Madrid, Spain (1995) 299-302
3. Beskow, J.: Animation of Talking Agents. In: Proceedings of AVSP'97, ESCA Workshop on Audio-Visual Speech Processing, Rhodes, Greece, (1997) 149-152
4. Parke, F. I.: Parameterized models for facial animation. IEEE Computer Graphics, 2(9) (1982) 61-68
5. Engwall, O.: Making the Tongue Model Talk: Merging MRI & EMA Measurements, In: Proc of Eurospeech 2001, (2001) 261-264
6. Cole, R., Massaro, D. W., de Villiers, J., Rundle, B., Shobaki, K., Wouters, J., Cohen, M., Beskow, J., Stone, P., Connors, P., Tarachow, A. and Solcher, D.: New tools for interactive speech and language training: Using animated conversational agents in the classrooms of profoundly deaf children. In: Proceedings of ESCA/Socrates Workshop on Method and Tool Innovations for Speech Science Education (MATISSE), London: University College London (1999) 45-52

7. Sjölander, K. and Beskow, J.: WaveSurfer - an Open Source Speech Tool. In: Proceedings of ICSLP 2000, Vol. 4, Bejing, China (2000) 464-467

8. Bertenstam, J., Beskow, J., Blomberg, M., Carlson R., Elenius, K., Granström, B., Gustafson, J., Hunnicutt, S., Högberg, J. Lindell, R., Neovius, L., de Serpa-Leitao, A., Nord L., and Ström, N.: The Waxholm system - a progress report. In: Proceedings of Spoken Dialogue Systems, Vigsø, Denmark (1995) 81-84

9. Beskow, J., Dahlquist, M., Granström, B., Lundeberg, M., Spens, K.-E. and Öhman, T.: The teleface project - multimodal speech communication for the hearing impaired. In: Proceedings of Eurospeech '97, Rhodos, Greece (1997) 2003-2006

10. Agelfors, E., Beskow, J., Dahlquist, M., Granström, B., Lundeberg, M., Spens K.-E., and Öhman, T.: Synthetic faces as a lipreading support. In: Proceedings of ICSLP'98, Sydney, Australia (1998) 3047-3050

11. Granström, B., Karlsson, I, and Spens, K-E.: SYNFACE – a project presentation. TMH-QPSR Vol. 44, Stockholm, KTH (2002) 93-96.

12. Gustafson, J., Lindberg, N. and Lundeberg, M.: The August spoken dialogue system. In: Proc of Eurospeech'99, Budapest, Hungary (1999) 1151-1154

13. Gustafson, J., Bell, L., Beskow, J., Boye, J., Carlson, R., Edlund, J., Granström, B., House, D., and Wirén, M.: AdApt - a multimodal conversational dialogue system in an apartment domain. In: Proceedings of ICSLP 2000, Vol. 2. Beijing, China (2000) 134-137

14. Cassell, J., Bickmore, T., Campbell, L., Vilhjálmsson, H. and Yan, H.: Human Conversation as a System Framework: Designing Embodied Conversational Agents. In: Cassell, J., Sullivan, J., Prevost, S., and Churchill, E. (eds.): Embodied Conversational Agents. The MIT Press, Cambridge MA. (2000) 29-63

15. Pelachaud C., Badler, N.I., and Steedman, M.: Generating Facial Expressions for Speech. Cognitive Science 28 (1996) 1-46

16. Nass C. and Gong, L.: Maximized modality or constrained consistency? In: Proceedings of AVSP'99. Santa Cruz, USA (1999) 1-5

17. Beskow, J., Granström, B., and Spens, K-E.: Articulation strength - Readability experiments with a synthetic talking face TMH-QPSR Vol. 44, Stockholm, KTH (2002) 97-100

18. Granström, B., House, D. and Lundeberg, M.: Prosodic cues in multi-modal speech perception. In: Proceedings of ICPhS-99. San Francisco, USA (1999) 655-658

19. House, D., Beskow. J. and Granström, B.: Timing and interaction of visual cues for prominence in audiovisual speech perception. In: Proceedings of Eurospeech 2001. Aalborg, Denmark (2001) 387-390

20. Ekman P.: About brows: Emotional and conversational signals. In: von Cranach, M., Foppa, K., Lepinies, W., and Ploog, D. (eds.): Human ethology: Claims and limits of a new discipline: Contributions to the Colloquium, Cambridge: Cambridge University Press. (1979) 169-248

21. Bell, L. and Gustafson, J.: Utterance types in the August System. In: Proceedings of IDS-99, Kloster Irsee, Germany (1999) 81-84

22. Granström, B., House, D., and Swerts, M.G.: Multimodal feedback cues in human-machine interactions. In: Bernard Bel and Isabelle Marlien (eds.): Proceedings of the Speech Prosody 2002 Conference. Aix-en-Provence: Laboratoire Parole et Langage (2002) 347-350

Efficient Relational Learning from Sparse Data

Luboš Popelínský

Faculty of Informatics, Masaryk University
Botanická 68a, CZ-602 00 Brno, Czech Republic
popel@fi.muni.cz

Abstract. This work deals with inductive inference of logic programs – relational learning – from examples. The work is, in the first place, application-oriented. It aims at building an easy-to-use relational learner and it focuses on the tasks that are solvable with the tool. Assumption-based learning, the new learning paradigm is introduced and the ABL system WiM is described. A methodology for experimental evaluation of ILP systems is introduced and experiments with WiM are displayed. Two classes of application – database schema redesign and mining in spatial data - that have been successfully solved with WiM are described.

Keywords: relational learning, database schema redesign, mining in spatial data

1 Motivation

Relational learning, or inductive logic programming(ILP) [16] explores inductive learning in first order logic. An inductive system learns if for a given set of instances of a particular concept it finds a general description of that concept. The main goal of ILP is then development of theory, algorithms and systems for inductive reasoning in first-order logic. Informally, for a given example set and background knowledge we aim at finding a hypothesis in first order logic that explain those examples using the background knowledge. In the general setting, examples, background knowledge and hypotheses may be any first-order formula. The main used setting in ILP is example setting, or 'specification by examples' where the evidence is restricted to true and false ground facts called examples. Background knowledge is a normal logic program.

The computational complexity of ILP algorithm is an important problem. In general there are three ways how to limit the size of the set generated by a refinement operator: to define bias (syntactic as well as semantic restrictions on the search space) [15], to accept assumptions on the quality of examples, or to use an oracle [21]. Even in the case of a finite relation we assume that the number of examples is (significantly) less than the number of all instances of the relation. Bias is usually split into two groups, language bias that narrows the space of possible solutions and search bias that defines how to search that space and when to stop. Language bias defines a form of possible solutions. More frequent

D. Scott (Ed.): AIMSA 2002, LNAI 2443, pp. 11–20, 2002.

constraints limit the maximal number of clauses in the solution or maximal number of literals in a clause body [7,14,21]. Languages were developed that enable to define almost any syntactic feature of the desirable solution. Search bias says how to search the graph of potential solutions. It also defines validation bias, the condition under which the search are to stop. Most of characteristics of bias – like the complexity of the intended solution, or the maximal number of nodes-hypotheses in the search space – may be expressed via parameters. Usually it is uneasy to set the parameters optimally. The techniques of the shift of bias can help.

The development of a new relational learner was motivated by some tasks that everybody must treat when using ILP. Except of building domain knowledge it is a selection of learning set (its cardinality and quality), and optimal settings of bias. Some general drawbacks of relational learners that motivated our work are as follows. It is very often that cardinality of a training set needed by ILP systems seems to be too big [2,14] and/or the needed quality of examples is extremely high [1,7,21] The used negative examples are more dependent on the used ILP system than on the solved task [7,14,21]. In the case of interactive systems, the obtained result very often depends on the order of examples [21]. Optimal settings of bias [15] can hardly be automatic. However, it should be as easy as possible. Finding the optimal parameters of bias is closer to art than to a science [7].

We focus here on exact learning. It means that no noise in input information (examples, domain knowledge) is allowed. We employ the generate-and-test top-down strategy. First a hypothesis is generated that is afterwards tested on examples. We solve only some of tasks that result in more efficient and more user–friendly ILP systems. We showed [20] how the number of hypotheses in generate–and–test paradigm can be lowered with bias settings. By this way, this 'brute force' top-down learning are becoming quite efficient. Here we bring experimental proof of it. When looking for the optimal bias settings we will aim at the minimal need of interaction with a user. As mentioned before, the useful negative examples are very often dependent on the used ILP system. We describe a semi-automatic method for finding negative examples. We show that the examples found are helpful. We describe classes of problems that can be solved with exact learners. We focus on the traditional class of problems – logic program synthesis, and database applications. We show that WiM system can be applied in the field of database schema redesign as well as in the process of knowledge discovery in geographic data.

Next three section are as a core of this work. Section 2 contains description of the basic algorithm of assumption-based learning. In Section 3 the WiM system, as the first implementation of this general paradigm, is introduced. Section 4 contains experimental results obtained with WiM on benchmark predicates. Section 5 displays the use of WiM in two application areas – database schema redesign and mining in geographic data. Props and cons of ABL and WiM are discussed in Section 6.

2   Assumption-Based Learning

We developed a new method called **assumption-based learning** (ABL) based
on [5,10]. A generic scenario of assumption-based learning consists of three parts,
an **inductive synthesiser**, a **generator of assumptions** which generates extensions of the input information and an **acceptability module** which evaluates acceptability of assumptions. That module is allowed to pose queries to the
teacher. It may happen that the inductive synthesiser have failed for any reason
to find a correct solution (e.g. because of missing examples, insufficient domain
knowledge or because of too strong bias). Then ABL system is looking for such
a minimal extension of the input - called **assumption** - which allows to find a
solution. The solution has to be correct and consistent with the input extended
by the new assumption. If an assumption is needed, it must be confirmed by
the acceptability module. It is true that a query to user is necessary to confirm
the assumption generated by the system. However, the number of queries, in
general, is smaller comparing to the other interactive systems [2,21]. A generic
algorithm of assumption-based learning is in Fig.1.

Given:
>   *domain knowledge BK, example set E, bias,*
>   *assumption $A = true$*
>   inductive engine I, overgeneral program P
>   function f, that computes an assumption A
>   acceptability module AM

1. Call I on $BK \cup P, E \cup A, bias$.
   - **if** I succeeds resulting in program P'
       then call AM to validate the assumption A.
       if A is accepted **then** return(P') **else go to** (2).
   - **else go to** (2).
2. Call f to generate a new assumption A. If it fails, return(fail) and stop else go to
   (1).

Fig. 1. A generic algorithm of assumption-based learning

3 WiM System

In this section, WiM system, the first implementation of the assumption-based
learning paradigm is introduced. Particular parts and functions of ABL are explained here. WiM [6,20] is a program for synthesis of normal logic programs
from a small example set. It further elaborates the approach of MIS [21] and
$Markus$ [7]. It works in top-down manner and uses shifting of bias and second-
order constraints. WiM is an instance of assumption-based learning. Assumptions are ground negative examples generated one-by-one. In every moment,
maximally one assumption is added into the example set. WiM consists of three
modules, inductive engine m^+, a generator of assumptions, and an acceptability
module. In the next three paragraphs we briefly describe these three modules.

3.1 Inductive Synthesiser m^+

We implemented m^+ that is based on *Markus* [7]. m^+ is a top-down synthesiser applying breath-first search in a refinement graph and controlling a search space with different parameters. A refinement operator is an improved version of *Markus'* one. m^+ employs only a subset of *Markus'* parameters. Those parameters concerns only language bias. We wanted to make the work with WiM as easy as possible. More advanced users, of course, can tune also other parameters of *Markus* . However, for most of tasks it is not necessary. m^+ employs **shifting of bias**. Four parameters are used for shifting — the maximal number of free variables in a clause, the maximal number of goals in the body of a clause, the maximal head argument depth ($X, [X|Y], [X, Y|Z]$, etc. are of depths 0, 1, 2, respectively), and the maximal number of clauses in a solution. The user defines the minimal and the maximal value of the parameters. m^+ starts with the minimal values of these parameters. If no acceptable result has been found, a value of one of the parameters is increased by 1 and m^+ is called again. In such a way all variations are being tried gradually. That choice of parameters implies that m^+ finds a simpler clause first. In some situations domain knowledge predicates may be defined extensionally. However, it is not realistic to assume that those definitions are complete enough. It would be appreciated if such extensional definition would be replaced by intensional one. We incorporated into WiM a **multiple predicate learning** algorithm which is sufficient in most situations for solving this task. A **second-order schema** can be defined which the learned program has to match. This schema definition can significantly increase an efficiency of the learning process because only the synthesised programs which match the schema are verified on the learning set.

3.2 Generator of Assumptions

An assumption is generated in the moment when the current example set is not complete enough to ensure that the inductive synthesiser is capable to find a definition of the target predicate. As an assumption, a near-miss to a chosen positive example is generated. The whole process of generation of assumptions consists of two steps:

Algorithm of assumption generation:

> **repeat**
>
> > 1. Find the preferable positive example in the example set. 2. Generate its near-miss.
> >
> > **until** a correct and complete program was found
> > **or** no more assumptions exist.

A **preference relation** on the set of examples is defined based on measure of complexity for atomic formulas (complexity of a list is equal to its length; complexity of terms in Peano arithmetics is equal to the corresponding value, e.g. $s(s(0))$ is of complexity 2). It enables to generate near-misses of less complex examples first. The relation of preference is an ordering on a set of examples. Thus it has a minimal elements. Now the preferable example can be computed.

First a complexity is computed for every positive example in the learning set. Then arbitrary example with a minimal complexity is chosen as preferable for computing near-misses.

A syntactic approach is used for computing **near-misses**. A minimal modification of the example chosen is computed (adding/removing/replacing one element in the list; increasing/decreasing by one the complexity of a term in Peano arithmetics). Whenever a new near-miss has been built, it is added into the example set as the negative example and learning algorithm is called. If no solution is found then the near-miss is replaced by another near-miss of the same positive example. If no near-miss of the example enables to learn a correct definition, next positive example (following the ordering given by the preference relation) is chosen for generation of near-misses.

3.3   Acceptability Module

For each assumption which has lead to a new predicate definition, acceptability module asks an oracle for a confirmation/rejection of the assumption. As WiM works with ground assumptions, a membership oracle is employed in WiM. The oracle answers *true* if the ground assumption is in the intended interpretation. Otherwise it answers *false*.

4   Experiments

WiM was examined on list processing predicates and on predicates for Peano arithmetics. We used both carefully chosen learning sets and learning sets generated randomly. The learned definitions of predicates were tested on randomly chosen example sets. Below we first introduce the methodology for generating random learning set. Then we display the results for the randomly generated learning sets. The other results can be found in [20].

Positive examples are generated as follows

1. Generate **input** arguments randomly as terms of depth 0..4 over a domain of constants ($\{a,b,c, \ \ldots \ ,z\}$ for lists, 0 for integers).
2. Compute the value of the **output** argument using the same domain.
3. If the depth of output argument is not greater than 4, and the example does not appear in the example set, add it there.

The input arguments are installed and then the output argument is computed, e.g. for append([_],[_,_],_) we may receive ([r],[g,b],[r,g,b]). As the length of [r,g,b] is not greater than 4, the example append([r],[g,b],[r,g,b]) is added into the example set. **Negative examples** are chosen in two steps.

1. Generate **all** arguments randomly as terms of depth 0..4 over a domain of constants ($\{a,b,c, \ \ldots \ ,z\}$ for lists, 0 for integers).
2. If it is a negative example, add it to the example set.

We used two criteria for evaluation, a success rate and a fraction of test perfect programs (see [20] for the results) over N learning sessions. For a given logic program and a test set we define **success rate** as a sum of covered positive examples and uncovered negative examples divided by a total number of examples. We generated a learning set as 2,3 and 5 positive examples and 10 negative examples. Then WiM was called to learn a program P. 50 positive and 50 negative examples were generated as a test set and a success rate was computed for P on this testing set. The whole process was repeated 10-times.

Table 1. Learning list processing predicates by Crustacean and WiM (average accuracy from 10 runs for 2,3 and 5 examples).

	Crustacean		WiM		
	2	3	2	3	5
member	0.65	0.76	0.80	0.97	0.97
last	0.74	0.89	0.76	0.89	0.94
append	0.63	0.74	0.77	0.95	0.95
delete	0.62	0.71	0.85	0.88	0.97
reverse	0.80	0.86	0.85	0.95	0.99
split	0.78	0.86	0.80	0.88	0.79
extractNth	0.60	0.78	0.74	0.80	0.98
plus	0.64	0.86	0.82	0.92	0.96
noneIsZero	0.73	0.79	0.72	0.46	0.58

4.1   Results

WiM can learn most of the ILP benchmark predicates on the mentioned domains from 2 positive examples, sometimes extended with one negative example. This negative example is generated automatically as the assumption. It never needs more than 4 examples for that class of predicates and more than one negative example. If the negative example is needed it can be generated with very good accuracy by WiM itself. We showed that the accuracy of the target definition increases with a number of positive example in the training set as well as with weakening of bias. Comparison with $CRUSTACEAN$ [1] is in Table 1. The table contains average accuracy obtained from 10 runs, for 2,3 and 5 examples that were generated randomly. For $CRUSTACEAN$ the results was taken from [1]; for 5 examples the results have not been published. We also compared WiM with $Markus$ as well as with other ILP systems $FILP$ [2], $SKILit$ [9] and $Progol$ [14] [20]. WiM outperforms $Markus$ - it never needs more positive examples than $Markus$ and needs less negative examples; bias is much more easy to set. WiM has higher efficiency of learning as well as smaller dependency on the quality of the example set than other exact learners. WiM is quite fast. CPU time needed for learning without assumptions was smaller than 8 seconds on SUN Sparc. Assumption-based learning is of course more time-consuming. The maximal CPU time was smaller than 4 seconds for list processing predicates and smaller than 33 seconds for Peano arithmetics ($\leq$ /2). Comparing WiM with MIS , MIS is not able to learn from only positive examples.

5   Applications

5.1   Inductive Redesign of Object-Oriented Database

Based on WiM, $DWiM$ [19] system has been implemented that can assist in object-oriented database schema redesign. In the first step, domain knowledge is being extracted from an object-oriented database schema described in F-logic [11]. Then positive examples are chosen by user from the database. Negative examples can be generated automatically as assumptions, using the closed world assumption, or can be assigned also by user.

```
japaneseCar:X        <-car:X[producer->F[place->
                       P[country->'Japan']]

factory:X            <-carFactory:X
factory:X            <-aircraftFactory:X

eVehicle:X           <-car:X[power->electricity]
eVehicle:X           <-pubTranVehicle:X[power->electricity]

family:F[hu->H,wi->W] <-person:H[spouse->W],
                       person:W[spouse->H]

person:X[managed->Y] <-person:X[boss->Y]
person:X[managed->Y] <-person:X[boss->Z],
                       person:Z[managed->Y]

person:X[mother->M]  <-not(person:X[father->M]),
                       person:M[son->X]
person:X[mother->M]  <-not(person:X[father->M]),
                       person:M[daughter->X]
```

Fig. 2. Class and attribute definitions

Limits of bias are generated automatically, too. The maximum complexity of head is set on 1 as well as number of free variables. Maximum clause length is equal to the number of attribute names and values which have appeared in input objects. Now WiM is run with the collected example set and background knowledge. $DWiM$ was examined on tasks that cover all frequent types of class and attribute definitions. $DWiM$ needed from 1 to 5 positive instances(objects) of classes. The number of the needed examples is small enough for user to be able to choose them. $DWiM$ program is quite fast so that it can be used in interactive design of deductive object-oriented databases. Some of the learned F-logic rules are in Figure 2.

5.2   Mining in Spatial Data

WiM system, is also a powerful tool for mining some of typical patterns in spatial data [8,13]. The general schema of $GWiM$ [18] system is a modification of $DWiM$ described earlier. The GENERATE module is replaced by a module that compiles rules of a spatial mining language into input of WiM. Then WiM is called. The inductive query language for spatial mining consists of three kinds of inductive queries. Two of them, that ask for characteristic and discriminate rules, are improved versions of $GeoMiner$ [8,3] rules. The dependency rules add a new quality to the inductive query language. The general syntactic form, adapted from $GeoMiner$ of the language is as follows. Semantics of those rule

> **extract** < KindOfRule > **rule**
> **for** < NameOfTarget >
> [**from** < ListOfClasses >]
> [< Constraints >]
> [**from point of view** < ExplicitDomainKnowledge >] .

Fig. 3. General form of rules

differs from that of $GeoMiner$. Namely < ExplicitDomainKnowledge > is a list of predicates and/or hierarchy of predicates. At least one of them have to appear in the answer to the query. The answer to those inductive queries is a first-order logic formula which characterises the subset of the database which is specified by the rule. We experimentally verified usability of the inductive query language and performance of $GWiM$. Cardinality of the learning sets is small enough for user to choose the learning examples. $GWiM$ outperforms in some aspects $GeoMiner$. Namely $GWiM$ can mine a richer class of knowledge, Horn clauses. Background knowledge used in $GeoMiner$ may be expressed only in the form of hierarchies, $GWiM$ accepts any Horn clause logic program.

6   Discussion

Although Progol is not proposed for logic program synthesis we compared WiM with it. For a comparison of WiM with PROGOL we used again randomly chosen examples. We focus only on $append/3$ predicate because the distribution package of PROGOL contains a training set for this predicate The set contains 17 positive and 8 negative examples. We also display results on this example set obtained with both systems (last columns - distr). Tab 2 contains the average success rate for 10 runs. PROGOL never found the correct solution for 2, 3, 5 and 7 examples neither any recursive solution. On the (distr) data and 5 runs, PROGOL did not stop once and 4-times it found an over-general definition `append([A|B],C,[A|D])` ; `append(A,B,B)`. In this case the success rates

Table 2. append/3, PROGOL and WiM

PROGOL					WiM				
2	3	5	7	distr	2	3	5	7	distr
0.68	0.81	0.89	0.97	0.89	0.77	0.95	0.95	1.00	1.00

varied between 0.96 and 0.99. When only positive examples appeared in the test set , the success rates were 0.39 , 0.69 , 0.79. *Progol* can also learn from positive examples only. However, this feature is not usable when learning from very small learning sets.

WiM overcomes other relational learners in the case that the number of learning examples is small (≤ 5) and it is not yet applicable for noisy data. We showed that even under these two conditions there are application areas where ABL was successfully employed. It is typical for these domains that learning data are being collected (or at least supervised) with human(in the case of program synthesis and/or object-oriented schema redesign), or the learning data are extracted from non-noisy data sources(e.g. some kinds of geographic data). Noisy data can be, at least partially, run employing oracles already implemented in *WiM* . However, this problem needs more exploration.

7 Conclusion

We introduced the new ILP paradigm called assumption-based learning. We experimentally proved that the implementation of the assumption-based paradigm, the system *WiM*, is less dependent on the quality of the learning set than other ILP systems. We showed how to decrease complexity of the search space in ILP setting. *WiM* system extends *Markus* [7] by shifting bias, multiple predicate learning, generating negative examples and employing second-order schema. We showed that even with a very small example set *WiM* is capable to learn most of the predicates which have been mentioned in ILP literature. We showed that *WiM* is feasible for solving real-world tasks. Our assumption-based approach can be combined with any existing ILP system.

We addressed the possibilities of ILP methods in object-oriented database schema modelling, i.e. in database schema design and restructuring. We showed that inductive logic programming could help in synthesis of those rules to support database schema redesign. We showed how to use the ABL technique for spatial data mining. Mining system *GWiM* was implemented based on *WiM*. *GWiM* overcomes, in expressive power, some other mining methods.

Acknowledgements. I would like to thank to Olga Štěpánková for her kind assistance and Pavel Brazdil and his group in Porto, Jaroslav Pokorný and Claire Nedellec for their comments. My thanks are also due to many colleagues from ILP community and anonymous referees. This work has been supported by the grant of Czech Ministry of Education MSMT 143300003.

References

1. Aha D.W., Lapointe S., Ling C.X., and Matwin S.: Inverting implication with small training sets. In Bergadano F., De Raedt L. (Eds.) Proc. of ECML'94, Catania, LNCS 784, pp. 31–48, Springer Verlag 1994.
2. Bergadano F. and Gunetti D.: An interactive system to learn functional logic programs. *Proc. of IJCAI'93*, Chambéry, pp. 1044–1049.

3. De Raedt L.: A Logical Database Mining Query Language. In: Cussens J., Frisch A.(Eds.): Proceedings of ILP'2000, LNAI 1866, pp.78–92, Springer-Verlag 2000.

4. De Raedt L., Lavrač N., Džeroski S.: Multiple predicate learning. In Proc. IJ-CAI'93. Morgan Kaufmann, San Mateo, CA.

5. DeKleer J.: An Assumption-Based TMS. Artificial Intelligence 18, 1986.

6. Flener P., Popelínský L. Štěpánková O.: ILP nad Automatic Programming: Towards three approaches. Proc. of 4th Workshop on Inductive Logic Programming (ILP'94), Bad Honeff, Germany, 1994.

7. Grobelnik M.: Induction of Prolog programs with Markus. In Deville Y.(ed.) Proceedings of LOPSTR'93. Workshops in Computing Series, pages 57-63,Springer-Verlag, 1994.

8. Han J. et al.: DMQL: A Data Mining Query Language for Relational Databases. In: ACM-SIGMOD'96 Workshop on Data Mining

9. Jorge A., Brazdil P.: Architecture for Iterative Learning of Recursive Definitions. In De Raedt L.(ed.): Advances in Inductive Logic Programming. IOS Press 1996.

10. Kakas A.C., Kowalski R.A., and Toni F.: Abductive logic programming. Journal of Logic and Computation 2, 6, pp. 719-770, 1992.

11. Kifer M., Lausen G., Wu J.: Logical Foundations of Object-Oriented and Frame-Based Languages. TR 93/06, Dept. of Comp. Sci. SUNY at Stony Brook, NY, March 1994 (accepted to Journal of ACM).

12. Koperski K., Han J., Adhikary J.: Mining Knowledge in Geographical Data. Comm.of ACM 1998

13. Malerba D., Lisi F.A.: Discovering Associations between Spatial Objects: An ILP Application In Proc of 11th Intl. Conf. ILP 2001, LNAI 2157, Springer Verlag 2001.

14. Muggleton S.: Inverse Entailment and Progol. New Generation Computing Journal, 13:245-286, 1995.

15. Nédellec C., Rouveirol C.: Specification of the HAIKU system. Rapport de Recherche n 928, L.R.I. Université de Paris Sud, 1994.

16. Nienhuys-Cheng S.-H., de Wolf R.: Foundations of Inductive Logic Programming. Lect. Notes in AI 1228, Springer Verlag Berlin Heidelberg 1997.

17. Popelínský L., Štěpánková O.: WiM: A Study on the Top-Down ILP Program . Technical report FIMU-RS-95-03, August 1995.

18. Popelínský L.: Knowledge Discovery in Spatial Data by Means of ILP. In: Zytkow J.M., Quafafou M.(Eds.): Proc. of 2nd European Symposium PKDD'98, Nantes France 1998. LNCS 1510, Springer-Verlag 1998.

19. Popelínský L.: Inductive inference to support object-oriented analysis and design. In: Proc. of 3rd Conf on Knowledge-Based Software Engineering, Smolenice 1998, IOS Press.

20. Popelínský L.: On Practical Inductive Logic Programming. PhD Thesis FEL CTU Prague 2001.// http://www.fi.muni.cz/usr/popelinsky/thesis/thesis.ps.gz

21. Shapiro Y.: Algorithmic Program Debugging. MIT Press, 1983.

22. Stahl I.: Predicate Invention in Inductive Logic Programming. In: L. De Raedt (Ed.), Advances of Inductive Logic Programming, IOS Press, 1996.

Efficient Instance Retraction

E.N. Smirnov, I.G. Sprinkhuizen-Kuyper, and H.J. van den Herik

IKAT, Department of Computer Science, Universiteit Maastricht,
P.O.BOX 616, 6200 MD Maastricht, The Netherlands
{smirnov, kuyper, herik}@cs.unimaas.nl

Abstract. Instance retraction is a difficult problem for concept learning by version spaces. In this paper, two new version-space representations are introduced: instance-based maximal boundary sets and instance-based minimal boundary sets. They are correct representations for the class of admissible concept languages and are efficiently computable. Compared to other representations, they are the most efficient practical version-space representations for instance retraction.

1 Introduction

Version spaces are an approach to the concept-learning task [5]. They are defined as sets of descriptions in concept languages that are consistent with training data. Version-space learning is an incremental process [3,4,5,7]:

− *If an instance i is added*, the version space is revised so that it consists of all the concept descriptions consistent with the processed training data *plus i*.
− *If an instance i is retracted*, the version space is revised so that it consists of all the concept descriptions consistent with the processed training data *minus i*.

For the learning process version spaces have to be represented. The standard representation is by boundary sets [5,7]. They are correct for the class of admissible concept languages [7], but their size can grow exponentially in the size of training data [1]. To overcome this problem alternative version-space representations were introduced in [2,3,4,6,7,8,10]. They extended the classes of concept languages for which version spaces are efficiently computable.

A shortcoming of most version-space representations is that they are inefficient for instance retraction. They lack a structure that determines the influence of an individual training instance. Hence, if a training instance is retracted, the representations are recomputed [7]. To avoid this problem two version-space representations were proposed. The first one is the training-instance representation [3]. By its definition it is efficient for instance retraction. However, the representation has only a theoretical value, since the classification of each instance requires search in the concept language using all the training data. The second representation is instance-based boundary sets (IBBS) [7,8]. It is correct and efficiently computable for the class of admissible concept languages. Moreover, its retraction algorithm is efficient: it does not recompute the representation. Therefore, at the moment the IBBS are the most efficient practical version-space representation for instance retraction.

D. Scott (Ed.): AIMSA 2002, LNAI 2443, pp. 21–30, 2002.

In this paper we address the challenging question whether it is possible to design version-space representations that are more efficient than the IBBS in terms of computability and retraction. To answer the question we introduce instance-based maximal boundary sets (IBMBS) as a new version-space representation in the next sections[1]. Section 2 provides the necessary formalisation. The IBMBS are defined in section 3. They are shown to be correct for admissible concept languages. The condition for finiteness and the complexity of the IBMBS are given. In section 4 four IBMBS algorithms, including the retraction algorithm, are presented together with their complexities. Section 5 provides an evaluation of the IBMBS. The dual representation of the IBMBS, instance-based minimal boundary sets (IBmBS), is given in section 6. The representations are compared with relevant work in section 7. Finally, in section 8 conclusions are given.

2   Formalisation

Let I be a set of descriptions of all possible entities. A concept $\mathfrak{C}$ is defined as a subset of I. Concepts are represented in a concept language Lc. The language Lc is defined as a set of descriptions c representing each exactly one concept.

The elements of concepts are called instances. They are related to concept descriptions by a cover relation M. The relation $M(c, i)$ holds for $c \in Lc$ and $i \in I$ iff the instance i is a member of the concept represented by c. A description $c \in Lc$ is said to cover an instance $i \in I$ iff the cover relation $M(c, i)$ holds.

As a rule any target concept $\mathfrak{C}$ is incompletely defined by training sets $I^+ \subseteq I$ and $I^- \subseteq I$ of positive and negative instances such that $I^+ \subseteq \mathfrak{C}$ and $I^- \cap \mathfrak{C} = \emptyset$. Hence, the concept-learning task in this case is to find descriptions of $\mathfrak{C}$ in Lc.

To find the descriptions of a target concept, we specify them by the consistency criterion: a description c is consistent iff c correctly classifies training data. The set of all consistent descriptions is called the version space [5].

Definition 1. (Version Space) *Given training sets* I^+ *and* I^- *of a target concept, the version space* $VS(I^+, I^-)$ *is defined as follows:*

$$VS(I^+, I^-) = \{c \in Lc \mid (\forall i \in I^+)M(c, i) \wedge (\forall i \in I^-)\neg M(c, i)\}.$$

To learn version spaces, they have to be compactly represented. It is possible usually if concept languages are ordered by a relation "more general" ($\geq$) [5]:

$$(\forall c_1, c_2 \in Lc)((c_1 \geq c_2) \leftrightarrow (\forall i \in I)(M(c_1, i) \leftarrow M(c_2, i))).$$

A concept language Lc with the relation "$\geq$" is partially ordered. In our study we are interested in sets $C \subseteq Lc$ that have maximal and minimal sets:

$$MAX(C) = \{c \in C \mid (\forall c' \in C)((c' \geq c) \rightarrow (c' = c))\}$$
$$MIN(C) = \{c \in C \mid (\forall c' \in C)((c \geq c') \rightarrow (c' = c))\}.$$

The maximal and minimal sets of version spaces are known as maximal and minimal boundary sets [5]. To refer to them we use the following notation.

---

[1] The paper is a short version of [9] where the omitted proofs can be found.

Notation 2. $MAX(VS(I^+, I^-))$ is denoted by $G(I^+, I^-)$. $MIN(VS(I^+, I^-))$ is denoted by $S(I^+, I^-)$.

One sub-class of concept languages ensures that version spaces are bounded by these sets. This is the class of admissible concept languages given below.

Definition 3. (Admissible Concept Language) *A partially-ordered concept language Lc is admissible iff each subset $C \subseteq Lc$ is bounded; i.e., for each element $c \in C$ there exist $g \in MAX(C)$ and $s \in MIN(C)$ such that $g \geq c$ and $c \geq s$.*

An admissible language has the following computational characteristics used in complexity analysis. They do not depend on the size of the training-data.

Γ_n: the maximal size of the set $G(\emptyset, \{n\})$ for $n \in I$;
$t_n^\uparrow$: the maximal time for generating the set $G(\emptyset, \{n\})$ for $n \in I$;
Σ_p: the maximal size of the set $S(\{p\}, \emptyset)$ for $p \in I$;
$t_p^\downarrow$: the maximal time for generating the set $S(\{p\}, \emptyset)$ for $p \in I$;
t_m: the maximal time of the operator of the relation $M(c, i)$ for $c \in Lc, i \in I$.

In this paper we perform a worst-case analysis of the representations proposed. The conditions for the worst case are as follows:

– the size of the sets $G(I^+, \{n\})$ equals the size Γ_n for all $n \in I, I^+ \subseteq I \setminus \{n\}$;
– the size of the sets $S(\{p\}, I^-)$ equals the size Σ_p for all $p \in I, I^- \subseteq I \setminus \{p\}$.

3 Instance-Based Maximal Boundary Sets

Definition 4. (Instance-Based Maximal Boundary Sets (IBMBS)) *Consider an admissible concept language Lc and nonempty training sets $I^+ \subseteq I$ and $I^- \subseteq I$. Then the instance-based maximal boundary sets of a version space $VS(I^+, I^-)$ are an ordered pair $\langle I^+, \{G(I^+, \{n\})\}_{n \in I^-} \rangle$.*

The IBMBS are "instance-based" since each of their elements corresponds to particular training instances. The IBMBS are "maximal boundary sets" since each of their elements in $\{G(I^+, \{n\})\}_{n \in I^-}$ is a maximal boundary set.

Theorem 5. (Correctness of IBMBS) *Let $VS(I^+, I^-)$ be a version space given by IBMBS: $\langle I^+, \{G(I^+, \{n\})\}_{n \in I^-} \rangle$. If the language Lc is admissible,*

$$(\forall c \in Lc)(c \in VS(I^+, I^-) \leftrightarrow ((\forall p \in I^+)M(c, p) \wedge (\forall n \in I^-)(\exists g \in G(I^+, \{n\}))(g \geq c))).$$

Given the IBMBS of a version space $VS(I^+, I^-)$ and an admissible concept language, theorem 5 states that the descriptions in $VS(I^+, I^-)$ are those that (1) cover all the positive instances in I^+, and (2) are more specific than an element of each maximal boundary set $G(I^+, \{n\})$. Thus, the size of IBMBS is not tied to the number of descriptions in $VS(I^+, I^-)$, i.e., the IBMBS are compact.

Since the IBMBS are compact, we can determine when they are finite.

Theorem 6. *The IBMBS are finite iff the training sets I^+ and I^- are finite and the maximal boundary set $G(\emptyset, \{n\})$ is finite for all $n \in I$.*

The worst-case space complexity of the IBMBS is $O(|I^+| + |I^-|\Gamma_n)$.

Learning **Algorithm**

   Input: i: a new training instance.

       $\langle\{I^+, \{G(I^+, \{n\})\}_{n \in I^-}\rangle$: IBMBS of $VS(I^+, I^-)$.

   Output:

       $\langle I^+ \cup \{i\}, \{G(I^+ \cup \{i\}, \{n\})\}_{n \in I^-}\rangle$: IBMBS of $VS(I^+ \cup \{i\}, I^-)$ if i is positive.

       $\langle I^+, \{G(I^+, \{n\})\}_{n \in I^- \cup \{i\}}\rangle$: IBMBS of $VS(I^+, I^- \cup \{i\})$ if i is negative.

   if instance i is positive **then**

      for $n \in I^-$ **do**

         $G(I^+ \cup \{i\}, \{n\}) = \{g \in G(I^+, \{n\}) \mid M(g, i)\}$

      return $\langle I^+ \cup \{i\}, \{G(I^+ \cup \{i\}, \{n\})\}_{n \in I^-}\rangle$

   if instance i is negative **then**

      Generate the set $G(\emptyset, \{i\})$

      $G(I^+, \{i\}) = \{g \in G(\emptyset, \{i\}) \mid (\forall p \in I^+) M(g, p)\}$

   return $\langle\{I^+, \{G(I^+, \{n\})\}_{n \in I^- \cup \{i\}}\rangle$.

Fig. 1. The Learning Algorithm.

4 Algorithms of the IBMBS

This section presents algorithms of the IBMBS together with their complexities.

4.1 Learning Algorithm

The learning algorithm of the IBMBS updates the representation given a new training instance. It is correct for the class of admissible concept languages. The algorithm consists of two parts for handling positive and negative training instances. They are based on theorem 7 and theorem 5, respectively.

Theorem 7. *Consider a version space $VS(I^+, I^-)$ represented by IBMBS: $\langle I^+, \{G(I^+, \{n\})\}_{n \in I^-}\rangle$, and a version space $VS(I^+ \cup \{i\}, I^-)$ represented by IBMBS: $\langle I^+ \cup \{i\}, \{G(I^+ \cup \{i\}, \{n\})\}_{n \in I^-}\rangle$. If the concept language Lc is admissible, then:*

$$G(I^+ \cup \{i\}, \{n\}) = \{g \in G(I^+, \{n\}) \mid M(g, i)\} \text{ for all } n \in I^-.$$

The learning algorithm is given in figure 1. *If the new training instance i is positive*, the algorithm forms the maximal boundary sets $G(I^+ \cup \{i\}, \{n\})$ for all $n \in I^-$. Each set $G(I^+ \cup \{i\}, \{n\})$ is formed from the elements of the set $G(I^+, \{n\})$ covering the instance i. The resulting IBMBS of $VS(I^+ \cup \{i\}, I^-)$ are formed from the set $I^+ \cup \{i\}$ and the maximal boundary sets $G(I^+ \cup \{i\}, \{n\})$ for all $n \in I^-$. *If the instance i is negative*, the algorithm generates the set $G(\emptyset, \{i\})$. The maximal boundary set $G(I^+, \{i\})$ is formed from the elements of $G(\emptyset, \{i\})$ covering the set I^+. The resulting IBMBS of $VS(I^+, I^- \cup \{i\})$ are formed from the set I^+ and the maximal boundary sets $G(I^+, \{n\})$ for all $n \in I^- \cup \{i\}$.

The worst-case time complexity of the algorithm, given one positive instance and one negative instance, is $O(t_n^\uparrow + (|I^+| + |I^-|)\Gamma_n t_m)$.

4.2 Retraction Algorithm

The retraction algorithm of the IBMBS updates the representation when an instance is removed from one of the training sets. It is correct for the class of admissible concept languages when the property G holds [7].

Definition 8. (Property G) *An admissible concept language Lc is said to have property G if for all $n_1, n_2 \in I$:*

$$\{g \in G(\emptyset, \{n_1\})|\neg M(g, n_2)\} = \{g \in G(\emptyset, \{n_2\})|\neg M(g, n_1)\}.$$

The retraction algorithm consists of two parts for handling positive and negative training instances. They are based on theorem 9 and theorem 5, respectively.

Theorem 9. *Consider a version space $VS(I^+, I^-)$ represented by IBMBS: $\langle I^+, \{G(I^+, \{n\})\}_{n \in I^-}\rangle$, and a second version space $VS(I^+ \setminus \{i\}, I^-)$ represented by IBMBS: $\langle I^+ \setminus \{i\}, \{G(I^+ \setminus \{i\}, \{n\})\}_{n \in I^-}\rangle$, where $i \in I^+$. If the concept language Lc is admissible and the property G holds, then:*

$$G(I^+ \setminus \{i\}, \{n\}) = G(I^+, \{n\}) \cup \{g \in G(I^+ \setminus \{i\}, \{i\})|\neg M(g, n)\} \text{ for all } n \in I^-.$$

The retraction algorithm is given in figure 2. *If an instance i is removed from the set I^+*, the algorithm executes two steps by theorem 9. In the first step it generates the set $G(\emptyset, \{i\})$. The set $G(I^+ \setminus \{i\}, \{i\})$ is formed from those elements of $G(\emptyset, \{i\})$ that cover the instances in $I^+ \setminus \{i\}$. In the second step the algorithm forms the maximal boundary set $G(I^+ \setminus \{i\}, \{n\})$ for each $n \in I^-$ as a union of the corresponding sets $G(I^+, \{n\})$ and $\{g \in G(I^+ \setminus \{i\}, \{i\}) | \neg M(g, n)\}$. The resulting IBMBS of $VS(I^+ \setminus \{i\}, I^-)$ are formed by the set $I^+ \setminus \{i\}$ and the maximal boundary sets $G(I^+ \setminus \{i\}, \{n\})$ for all $n \in I^-$. *If the instance i is removed from the set I^-*, the algorithm forms the resulting IBMBS of $VS(I^+, I^- \setminus \{i\})$ from the set I^+ and the maximal boundary sets $G(I^+, \{n\})$ for all $n \in I^- \setminus \{i\}$.

The worst-case time complexity of the algorithm, given one positive instance and one negative instance, is $O(t_n^\uparrow + (|I^+| + |I^-|)\Gamma_n t_m)$.

4.3 Algorithm for Version-Space Collapse

The algorithm for version-space collapse checks whether a version space given by IBMBS is empty. It is proposed for admissible concept languages when the intersection-preserving property holds [7]. The property is given below.

Definition 10. (Intersection-Preserving Property (IP)) *An admissible concept language is said to have the intersection-preserving property if for each nonempty set $C \subseteq Lc$ there exists a description $c \in Lc$ such that an instance $i \in I$ is covered by all the elements of C iff i is covered by the description c.*

The property IP is introduced because it guarantees that if the training set I^- is not empty, the version space $VS(I^+, I^-)$ is not empty iff for each $n \in I^-$ the version space $VS(I^+, \{n\})$ is not empty (see theorem 11).

Retraction **Algorithm**

Input: i: a training instance such that $i \in I^+ \cup I^-$.

$\langle \{I^+, \{G(I^+, \{n\})\}_{n \in I^-}\rangle$: IBMBS of $VS(I^+, I^-)$.

Output: $\langle \{I^+ \setminus \{i\}, \{G(I^+ \setminus \{i\}, \{n\})\}_{n \in I^-}\rangle$: IBMBS of $VS(I^+ \setminus \{i\}, I^-)$ if $i \in I^+$.

$\langle \{I^+, \{G(I^+, \{n\})\}_{n \in I^- \setminus \{i\}}\rangle$: IBMBS of $VS(I^+, I^- \setminus \{i\})$ if $i \in I^-$.

Precondition: $|I^+| > 1$ if $i \in I^+$ and $|I^-| > 1$ if $i \in I^-$.

if $i \in I^+$ then

    Generate the set $G(\emptyset, \{i\})$

    $G(I^+ \setminus \{i\}, \{i\}) = \{g \in G(\emptyset, \{i\}) | (\forall p \in I^+ \setminus \{i\}) M(g, p)\}$

    for $n \in I^-$ do

        $G(I^+ \setminus \{i\}, \{n\}) = G(I^+, \{n\}) \cup \{g \in G(I^+ \setminus \{i\}, \{i\}) | \neg M(g, n)\}$

    return $\langle I^+ \setminus \{i\}, \{G(I^+ \setminus \{i\}, \{n\})\}_{n \in I^-}\rangle$

if $i \in I^-$ then

    return $\langle I^+, \{G(I^+, \{n\})\}_{n \in I^- \setminus \{i\}}\rangle$.

Fig. 2. The Retraction Algorithm.

Theorem 11. *Consider an admissible concept language Lc such that the property IP holds. If the set I^- is nonempty, then:*

$$(VS(I^+, I^-) \neq \emptyset) \leftrightarrow (\forall n \in I^-)(VS(I^+, \{n\}) \neq \emptyset).$$

To check a version space $VS(I^+, I^-)$ for collapse, by theorem 11 we can check for collapse of the version spaces $VS(I^+, \{n\})$ for $n \in I^-$. Since $VS(I^+, \{n\})$ are given by sets $G(I^+, \{n\})$ in the IBMBS of $VS(I^+, I^-)$, we give a relation between the sets $G(I^+, \{n\})$ and version spaces $VS(I^+, \{n\})$ [7].

Theorem 12. $(VS(I^+, I^-) \neq \emptyset) \leftrightarrow (G(I^+, I^-) \neq \emptyset)$.

Theorems 11 and 12 imply corollary 13 below. It states that if the property IP holds and the training set I^- is nonempty, the version space $VS(I^+, I^-)$ is nonempty iff for each $n \in I^-$ the set $G(I^+, \{n\})$ is nonempty.

Corollary 13. *Consider an admissible concept language Lc such that the property IP holds. If the set I^- is nonempty, then:*

$$(VS(I^+, I^-) \neq \emptyset) \leftrightarrow (\forall n \in I^-)(G(I^+, \{n\}) \neq \emptyset).$$

The version-space collapse algorithm uses corollary 13 and is given in figure 3. If a version space $VS(I^+, I^-)$, given by IBMBS, is checked for collapse, the algorithm visits the sets $G(I^+, \{n\})$ for $n \in I^-$. If none of the sets $G(I^+, \{n\})$ is empty, by corollary 13 $VS(I^+, I^-)$ is not empty and the algorithm returns false. Otherwise, by corollary 13 $VS(I^+, I^-)$ is empty and the algorithm returns true. The worst-case time complexity of the algorithm is $O(|I^-|)$.

VS-Collapse **Algorithm**
   Input: $\langle\{I^+, \{G(I^+, \{n\})\}_{n \in I^-}\rangle$: IBMBS of $VS(I^+, I^-)$.
   Output: true if $VS(I^+, I^-) = \emptyset$.
          false if $VS(I^+, I^-) \neq \emptyset$.
     for $n \in I^-$ **do**
       if $G(I^+, \{n\}) = \emptyset$ **then**
          return true
    return false.

Fig. 3. The Algorithm for Version-Space Collapse.

4.4   Classification Algorithm

The classification algorithm of the IBMBS implements the unanimous-voting rule: an instance is classified iff all the descriptions in a version space agree on a classification [5]. The positive instance classification is based on theorem 14. Theorem 14 states that all the descriptions of a version space $VS(I^+, I^-)$ cover an instance $i \in I$ iff the version space $VS(I^+, I^- \cup \{i\})$ is empty.

Theorem 14. $(\forall i \in I)((\forall c \in VS(I^+, I^-))M(c, i) \leftrightarrow (VS(I^+, I^- \cup \{i\}) = \emptyset))$.

The negative instance classification is based on theorem 15. Theorem 15 states that if the concept language is admissible and the property IP holds, then none of descriptions of a version space $VS(I^+, I^-)$ covers an instance $i \in I$ iff a version space $VS(I^+, \{n\})$ exists of which the descriptions do not cover i.

Theorem 15. *If the concept language Lc is admissible such that the property IP holds, and $I^- \neq \emptyset$, then:*

$$(\forall i \in I)((\forall c \in VS(I^+, I^-))\neg M(c, i) \leftrightarrow (\exists n \in I^-)(\forall c \in VS(I^+, \{n\}))\neg M(c, i)).$$

By theorem 15 a negative instance classification can be obtained by the version spaces $VS(I^+, \{n\})$ as well. Since $VS(I^+, \{n\})$ are given with sets $G(I^+, \{n\})$ in the IBMBS of $VS(I^+, I^-)$, we show how to use these sets for the classification.

Theorem 16. $(\forall c \in VS(I^+, I^-))\neg M(c, i) \leftrightarrow (\forall g \in G(I^+, I^-))\neg M(g, i)$.

Theorems 15 and 16 imply corollary 17 below. Corollary 17 states that if the concept language is admissible such that the property IP holds, then none of the descriptions of a version space $VS(I^+, I^-)$ covers an instance $i \in I$ iff there exists a set $G(I^+, \{n\})$ of which all the descriptions do not cover the instance i.

Corollary 17. *If the concept language Lc is admissible such that the property IP holds, and $I^- \neq \emptyset$, then:*

$$(\forall i \in I)((\forall c \in VS(I^+, I^-))\neg M(c, i) \leftrightarrow (\exists n \in I^-)(\forall g \in G(I^+, \{n\}))\neg M(g, i)).$$

Classify **Algorithm**
> **Input:** i: an instance to be classified.
> $\langle I^+, \{G(I^+, \{n\})\}_{n \in I^-} \rangle$: IBMBS of $VS(I^+, I^-)$.
> **Output:** "+" if $(\forall c \in VS(I^+, I^-))M(c, i)$.
> "−" if $(\forall c \in VS(I^+, I^-))\neg M(c, i)$.
> "?" otherwise.
> **Precondition:** $VS(I^+, I^-) \neq \emptyset$.
>> label i as negative
>> $\langle \{I^+, \{G(I^+, \{n\})\}_{n \in I^- \cup \{i\}} \rangle = Learning(i, \langle \{I^+, \{G(I^+, \{n\})\}_{n \in I^-} \rangle)$
>> **if** $VS\text{-}Collapse(\langle I^+, \{G(I^+, \{n\})\}_{n \in I^- \cup \{i\}} \rangle)$ **then**
>>> **return** "+"
>> **for** $n \in I^-$ **do**
>>> **if** $(\forall g \in G(I^+, \{n\}))\neg M(g, i)$ **then**
>>>> **return** "−"
>> **return** "?".

Fig. 4. The Classification Algorithm.

The classification algorithm of the IBMBS is given in figure 4. Given a nonempty version space $VS(I^+, I^-)$, it classifies an instance $i \in I$ in two steps. In the first step the algorithm forms the IBMBS of the version space $VS(I^+, I^- \cup \{i\})$ using the learning algorithm applied on the IBMBS of $VS(I^+, I^-)$ with the instance i labeled as negative. If $VS(I^+, I^- \cup \{i\})$ is empty, by theorem 14 all the descriptions in $VS(I^+, I^-)$ cover the instance. Hence, the instance i is positive and the algorithm returns "+". If $VS(I^+, I^- \cup \{i\})$ is not empty, the algorithm executes the second step. It visits the sets $G(I^+, \{n\})$ for $n \in I^-$. If none of the elements of one of these sets covers the instance i, by corollary 17 all the descriptions in $VS(I^+, I^-)$ do not cover the instance. Thus, the instance i is negative and the algorithm returns "−". Otherwise, the algorithm returns "?".

The worst-case time complexity of the algorithm is $O(t_n^\uparrow + (|I^+| + |I^-|)\Gamma_n t_m)$.

5   Evaluation of the IBMBS

From the previous sections we conclude that *the IBMBS are efficiently computable for the class of admissible concept languages* because:

(1) the worst-case space complexity of the IBMBS is polynomial in the computational characteristic Γ_n, and the sizes $|I^+|$ and $|I^-|$;
(2) the worst-case time complexity of the learning algorithms is polynomial in the computational characteristics $t_n^\uparrow$, Γ_n, t_m, and the sizes $|I^+|$ and $|I^-|$.

In addition we note that:

(3) the worst-case time complexities of the retraction algorithm, the algorithm for version-space collapse and the classification algorithm are polynomial in the computational characteristics $t_n^\uparrow$, Γ_n, t_m, and the sizes $|I^+|$ and $|I^-|$;
(4) *the retraction algorithm does not recompute the IBMBS.*

6   Instance-Based Minimal Boundary Sets

Instance-based minimal boundary sets (IBmBS) and their algorithms can be derived by duality from the previous sections[2]. Due to space limitations we refrain from providing details. The complexities of the IBmBS representation and of its algorithms are given in table 1.

7   Comparison with Relevant Work

Below we compare the IBMBS and the IBmBS with the training-instance representation [3] and the instance-based boundary-set representation [7,8], i.e., with version-space representations that are efficient for instance retraction.

The training-instance representation is efficiently computable and efficient for instance retraction [3]. Nevertheless, it is not practical: the classification of each instance is realised as a search in the concept language using all the training data and the instance. This contrasts with the IBMBS and the IBmBS where the classification process is more based on the representations than on search.

Table 1. Worst-Case Complexities of IBMBS, IBmBS, IBBS and their Algorithms.

	IBMBS
Space:	$O(|I^+| + |I^-||\Gamma_n)$
Time: Learning Algorithm	$O(t_n^\uparrow + (|I^+| + |I^-|)\Gamma_n t_m)$
Time: Retraction Algorithm	$O(t_n^\uparrow + (|I^+| + |I^-|)\Gamma_n t_m)$
Time: Version-Space Collapse Algorithm	$O(|I^-|)$
Time: Classification Algorithm	$O(t_n^\uparrow + (|I^+| + |I^-|)\Gamma_n t_m)$
	IBmBS
Space:	$O(|I^+|\Sigma_p + |I^-|)$
Time: Learning Algorithm	$O(t_p^\downarrow + (|I^+| + |I^-|)\Sigma_p t_m)$
Time: Retraction Algorithm	$O(t_p^\downarrow + (|I^+| + |I^-|)\Sigma_p t_m)$
Time: Version-Space Collapse Algorithm	$O(|I^+|)$
Time: Classification Algorithm	$O(t_p^\downarrow + (|I^+| + |I^-|)\Sigma_p t_m)$
	IBBS
Space:	$O(|I^+|\Sigma_p + |I^-||\Gamma_n)$
Time: Learning Algorithm	$O(t_p^\downarrow + t_n^\uparrow + (|I^+| + |I^-|)(\Sigma_p + \Gamma_n)t_m)$
Time: Retraction Algorithm	$O(t_n^\uparrow + t_p^\downarrow + (|I^+| + |I^-|)(\Gamma_n + \Sigma_p)t_m)$
Time: Version-Space Collapse Algorithm	$O(|I^+| + |I^-|)$
Time: Classification Algorithm	$O(t_p^\downarrow + t_n^\uparrow + (|I^+| + |I^-|)(\Sigma_p + \Gamma_n)t_m)$

The instance-based boundary-set representation (IBBS) is efficiently computable and efficient for instance retraction for the class of admissible concept languages when both properties G and S hold [7,8]. This is confirmed by the

---

[2] We note that the dual of the property G is the property S, and the dual of the intersection-preserving property (IP) is the union-preserving property (UP) [7].

worst-case complexities of the representation and its algorithms given in table 1. An analysis of these complexities shows that each of them is equal to the sum of the corresponding complexities of the IBMBS and IBmBS. Thus, the IBMBS and the IBmBS have two advantages: (1) they are more efficiently computable than the IBBS, and (2) the IBMBS and the IBmBS have more efficient algorithms for learning, retraction, version-space collapse, and classification.

8 Conclusion

This paper introduces the IBMBS and the IBmBS as new version-space representations. It shows that the representations are compact and efficiently computable. The four most important version-space algorithms are given. These results of the IBMBS and the IBmBS are compared with those of other existing version-space representations that are efficient for instance retraction. From the comparison it is concluded that the IBMBS and the IBmBS are the most efficient practical version-space representations for instance retraction.

References

1. Haussler, D.: Quantifying Inductive Bias: AI Learning Algorithms and Valiants Learning Framework. Artificial Intelligence **36** (1988) 177-221
2. Hirsh, H.: Polynomial-Time Learning with Version Spaces. In: Proceedings of the Tenth National Conference on Artificial Intelligence, AAAI Press, Menlo Park, CA (1992) 117-122
3. Hirsh, H., Mishra, N., Pitt, L.: Version Spaces without Boundary Sets. In: Proceedings of the Fourteenth National Conference on Artificial Intelligence, AAAI Press, Menlo Park, CA (1997) 491-496
4. Idemstam-Almquist, P.: Demand Networks: An Alternative Representation of Version Spaces. Master's Thesis, Department of Computer Science and Systems Sciences, Stockholm University, Stockholm, Sweden (1990)
5. Mitchell, T.: Machine Learning. McGraw-Hill, New York, NY (1997)
6. Sablon, G., DeRaedt, L., Bruynooghe, L.: Iterative Versionspaces. Artificial Intelligence **69** (1994) 393-410
7. Smirnov, E.N.: Conjunctive and Disjunctive Version Spaces with Instance-Based Boundary Sets. Ph.D. Thesis, Department of Computer Science, Universiteit Maastricht, Maastricht, The Netherlands (2001)
8. Smirnov, E.N., Braspenning, P.J.: Version Space Learning with Instance-Based Boundary Sets. In: Proceedings of The Thirteenth European Conference on Artificial Intelligence. Jonh Willey and Sons, Chichester, UK (1998) 460-464
9. Smirnov, E.N., Sprinkhuizen-Kuyper, I.G., van den Herik, H.J.: Further Developments in Efficient Instance Retraction. Technical Report CS 02-02, Department of Computer Science, Universiteit Maastricht, Maastricht, The Netherlands (2002)
10. Smith, B.D., Rosenbloom, P.S.: Incremental Non-Backtracking Focusing: A Polynomially Bounded Algorithm for Version Spaces. In: Proceedings of the Eight National Conference on Artificial Intelligence, MIT Press, MA (1990) 848-853

Learning Patterns in Multidimensional Space Using Interval Algebra

A. Osmani

LIPN-CNRS UMR 7030,
99, Avenue J.-B. Clément 93430 Villetaneuse- FRANCE
ao@lipn.univ-paris13.fr

Abstract. In this paper we propose a machine learning formalism based on generalized intervals. This formalism may be used to diagnose breakdown situations
in telecommunication networks. The main task is to discover significant temporal patterns in the large databases generated by the monitoring system. In this
kind of applications, time duration is relevant to the alarms identification process.
The shapes of the decision boundaries are usually axis-parallel with constraints.
The representation of examples in our formalism is similar to the representation described in the Nested Generalized Exemplar theory [Sal91]. This theory of
generalization produces an excellent generalization with interpretable hypotheses
[WD95] in domains where the decision boundaries are axis-parallel.
Using Allen qualitative relations between intervals, firstly we will give an adapted
organization of the set of relations, then we will define an operator of generalization and we will give a table of qualitative generalization. Finally we suggest two
learning algorithms. The second one uses a topologic lattice between relations to
optimize the first one.

1 Introduction

One interesting solution to predict or to explain the behavior of a system is to build
a general model able to imitate the system. It is typically the case in model-based
diagnosis approaches where the problem is to detect, to localize and to identify failures
in the system. In several approaches, breakdown situations are simulated in the model
[Osm99b], and a set of observations is treated, and then archived. These observations are
ordered in time. Sometimes, durations are required: the alarm CT1(technique center) is
happened 5 minutes 3 seconds before the alarm CM2(switch). In other situations only
the order is required: the alarm SCS is observed after CT1. In this paper, we propose a
machine learning approach based on generalized intervals[BCdCO98,Lig91,Lad86] to
treat the observations in order to simplify the identification process.

In 1991, Salzberg [Sal91] proposed a learning theory, using hyperrectangles, and
showed the relevance of this theory in three cases. In the model of representation NGE
(Nested Generalized Exemplar), Salzberg proposed a new way to describe concepts by
using hyperrectangles. He associates a weight parameter for each hyperrectangle He
considers that the function of distance between hyperrectangles can change dynamically
and he takes into account the generalization with exception by using the Thornton
[Tho87] results. The work proposed in [WD95] analyses the performance of the NGE

D. Scott (Ed.): AIMSA 2002, LNAI 2443, pp. 31–40, 2002.

approach compared to the $k-$nearest neighbors (knn) approach in 11 domains. He shows that the performance of the hyperrectangle approach is poor, except when the application is adapted; in which case the approach presents good performances with some appreciates advantages like the level of abstraction and the quantity of information necessary to describe the examples.

It is especially the case with the applications related to the learning of alarm sequences for the faults discrimination in a telecommunication network. In order to model the behavior of the telecommunication network when an abnormal operation occurs, we use the simulator proposed in [Osm99a]. This simulator of breakdown situations in telecommunication networks can reproduce components behavior and messages propagation between components in the network. This simulator builds generalized intervals (see example 2), each generalized interval became a learning example of an abnormal situation. This application is an excellent example for the use of the learning approach based on generalized intervals.

In this paper, we introduce a learning approach based on generalized intervals and which uses both quantitative and qualitative relations between intervals. Our goal is to implement a global solution of learning using generalized intervals with constraints.

In section 1, we give a real example that justifies our interest in the machine learning approach using this kind of representation. Section 2 gives some definitions and shows our relations between intervals extracted from Allen's relations. Section 3 defines the operator of generalization and introduces the table of generalization using our relations between intervals. Section 4 presents two learning algorithms; the first one uses naively the operator of generalization, the second one uses the property of the relation's lattice between interval relations defining a conceptual neighborhood structure to organize examples in order to optimize the first learning algorithm. Section 5 concludes this paper.

Related Work

Several works focus on machine learning using intervals and/or rectangles. Methods that induce logical conjunctions are a good example of orthogonal rectangle bias. The induction of logical conjunctions is one the early machine learning approaches. The original idea was presented by Bruner and al. [BA56], while the first popular implemented IGS (Incremental general-to-specific) algorithm was proposed by Winston [Win75]. This framework has been extended by Mitchell [Mit77] by combining ISG and IGS approaches. Langley's Book [Lan96] gives some complements about this learning approach.
PAC learning of rectangles, have been also studied because they have been experimentally showed to yield excellent hypotheses for several applied problems [ALS97,WD95, WK91].
Nested generalized exemplar theory accomplishes the learning task by storing objects in Euclidian space as hyperrectangle [Sal91]. The hyperrectangles may be nested inside another to arbitrary depth. Some applications results are presented in [WD95].

Other works deal with intervals to learn and to classify patterns in Euclidian space: In Koc[Koc95] an algorithm (COFI) for classification with overlapping feature intervals is proposed. COFI algorithm is an exemplar-based concept-learning algorithm where learning concepts are represented as intervals on the class dimensions for each feature. The knowledge representation is similar to the NGE method, no domain theory is used. In COFI algorithm, learning task is performed in a dynamic environment. The prediction step is based on a majority voting taken among individual predictions based on the votes of the features. The nearest work to the one presented in this paper is the paper presented by Hoppner[Hop01]. Hoppner uses interval algebra to discover temporal rules behavior of multivariate time series.

2   Application Example

This section gives some "generalized examples" from the learning database generated by AutModSim tool[1] describing breakdown situations in telecommunication network. The interpretation of the first line of the matrix is done as follow: if the supervisor of the telecommunication network receives the alarms a_1 in the interval [2,7], a_2 in the interval [2,4] and a_3 in the interval [0,1], probably the network center P_{ct} is in breakdown situation.

$$
\begin{bmatrix} & a_1 & a_2 & a_3 & \end{bmatrix}
$$

$$
\begin{bmatrix} p\_ct \\ p_{ct} \\ p_{cm} \end{bmatrix} \begin{bmatrix} [2,7] & [2,4] & [0,1] \\ [1,2] & [3,4] & \\ [0,1] & [0,1] & [2,5] \end{bmatrix}
$$

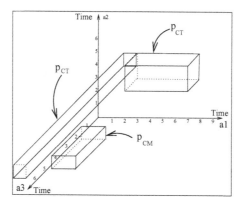

Fig. 1. Illustration.

More generally, the learning database can contain simple examples or generalized examples[2] in the form (breakdown situation, alarm sequence). Initially, we have m known breakdown situations (m is a subset of possible breakdown situations): $\{P_1, \ldots, P_m\}$ and n types of alarms: $\{a_1, \ldots, a_n\}$. These alarms define the dimension

---

[1] AutModSim simulates breakdown situations in telecommunication networks and generates alarm sequences with time intervals [OL].

[2] A simple example is represented with point in multidimensional space. A generalized interval is represented by generalized interval.

of our Euclidian space. For each breakdown situation P_i, we associate a set of generalized example: the example j of the breakdown situation P_i is the sequence $(a_1, X_{i1}^j, \ldots, X_{in}^j)$ where X_{ij} is an interval. In this paper we consider the generalized interval $X_i^j = (X_{i1}^j, \ldots, X_{in}^j)$ as the representative of the example j of P_i.

The learning database will be in the following form:

$$
\begin{bmatrix} a_1 & \ldots & a_n \end{bmatrix}
$$

$$
\begin{bmatrix} P_1 \\ \vdots \\ P_1 \\ \vdots \\ P_m \\ \vdots \\ P_m \end{bmatrix}
\begin{bmatrix} X_{11}^1 & \ldots & X_{1n}^1 \\ \vdots & & \vdots \\ X_{11}^{m_1} & \ldots & X_{1n}^{m_1} \\ \vdots & & \vdots \\ X_{m1}^1 & \ldots & X_{mn}^1 \\ \vdots & & \vdots \\ X_{m1}^{m_m} & \ldots & X_{mn}^{m_m} \end{bmatrix}
$$

This example gives one possible application of our formalism. In this paper, we will present the operator of generalization and the training algorithm.

3   Definitions

An interval x can be identified by these two ends $[x^-, x^+]$. In this case, it is called: instantiated interval.

Definition 1. *A generalized interval X is defined by a sequence of instantiated intervals or by a sequence of intervals and a constraints network between these intervals.*

The constraints are expressed by disjunctions of relations representing a subset of Allen's thirteen relations [All83]. These relations are {precedes(p), meets(m), overlaps(o), finish(f), stard(s), during(d) }, their opposites and the relation of equality.

Example 1. Each of the two following examples illustrates the definition of a generalized interval defined by a sequence of instantiated intervals and a generalized interval defined by a sequence of intervals and a constraints network.

$$ X = ([1,2], [3,5], [2,6]), \ X = \{(x_1, x_2, x_3), R_X\}, \ R_X = \{x_1\, p\, x_2, x_1\, m\, x_3, x_2\, d\, x_3\} $$

Definition 2. *A generalized example is a set of examples describing the same concept. If a point represents a training example of a concept in a given space, an interval, a rectangle, and a cube that describe the same concept are generalized examples*[3].

Allen's relations between intervals [All83] are not necessary used for our learning problem. The figure 2 presents considered relationships between intervals. We consider four groups of relations: the relation disconnect ($disc$) which correspond to the relation precedes, the relation intersect ($inter$) which corresponds to the Allen's relations *meets* and *overlaps*, the relation contain ($cont$) which groups together the relations $finish$,

---

[3] A simple example is a particular case of a generalized interval. In the rest of the paper, example will indicate both simple and generalized example.

$start$ and $during$ and the relation of equality eq. We note the opposite relations of the relations $disc$, $inter$ and $cont$ by $disc^{-1}$, $inter^{-1}$ and $cont^{-1}$, respectively. The relations $DISC$, $CONT$ and $INTER$ indicate the relations $(disc \vee disc^{-1})$, $(cont \vee cont^{-1})$, $(inter \vee inter^{-1})$, respectively. The properties of this cutting will be detailed in the next section.

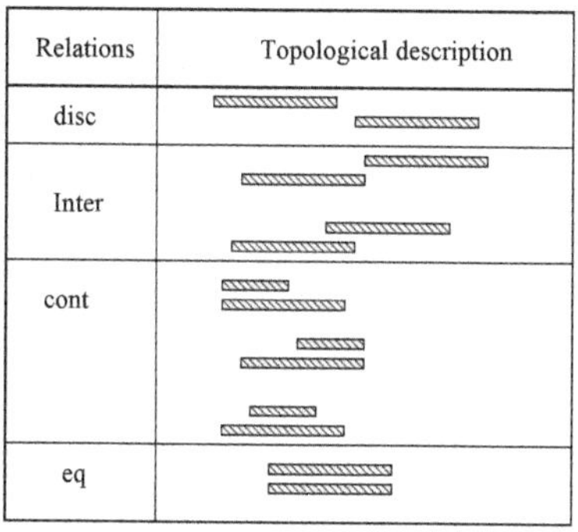

Relations	Topological description
disc	
Inter	
cont	
eq	

Fig. 2. $disc$, $cont$ and $inter$ relations between simple intervals.

Definition 3. *A minimal covering set of parts of the attributes space for a given concept is a space described by a set of generalized intervals E(X), such that any example describing the concept is member, at least, a generalized interval and the intersection of each side of each element of E(X) with one of the examples which it contains is nonempty. The operator of generalization presented in the next section respect this property.*

4   The Operator of Generalization ψ

This section introduces the operator of generalization ψ. This operator allows making a minimal recovery of the space of the attributes by minimizing the number of generalized intervals characterizing each concept and also by minimizing the recoveries of counterexamples during generalization.

Notation 1 *Let us consider $X = (x_1..., x_n)$. We note Gx_i an unspecified interval which generalizes x_i. We note $x_{(i)}$ the generalized interval defined as follow: $X_{(i)} = (x_1...x_{i-1}, Gx_i, x_{i+1}...x_n)$, and we note $X_{(i_1...,i_k)}$ the generalized interval X for which the components x_{i_1}, x_{i_k} are generalized before.*

Let us consider $X = (x_1, ..., x_n)$ and $Y = (y_1, ..., y_n)$ two generalized intervals with the same dimension and defined in the same space.

4.1 $\psi(X, Y)$ Operator

The operator of generalization $\psi_i(x, y)$ defines the generalization of the example X compared to the example Y as follows: $\psi_i(x, y) = x_{(i)}$ such as:

- $Gx_i = [min(x_i^-, y_i^-), max(x_i^+, y_i^+)]$ if X and Y are instantiated and
- $cont(Gx_i, x_i) \wedge cont(Gxi, y_i) \wedge (\forall z_i(\neg cont(G_{x_i}, z_i) \vee \neg disc(x_i, z_i) \vee \neg disc(z_i, y_i)) \wedge (\forall z_i(\neg cont(G_{x_i}, z_i) \vee \neg disc(y_i, z_i) \vee \neg disc(x_i, y_i)))$.

The application of the operator ψ_i on X and Y makes possible to replace X in the database by the generalized example $\psi_i(x, y)$.

According to the same principle, $\psi_{i_1...,i_k}(x, y)$ defines the operator of generalization of X compared to Y for the sequence of attributes $x_{i_1}..., x_{i_k}$.

$$\psi_{i_1...,i_k} = \psi_{i_1} \circ ... \circ ...\psi_{i_k} = \circ_{l=i_1}^{i_k} \psi_l$$

Example 2. Let us consider two generalized examples $X = ([2,3],[5,6])$ and $Y = ([5,7],[1,3])$. Figure 3 illustrates the application of the operators ψ_1 and $\psi_{1,2}$.

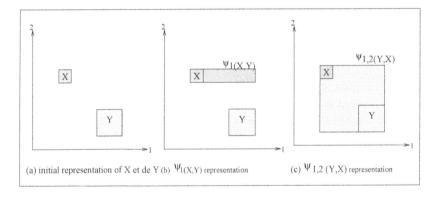

(a) initial representation of X et de Y (b) $\Psi_{1(X,Y)}$ representation   (c) $\Psi_{1,2}$ (Y,X) representation

Fig. 3. Illustration of the operators ψ_i et $\psi_{i_1,...,i_k}$.

The operator $\psi(X, Y)$ generalizes the two generalized examples X and Y and produces only one example Z as follows:

$$\psi(X,Y) = Z = ([min(x_1^-, y_1^-), max(x_1^+, y_1^+)]...,[min(x_n^-, y_n^-), max(x_n^+, y_n^+)])$$

Proposition 1. $\psi(X,Y) = GX$ *such that* $GX = \circ_{i=1}^{i=n} \psi_i(X, Y)$

Property 1 *The operators ψ_i and $\psi_{i_1...,i_k}$ are not commutative. The operator ψ is commutative.*

Example 3. The figure 3(c) gives an example of generalization of Y with X on two attributes. If the description space of the examples contains only two attributes then $\psi(x, y) = \psi_{1,2}(y, x)$.

4.2 $\psi(X, Y, Z)$ **Operator**

Generalization process operates in a universe of examples and counterexamples. The operator $\psi(x, y, z)$ defines the concept of generalization of two examples X and Y of the same concept, knowing that Z is a counterexample for this same concept.

Before defining this operator, I will start with the definition of the operator $\psi_i(x, y, z)$. This operator defines the generalization of the example X compared to the example Y describing the same concept by knowing the counterexample Z.

- **dimension 1:** it indicates the behavior of $\psi_i(x, y, z) = \psi(x, y, z)$ in an one-dimensional space(i=1). Generalization is done as follows: $(\forall X)(\forall Z)(\forall Y)$
  1. $(cont(X, Y) \vee cont(Y, X) \vee inter(Y, X) \vee inter(X, Y)) \Rightarrow (\psi_i(X, Y, Z) = \psi_i(X, Y))$
  2. $(\forall Z)((disc(X, Z) \wedge disc(Y, Z)) \vee (disc(Z, X) \wedge disc(Z, Y))) \Rightarrow (\psi_i(X, Y, Z) = \psi_i(X, Y))$

  If none of the two premises is valid, generalization fails.
- **high dimensions** The definition of $\psi_i(X, Y, Z)$ $i \in \{1, .., n\}$ is done as follow: $\psi_i(X, Y, Z) = \psi_i(X, Y)$ if, and only if, one of the following expressions is checked:
  1. $(\exists j)(j \neq i)DISC(x_j, z_j)$ or
  2. $(R(x_i, z_i) \wedge R(y_i, z_i) \wedge R(x_i, y_i))) = ok$ in the table 1.

  Otherwise generalization fails.

As for the operator $\psi_{i_1, .., i_k}(X, Y)$:

$$\psi_{i_1, ..., i_k}(X, Y, Z) = \circ_{m=i_1}^{m=i_k} \psi_m(X, Y, Z)$$

Table 1 gives the list of the possible situations which can occur between the examples X, Y and Z, knowing that X and Y describe the same concept and Z a different concept. The table 1 indicates when generalization is possible, i.e. $\psi_i(x, y, z) = \psi_i(x, y)$, by the word: ok, when generalization is not possible, i.e. no modification is brought to the base of the examples, by the word $\neg ok$ and when the relation between X, Y and Z is inconsistency by the word 0.

The first column indicates relations $R(X, Z)$ and $R(Y, Z)$, respectively. The first line indicates the relation $R(X, Y)$. The relations $cont$ and eq are not represented in the first line because the generalization process make no modification for X.

Proposition 2. $(\forall i)(R(x_i, z_i)R(y_i, z_i)R(x_i, y_i) = ok) \rightarrow \psi(X, Y, Z) = \psi(X, Y)$

Proposition 3. $\psi(X, Y, Z) = GX$ such that:

1. $GX = \circ_{i=1}^{i=n}\psi_i(X, Y)$
2. $(\forall i)\; \psi_i(\circ_{j=1}^{j=i-1}\psi_j(X, Y), Y, Z) = \psi_i(\circ_{j=1}^{j=i-1}\psi_j(X, Y), Y)$

Let us consider $S = (Z_1, \ldots Z_l)$ the ordered set of the counterexamples for the concept described by the examples X and Y.

$$\psi(X, Y, S) = \circ_{i=1}^{i=l}\psi(X, Y, Z_i)$$

Table 1. Generalization of an example X compared to Y knowing the counterexample Z.

	disc	inter	$cont^{-1}$	$inter^{-1}$	$disc^{-1}$
disc disc	ok	ok	ok	ok	ok
disc int	ok	ok	ok	0	0
disc cont	ok	ok	ok	0	0
disc eq	ok	0	0	0	0
disc $cont^{-1}$	¬ok	0	0	0	0
disc $inter^{-1}$	¬ok	0	0	0	0
disc $disc^{-1}$	¬ok	0	0	0	0
inter disc	0	0	0	ok	ok
inter int	0	ok	ok	ok	0
inter cont	0	ok	ok	0	0
inter eq	0	ok	0	0	0
inter $cont^{-1}$	¬ok	0	0	0	0
inter $inter^{-1}$	¬ok	ok	0	0	0
inter $disc^{-1}$	¬ok	0	0	0	0
cont disc	0	0	0	ok	ok
cont int	0	0	0	ok	0
cont cont	0	ok	ok	ok	0
cont eq	0	0	0	0	0
cont $cont^{-1}$	0	0	0	0	0
cont $inter^{-1}$	0	ok	0	0	0
cont $disc^{-1}$	ok	ok	0	0	0

	disc	inter	$cont^{-1}$	$inter^{-1}$	$disc^{-1}$
$cont^{-1}$ disc	0	0	0	0	¬ok
$cont^{-1}$ int	0	0	ok	ok	¬ok
$cont^{-1}$ cont	0	0	ok	0	0
$cont^{-1}$ eq	0	0	ok	0	0
$cont^{-1}$ $cont^{-1}$	¬ok	ok	ok	ok	¬ok
$cont^{-1}$ $inter^{-1}$	¬ok	ok	ok	0	0
$cont^{-1}$ $disc^{-1}$	¬ok	ok	0	0	0
$inter^{-1}$ disc	0	0	0	0	¬ok
$inter^{-1}$ int	0	0	0	ok	¬ok
$inter^{-1}$ cont	0	0	ok	ok	0
$inter^{-1}$ eq	0	0	0	ok	0
$inter^{-1}$ $cont^{-1}$	0	0	0	ok	¬ok
$inter^{-1}$ $inter^{-1}$	0	ok	ok	ok	0
$inter^{-1}$ $disc^{-1}$	ok	ok	0	0	0
$disc^{-1}$ disc	0	0	0	0	¬ok
$disc^{-1}$ int	0	0	0	0	¬ok
$disc^{-1}$ cont	0	0	ok	ok	ok
$disc^{-1}$ eq	0	0	0	0	ok
$disc^{-1}$ $cont^{-1}$	0	0	0	0	¬ok
$disc^{-1}$ $inter^{-1}$	0	0	ok	ok	ok
$disc^{-1}$ $disc^{-1}$	ok	ok	ok	ok	ok

5   Learning Algorithms

This section presents two training algorithms: a naive learning algorithm (NLAGI) and an optimized learning algorithm (OLAGI) which reduce the training time.

Algorithm 1   *algorithm NLAGI*

Input : $S = (E_1, ..., E_m)$ *and* $C = (C_1, ..., C_n)$
begin
1     $Result = \emptyset$;
2   *for (i=1 to n) do* $generalized_i$ =*false* ;
3   *for (i=1 to n) do {*
4   *for (j=i+1 to n) do {*
5   *if* $(\psi(C_i, C_j, S) = \psi(C_i, C_j))$
6   *{ generalized$_i$ =true ; generalized$_j$ =true ;*
8              $C = C + \psi(C_i, C_j)$; *n++ ;*
10   *generalized$_n$ =false;*
11   *}*
12   *}*
13       $C = C - \{C_i\}$;
14   *if (generalized$_i$ =false){result+=C$_i$;}*
15   *}*
EndAlgorithm

Algorithm OLAGI exploits the lattice structure between interval relations [Lig96] to define a partial order $\preceq$ between the training base of examples. In fact, examples are ordered sequentially in the database. To obtain this total ordering starting from the partial ordering, we take into account the fact that the operator ψ is noncommutative.

Figure 4(a) shows the lattice between interval relations. Figure 4(b) uses this result to define a lattice between our defined relations. We call the obtained lattice: an increased lattice. The dotted lines extract a total order between the relations by using ψ previous defining properties. In the increased lattice, $X \preceq Y$ if there is a path from X to Y.

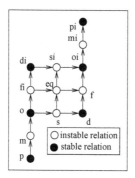 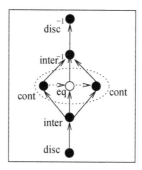

Fig. 4. (a) Simplified lattice   (b) Lattice of interval relations

The extension of this relation lattice between intervals to a relation lattice between generalized intervals uses a simplified version of the generalized lattice defined in [BCdCO98].

The contribution of this property is to make the training local. Indeed, by ordering the examples of training (cost $O(n^2)$, N is the number of examples in the database), we obtain the following result:

Let us consider $X_1, \ldots, X_m$ the sequence of training examples of training such that:
$$(\forall i)(\not\exists j)/(i < j) \ and \ X_j \preceq X_i$$

Property 2 $(\forall i)(\forall j > i)$ such that $X_i, X_{i+1}, \ldots, X_j$ describe the same concept, for all Z in the sequence of learning examples describing another concept than X_i,

$$\psi_{t,1 \leq t \leq n}(X_{k,i \leq k \leq j}, X_{l,i \leq l \leq j}, Z) = \psi_t(X_k, X_l)$$

and more generally : $\psi(X_{k,i \leq k \leq j}, X_{l,i \leq l \leq j}, Z) = \psi(X_k, X_l)$

The OLAGI learning algorithm uses this propriety to reduce learning time.

6   Conclusion

In our considered application sequences of alarms are generated by the telecommunication network. Each sequence describes a particular state of the system. We have proposed a technique to represent these sequences by generalized intervals each one describing a generalized example of a breakdown situation. This technique uses temporal CSP and translates some known results to propose an interesting generalization algorithm. In this paper we describe our contribution but the developed framework include a large part of related work (see section 2). The learning techniques are used more and more for the telecommunication management network. This article presents a formalism to learn temporal patterns with interval.

References

[All83]   J.F. Allen. Maintaining knowledge about temporal intervals. *Journal of the Association for Computing Machinery*, 26:832–843, 1983.

[ALS97]   P. Auer, P.M. Long, and A. Srinivasan. Approximating hyperrectangles: Learning and pseudo-random sets. In *ACM. Symposium on the Theory of Computing*, pages 314–323, 1997.

[BA56]   J.S. Bruner and G.A. Auster. A study of thinking. In *New York: John Wiley*, 1956.

[BCdCO98]   P. Balbiani, J.-F Condotta, L. Fariñas del Cerro, and A. Osmani. Reasoning about generalized intervals. In *LNAI 1480*, pages 50–61. Springer, AIMSA-98, 1998.

[Hop01]   F. Hoppner. Discovery of temporal patterns -learning rules about the qualitative behaviour of time series. In *LNAI 2168 PKDD*, pages 192–203. Springer-Verlag Berlin, 2001.

[Koc95]   H.U. Koc. *Classification with overlapping feature intervals*. Phd thesis, Bilkent University (department of computer engineering and information science), 1995.

[Lad86]   P.B. Ladkin. Time representation: A taxonomy of interval relations. In *Proceedings of the AAAI National Conference on Artificial Intelligence*, pages 360–366, 1986.

[Lan96]   P. Langley. *Elements of machine learning*. Morgan Kaufmann Publishers, 1996.

[Lig91]   G. Ligozat. On generalized interval calculi. In *Proceedings of the AAAI National Conference on Artificial Intelligence*, pages 234–240, 1991.

[Lig96]   G. Ligozat. A new proof of tractability for ORD-HORN relations. In *Proceedings of the AAAI National Conference on Artificial Intelligence*, pages 395–401, 1996.

[Mit77]   T.M. Mitchell. Version spaces: A candidate elimination approach to rule learning. In *Proceedings of the International Joint Conference on Artificial Intelligence*, pages 305–310, 1977.

[OL]   A. Osmani and F. Lévy. Generation d'une base d'apprentissage pour l'apprentissage de pannes dans un reseau de télécommunications. In *(RFIA'2000)*.

[Osm99a]   A. Osmani. *Diagnostic à base de modèles pour la supervision de pannes dans un réseau de télécommunications & raisonnement sur les intervalles*. PhD thesis, Laboratoire LIPN, Institut Galilée, Université de Paris XIII, 1999.

[Osm99b]   A. Osmani. Modeling and simulating breakdown situations in telecommunication networks. In *LNAI 1611*, pages 698–707, IEA/AIE-99, 1999.

[Sal91]   S. Salzberg. A nearest hyperrectangle learning method. In *Machine Learning*, volume 6(3), pages 251–276, 1991.

[Tho87]   C. Thornton. Hypercuboid formation behavior of two learning algorithms. In *Proceedings of the International Joint Conference on Artificial Intelligence*, pages 301–313, 1987.

[WD95]   Dietrich Wettschereck and Thomas G. Dietterich. An experimental comparison of the nearest-neighbor and nearest-hyperrectangle algorithms. *Machine Learning*, 19(1):5–27, 1995.

[Win75]   P.H. Winston. Learning structural descriptions from examples. In *In P.H. Winston (ed.). The psychology of computer vision, optADDRESS =*, 1975.

[WK91]   S.M. Weiss and C.A. Kulikowski. *Computer System that learn*. San Mateo CA: Morgan Kaufmann Publishers, INC, 1991.

A Machine Learning Approach to Automatic Production of Compiler Heuristics

Antoine Monsifrot, François Bodin, and René Quiniou

IRISA-University of Rennes France
{amonsifr,bodin,quiniou}@irisa.fr

Abstract. Achieving high performance on modern processors heavily relies on the compiler optimizations to exploit the microprocessor architecture. The efficiency of optimization directly depends on the compiler heuristics. These heuristics must be target-specific and each new processor generation requires heuristics reengineering.

In this paper, we address the automatic generation of optimization heuristics for a target processor by machine learning. We evaluate the potential of this method on an always legal and simple transformation: loop unrolling. Though simple to implement, this transformation may have strong effects on program execution (good or bad). However deciding to perform the transformation or not is difficult since many interacting parameters must be taken into account. So we propose a machine learning approach.

We try to answer the following questions: is it possible to devise a learning process that captures the relevant parameters involved in loop unrolling performance? Does the Machine Learning Based Heuristics achieve better performance than existing ones?

Keywords: decision tree, boosting, compiler heuristics, loop unrolling.

1 Introduction

Achieving high performance on modern processors heavily relies on the ability of the compiler to exploit the underlying architecture. Numerous program transformations have been implemented in order to produce efficient programs that exploit the potential of the processor architecture. These transformations interact in a complex way. As a consequence, an optimizing compiler relies on internal heuristics to choose an optimization and whether or not to apply it. Designing these heuristics is generally difficult. The heuristics must be specific to each implementation of the instruction set architecture. They are also dependent on changes made to the compiler.

In this paper, we address the problem of automatically generating such heuristics by **a machine learning approach**. To our knowledge this is the first study of machine learning to build these heuristics. The usual approach consists in running a set of benchmarks to setup heuristics parameters. Very few

D. Scott (Ed.): AIMSA 2002, LNAI 2443, pp. 41–50, 2002.
© Springer-Verlag Berlin Heidelberg 2002

papers have specifically addressed the issue of building such heuristics. Nevertheless approximate heuristics have been proposed [8,11] for *unroll and jam* a transformation that is like unrolling (our example) but that behaves differently.

Our study aims to simplify compiler construction while better exploiting optimizations. To evaluate the potential of this approach we have chosen a simple transformation: loop unrolling [6]. Loop unrolling is always legal and is easy to implement, but because it has many side effects, it is difficult to devise a decision rule that will be correct in most situations.

In this novel study we try to answer the following questions: is it possible to learn a decision rule that selects the parameters involved in loop unrolling efficiency? Does the Machine Learning Based Heuristics (denoted MLBH) achieve better performance than existing ones? Does the learning process really take into account the target architecture?

To answer the first question we build on previous studies [9] that defined an abstract representation of loops in order to capture the parameters influencing performance. To answer the second question we compare the performance of our Machine Learning Based Heuristics and the GNU Fortran compiler [3] on a set of applications. To answer the last question we have used two target machines, an UltraSPARC machine [12] and an IA-64 machine [7], and used on each the MLBH computed on the other.

The paper is organized as follows. Section 2 gives an overview of the loop unrolling transformation. Section 3 shows how machine learning techniques can be used to automatically build loop unrolling heuristics. Section 4 illustrates an implementation of the technique based on the OC1 decision tree software [10].

2 Loop Unrolling as a Case

The performance of superscalar processors relies on a very high frequency[1] and on the parallel execution of multiple instructions (this is also called *Instruction Level Parallelism* –ILP). To achieve this, the internal architecture of superscalar microprocessors is based on the following features:

Memory hierarchy: the main memory access time is typically hundreds of times greater than the CPU cycle time. To limit the slowdown due to memory accesses, a set of intermediate levels are added between the CPU unit and the main memory; the level the closest to the CPU is the fastest, but also the smallest. The data or instructions are loaded by blocks (sets of contiguous bytes in memory) from one memory level of the hierarchy to the next level to exploit the following fact: when a program accesses some memory element, the next contiguous one is usually also accessed in the very near future. In a classical configuration there are 2 levels, L1 and L2 of cache memories as shown on the figure 1. The penalty to load data from main memory tends to be equivalent to executing 1000 processor cycles. If the data is already in L2, it is one order of magnitude less. If the data is already in L1, the access can be done in only a few CPU cycles.

---

[1] typically 2 gigahertz corresponding to a processor cycle time of 0.5 nanosecond

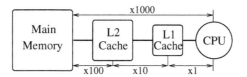

Fig. 1. Memory hierarchy

Multiple Pipelined Functional Units: the processor has multiple functional units that can run in parallel to execute several instructions per cycle (typically an integer operation can be executed in parallel with a memory access and a floating point computation). Furthermore these functional units are pipelined. This divides the operation in a sequence of steps that can be performed in parallel. Scheduling instructions in the functional units is performed in an *out-of-order* or *in-order* mode. Contrary to the *in-order*, in the *out-of-order* mode instructions are not always executed in the order specified by the program. When a processor runs at maximum speed, each pipelined functional unit executes one instruction per cycle. This requires that all operands and branch addresses are available at the beginning of the cycle. Otherwise, functional units must wait during some delays. The processor performance depends on these waiting delays.

The efficiency of the memory hierarchy and ILP are directly related to the structure and behavior of the code. Many program transformations reduce the number of waiting delays in program execution.

Loop unrolling [6] is a simple program transformation where the loop body is replicated many times. It may be applied at source code level to benefit from all compiler optimizations. It improves the exploitation of ILP: increasing the size of the body augments the number of instructions eligible to *out-of-order* scheduling. Loop unrolling also reduces loop management overhead but it has also some beneficial side effects from later compiler steps such as common sub-expression elimination. However it also has many negative side effects that can cancel the benefits of the transformation:

- the instruction cache behavior may be degraded (if the loop body becomes too big to fit in the cache),
- the register allocation phase may generate spill code (additional load and store instructions),
- it may prevent other optimization techniques.

As a consequence, it is difficult to fully exploit loop unrolling. Compilers are usually very conservative. Their heuristics are generally based on the loop body size: under a specific threshold, if there is no control flow statement, the loop is unrolled. This traditional approach under-exploits loop unrolling [5] and must be adapted when changes are made to the compiler or to the target architecture.

The usual approach to build loop unrolling heuristics for a given target computer consists in running a set of benchmarks to setup the heuristics parameters. This approach is intrinsically limited because in most optimizations such as loop unrolling, too many parameters are involved. Microarchitecture characteristics (for instance the size of instruction cache, ...) as well as the other optimizations (for instance instruction scheduling, ...) that follow loop unrolling during the compilation process should be considered in the decision procedure. The main parameters, but not all (for instance number instruction cache misses), which influence loop unrolling efficiency directly depend on the loop body statements. This is because loop unrolling mainly impacts code generation and instruction scheduling. As a consequence, it is realistic to base the unrolling decision on the properties of the loop code while ignoring its execution context.

3   Machine Learning for Building Heuristics

Machine learning techniques offer an automatic, flexible and adaptive framework for dealing with the many parameters involved in deciding the effectiveness of program optimizations. Classically a decision rule is learnt from feature vectors describing positive and negative applications of the transformation. However, it is possible to use this framework only if the parameters can be abstracted statically from the loop code and if their number remains limited. Reducing the number of parameters involved in the process is important as the performance of machine learning techniques is poor when the number of dimensions of the learning space is high [10]. Furthermore learning from complex spaces requires more data.

To summarize the approach, the steps involved in using a machine learning technique for building heuristics for program transformation are:

1. finding a loop abstraction that captures the "performance" features involved in an optimization, in order to build the learning set,
2. choosing an automatic learning process to compute a rule in order to decide whether loop unrolling should be applied,
3. setting up the result of the learning process as heuristics for the compiler.

In the remainder of this section, we present the representation used for abstracting loop properties. The next section shows how to sort the loop into winning and loosing classes according to unrolling. Finally, the learning process based on learning decision trees is overviewed.

3.1   Loop Abstraction

The loop abstraction must capture the main loop characteristics that influence the execution efficiency on a modern processor. They are represented by integer **features** which are relevant static loop properties according to unrolling. We have selected 5 classes of integer features:

Memory access: number of memory accesses, number of array element reuses from one iteration to another.
Arithmetic operations count: number of additions, multiplications or divisions excepting those in array index computations.
Size of the loop body: number of statements in the loop.

Control statements in the loop: number of if statements, goto, etc. in the
loop body.

Number of iterations: if it can be computed at compile time.

In order to reduce the learning complexity, only a subset of these features are
used for a given compiler and target machine. The chosen subset was determined
experimentally by cross validation (see Section 4). The quality of the predictions
achieved by an artificial neural network based on 20 indices was equivalent to
the predictive quality of the 6 chosen features.

Figure 2 gives the features that were selected and an example of loop abstraction.

```
do i=2,100
  a(i) = a(i)+a(i-1)*a(i+1)
enddo
```

Number of statements	1
Number of arithmetic operations	2
Minimum number of iterations	99
Number of array accesses	4
Number of array element reuses	3
Number of if statements	0

Fig. 2. Example of features for a loop.

3.2   Unrolling Beneficial Loops

A learning example refers to a loop in a particular context (represented by
the loop features). To determine if unrolling is beneficial, each loop is executed
twice. Then, the execution times of the original loop and of the unrolled loop
are compared. Four cases can be considered:

not significant: the loop execution time is too small and therefore the timing
is not significant. The loop is discarded from the learning set.

equal: the execution times of the original and of the unrolled loop are close. A
threshold is used to take into account the timer inaccuracy. Thus, the loop
performance is considered as invariant by unrolling if the benefit is less than
10%.

improved: the speedup is above 10%. The loop is considered as being **beneficial** by unrolling.

degraded: there is a speed-down. The loop is considered as a degraded loop by
unrolling.

The loop set is then partitioned into equivalence classes (denoted loop classes
in the remainder). Two loops are in the same loop class if their respective abstractions are equal.

The next step is to decide if a loop class is to be considered as a positive or
a negative example. Note that there can be beneficial and degraded loops in the
same class as non exhaustive descriptions are used to represent the loops. This
is a natural situation as the loop execution or compilation context may greatly
influence its execution time, for instance due to instruction cache memory effects.
The following criterion has been used to decide whether a class will represent a
positive or a negative example:

1. In a particular class, a loop whose performance degrades by less than 5% is counted once, a loop that degrades performance by 10% is counted twice. A loop that degrades performance more than 20% is counted three times.
2. if the number of unrolling beneficial loops is greater than the number of degraded loops (using the weights above), then the class represents a positive example, else the class represents a negative example.

3.3   A Learning Method Based on Decision Trees and Boosting

We have chosen to represent unrolling decision rules as decision trees. Decision trees can be learnt efficiently from feature based vectors. Each node of the decision tree represents a test checking the value(s) of one (or several) feature(s) which are easy to read by an expert. This is not the case for statistical methods like Nearest Neighbor or Artificial Neural Network for instance, which have comparable or slightly better performance.

We used the OC1 [10] software. OC1 is a classification tool that induces oblique decision trees. Oblique decision trees produce polygonal partitionings of the feature space. OC1 recursively splits a set of objects in a hyperspace by finding optimal hyperplanes until every object in a subspace belongs to the same class.

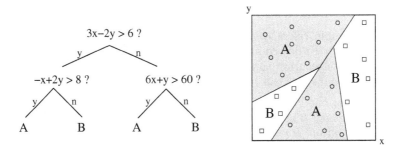

Fig. 3. The left side of the figure shows an oblique decision tree that uses two attributes. The right side shows the partitioning that this tree creates in the attribute space.

A decision tree example is shown in Figure 3, together with its 2-D related space. Each node of the tree tests a linear combination of some indices (equivalent to an hyperplane) and each leaf of the tree corresponds to a class. The main advantages of OC1 is that it finds smaller decision trees than classical tree learning methods. The major drawback is that they are less readable than classical ones.

The classification of a new loop is equivalent to finding a leaf loop class. Once induced, a decision tree can be used as a classification process. An object represented by its feature vector is classified by following the branches of the tree indicated by node tests until a leaf is reached.

To improve the accuracy obtained with OC1 we have used boosting [13]. Boosting is a general method for improving the accuracy of any given algorithm.

Boosting consists in learning a set of classifiers for more and more difficult problems: the weights of examples that are misclassified by the classifier learnt at step n are augmented (by a factor proportional to the global error) and at step $n + 1$ a new classifier is learnt on this weighted examples. Finally, the global classification is obtained by a weighted vote of the individual classifier according to their proper accuracy. In our case 9 trees were computed.

4   Experiments

The learning set used in the experiments is made of loops extracted from programs in Fortran 77. Most of them were chosen in available benchmarks [4,1]. We have studied two types of programs: real applications (the majority comes from SPEC [4]) and computational kernels. Table 1 presents some characteristics of a loop set (cf section 3.2).

Table 1. IA-64 learning set.

Number of loops	1036
Discarded loops	177
Unrolling beneficial loops	233
Unrolling invariant loops	505
Unrolling degraded loops	121
Loop classes	572
Positive examples	139
Negative examples	433

The accuracy of the learning method was assessed by a 10-fold cross-validation. We have experiment with pruning. We have obtained smaller trees but the resulting quality was degraded. The results without pruning are presented in Table 2. Two factors can explain the fact that the overall accuracy cannot be better than 85%:

1. since unrolling beneficial and degraded loops can appear in the same class (cf section 3.2) a significant proportion of examples may be noisy,
2. the classification of positive examples is far worse than the classification of negative ones. Maybe the learning set does not contain enough beneficial loops.

To go beyond cross validation another set of experiments has been performed on two target machines, an UltraSPARC and an IA-64. They aim at showing the technique does catch the most significant loops of the programs. The g77 [3] compiler was used. With this compiler, loop unrolling can be globally turned on and off. To assess our method we have implemented loop unrolling at the source

Table 2. Cross validation accuracy

	UltraSPARC		IA-64	
	normal	boosting	normal	boosting
Accuracy of **overall** example classification	79.4%	85.2%	82.6%	85.2%
Accuracy of **positive** example classification	62.4%	61.7%	73.9%	69.6%
Accuracy of **negative** example classification	85.1%	92.0%	86.3%	92.3%

code level using TSF [2]. This is not the most efficient scheme because in some cases this inhibits some of the compiler optimizations (contrary to unrolling performed by the compiler itself). We have performed experiments to check whether the MLB heuristics are at least as good as compiler heuristics and whether the specificities of a target architecture can be taken into account. A set of benchmark programs were selected in the learning set and for each one we have:

1. run the code compiled by g77 with -O3 option,
2. run the code compiled with -O3 -funroll options : the compiler uses its own unrolling strategy,
3. unroll the loops according to the result of the MLB heuristics and run the compiled code with -O3 option. The heuristics was learned for the target machine from learning set where the test program was removed.
4. unroll the loops according to the result of the MLB heuristics learnt for the **other** target machine and run the compiled code with -O3 option.

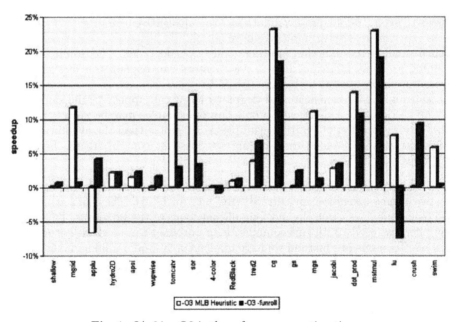

Fig. 4. IA-64 : -O3 is the reference execution time.

The performance results are given in Figure 4 and Figure 5 respectively for the IA-64 and UltraSPARC targets.

The average execution time of the optimized programs for the IA-64 is 93.8% of the reference execution time (no unrolling) using the MLB heuristics and 96.8% using the g77 unrolling strategy. On the UltraSPARC we have respectively 96% and 98.7% showing that our unrolling strategy performs better. Indeed,

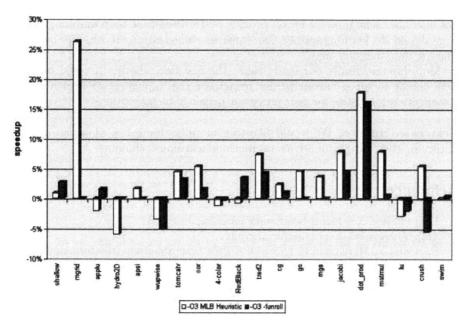

Fig. 5. UltraSPARC : -O3 is the reference execution time.

gaining a few percent on average execution time with one transformation is significant because each transformation is not often beneficial. For example, only 22% of the loops are beneficial by unrolling on IA-64 and 17% on UltraSPARC.

In the last experiment we exchanged the decision trees learnt for the two target machines. On the UltraSPARC, the speedup is degraded from 96% to 97.9% and on the IA-64 it is degraded from 93.8% to 96.8%. This shows that the heuristics are effectively tuned to a target architecture.

5   Conclusion

Compilers implement a lot of optimization algorithms for improving performance. The choice of using a particular sequence of optimizations and their parameters is done through a set of heuristics hard coded in the compiler.

At each major compiler revision, but also at new implementations of the target Instruction Set Architecture, a new set of heuristics must be reengineered.

In this paper, we have presented a new method for addressing such reengineering in the case of loop unrolling. Our method is based on a learning process which adapts to new target architectures or new compiler features. Using an abstract loop representation we showed that decision trees that provide target specific heuristics for loop unrolling can be learnt.

While our study is limited to the simple case of loop unrolling it opens a new direction for the design of compiler heuristics. Even for loop unrolling, there are still many issues to consider to go beyond this first result. Are there better abstractions that can capture loop characteristics? Can hardware counters (for instance cache miss counters) provide better insight on loop unrolling? How large should the learning set be? Can other machine learning techniques be more efficient than decision trees?

More fundamentally our study raises the question whether it could be possible or not to quasi automatically reengineer the implementation of a set of optimization heuristics for new processor target implementations.

Acknowledgments. We would like to gratefully thank I. C. Lerman and L. Miclet for their insightful advice on machine learning techniques.

References

1. David Bailey. Nas kernel benchmark program, June 1988. http://www.netlib.org/benchmark/nas.
2. F. Bodin, Y. Mével, and R. Quiniou. A User Level Program Transformation Tool. In *Proceedings of the International Conference on Supercomputing*, pages 180–187, July 1998, Melbourne, Australia.
3. GNU Fortran Compiler. http://gcc.gnu.org/.
4. Standard Performance Evaluation Corporation. http://www.specbench.org/.
5. Jack W.Davidson and Sanjay Jinturkar. Aggressive Loop Unrolling in a Retargetable, Optimizing Compiler. In *Compiler Construction*, volume 1060 of *Lecture Notes in Computer Science*, pages 59–73. Springer, April 1996.
6. J. J. Dongarra and A. R. Hinds. Unrolling loops in FORTRAN. *Software Practice and Experience*, 9(3):219–226, March 1979.
7. IA-64. http://www.intel.com/design/Itanium/idfisa/index.htm.
8. A. Koseki, H. Komastu, and Y. Fukazawa. A Method for Estimating Optimal Unrolling Times for Nested Loops. In *Proceedings of the International Symposium on Parallel Architectures, Algorithms and Networks*, 1997.
9. A. Monsifrot and F. Bodin. Computer Aided Hand Tuning (CAHT): "Applying Case-Based Reasoning to Performance Tuning". In *Proceedings of the 15th ACM International Conference on Supercomputing (ICS-01)*, pages 196–203. ACM Press, June 17–21 2001, Sorrento, Italy.
10. Sreerama K. Murthy, Simon Kasif, and Steven Salzberg. A System for Induction of Oblique Decision Trees. *Journal of Artificial Intelligence Research*, 2:1–32, 1994.
11. Vivek Sarkar. Optimized Unrolling of Nested Loops. In *Proceedings of the 14th ACM International Conference onSupercomputing (ICS-00)*, pages 153–166. ACM Press, May 2000.
12. UltraSPARC. http://www.sun.com/processors/UltraSPARC-II/.
13. C. Yu and D.B. Skillicorn. Parallelizing Boosting and Bagging. Technical report, Queen's University, Kingston, Ontario, Canada K7L 3N6, February 2001.

Using Failed Local Search for SAT as an Oracle for Tackling Harder A.I. Problems More Efficiently*

Éric Grégoire, Bertrand Mazure, and Lakhdar Saïs

CRIL-CNRS – Université d'Artois
Rue Jean Souvraz SP-18
F-62307 Lens Cedex France
{gregoire,mazure,sais}@cril.univ-artois.fr

Abstract. Local search is often a suitable paradigm for solving hard decision problems and approximating computationally difficult ones in the artificial intelligence domain. In this paper, it is shown that a smart use of the computation of a local search that *failed* to solve a NP-hard decision problem $\mathcal{A}$ can sometimes slash down the computing time for the resolution of computationally *harder* optimization problems containing $\mathcal{A}$ as a sub-problem. As a case study, we take $\mathcal{A}$ as SAT and consider some $P^{NP[\mathcal{O}(\log m)]}$ symbolic reasoning problems. Applying this technique, these latter problems can often be solved thanks to a small constant number of calls to a SAT-solver, only.

Keywords. SAT, local search, minimal models, logic and AI.

1 Introduction

Many hard instances of the NP-complete SAT decision problem can be solved using local search algorithms [20,19,15,12]. Actually, these latter algorithms for SAT were fist developed to approximate the MAXSAT optimization problem [9]. Indeed, when the local search fails to solve a decision problem, its result or some of its computations deliver an approximate solution of the corresponding optimization problem.

In this paper, this idea is pushed a step further: failing to prove a decision problem $\mathcal{A}$ can sometimes help us in solving some *harder*[1] symbolic reasoning problems more efficiently. As a case study, we take $\mathcal{A}$ as SAT and consider some $P^{NP[\mathcal{O}(\log m)]}$ optimization problems: namely, computing a preferred maximal consistent subset of clauses and computing a preferred minimal model, respectively. It is shown that a smart use of the computation of a local search that failed to solve a SAT instance can sometimes slash down the computing time for the resolution of these optimization problems. More precisely, it appears that

---

* This work has been funded in part by the CNRS, the IUT de Lens, the *Région Nord/Pas-de-Calais* and by the EC under a FEDER program.
[1] Unless P=NP

D. Scott (Ed.): AIMSA 2002, LNAI 2443, pp. 51–60, 2002.

they can often be solved in this way thanks to a small constant number of calls to a SAT-solver, only.

But let us start back from the basic consideration that local search algorithms do not cover the whole search space. Accordingly, they cannot conclude that a SAT instance is insatisfiable, i.e. they cannot solve the dual co-NP-complete UN-SAT problem. Recently, we have discovered the following two heuristics about the work performed by local search techniques when they fail to prove the consistency of SAT instances [13].

HEURISTIC 1

Let us count the number of times each clause has been falsified during the failed local search and count the number of times a Boolean variable has occurred in the unsatisfied clauses. The clauses with the highest scores form an approximation of the set-theoretic union of the minimal inconsistent subsets of the instance. Likewise, the Boolean variables with the highest scores take part in these subsets, most probably.

HEURISTIC 2

Focusing a further complete search algorithm on the clauses and on the Boolean variables with the highest scores can often make the instance solved efficiently.

We refer the reader to [13,11] for the experimental work that gave rise to these heuristics. In order for Heuristic 1 to provide the best possible approximation, the parameters of the local search algorithm should be fine-tuned as to give a good coverage of the search space (mainly, the number of tries should be large and the distance between initial configurations should be maximized). The second heuristic has been introduced independently and in some implicit way by Crawford in the context of hard 3-SAT instances [3]. However, this failed as Heuristic 2 is generally only helpful when Heuristic 1 delivers an approximation of the minimal inconsistent subsets that can be handled by the best complete techniques for SAT. Clearly, this is not the case for large random k-SAT instances at the phase transition, since the size of these subsets does not diverge significantly enough from the size of the initial instances [13,2].

2   Basic Applications to SAT and MAX-SAT

Before we climb the polynomial hierarchy and show how these SAT-related heuristics can help with respect to harder optimization problems, let us briefly review how using failed local search can help with respect to MAX-SAT and SAT themselves.

When a local search algorithm fails to prove that a SAT instance is satisfiable, the largest set of simultaneously satisfied clauses during the failed search is an approximation of the largest consistent subset of the instance, i.e. gives an approximate solution to the MAXSAT problem [9]. Obviously enough, when the search succeeds in showing that the instance is satisfiable, then the MAXSAT problem is solved.

The local search technique can itself take its previous failed steps into account. For instance, [17] attached a dynamic weight on clauses that increases with the number of times these latter ones have been previously falsified. Focusing on these clauses, a steepest descent towards and a better approximation of the solution can be obtained, as illustrated in Table 1, where GSAT [20] and GSAT+weight [17] are compared on DIMACS instances [5]. In the table, #unsat represents the lowest number of falsified clauses during the search.

Table 1. GSAT vs GSAT+weight[2]

Instances	Sat	Size		GSAT		GSAT+Weight	
		Var.	Cla.	time	#unsat	time	#unsat
BF series:							
0432-077	No	1044	3685	5s99	18	6s11	1
1355-240	No	2298	7307	91s42	89	57s94	2
2670-208	No	1379	3423	12s80	25	16s08	1
SSA series:							
0432-001	No	435	1027	0s49	6	0s43	1
2670-128	No	1359	3296	12s78	29	7s92	2
6288-047	No	10410	34238	102s78	425	101s17	56
7552-083	Yes	1448	3298	13s72	32	0s06	0
AIM series:							
200-1_6-yes1-1	Yes	200	320	0s07	1	0s02	0
200-1_6-no-3	No	200	320	0s06	1	0s08	1
II series:							
8b4	Yes	1068	8214	3s42	1	0s08	0
16a1	Yes	1650	19368	33s27	1	0s09	0
32d3	Yes	824	19478	11s94	36	1s70	0

In [13,11] several ways to exploit Heuristic 2 in order to solve SAT instances efficiently have been proposed. For instance, DP+TSAT is a combination of a Davis, Logemann and Putnam [4] complete procedure (in short, DP) that proves competitive in most situations. It starts with a call to a tabu-based local search algorithm (TSAT) [12,14]. If this one fails to prove consistency, then a DP procedure is run. The branching heuristic of DP selects the most often falsified literal by a previous call to a local search algorithm. In Table 2, the very good performance of DP+TSAT is illustrated on various benchmarks from [5].

3   Computing Preferred Maximal Consistent Subsets of Clauses

Let us now climb the polynomial hierarchy and select some recurrent combinatorial optimization problems in the artificial intelligence community as a case

---

[2] All experimental results in this paper have been obtained on Pentium III 350Mhz under linux kernel 2.2.12. All experimental data are available at:
   http://www.cril.univ-artois.fr/~mazure.

Table 2. DIMACS problems

Instances	Sat	Size Var.	Cla.	Classical DP #A	#CH	time	DP+TSAT #A	#CH	time
AIM series:									
100-1_6-no-3	No	100	160	3E+07	2E+06	214s71	178	16	0s26
100-1_6-yes1-2	Yes	100	160	495858	30052	4s39	77	6	0s08
100-2_0-no-1	No	100	200	4E+07	2E+06	349s52	46	5	0s10
100-2_0-yes1-1	Yes	100	200	706388	31274	7s41	81	8	0s15
200-1_6-no-1	No	200	320	***	***	>8h	240	16	0s58
200-1_6-yes1-3	Yes	200	320	***	***	>9h	232	11	0s32
200-2_0-no-3	No	200	400	***	***	>15h	120	10	0s42
200-2_0-yes1-1	Yes	200	400	2E+09	7E+07	21859s45	291	27	1s21
50-1_6-no-1	No	50	80	12072	895	0s09	72	8	0s06
50-1_6-yes1-1	Yes	50	80	1540	84	0s01	37	6	0s05
50-2_0-no-1	No	50	100	54014	2759	0s43	52	5	0s05
50-2_0-yes1-1	Yes	50	100	2878	176	0s03	11	3	0s03
BF series:									
0432-007	No	1040	3668	9E+08	6E+06	19553s44	115766	870	85s25
1355-075	No	2180	6778	317628	2047	18s88	4602	28	26s23
1355-638	No	2177	4768	***	***	>17h	6192	32	32s57
2670-001	No	1393	3434	***	***	>25h	490692	4822	519s40
SSA series:									
0432-003	No	435	1027	133794	1570	1s79	1338	16	0s80
2670-130	No	1359	3321	***	***	>33h	2E+07	79426	8040s64
2670-141	No	986	2315	3E+08	2E+06	6350s77	1E+07	92421	6639s44
7552-038	Yes	1501	3575	***	***	>13h	29	1	0s34
7552-158	Yes	1363	3034	1639	78	0s19	12	1	0s29
7552-159	Yes	1363	3032	1557	84	0s21	12	1	0s25
7552-160	Yes	1391	3126	1457	76	0s18	1	1	0s30

(#A = Number of assignments   #CH = Number of choices)

study. A first one consists in computing maximal (set-theoretic) consistent sub-sets of clauses, while obeying a preference relation between clauses.

For clarity of presentation, we first need to recall the concept that is dual to the notion of maximal consistent subset of clauses, namely the concept of *minimal inconsistent kernel*. In the following, $\mathcal{C}$ is a finite set of Boolean clauses.

DEFINITION 1

A minimal inconsistent kernel *(in short, kernel) of $\mathcal{C}$ is a subset of $\mathcal{C}$ that is both inconsistent and minimal with respect to set-theoretic inclusion.*

Clearly, $\mathcal{C}$ might contain several different kernels in the general case. Also, dropping one clause belonging to a kernel of $\mathcal{C}$ is enough to *break* the kernel, i.e. to suppress it from the set of kernels of $\mathcal{C}$.

DEFINITION 2

The inconsistent part *of $\mathcal{C}$, noted $\cup$MIN-UNSAT$(\mathcal{C})$, is the set-theoretic union of all kernels of $\mathcal{C}$.*

The dual concept is thus the notion of maximal consistent subset of $\mathcal{C}$; computing one of them is the target of the MAXSAT optimization problem. Let us redefine this notion when a preference pre-ordering applies on clauses of $\mathcal{C}$, which is often the case in many artificial intelligence applications. Accordingly, this gives rise to an extended form of MAXSAT that accommodates a preference relation between clauses.

Assume thus that the m clauses in $\mathcal{C}$ are partitioned inside n strata $S_1 \cup \ldots \cup S_n$. For simplicity of presentation, we assume that the m clauses are numbered in a way that follows the strata, i.e. when $c_i \in S_k$, $c_j \in S_r$ and $k > r$, then $i > j$. When $c_i \in S_k$ and $c_j \in S_r$ such that $k > r$ that means that c_j is preferred over c_i, i.e. if we must choose to drop one of the two clauses to get a maximal consistent subset then we drop c_i. Accordingly, the strata translate a preference complete pre-ordering on the clauses of $\mathcal{C}$. Let $A = A_1 \cup \ldots A_n$ and $B = B1 \cup \ldots \cup B_n$ be two consistent subsets of $\mathcal{C}$, where $A_i = A \cap S_i$ and $B_i = B \cap S_i$.

DEFINITION 3 *(Benferhat et al.)[1]*
$A <<_{\{S_1 \cup \ldots \cup S_n\}} B$ iff $\exists i$ s.t. $A_i \subset B_i$ and $\forall j < i$, $A_j = B_j$. A consistent subset of $\mathcal{C}$ that is maximal w.r.t. $<<_{\{S_1 \cup \ldots \cup S_n\}}$ is called a preferred maximal consistent subset of $\mathcal{C}$ (w.r.t. $S_1 \cup \ldots \cup S_n$).

In some artificial intelligence problems, like model-based diagnosis [18,8], a *single kernel* assumption is often assumed. In this respect, the following definition will prove useful.

DEFINITION 4
The set of highest cancelable clauses of $\mathcal{C}$, noted $\cup$MIN-UNSAT$(\mathcal{C})_{highest}$ is the set of clauses that are maximal according to the complete pre-ordering $<$ between clauses in $\cup$MIN-UNSAT$(\mathcal{C})$.

Under the single kernel assumption, dropping one element of $\cup$MIN-UNSAT$(\mathcal{C})_{highest}$ delivers a preferred maximal consistent subset of $\mathcal{C}$. Computing one element of $\cup$MIN-UNSAT$(\mathcal{C})_{highest}$ is however computationally heavy in the worst case; it is easy to show that it is polynomial under a number of calls to an NP-oracle that is logarithmic with respect to the number of strata (which, in the worst case, is the number of clauses of $\mathcal{C}$).

PROPOSITION 1
When the single kernel assumption applies, computing a preferred maximal consistent subset of $\mathcal{C}$ belongs to $P^{NP[\mathcal{O}(\log n)]}$, where n is the total number of strata.

However, when Heuristics 1 and 2 apply, this task can be achieved more efficiently for most sets of clauses, reducing the logarithmic number of calls to an NP-oracle to only 4 calls to a fast satisfiability check very often.

PROPOSITION 2
When both the single kernel assumption and Heuristics 1 and 2 apply, computing a preferred maximal consistent subset of $\mathcal{C}$ is polynomial under 4 calls to an NP-oracle.

The algorithm is given in the [6]. The main idea is the following. A local search algorithm is run on $\mathcal{C}$. If it fails to prove the consistency of $\mathcal{C}$ after a preset computing time, a complete DP-based search is performed. When $\mathcal{C}$ is inconsistent, the trace of the search delivers a list $\mathcal{L}$ of clauses c that are sorted in decreasing order w.r.t. the number of times they have been falsified during the search. $\mathcal{L}$ is re-organized in such a way that a clause that belongs to the most often falsified ones and that exhibits the highest stratum among these latter ones appears first. Under the single kernel assumption, the first clause c in the list $\mathcal{L}$ belongs to $\cup$MIN-UNSAT$(\mathcal{C})_{highest}$, most probably. Accordingly, we check the consistency of $\mathcal{C}\backslash\{c\}$ and retract c from $\mathcal{L}$. If this leads to consistency, we just need one more consistency check to make sure that no preferable clause would lead to consistency when dropped. If this fails, we try the next elements of $\mathcal{L}$, successively.

In table 3, some typical experimental results are given. Large benchmarks were built, merging several DIMACS benchmarks [5] (sharing a same set of variables). A total order between clauses are assumed. Table 3 gives the initial DIMACS instances that were merged, the size of the final instances, the clauses to be dropped to obtain a maximal consistant preferred subset, and the global computing time.

Table 3. Maximal consistant preferred sub-base

Instances	Size		#Cla. tested	Time to		
	Var.	Cla.		compute the trace	find c	prove it gives a preferred sub-base
ssa7552-160+dubois10	1391	3206	41	88s62	52s35	4s13
ssa7552-094+pret150-60	1473	3842	400	89s77	869s14	2s68
ssa7552-156+aim-50-2_0-no-2	1444	3382	100	93s76	139s87	1s20

When we cannot assume that the single kernel assumption applies, then the problem becomes even harder.

PROPOSITION 3
Computing one preferred maximal consistent subset of $\mathcal{C}$ belongs to $P^{NP[\mathcal{O}(m)]}$, where m is the total number of clauses in $\mathcal{C}$.

In [6], a basic algorithm that computes an approximate preferred maximal consistent subset of $\mathcal{C}$ is given. Once again, it makes use of the failed local search intensively. It delivers a right set of clauses under the condition that Heuristic 1 allows us to extract a superset of $\cup$MIN-UNSAT$(\mathcal{C})$, which is often the case.

PROPOSITION 4
When the trace of the local search allows us to extract a superset of $\cup$MIN-UNSAT$(\mathcal{C})$ as the part of L that is interpreted as containing the most often falsified clauses, then Procedure 1 in [6] computes a preferred maximal consistent subset of $\mathcal{C}$.

In most realistic situations, the number of kernels is bounded by a small constant k. In this case, the computation of a preferred maximal consistent subset of $\mathcal{C}$ can be reduced dramatically when the trace of the local search that runs on $\mathcal{C}$ allows us to extract a superset of $\cup$MIN-UNSAT($\mathcal{C}$).

PROPOSITION 5
When the trace of the local search allows us to extract a superset of $\cup$MIN-UNSAT(C) and when the number of kernels of C is bounded by k, then computing one preferred maximal consistent subset of C is polynomial under k calls to a NP-oracle.

4   Computing Preferred Models of Sets of Clauses

Let us now turn our attention to another hard optimization problem. Let us illustrate it by means of an artificial intelligence application. The knowledge about a physical device is represented using a finite set $\mathcal{C}$ of Boolean clauses. To represent possible faulty behaviors of the device, a pre-ordered set $(AB, <)$ of specific Boolean variables Ab_i [16] is used. For instance, the rule asserting that, under normal circumstances, when the switch is on then the lights should be on is represented by the formula $switch\_on \wedge \neg Ab_{37} \Rightarrow lights\_on$, and in clausal form by $\neg switch\_on \vee Ab_{37} \vee lights\_on$ (where $\wedge$, $\vee$, $\neg$, $\Rightarrow$ represent the standard conjunctive, disjunctive, negation and material implication connectives, respectively). If at the same time we also have that both $switch\_on$ and $\neg lights\_on$ are *true*, then Ab_{37} must also be *true* in order for the whole set of formulas to remain consistent. In the normal circumstances of affairs, all markers can be assumed *false* while the system remains consistent. When the system requires some markers to be *true* in order to be consistent, then these latter markers indicate one possible failure.

Let us recall that a model is a truth assignment that satisfies all clauses from $\mathcal{C}$. A model is represented by the set of Boolean variables that it sets to *true*. Here, we are interested in finding a model of $\mathcal{C}$ where no marker Ab_i from AB is *true*. If such a model does not exist, then we want to provide the user with the marker with the lowest index that <u>must</u> be *true* in order for the system to be consistent. The motivation is that we want to inform the user of the most important failure, which are supposed to be represented by markers Ab_i with lowest possible index i. This specific form of model-based reasoning is used to solve the Christmas Tree Syndrome (as it is called by airforce pilots when many alarms flash at the same time due to a single source problem, which is often vital to localize quickly). Such a problem is described in e.g. [7].

In the following, $\mathcal{C}$ is assumed consistent. Let M_1, M_2 and M_3 be models of $\mathcal{C}$.

DEFINITION 5
M_1 is a preferred model of $\mathcal{C}$ iff

1. *M_1 does not contain any Ab_i*
2. *or M_1 contains at least one Ab_i and, at the same time,*

- there does not exist a model M_2 of C that does not contain any Ab_j ;
- there does not exist a model M_3 of C containing an Ab_j such that $Ab_j < Ab_i$ for all Ab_i in M_1.

Computing one such preferred model is an heavy task in the general case.

PROPOSITION 6
Computing one preferred model of C is in $P^{NP[\mathcal{O}(\log m)]}$, where m is the total number of strata in AB.

Fortunately, the technique that is proposed in this paper allows us to find a preferred model (and thus one most important failure) using a small constant number (often 3) calls to a fast propositional satisfiability prover (very often). It works as follows. First, we try to prove the absence of device failure by assigning all markers to *false* and showing that C remains consistent under these circumstances. To this end, a combination of a local search technique with a complete DP algorithm is used. More precisely, if the local search technique delivers a model, then this proves the absence of failure. Else, a complete DP technique is run (possibly focusing on the trace delivered by the previous call to the local search algorithm). If a model is found, no failure is exhibited. Else, the algorithm takes the trace delivered by the local search into account. In order to be consistent, at least one marker should be *true*. In this respect, the following result proves essential.

PROPOSITION 7
Let D be any superset of $\cup MIN\text{-}UNSAT(C \cup \{\neg Ab_i\}_{(\forall Ab_i \in AB)})$. Any model of C contains at least one marker occurring in D.

Accordingly, if the heuristic about the trace is correct, then it indicates by means of the score of the clauses to which they belong, which markers should be *true* to get a model of C. Fortunately, this heuristic is experimentally correct extremely often for realistic sets of clauses representing physical devices.

HEURISTIC 3
The trace of the failed (local) search of a model of $C \cup \{\neg Ab_i\}_{(\forall Ab_i \in AB)}$ is a good oracle of the markers that are required to be true *in order for C to be consistent.*

The idea is thus to select the marker with the lowest index in the clauses with the highest scores and set it to *true*. Assume it is Ab_i: if this leads to a model, it remains to check that no model containing a marker with a strictly lower index exists. This can be checked by testing the consistency of $C \cup \{\neg Ab_i\} \cup \{Ab_1 \vee Ab_2 \vee \dots Ab_r\}$, where the last clause is formed from all markers Ab_k such that $Ab_k < Ab_i$. If this leads to a model (low probability), then the process is iterated with the marker *true* with the lowest index in this last clause. If no model can be found, then Ab_i is the *most important* failure to be reported to the user.

Obviously enough, this process might lead all markers to be considered successively and yield a $P^{NP[\mathcal{O}(\log m)]}$ complexity where n is the number of markers (although a dichotomy-based approach could reduce it to the logarithmic result of Proposition 6). Fortunately, applying the heuristic often leads us to the result immediately.

In Table 4, typical experimental results are given for ISCAS [10] benchmarks, translated into the DIMACS format [5]. The time to compute a preferred model in case of device failure, and the total number of candidates Ab_i that had to be considered are given.

Table 4. ISCAS problems

| Instances | Size | | | $\#Ab_i$ | Time to obtain | |
	Var.	Cla.	Ab_i	tested	trace	pref. model
c17	29	73	6	2	0s00	0s02
c432	692	1903	160	5	0s02	1s61
c1355	2165	5293	514	0	0s00	0s12
c1908	3129	7880	718	3	1s00	16s75
c2670	4499	11200	997	3	1s05	27s48
c3540	6104	15720	1446	3	3s02	66s51
c5315	8865	23201	1994	2	6s06	76s91

5 Conclusion

In this paper, it has been shown how the computation of a local search that failed to solve a SAT instance can prove useful in allowing *harder* symbolic reasoning problems to be solved more efficiently. We believe that similar results could be obtained with respect to other decision and optimization problems.

Obviously enough, the price to pay is the restricted applicability of the approach. In particular Heuristic 2 does not work well for large random instances at the transition phase, where really hard problems are often thought to be found. On the other hand, the heuristics that are used in this paper appear to work very often for realistic real-world problem instances.

References

1. S. Benferhat, C. Cayrol, D. Dubois, J. Lang, and H. Prade. Inconsistency management and prioritized syntax-based entailment. In *Proceedings of the Thirteenth International Joint Conference on Artificial Intelligence (IJCAI'93)*, pages 640–645, 1993.
2. Yacine Boufkhad and Olivier Roussel. Redundancy in random sat formulas. In *Proceedings of the Seventeenth National Conference on Artificial Intelligence (AAAI'00)*, pages 273–278, 2000.
3. James M. Crawford. Solving satisfiability problems using a combination of systematic and local search. In *Working notes of the DIMACS Workshop on Maximum Clique, Graph Coloring, and Satisfiability*, 1993.
4. Martin Davis, George Logemann, and Donald Loveland. A machine program for theorem proving. *Journal of the Association for Computing Machinery*, 5:394–397, 1962.

5. Second Challenge on Satisfiability Testing organized by the Center for Discrete Mathematics and Computer Science of Rutgers University, 1993. http://dimacs.rutgers.edu/Challenges/.

6. Éric Grégoire. Handling inconsistency efficiently in the incremental construction of stratified belief bases. In A. Hunter and S. Parsons, editors, *Proceedings of the Fifth European Conference on Symbolic and Quantitative Approaches to Reasoning and Uncertainty (ECSQARU'99)*, volume 1638 of *Lecture Notes in Computer Science*, pages 168–178, London (UK), July 1999. Springer.

7. Éric Grégoire and David Ansart. Overcoming the christmas tree syndrome. *International Journal on Artificial Aintelligence Tools (IJAIT)*, 9(2):97–111, 2000.

8. W. Hamscher, L. Console, and J. De Kleer. *Readings in Model-Based Diagnosis*. Morgan Kaufmann, 1992.

9. Pierre Hansen and Brigitte Jaumard. Algorithms for the maximum satisfiability problem. *Journal of Computing*, 22:279–303, 1990.

10. International Symposium on Circuits And Systems, 1985. http://www.eecs.umich.edu/~mhansen/imodels/ISCAS_HLM.html.

11. Bertrand Mazure. *De la Satisfaisabilité à la Compilation de Bases de Connaissances Propositionnelles*. Thèse de doctorat, Université d'Artois, Centre de Recherche en Informatique de Lens (Faculté Jean Perrin), January 1999.

12. Bertrand Mazure, Lakhdar Saïs, and Éric Grégoire. Tabu search for SAT. In *Proceedings of the Fourteenth National Conference on Artificial Intelligence (AAAI'97)*, pages 281–285, Providence (Rhode Island, USA), July 1997.

13. Bertrand Mazure, Lakhdar Saïs, and Éric Grégoire. Boosting complete techniques thanks to local search methods. *Annals of Mathematics and Artificial Intelligence*, 22:319–331, 1998.

14. Bertrand Mazure, Lakhdar Saïs, and Éric Grégoire. System Description: CRIL Platform for SAT. In *Proceedings of the Fifteenth International Conference on Automated Deduction (CADE'15)*, volume 1421 of *Lecture Notes in Artificial Intelligence*, pages 116–119, Lindau (Germany), July 1998.

15. David A. McAllester, Bart Selman, and Henry A. Kautz. Evidence for invariants in local search. In *Proceedings of the Fourteenth National Conference on Artificial Intelligence (AAAI'97)*, pages 321–326, August 1997.

16. J. McCarthy. Applications of circumscription to formalizing common-sense knowledge. *Artificial Intelligence*, 28:89–116, 1986.

17. P. Morris. The break out method for escaping from local minima. In *Proceedings of the Eleventh National Conference on Artificial Intelligence (AAAI'93)*, pages 40–45, 1993.

18. R. Reiter. A theory of diagnosis from first principles. *Artificial Intelligence*, 32:57–95, 1987.

19. Bart Selman, Henry A. Kautz, and B. Cohen. Local search strategies for satisfiability testing. In *Working notes of the DIMACS Workshop on Maximum Clique, Graph Coloring, and Satisfiability*, 1993.

20. Bart Selman, Hector J. Levesque, and David Mitchell. Gsat: A new method for solving hard satisfiability problems. In *Proceedings of the Tenth National Conference on Artificial Intelligence (AAAI'92)*, pages 440–446, 1992.

A Heuristic for Planning Based on Action Evaluation

Dimitris Vrakas and Ioannis Vlahavas

Department of Informatics
Aristotle University of Thessaloniki
54006, Thessaloniki Greece
{dvrakas,vlahavas}@csd.auth.gr

Abstract. This paper proposes a domain independent heuristic for regression planners, which is based on action evaluation. The heuristic obtains estimates for the cost of applying each action of the domain by performing a forward search in a relaxed version of the initial problem. The estimates for the actions are then utilized in a backward search on the original problem. The heuristic, which has been further refined by a fact ordering and several domain-analysis techniques, has been implemented in AcE (Action Evaluation), a regression, heuristic planner. AcE has been thoroughly tested on a variety of planning problems, from the AIPS competitions with quite promising results.

1 Introduction

State space planning is the simplest form of planning and has been an active research area for many years. However, a large part of the AI researchers in Planning, abandoned it and focused on other areas, since they regarded it to be non promising. This was totally justifiable, since even with the heuristics that were available at that time the search in the space of states was combinatorial explosive. However, 6-7 years ago, McDermott with his work on UNPOP and later Geffner with ASP/HSP, urged a large part of the planning community to re-consider state space planning. They showed that with the appropriate heuristics, state space planning can be very efficient.

In this paper we propose a different approach in state-space, heuristic planning, which is based on estimated distances between the domain's actions, rather than facts, and the goals. Basing the estimates on actions rather than facts, enables the heuristic to keep better track of the various interactions between the facts, and therefore produce better estimates. The proposed heuristic is embodied in a regression planner employing a weighted A* search strategy, which is thoroughly tested on a large variety of problems, adopted from the last AIPS-00 planning competition. The efficiency of the new planner, called AcE, is assessed through comparative tests with 5 of the most efficient planners in this category.

The rest of the paper is organized as follows: Section 2 presents an overview of the research in the area of heuristic planning. Section 3 describes the heuristic of AcE among with an extension based on fact ordering. Section 4 addresses certain implementation issues and section 5 presents experimental results of Ace and most of the state-of-the-art planners presented over the last years. Finally section 6 concludes the paper and poses future directions.

D. Scott (Ed.): AIMSA 2002, LNAI 2443, pp. 61-70, 2002.
© Springer-Verlag Berlin Heidelberg 2002

2 Related Work

Two of the most promising trends in domain-independent planning were presented over the last few years.

The first one consists of the transformation of the classical search in the space of states to other kinds of problems, which can be solved more easily. Examples of this category are the SATPLAN [6] and BLACKBOX [14] planning system, the evolutionary GRAPHPLAN [1] and certain extensions of GRAPHPLAN as the famous STAN [9] planner.

SATPLAN and BLACKBOX transform the planning problem into a satisfiability problem, which consists of a number of boolean variables and certain clauses between these variables. The goal of the problem is to assign values to the variables in such a way that establishes all of the clauses.

GRAPHPLAN on the other hand creates a concrete structure, called the planning graph, where the nodes correspond to facts of the domain and edges to actions that either achieve or delete these facts. Then the planner searches for solutions in the planning graph. GRAPHPLAN has the ability to produce parallel plans, where the number of steps is guaranteed to be minimum.

Fox and Long developed STAN, a powerful planning system, extending GRAPHPLAN with *State Analysis* techniques. Apart from the *State Analysis* techniques, the efficiency of STAN is due to the construction of the planning graph in STAN, which is done very efficiently through bit-wise operators on vectors of bits. In its latest version, called Hybrid STAN [4], the system is cable of identifying specific sub-problems (e.g. TSP sub-problems) from the definition of the original problem. The planner then uses specialized techniques to tackle each of the sub-problems separately.

The second category is based on a relatively simple idea where a general domain independent heuristic function is embodied in a heuristic search algorithm such as Hill Climbing, Best-First Search or A*. A detailed survey of search algorithms can be found in [8]. Examples of planning systems in this category are UNPOP [10], the ASP/HSP family [2,3], GRT [12,13], AltAlt [11], FF [5], which was awarded for outstanding performance in the last AIPS-00 planning competition and BP [15].

The planners of the latter category rely on the same idea to construct their heuristic function. They relax the planning problem by ignoring the delete lists of the domain operators and starting either from the Initial State or the Goals they construct a leveled graph of facts, noting for every fact f the level at which it was achieved $L(f)$. In order to evaluate a state S, the heuristic function takes into account the values of $L(f)$ for each $f \in S$.

3 Evaluating Actions

Most of the state-of-the-art planners in this category, such as GRT, HSP/ASP, HSPr and AltAlt, note for every fact of the domain its estimated distance from the goals (or from the initial state) and then use these values in order to evaluate a whole state (usually by summing up the values of the included facts).

Their main inefficiency sources from the facts that they consider the facts of the domain to be completely independent and the cost of achieving a set of facts is equal to the sum of the costs of achieving each one of them separately. However, this is rarely the case since in the attempt to achieve a certain fact many other facts are also achieved in the way.

GRT partially deals with this problem with the introduction of *related facts*. Two facts p and q are related with each other if:

a)   The action that achieved p, during the construction of the heuristic, also achieves q or the opposite.

b) q is already noted as related with one of the preconditions of the action achieving p.

Although, the *related facts* are able to track only a small subset of the interactions between the facts of the domain, they manage to refine the heuristic of GRT and they prove to be useful in many domains.

FF, adopts a different strategy for keeping track of the possible interactions between the facts of the domain. In order to construct its heuristic, FF builds a graph similar to that of GRAPHPLAN and uses this graph to extract a relaxed partially ordered relaxed plan, the size of which is the estimated distance between the current state and the goals. From the way in which the relaxed plan is constructed FF is able to discover a large portion of the interactions. However, the fact that FF has to search in both directions in order to construct its heuristic, enforces it to reconstruct it at each state (or at least in a large number of states) during the actual search.

This paper proposes a different approach in the construction of the heuristic function, based on action evaluation, which is able to keep track of the great majority of interactions between the domain's facts and yet needs to be constructed only once at the beginning.

The heuristic of AcE is constructed in the forward direction, starting from the initial state and proceeds towards the goals, calculating the distances between the initial state and all the actions of the domain (or at least all the actions that can be achieved from the initial state). The distance, noted as *dist*, for a given action A is calculated by the following rules:

$$dist(A) = \begin{cases} 1, \; if \; prec(A) \subseteq I \\ 1 + \sum_{X \in MPS(prec(A))} dist(X), if \; prec(A) \not\subseteq I \end{cases}$$

where *MPS(S)* is a function returning the set of actions $\{A_p\}$ achieving all the facts of S with the minimum accumulated cost of $dist(A_p)$. Note that MPS never returns actions with undefined dist.

In order to find the minimum set of actions achieving a specific state, *MPS(S)* has to calculate all the possible combinations of actions achieving S, and this process is combinatorial explosive. In AcE, *MPS(S)* is approximated using a greedy algorithm, which is outlined in figure 1.

```
Function MPS(S)
Input: a set of facts S
Output: a set of actions achieving S with near minimum
accumulated dist
```

Set $G = \emptyset$
$S = S - S \cap I$
Repeat
  f is the first fact in S
  Let $act(f)$ be the set of actions achieving f
  for each action A in $act(f)$ do
    $val(A) = dist(A) \ / \ | \ add(A) \cap S \ |$
Let A' be an action in $act(f)$ that minimizes val
Set $G = G \cup A$'
  Set S = S - $add(A') \cap S$
Until $S = \emptyset$
Return G

Fig. 1. *MPS* Function

In the worst case, each action A' selected by MPS will only achieve one fact of S and therefore the complexity of MPS will be |S|*N, where N is the number of the domain's actions. Since |S|<<N the order of the complexity is $O(N^2)$.

In the average case, the actions achieving a fact f are a small subset of the domain's actions and the size of the subset is N/K, where K is comparable to |S| for each state S of the domain. Therefore the complexity of MPS is |S|*N/K, which is in the order of O(N).

We will illustrate the heuristic function of AcE with a concrete example of the Blocks-world domain. Suppose that the initial state of the problem is the one shown in figure 2.

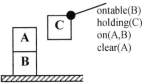

ontable(B)
holding(C)
on(A,B)
clear(A)

Fig. 2. Example of the Blocks wordl

The actions that can be applied to the initial state of the problem in figure 2 are: put-down(C) and stack(C,A) and therefore: dist(put-down(C))=1 and dist(stack(C,A))=1. In order to calculate dist(un_stack(A,B)) we need *MPS(prec(un_stack(A,B))):*
S= {handempty,on(A,B),clear(A)}
$S = S - S \cap I$ = {handempty}
f=handempty
act(f) = {put_down(C), stack(C,A)}, *note here that all the other actions achieving f have undefined dist, so they are not taking into account.*
A' = put_down(C) both actions in act(f) have the same val, so one of them is arbitrarily selected.
$G = \{put\_down(C)\}$
$S = \emptyset$

MPS({handempty,on(A,B),clear(A)})={put_down(C)} and dist(un_stack(A,B))= 1+
dist(put_down(C)) =1+1 = 2.

Similarly the algorithm proceeds with the rest of the domain's actions. When
distances have been assigned to all the domain's actions, AcE starts searching the
state-space starting from the goals. During the search, the estimated distances of the
actions are used to evaluate all the intermediate states.

In order to calculate the heuristic value a given state S_1 ($h(S_1)$), AcE uses $MPS(S_1)$
to find the near minimum set of actions achieving the facts of S_1 and then sums up the
distances of the actions in $MPS(S_1)$. This can be seen as the process of evaluating an
action A_{S1} for which: $prec(A_{S1}) = S_1$.

For example, in order to evaluate state S_a of figure 3, we calculate MPS(S_a):

$S=$ *{ontable(B),ontable(C),holding(A),clear(B),clear(C)}*

$S = S - S \cap I =${ontable(C),holding(A),clear(B),clear(C)}*

f=ontable(C)

act(f)={put_down(C)}

A' = put_down(C)

G={put_down(C)}

S={ holding(A),clear(B)}

f=holding(A)

act(f)={pick-up(A),unstack(A,B),unstack(A,C)}

A'=unstuck(A,B)

G={put_down(C), unstuck(A,B)}

$S = \varnothing$

MPS(S_a)={put_down(C), unstuck(A,B)} and

$h(S_1)$=dist(*put_down(C)*) + dist(*unstuck(A,B)*) = 1 + 2 =3

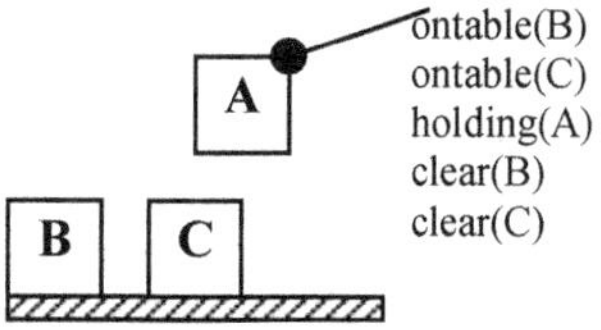

ontable(B)
ontable(C)
holding(A)
clear(B)
clear(C)

Fig. 3. State S_a

Similarly, $h(S_b)$ for S_b={*ontable(A), ontable(C), holding(B), clear(A), clear(C)*} is equal to
dist(put_down(C)) + dist(put_down(A)) + dist(pick_up(B)) = 1 + 3 + 4 = 8

It is clear from the above examples that the heuristic of AcE still produces
overestimates. This can be overcome by keeping track of the MPS for all the
domain's actions, apart from the distances, and taking also into account part of the
delete lists. It remains in our direct future plans to investigate this type of heuristic
refinement. However, the heuristic as it is behaves satisfactory and it generally
succeeds in guiding the search to the most promising states.

3.1. Ordering the Facts of the Initial State

Goal ordering for planning has been an active research topic over the last years and a
number of techniques have been successfully adopted by state-of-the-art planning
systems [7]. AcE adopts a variation of Goal ordering, which is suitable for regression
planners and is very fast to compute. This technique was also adopted by BP[15],
offering a significant speedup in its approach. The technique is based on mutual
exclusions between facts of the domain. Since the planner calculates the set of binary
mutual exclusions, in order to use them for the regression phase, the overhead
imposed by the calculation of reasonable orderings is negligible. Function *OB-R*
(Ordered Before for Regression), which is outlined in Figure 4, is iteratively ran on
every pair of facts in the initial state in order to identify the possible orderings.

```
Function OB-R
Input: Initial facts a and b
Output: True (a should be ordered before b) or False (a
should not be ordered before b)
For each action O: a∈ del(O)
        Result =true
        For each fact f: f∈ (prec(O)-del(O) ∪ add(O))
                If mx(a,f)=true
                        Result=false
        If result = true return false
Return true
```

Fig. 4. The OB-R Function

The orderings extracted by OB-R are used in the planning phase, in order to refine the results of the heuristic function. More specifically, after the evaluation of a state S by the heuristic function, AcE searches state S for possible violations of the orderings. Fact f of a state S is violating an ordering if:

$f∈ I$ and $∃$ fact g: $g∉ S$ and OB-R(g,f)=true

For every ordering violation in state S, the estimated distance between S and the Goals is increased by a constant number (10 at the current implementation), since at a later point the ordering breaches will have to destroyed and re-achieved after the correct ordering has been reinstated.

4 Implementation Issues

This section discusses certain implementation issues of the AcE planning system, concerning the adopted search strategy and the internal representation of the important information. It also addresses certain problems that arise during the application of the planner in specific domains and presents two techniques for enriching and simplifying the problems definitions that deal with the above problems.

4.1. Search Strategy

AcE employs a weighted A* search strategy which starts from the goals of the problem and moves backwards until it reaches the initial state. A state S in weighted A* is evaluated using the following formula:

$$e(S) = w*h(S) + d(S),$$

where h(S) is the value of the heuristic function for state S, d(S) is the number of steps that were performed to reach S and w is a constant real number between 0 and 1.

Ace has a closed list, which is index by a hash table, in which it keeps all the already expanded states, in order to avoid revisiting them in the future.

The states that have not yet been expanded are kept in an agenda, the size of which is limited to a constant number N. If the size of the agenda grows larger than N at some point during search, only the N best states (according to the heuristic function) will remain in the agenda, while the rest will be pruned.

By pruning states from the agenda, AcE risks its completeness (i.e. the pruned states may be leading to a solution), but this is a necessary concession since otherwise the memory requirements may grow outside the available resources.

4.2. Representation

After the parsing of the input files (domain file and problem file) and in order to speed up the planning process, AcE creates all the (grounded) facts of the domain and the (grounded) actions that can be achieved from the initial state of the problem. These facts and actions are stored in tables and AcE assigns to each fact and actions a unique integer number, Based on these numbers Ace makes all the necessary links between facts and actions. For example, for each fact f it creates four lists of actions containing:

    a)   The actions that have f in their preconditions
    b)   The actions that have f in their add-effects
    c)   The actions that have f in their delete lists
    d)   The actions that have f in their preconditions and not in their delete lists.

These integers and the appropriate lists are then utilized during the search. A state is represented as a one-dimensional table of integers and in order to find the actions that are applicable to a state S, AcE performs a limited search in the appropriate lists of actions of the facts in S.

5 Experimental Results

In order to evaluate the efficiency of AcE we compared it, on a large variety of problems used in the two AIPS planning competitions, with three state-of-the-art planning systems. These are: FF, GRT and HSPr. Figures 5-12 present experimental results from the blocks-world, the Logistics, the Mic-10 and the Gripper domain respectively.

The platform used for the results is a SUN ULTRA ENTERPRISE 450 Unix server with 2 GB of shared memory and 4 processors running at 400 MHz. The underlying operating system is SUN Solaris 2.8. For each experiment we limited the available cpu time to 120 seconds.

5.1. Blocks

FF managed to solve a few more problems than the other three contestants and except for a few problems it was quite faster, taking less than 0.1 sec for most of the problems. AcE had a quite uniform performance in most of the problems, taking much less time than HSPr and GRT. Concerning plan length AcE and FF behaved equally producing shorter plans than HSPr and especially GRT.

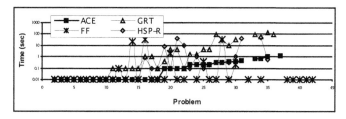

Fig. 5. Execution time for Blocks-world problems

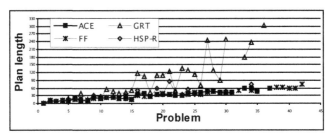

Fig. 6. Plan lengths for Blocks-world problems

5.2. Logistics

FF was also faster in the Logistics domain, but AcE was very close to it concerning execution time. GRT and HSPr did not scale up effectively to the hard instances of Logistics, taking much more time than FF and AcE. Concerning plan length, FF and GRT produced a little bit smaller plans than AcE and HSPr.

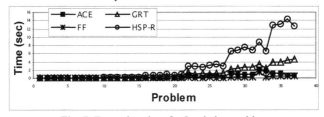

Fig. 7. Execution time for Logistics problems

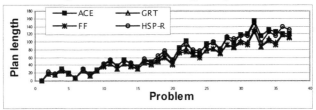

Fig. 8. Plan lengths for Logistics problems

5.3. Mic-10

In MIC-10 the situation concerning execution time was quite similar to that of the Logistics domain. FF and AcE took less than a second to solve almost every problem, with a few exceptions by the latter. The plans created by all planners were of similar quality, with HSPr producing a little larger plans.

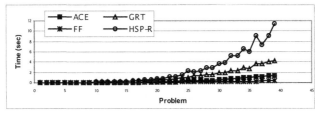

Fig. 9. Execution time for MIC-10 problems

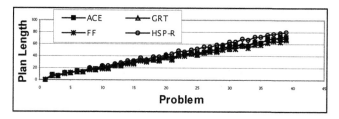

Fig. 10. Plan length for MIC-10 problems

5.4. Gripper

AcE was quite faster than the other contestants in the Gripper domain. It took less than a second to solve all the problems. GRT and FF behaved almost similarly and HSPr took much more time to solve the hard instances. However, HSPr produced the shortest plans, which however were quite close to those produced by AcE and GRT. GRT and AcE produced plans of exactly the same length for each of the problem. FF did not behave well in the Gripper domain, producing the lengthiest plans in all instances and it was lower than AcE and GRT.

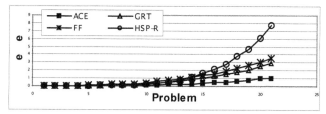

Fig. 11. Execution time for Gripper problems

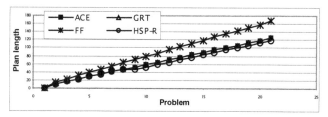

Fig. 12. Plan length for Gripper problems

6 Conclusion and Future Work

This paper presented a different approach to domain-independent heuristic planning. The proposed heuristic is not based on distances between independent facts and the goals, but on distances between actions and the goals. This enables the heuristic to keep track of more interactions and yet remain simple enough to be executed with little computational cost.

The proposed heuristic has been embodied in a weighted A* regression planner, called AcE, and the planner has been tested on a variety of toy problems and compared with state-of-the-art planning systems. The results are quite promising, since they show that AcE is at least a fair match the planners excelling in the planning competitions.

It is in our direct future planners to investigate ways of further refining the heuristic. One possible way of doing this is by keeping track of more information for every action, than just its estimated distance, and taking also into account part of the information provided by the delete lists of the actions. Furthermore, we plan to extend AcE to handle many of the new features in PDDL 2.1, such as time and resources.

Acknowledgements. This project has been partially supported by SUN Micro-systems, grant number EDUD-7832-010326-GR.

References

[1]   Blum, L., and Furst M., Fast planning through planning graph analysis, In Proceedings of the 14th Int. Joint Conference on Artificial Intelligence, 636-642. Montreal, Canada. (1995)

[2]   Bonet, B. and Geffner, H. Planning as Heuristic Search: New Results, In Proceedings of the 5th European Conference on Artificial Intelligence. Durham UK. (1999)

[3]   Bonet, B., Loerincs, G., and Geffner, H., A robust and fast action selection mechanism for planning, In Proceedings of the 14th Int. Conference of the American Association of Artificial Intelligence (AAAI-97), 714-719. Providence, Rhode Island. (1997)

[4]   Fox, M. and Long, D., Hybrid STAN: Identifying and Managing Combinatorial Subproblems in Planning. *In Proceedings of 19th UK Planning and Scheduling SIG Workshop*, (2000)

[5]   Hoffmann, J. A Heuristic for Domain Independent Planning and its Use in an Enforced Hill-climbing Algorithm, In Proceedings of the 12th Int. Symposium on Methodologies for intelligent Systems. (2000)

[6]   Kautz, H. and Selman, B., Pushing the Envelope: Planning, Propositional Logic, and Stochastic Search. *In Proceedings of the Thirteen National Conference on Artificial Intelligence (AAAI-96)*. Portland, Oregon, USA. (1996)

[7]   Koehler, J. and Hoffmann, J. On Reasonable and Forced Goal Orderings and their Use in an Agenda-Driven Planning Algorithm, *Journal of Artiicial Intelligence Research* 12. (2000)

[8]   Korf, R. *Artificial intelligence search algorithms*, CRC Handbook of Algorithms and Theory of Computation, Atallah, M. J. (Ed.), CRC Press, Boca Raton, FL, pp. 36-1 to 36-20. (1998)

[9]   Long, D. and Fox, M. Efficient Implementation of the Plan Graph in STAN, JAIR, 10, pp. 87-115.(1998)

[10] McDermott, D. A Heuristic Estimator for Means-End Analysis in Planning, In Proceedings, AIPS (1996)

[11] Nguyen, X., Kambhampati, S. and Nigenda, R. AltAlt: Combining the advantages of Graphplan and Heuristics State Search, In Proceedings, International Conference on Knowledge-based Computer Systems, Bombay, India. (2000)

[12] Refanidis, I., and Vlahavas, I., *GRT:* A Domain Independent Heuristic for STRIPS Worlds based on Greedy Regression Tables, In *Proceedings, 5th European Conference on Planning*, Durham, UK, pp. 346-358. (1999)

[13] Refanidis, I. and Vlahavas, I., The GRT Planner: Backward Heuristic Construction in Forward State-Space Planning, *Journal of Artificial Intelligence Research* 15:115-161. (2000)

[14] Selman, B., Levesque, H. and Mitchell, D., A New Method for solving Hard Stisfiability Problems. *In Proceedings of the Tenth National Conference on Artificial Intelligence (AAAI-92)*, 440-446. San Jose, California, USA. (1992)

[15] Vrakas, D. and Vlahavas, I. Combining Progression and Regression in State-Space Heuristic Planning, *In Pre-Proceedings of the 6th European Conference on Planning*, 1-12. Toledo, Spain. (2001)

WHAT: Web-Based Haskell Adaptive Tutor*

Natalia López, Manuel Núñez, Ismael Rodríguez, and Fernando Rubio

Dept. Sistemas Informáticos y Programación.
Universidad Complutense de Madrid, E-28040 Madrid. Spain.
{natalia,mn,isrodrig,fernando}@sip.ucm.es

Abstract. In this paper we introduce WHAT, an intelligent tutor for learning the functional programming language Haskell. WHAT adapts its behavior not only *individually* for each student but also by considering the performance of *similar* students. The core of its adaptive part is based on the classification of students into *classes* (groups of students sharing some attributes). By doing that, the behavior of past students of the same class determines how WHAT interacts, in the future, with students of that class. That is, WHAT *learns* how to deal with each type of student. Besides, the general model of each class is instantiated for each student in order to better fit the particular learning needs.

Keywords: Intelligent Tutors, Education, e-learning.

1 Introduction

During the last years, and due to the wide implantation of the WWW, there has been a proliferation of web-based courses. The first systems were quite rudimentary and rather rigid, that is, they were mainly based on a fix set of questions; usually, multiple-choice questions. In particular, it was rather difficult to evaluate the profit gained by the users of the course. The situation changed in the moment that artificial intelligence techniques appeared in the development of this kind of systems. Good examples of these new generation tutoring systems are [3,1,12,6] among many others. Besides, by using adaptive hypermedia techniques (e.g. [2,5,13]) when developing intelligent tutors, we get a system that is automatically adapted according to the responses of students (e.g. [11]).

In this paper we present WHAT: Web-based Haskell Adaptive Tutor. In short, WHAT represents a system which can be used by students as a complement to the classroom learning of the functional programming language Haskell [9]. During the last years, in order to introduce programming to first-year students of Mathematics, different languages (actually, Pascal, Haskell, and Java) have been used in our department. Unfortunately, no common agreement has been reached and the question of which language is more suitable for Mathematics students is still open. The main reason for developing a Haskell tutor, and not a Java or a Pascal one, is that the existing environments for Haskell are not *friendly.* Most Haskell compilers/interpreters only allow the user to interact with a text-based interface and only a programming environment (`winhugs`

---

* Work partially supported by the CICYT project TIC2000-0701-C02-01.

D. Scott (Ed.): AIMSA 2002, LNAI 2443, pp. 71–80, 2002.

at `http://www.haskell.org/hugs`) provides a simple graphical interface. Thus, one of the main disadvantages of using Haskell to teach first-year students is that they do not feel comfortable with the environment: Even though the language could be a good choice, the environments are certainly not. Therefore, in order to fairly compare the difficulties the students have to deal with each language, a better interface is needed for Haskell.

Next we briefly sketch the main characteristics of WHAT. First, WHAT combines individual profiles for each student with general profiles for each *class* of students (the class mechanism is explained in Section 3). By doing so, WHAT is able to adapt its behavior with respect to a student not only *individually*, on the basis of her[1] previous fails and successes, but also by taking into account the performance of the rest of students (current as well as former students). That is, the system *learns* how to interact with a student by adapting the general profile of her class(es) to her necessities. However, the progress of the users while experimenting with the system is individually controlled. WHAT keeps profiles for each student where all the relevant information (from her previous sessions) is recorded. In particular, the system points to the next topic that the user should explore once she has reached a certain command in the current topic. Another important feature of WHAT is given by its skill to (automatically) generate new problems. Exercises are randomly created according to the knowledge that the student has obtained so far.

We think that WHAT may increase the success rate of students in two ways. On the one hand, students can regularly check their progress by self-evaluation. On the other hand, teachers can find out which parts of the course are more difficult for the students (WHAT provides the teacher with a private interface that allows her to access to information about students performance). In the presentation of WHAT we have tried to avoid Haskell details, so that the main ideas (how WHAT has been developed) can be followed even if the reader is not an expert in functional programming. The rest of the paper is organized as follows. In Section 2 we describe the behavior of WHAT from a user point of view. In Section 3 we explain the adaptive behavior of our tutor. We concentrate on the class mechanism underlying WHAT. In Section 4 we present some implementation details. Finally, in Section 5 we present our conclusions and some lines for future work.

2   An Overview of WHAT

In this section we explain the main functionalities of our adaptive tutor. Technicalities about the implementation are presented in the next sections. The main aim of our web-based system is to provide students with an *easy-to-use* tool where they can practice the knowledge previously gained in the classroom. So, students will be able to check whether they have fully assimilated the concepts they were supposed to. Even though we have designed our system to help students having another (main) source of learning (i.e. a teacher) the current system

---

[1] During the rest of the paper we suppose a generic female student.

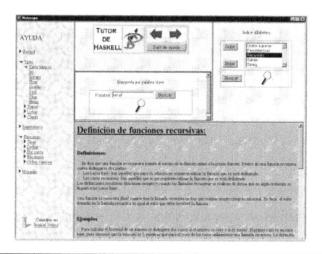

Fig. 1. Help page in WHAT.

could be used as a completely independent tutor. Actually, all the concepts covered by the course are already documented by means of a friendly navigation interface (see Figure 1). Topics can be accessed in three different ways: By using an index of topics (left frame), by incremental searches (center frame), or by an alphabetic list of keywords (right frame).

In order to ensure a personalize treatment, students access the system through a login page. This allows the system to recover the data from previous sessions. At the beginning of the course, students are provided with a password. They log in by giving their ID-number and password. This mechanism tries to avoid *attacks* to previous sessions of students. For example, an attacker could ask the system for previous exercises and provide wrong answers. Then, when the real student logs in, she will find out that the system thinks that she did not understand the concepts covered in previous sessions.

Once a student has been recognized by the system, a new session starts. The initial page allows the student to choose among three different types of problems:

- Evaluation of expressions.
- Typing functions.
- Solving programming assignments.

Let us remark that these three parts are not taught sequentially, but in parallel. For example, students will be able to define a function adding or multiplying two numbers before they are able to type/evaluate an expression as

```
foldr (&&) True (zipWith (==) "hello" ['h','e','l','l','o'])
```

As it is widely recognized, any intelligent tutoring system should have a good underlying curriculum model (see for example [7]). In order to avoid incoherences, the curriculum model should be carefully organized according to some rules (see [4]). We have designed our system taking into account the following considerations. At each moment, the student will be able to choose which category of exercises she would like to practice. After reaching a certain level in a type of problems, WHAT suggests the student to solve exercises from a different type. However, the student may continue practicing exercises from the same category. In this case, the curricular dependencies restrict the level she can reach in this category. Even though the student can choose freely the type of exercises, the difficulty of them will be constrained by two main factors:

- It will increase according to the level that the student has reached in previous sessions.
- A student will not be allowed to practice topics which have not been covered yet in the classroom, even if she has correctly learnt all of the previous topics.

These two restrictions are strongly related to the curriculum theory underlying our system. Let us remark that even though the first restriction is applied, the system will sometimes ask for exercises which the student is supposed to know already (according to her previous sessions). We pretend to control that students do not forget topics that were covered at the beginning of the course. By using the second restriction we try to avoid that students simply guess the answers to questions that have not been already taught. There is an exception to this constraint. If a student took the course in previous years but she did not pass it, then she will have access to any topic. Let us remark that, even in this case, the first limitation will be applied. Nevertheless, this second restriction could be easily removed in order to allow good students (that is, the ones having an acceptable rate of right answers) to speed up their learning. In this case, the help system (that covers all the course) can (somehow) substitute the teacher.

Finally, WHAT includes an extra option: *Review*. The students will be able to use this possibility to review the lessons learnt so far. So, they will be confronted with assignments similar to those that have been already covered by them in previous sessions. This option can be very interesting (from a student point of view) when the exam is approaching.

Now we will briefly sketch what the student will find in each part of the course. Firstly, in order to gently introduce the language, the capabilities of the programming language will be restricted to the power of a complex calculator. Thus, the first exercises will be only devoted to handle simple numerical operations. So, students will get familiar with the syntax of the language. The difficulty will start increasing, taking into account the precedence of operators, asking for the answer to questions like

```
4-5+7*3-2
```

Both integer and real numbers will be used, but considering the type of operations that can be used with each of them. After dealing with numerical values, other simple types like characters and booleans will be used. Then tuples will be introduced. At this point, the student is able to start working with lists. First, strings of characters will be considered, as they are more intuitive. Then, they will be generalized to deal with lists of any type.

Regarding the definition of functions, at the beginning only very easy operations will be considered (e.g. adding two numbers). By doing so, we expect the students to avoid the usual mistakes of a beginner when declaring functions. Then, the system will concentrate on recursive programming. A next step is given by introducing simple higher order functions like `map`, `filter`, and `zipWith`. Finally, the student will be able to define her own higher order functions.

2.1 Wrong Answers and Hints

A very important part of any tutoring system is the feedback that the user receives. While designing our system, we have been specially careful at this point. Let us consider what our system returns after a question is answered. If the student provides the right answer then the system returns a congratulations message. The difficulties start when managing wrong answers. The easy solution consists in notifying that the answer was wrong and provide the right answer. We consider that this is *not* a good practice. In the best scenario, the student will try to understand what she was doing wrong by pattern matching. We have preferred to return a suggestion about what the student should do (indicating what the error was) instead of giving the right answer. We have also paid special attention to avoid cheating. As it is pointed out for example in [10], some students tend to learn how to cheat the system instead of learning the current contents. We do not claim that our system is totally fool-proof (actually, we do not think so!) but we have tried to detect some *funny* answers. For instance, if we ask for the value of 3+4 a student may answer 5+2 (non so trivial examples include the application of higher order functions in an unexpected way). Actually, this is a right answer, but it is not what it is expected. If WHAT detects such a *right* answer, it will indicate that it is correct but it will ask for the *most correct* answer. Finally, even though the management of answers has been a specially hard part to develop, we think that the effort has been worth. Firstly, students will see their mistakes and try to correct them. Secondly, they will be soon convinced (we hope) that it is senseless to spend time trying to fool the system.

Students will be also allowed to ask for hints. The type of hints, that the system provides, depends on the number of hints the student has already asked for in the current exercise. For instance, if the student has provided a wrong answer, a first hint will only provide a message saying which type of error it was, that is, whether it was a syntactic error, a type error, or a semantic error. Afterwards, in case the student needs more hints, the error will be explained more precisely. Finally, if a student is not able to provide the right answer, she can press the *give up* button and the answer will be presented. In our system, the student may ask for a hint, give a wrong answer, fail again, etcetera.

3   Adaptive Behavior of the System

The main advantage of using an intelligent tutor with adaptive capabilities is that it can be automatically adapted to the students. WHAT can adapt its behavior not only on the basis of the fails and successes of the current student, but also on the experiences of the rest of students. Thus, there will be a module of the implementation dealing with the *class adaptive* part, while a different module will be responsible of the *user adaptive* part.

The *Class Adaptive Module* (CAM) gathers statistics about the interaction of the users with WHAT. The ID number of users will not be relevant, but only the *class(es)* of the student. This module manages a fix set of classes, that is, it does not generate new classes. For example, CAM will distinguish between students who were taking the course in previous years and fresh students. By doing so, the system will learn how to interact with the *typical* student of each class, creating different models for different classes. For instance, students with previous knowledge of an imperative language will not need many questions about evaluating simple numerical expressions, while the rest of students will need to work harder on this issue.

It is important to note that a student may be located in more than a single class. For example, a student can take the course for the second year and, in addition, she can also know an imperative programming language. In such cases, it seems that the fails and successes of the student should be taken into account in both of her classes. However, this would be an erroneous solution, as this student is not a good representative of any of them. The correct solution is to use a new class for the intersection of both classes. Note that there is no risk of class explosion, as the set of primitive classes is quite small.

The previous classes are *static*, that is, a student is located in a class(es) at the beginning of the course and these attributes do not change during the academic year. In addition to static classes, WHAT also handles *dynamic* classes of students. Currently, WHAT considers two dynamic classes. The first one classifies the students according to their *learning speed*, while the second one does it on the basis of their *memory*.

It is well known that not all students need the same effort to learn a new topic. Some people need to practice many times the same type of problems before mastering it, while others only need to work on it during a small amount of time. *Fast learning* students use to get bored after solving several similar problems. Thus, by repeating them, their motivation is dramatically reduced. So, they do not achieve the goals they should. On the other hand, *slow learning* students get depressed if they continuously fail the questions. Thus, WHAT will interleave easier questions while asking them new problems. By doing so, the motivation of the students will not be lost and the overall results will be improved.

It is also a fact that not everybody has the same memory. Some students easily forget concepts learnt in previous lessons, while others obtain more solid backgrounds. Students with weaker memories will be asked questions about old lessons more frequently than those with better memories.

Once we have explained the class mechanism, we briefly sketch how CAM adapts itself. The statistics recorded for each class of student and each type of assignments are used by CAM to modify the original information. This is done in two ways. First, for each class of students, CAM keeps values (one for each topic of the course) about the number of exercises that students are supposed to solve before they know the topic. These values will be readapted according to the performance of students. The second task of CAM consists in classifying the difficulty of programming assignments. Each programming assignment has associated with it a value indicating its difficulty. A difficult programming assignment will not be asked until enough easier exercises are correctly solved. As in the previous case, CAM uses its statistics to modify the difficulty of assignments. The new values are computed by taking into account the response of all the students (regardless of their attributes). However, difficulty is a relative concept. For example, a difficulty value v will not have the same meaning for fresh students that it has for second year students knowing Java. So, the corresponding values v's are normalized for each class of students.

The *User Adaptive Module* (UAM) deals with concrete information about each individual student. As the static attributes of each student will be recorded at the beginning of the academic year, the main tasks of UAM are:

- To compute the dynamic classes in which the student is included at each moment.
- To adapt the models created by CAM to better fit the characteristics of the individual student.

Let us remark that while CAM creates models for each class (both static and dynamic), UAM classifies students inside a class. This is so because only UAM has the appropriate information about individual students. Regarding dynamic classes, WHAT is able to classify students according to both the *speed* and the *memory* of every student. Initially, all the students are located in the same classes. Afterwards, the speed of each student is obtained by computing the number of questions that were necessary before she started to answer correctly all the questions on the same topic. Let us note that we do not take into account the time of response because this would lead to some erroneous results (for example, a bad Internet connection could indicate that the student is very *slow*). The *memory* factor is computed on the basis of the questions about previously learnt lessons. Besides, some students learn slower at the beginning and faster afterwards, while other students have the opposite behavior. If WHAT detects these situations, it will be the task of UAM to modify the dynamic attributes of the student. Let us note that the modification of dynamic attributes should be done very carefully. For example, a student should not be considered memory-weak just because of a simple mistake, that is, the system is *noise tolerant*.

The second task of UAM consists in adapting the models obtained by CAM. If a student s belongs to a class c, UAM will adapt the general model for c so that it will better fit to the peculiarities of s. For instance, UAM will record errors that the student has performed in the past. When the student has an error and ask for help, the system will be able to relate the current error with previous ones. Then, the student will remember the reason of the past error, and she will better understand the reason of the current one. Finally, let us remark that UAM does not create a complete individual model for s: it only adapts the model corresponding to the class c (designed by CAM). By doing so, we increase the efficiency of the system and we also provide a hierarchical organization. Thus, it will be easier for the teacher to understand the evolution of the students.

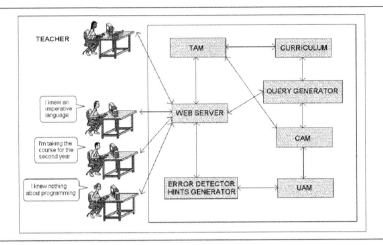

Fig. 2. The WHAT system architecture.

3.1 Non-adaptive Behavior of WHAT

As we have already explained, WHAT can automatically adapt itself to improve its ability to help students to learn. But the capabilities of an intelligent tutor cannot be compared to those of an expert human teacher. Thus, even though WHAT is a powerful tool to help teaching, we think that the overall control of the course should be taken by the human professor.

From the teacher point of view, WHAT provides information about the skills the students are getting, but also about *how* they are obtaining the skills: Their main difficulties with each type of problems. Thus, the teacher can adapt the classroom lessons to explain with more detail the parts of the course that seemed to be harder for previous students. So, by using WHAT, the teacher learns *from* the students how to improve the lessons.

Not only the classroom lessons can be modified depending on the results provided by WHAT, but also WHAT itself can be modified by the teacher. In fact, WHAT contains an additional module: *Teacher Adaptive Module* (TAM). This module allows the teacher to change the teaching strategies of the system. For instance, it allows to add/modify/remove programming problems from a given lesson. More importantly, it allows to modify by hand both the design of the curriculum and the basic models for each class of students.

4 Implementation

In this section we sketch some implementation details. In particular, we will concentrate on how assignments are generated. First, we present the architecture of WHAT (see Figure 2). From the teacher point of view, she accesses the TAM through the web server. From the TAM the teacher is allowed to modify the curriculum model. Besides, she can also consult CAM to check the current models for the corresponding classes. The web server generates new queries by taking into account both the curriculum model and the models corresponding to the classes of the current student.

The generation of new exercises is automatically done for the first two classes of problems (evaluation and typing of expressions). There is a set of predefined functions, and they are combined randomly, by taking into account that the corresponding types fit. The complexity of the expressions will depend on several factors: the set of types that can be used, the functions that have been taught so far, the number of functions that can be combined in each expression, and also the number of levels of higher-order that can be used, that is, the number of nested higher-order functions that can be used in a single function. The implementation of this generator of problems has been done in Haskell because this language is very suitable for this kind of programs. Let us remark that this choice is not related to the fact that WHAT teaches Haskell. Actually, any programming language could be used to write this part of the system.

Unfortunately, it is not possible to automatically generate programming assignments. So, they are randomly selected from a wide set of predefined problems. The problems are classified according to their characteristics, so that they are only proposed to the student when they have reached the appropriate level. Even though it is not possible to automatically generate new problems, it is possible to automatically generate variations of the predefined problems, modifying the parameters of the problems. Functional languages are very adequate for that because programs can be written by combining higher order functions.

In order to check the programs that students have developed, we provide an automatic connection to a Haskell environment where the program is tested over a set of input data. These data will represent the most relevant cases of the (class of) function, that is, the values that are more difficult to deal with. These values are not known by students. In addition to the most relevant cases, there will be some randomly selected cases, just to increase the set of tests. By doing so, we will be able to detect most of the errors introduced by the student. Moreover, in the case of a wrong answer, a good hint about the source of error can be given because WHAT will know the cases that are not correctly covered. Let us remind that it is not possible to automatically *verify* that any given program is correct, as it is well known that such a task is undecidable. So, the best that we can do is just to *test* the programs.[2]

Regarding the web interface, the implementation uses both CGIs and JavaScript. The server side of the system is implemented using CGIs. The CGIs (written in C) control the interaction of the user with the system, generating appropriate web pages. These pages include JavaScript code, so that the user may perform most of the operations without actually connecting to the server.

---

[2] This is an easy way of cheating WHAT. However, we think that the probability of such an error is rather low because of the careful selection of the test cases.

5   Conclusions and Future Work

In this paper we have presented WHAT. We have described its features and we have given some implementation details. In particular, we have explained the class mechanism underlying WHAT. This classification of students allows WHAT to adapt itself to the necessities of each particular type of student.

As future work, we plan to provide similar systems for Pascal and Java. This will allow us to study their learning curves by using comparable tools. Finally, we would also like to apply the experience gained after constructing WHAT to a different field of expertise. Actually, we are already developing a tutor to teach process algebras. In this case, we will consider PAMR [8] because it allows to *abstract* some of the usual difficulties when specifying real systems.

References

1. A. Baena, M.V. Belmonte, and L. Mandow. An intelligent tutor for a web-based chess course. In *AH 2000, LNCS 1892*, pages 17–26. Springer, 2000.
2. P. Brusilovsky. Efficient techniques for adaptive hypermedia. *User Modeling and User-Adapted Interaction*, 6(2-3):87–129, 1996.
3. P. Brusilovsky, E. Schwarz, and G. Weber. ELM-ART: An intelligent tutoring system on the World Wide Web. In *3rd Int. Conf. on Intelligent Tutoring Systems, LNCS 1086*, pages 261–269. Springer, 1996.
4. H. Dufort, E. Aïmeur, C. Frasson, and M. Lalonde. Curriculum evaluation: A case study. In *4th Int. Conf. on Intelligent Tutoring Systems, LNCS 1452*, pages 106–115. Springer, 1998.
5. S. Ferrandino, A. Negro, and V. Scarano. CHEOPS: Adaptive hypermedia on World Wide Web. In *IDMS'97, LNCS 1309*, pages 210–219, 1997.
6. N. López, M. Núñez, I. Rodríguez, and F. Rubio. Including malicious agents into a collaborative learning environment. In *6th Int. Conf. on Intelligent Tutoring Systems, LNCS 2363*, pages 51–60. Springer, 2002.
7. G.I. McCalla. The search for adaptability, flexibility, and individualization: Approaches to curriculum in intelligent tutoring systems. In M. Jones and P.H. Winne, editors, *Foundations and Frontiers of Adaptive Learning Environments*, pages 91–122. Springer, 1992.
8. M. Núñez and I. Rodríguez. PAMR: A process algebra for the management of resources in concurrent systems. In *FORTE 2001*, pages 169–185. Kluwer Academic Publishers, 2001.
9. S. L. Peyton Jones and J. Hughes. Report on the programming language Haskell 98, 1999. http://www.haskell.org.
10. R. Schank and A. Neaman. Motivation and failure in educational simulation design. In K.D. Forbus and P.J. Feltovich, editors, *Smart Machines in Education*, chapter 2. AAAI Press/The MIT Press, 2001.
11. G. Weber. Adaptive learning systems in the World Wide Web. In *7th Int. Conf. on User Modelling, UM'99*, pages 371–378. Springer, 1999.
12. B.P. Woolf, J. Beck, C. Elliot, and M. Stern. Growth and maturity of intelligent tutoring systems: A status report. In K.D. Forbus and P.J. Feltovich, editors, *Smart Machines in Education*, chapter 4. AAAI Press/The MIT Press, 2001.
13. H. Wu, P. De Bra, A. Aerts, and G.J. Houben. Adaptation control in adaptive hypermedia systems. In *AH 2000, LNCS 1892*, pages 250–259. Springer, 2000.

Decomposing and Distributing Configuration Problems

Diego Magro and Pietro Torasso

Dipartimento di Informatica, Università di Torino
Corso Svizzera 185; 10149 Torino; Italy
{magro, torasso}@di.unito.it

Abstract. In the present work the issue of decomposing and distributing a configuration problem is approached in a framework where the domain knowledge is represented in a structured way by using a KL-One like language, where *whole-part relations* play a major role in defining the structure of the configurable objects. The representation formalism provides also a constraint language for expressing complex relations among components and subcomponents.

The paper presents a notion of *boundness* among constraints which specifies when two components can be independently configured. *Boundness* is the basis for partitioning constraints and such a partitioning induces a decomposition of the configuration problem into independent subproblems that are distributed to a pool of configurators to be solved in parallel.

Preliminary experimental results in the domain of PC configuration showing the effectiveness of the decomposition technique in a sequential approach to configuration are also presented.

1 Introduction

In recent years configuration has attracted a significant amount of attention not only from the application point of view but also from the methodological one [12]. In particular, logical approaches such as [13,4] and approaches based on CSP have emerged [10,3,11, 14]. In CSP approaches, configuration can exploit powerful constraint problem solvers for solving complex problems [5,1]. From the other hand, logical approaches make use of a more explicit and structured representation of the entities to be configured (e.g. [9]). Logical approaches seem to offer significant benefits when interaction with the user (e.g. [7]) and explainability of the result (or failure) are major requirements.

Configuration, as many other tasks, can be computationally expensive; therefore, the idea of problem decomposition looks attractive since, from the early days of AI, problem decomposition has emerged as one of the most powerful mechanisms for controlling complexity. Ideally, the solution of a complex configuration problem should be easily assembled by combining the solutions of the subproblems the initial problem has been decomposed into. Moreover, decomposing a configuration problem into a set of mutually independent subproblems allows the configuration process to be distributed among a set of configurators working in parallel. Unfortunately, in many cases it is not obvious at all how to perform such a decomposition.

In the present work the issue of decomposing a configuration problem is approached in a framework where knowledge about the entities is represented in a structured way by using a KL-One like language augmented with a constraint language for expressing

D. Scott (Ed.): AIMSA 2002, LNAI 2443, pp. 81–90, 2002.

complex inter-role relations (see section 2 for a summary of the representation language). Partonomic relations provide the basic knowledge for decomposing the configuration problem. In fact, two subparts involved into two partonomic relations can not be independently configured if there is at least a constraint that links them together. For this reason we have introduced a notion of boundness among constraints (section 3) which assures that two components not involved in a same set of *bound* constraints can be independently configured.

Section 4 provides a high-level description of the configuration algorithm and of the decomposition strategy, while an example of an application of the algorithm is shown in section 5. Section 6 reports preliminary experimental results concerning the reduction of the computational effort. A discussion of the approach is reported in section 7.

2   The Conceptual Language

In the last few years we have developed a representation formalism called $\mathcal{FPC}$ [6,7] (Frames, Parts and Constraints) for modeling configuration problems. Basically, $\mathcal{FPC}$ is a frame-based KL-One like formalism augmented with a constraint language.

In $\mathcal{FPC}$, there is a basic distinction between *atomic* and *complex* components. *Atomic components* are described by means of a set of features characterizing the component itself, while *complex components* can be viewed as structured entities whose characterization is mainly given in terms of their (sub)components, which can be complex components in their turn or atomic ones. $\mathcal{FPC}$ offers the possibility of organizing classes of (both atomic and complex) components in *taxonomies* as well as the facility of building *partonomies* that (recursively) express the *whole-part relations* between each complex component and any one of its (sub)components. Moreover, in any complex component, a set of *constraints* restricts the set of valid combinations of its (sub)components.

Frames and Parts. In $\mathcal{FPC}$, each *frame* represents a *class* of components (either *atomic* or *complex*) and it has a set of *member slots* associated with it. Each slot represents a *property* of the components belonging to the class and it can be of type either *partonomic* or (alternatively) *descriptive*. Any slot p of a class C is described via a value restriction D(that can be another class or a set of values of a predefined kind) and a number restriction (i.e. an integer interval $[m,n]$ with $m \leq n$), as usual in the KL-One like representation formalisms. A slot p with value restriction D and number restriction $[m,n]$ captures the fact that the property p for any component of type C is expressed by a (multi)set of values of type D whose cardinality belongs to the interval $[m,n]$.

In the following we restrict our attention to partonomic slots since in this framework they represent the basic knowledge for problem decomposition.

Partonomic slots are used for capturing the *whole-part relation* among components. In $\mathcal{FPC}$ this relation is assumed to be asymmetric and transitive. Formally, any partonomic slot p of a class C is interpreted as a relation $p : C \rightarrow D$ such that $(\forall c \in C)(m \leq |p(c)| \leq n))$, being D and $[m,n]$, respectively, its value and its number restrictions; the meaning is straightforward: any complex component of type C has from a minimum of m up to a maximum of n direct parts of type D via a whole-part relation named p.

It is worth noting that in each configuration a component can neither be a direct part of two different complex components nor a direct part of the same complex component via two different whole-part relations (*exclusiveness assumption on parts*).

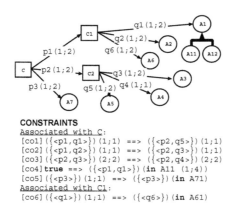

CONSTRAINTS
Associated with C:
[co1] ({<p1,q1>}) (1;1) ==> ({<p2,q5>}) (1;1)
[co2] ({<p1,q2>}) (1;1) ==> ({<p2,q3>}) (1;1)
[co3] ({<p2,q3>}) (2;2) ==> ({<p2,q4>}) (2;2)
[co4] **true** ==> ({<p1,q1>}) (**in** A11 (1;4))
[co5] ({<p3>}) (1;1) ==> ({<p3>}) (**in** A71)
Associated with C1:
[co6] ({<q1>}) (1;1) ==> ({<q6>}) (**in** A61)

Fig. 1. A toy conceptual model

Figure 1 contains a toy conceptual model that we use here as a simple example. Each rectangle represents a class of complex components, each oval represents a class of atomic components and any thin solid arrow corresponds to a partonomic slot. In the figure, it is stated, for instance, that C is a class of complex components and the partonomic slot $p1$ specifies that each instance of C has to contain one or two (complex) components of type $C1$; whereas the partonomic slot $p3$ states that any instance of C has to contain one or two (atomic) components of type $A7$.

In any conceptual model, a *slot chain* $\gamma = \langle p_1, \ldots, p_n \rangle$, starting in a class C and ending in a class D is interpreted as the relation composition $p_n \circ p_{n-1} \circ \ldots \circ p_1$ from C to D. The chain represents the subcomponents of a complex component $c \in C$ via the *whole-part* relations named $p_1, \ldots, p_n$. In figure 1, for example, $\langle p1, q1 \rangle$ denotes the subcomponents (of type $A1$) of each instance of C through the partonomic slots $p1$ and $q1$. Similarly, a set of slot chains $R = \{\gamma_1, \ldots, \gamma_m\}$ (where each γ_i starts in C and ends in D_i) is interpreted as the relation union $\bigcup_{i=1}^{m} \gamma_i$ from C to $\bigcup_{i=1}^{m} D_i$.

Besides the partonomies, also the taxonomies are useful in the conceptual models. In figure 1 the subclass links are represented by thick solid arrows. In that toy domain we assume that each class of atomic components Ai is partitioned into two subclasses $Ai1$ and $Ai2$. Only the partitioning of $A1$ into $A11$ and $A12$ is reported in figure.

Constraints. A set (possibly empty) of *constraints* is associated with each class of complex components. These constraints allow one to express those restrictions on the components and the subcomponents of the complex objects that can't be expressed by using only the frame portion of $\mathcal{FPC}$, in particular the inter-slot constraints that cannot be modeled via the number restrictions or the value restrictions.

Each constraint cc associated with C is of the form $\alpha \Rightarrow \beta$, where α is a conjunction of predicates or the boolean constant *true* and β is a predicate or the boolean constant *false*. The meaning is that for every complex component $c \in C$, if c satisfies α then it must satisfy β. It should be clear that if $\alpha = true$, then, for each $c \in C$, β must always hold, while if $\beta = false$, then, for each $c \in C$, α can never hold.

In the following we present only a simplified version of some predicates available in $\mathcal{FPC}$. For a more complete description of them see [6].

Let $R = \{\gamma_1, \ldots, \gamma_m\}$, where each $\gamma_i = \langle p_{i_1}, \ldots p_{i_n} \rangle$ is a slot chain starting in a class of C complex components. For any $c \in C$, $R(c)$ denotes the values of the relation R computed for c.

1) $(R)(h; k)$. $c \in C$ satisfies the predicate *iff* $h \leq |R(c)| \leq k$, where h, k are non negative integers with $h \leq k$.

2) $(R)(inI)$. $c \in C$ satisfies the predicate *iff* $R(c) \subseteq I$, where I is a union of classes in the conceptual model.

3) $(R)(inI(h; k))$. $c \in C$ satisfies the predicate *iff* $h \leq |R(c) \cap I| \leq k$, where h, k are non negative integers with $h \leq k$ and I is a union of classes in the conceptual model.

For example, the constraint $co5$ states that if only one component playing the partonomic role $p3$ is present in a configuration of an object of type C, then this component must be of type $A71$. It is worth noting that the user's requirements are automatically translated into the $\mathcal{FPC}$ constraint language. For example, the (user's) requirement of inserting in a configuration of an object of type C from 1 up to 4 subcomponents of type $A11$ is expressed by the constraint $co4$.

3   The Role of Partonomic Knowledge in Problem Decomposition

Given this framework, configuring a complex object of type C means to completely determine an instance c of C in which all the partonomic slots of C are instantiated and each direct component of c is completely configured too. c has to respect both the conceptual model (number and value restrictions imposed by the taxonomy and the partonomy as well as the constraints associated with the classes of components involved in c) and the user's requirements.

Configuring a complex component by taking into consideration only its taxo- partonomic description would be a straightforward activity. In fact, for any well formed model expressed in $\mathcal{FPC}$ in which no constraints are associated with any class, a configuration respecting that model would always exist. A simple algorithm could find it without any search and by simply starting from the class of the target object (i.e. the one for which the configuration has to be built), considering each slot p of that class and, for it, choosing its cardinality, i.e. choosing the number of components playing the partonomic role p to introduce into the configuration, and the type for each such component. This process must be recursively repeated for each complex component introduced in the configuration, until all the atomic ones are reached. In this process the algorithm needs only to respect the number and the value restrictions of the slots. Unfortunately, this is not realistic. The conceptual model usually contains complex constraints that link together different slots. In this more realistic situation a solution can't be generally found by making only a set of local choices and without resorting to search in a large space of alternatives.

Moreover, the requirements usually imposed by the user to the target artifact further restrict the set of legal configurations. This means that the search for a configuration is not guaranteed to be fruitful any more. In fact, even assuming the consistency of the conceptual model, the user's requirements could be inconsistent w.r.t. it and in such a case no configuration respecting the model and satisfying the requirements exists.

Therefore, in general, the task of solving a configuration problem can be rather expensive from a computational point of view. As we have mentioned above, in $\mathcal{FPC}$ framework this is mainly due to the constraints (both those that are part of the conceptual model and those imposed as user's requirements) that link together different components and subcomponents. In these situations a choice made for a component during the configuration process might restrict the choices actually available for another one, possibly preventing the latter to be fully configured. In such cases the configuration process has to revise some decision that it previously took and to explore a different path in the search space. Usually, in real cases the search space is rather huge and many paths in it don't lead to any solution.

However, in many cases it does not happen that every constraint interacts with each other and the capability of recognizing the sets of (potentially) interacting constraints can constitute the basis for decomposing a problem into independent subproblems.

Once a problem has been decomposed into a set of independent subproblems, these could be solved concurrently and with a certain degree of parallelism, potentially reducing the overall computational time. However, also a sequential configuration process can take advantage of the decomposition. In fact, if two subproblems are recognized to be independent, the configurator is aware that no choice made during the configuration process of the first one needs to be revised if it enters a failure path while solving the second one.

To be effective, the task of recognizing the decomposability of a problem (and of actually decomposing it) should not take too much time w.r.t. the time requested by the whole resolution process.

In our approach, the partonomic knowledge can be straightforwardly used in recognizing the interaction among constraints (with an acceptable precision) and in defining a way of decomposing a configuration problem into independent subproblems. With this aim, we introduce the *bound* relation among constraints. Intuitively, two constraints are *bound* iff the choices made during the configuration process in order to satisfy one of them *can* interact with those actually available for the satisfaction of the second one. If c is a complex component in a (tentative) configuration, the **bound relation** $\mathcal{B}_c$ is defined in the set $CONSTRS(c)$ of the constraints that c must satisfy, as follows: let $u, v, w \in CONSTRS(c)$. **If** u and v contain both a *same* partonomic slot p of $class(c)$ **then** $u\mathcal{B}_c v$ (i.e. if u and v refer to a same part of c, they are bound); **if** $u\mathcal{B}_c v$ **and** $v\mathcal{B}_c w$ **then** $u\mathcal{B}_c w$ (transitivity).

It is easy to see that $\mathcal{B}_c$ is an equivalence relation. If U is an equivalence class in the quotient set $CONSTRS(c)/\mathcal{B}_c$, every constraint in U might interact with any other constraint in the same class during the configuration process of c. On the contrary, given the *exclusiveness assumption on parts*, if $V \in CONSTRS(c)/\mathcal{B}_c$ is different from U, it means that in c the constraints belonging to V don't interact in any way with those in U. This means that the problem of configuring c by taking into consideration $CONSTRS(c)$ can be split into the set of independent subproblems of configuring c by considering the set W of constraints, for each $W \in CONSTRS(c)/\mathcal{B}_c$.

4   Configuration via Decomposition and Distribution

As said in the section above, *bound* relation can be used for singling out independent subproblems in the configuration process. A sequential algorithm for configuration exploiting decomposition is described in [8]. In the present paper we describe a general configuration technique which exploits the decomposition mechanism for distributing independent subproblems among a set of configurators working in parallel.

Let $\mathcal{P}$ be a pool of m configurators ($m \geq 1$). In the following we assume that each configuration request is sent to $\mathcal{P}$. If no configurator is available, the request is enqueued and it is assigned to a configurator as soon as one becomes available.

Each *configuration request* is a 4-TUPLE $\langle CM, T, c, V \rangle$, where CM is the $\mathcal{FPC}$ conceptual model describing the domain; T is a tentative configuration "under construction"; c is a complex component occurring in T and V is a set of $\mathcal{FPC}$ constraints holding for c. Such a 4-TUPLE corresponds to the request of extending the tentative configuration T (in the domain modeled by CM) by configuring only those direct parts of the complex component c involved in the constraints in V.

Each configurator in $\mathcal{P}$ runs the $configure$ procedure in figure 2. $configure$ procedure accepts as input a configuration request $\langle CM, T, c, V \rangle$ and it returns either the $FAILURE$ message or a tentative configuration in which the complex component c has been successfully extended.

The problem of extending c by taking into consideration the constraints in V requires the introduction in T of a set of direct components of c (first instruction of the procedure in fig. 4) and, then, the extension of each *complex* component introduced in this first step (WHILE loop).

Procedure $insertDirectComponents(CM, T, c, V)$ tries to introduce in T the direct components of c that might be critical for the satisfaction of the constraints in V. To do this, among the partonomic slots of the most specific class (w.r.t. the taxonomy) in CM to which c belongs (let's call it $class(c)$), it considers only those occurring in some constraint of the set V (in fact, the other partonomic slots possibly associated with $class(c)$ are not critical for the satisfaction of the constraints in V). For each such partonomic slot p, this procedure chooses both the number of the components playing the partonomic role p that should be inserted into the tentative configuration T and the type for each of them. Such choices are done by taking into account both the number and value restrictions associated with the partonomic slot p. Since, in general, there are more than one alternatives, the configurator records all the open choices. Whenever a direct *complex* component of c is introduced, it is inserted in the queue $dirC\_comps(c)$.

```
procedure configure(CM,T,c,V){
  T = insertDirectComponents(CM,T,c,V);
  if(T == FAILURE){return FAILURE;}
  /*T ≠ FAILURE*/
  while(dirC_comps(c)≠ <>){
    c' = dequeue(dirC_comps(c));
    CONSTRS(c') = I_Constrs(c') ∪ L_Constrs(c');
    {V₁,...,Vₙ}  = CONSTRS(c')/Bₑ' ;
    {T₁,...,Tₙ}  = send( {⟨T,c',Vᵢ⟩}ⁿᵢ₌₁ ,P );
    if( (∃i)(Tᵢ == FAILURE) ){
      if(no open choice for c){
        return FAILURE;
      }else{BACKTRACK;}
    }else{T = merge({T₁,...,Tₙ} );}
  }//while
  return T;
}//configure
```

Fig. 2. High level description of the configuration algorithm

It can happen that in this phase there is no way to insert these direct components of c into T without violating any constraint in V: in this case, the process fails.

The WHILE loop considers each *complex* direct component c' of c that was introduced (and enqueued in $dirC\_comps(c)$) in the previous step. The set of constraints that have to be considered for c' is $CONSTRS(c') = I\_Constrs(c') \cup L\_Constrs(c')$. $I\_Constrs(c')$ is the set of constraints that c' inherits from c, namely the constraints in V in which some partonomic slot associated with $class(c')$ occurs (i.e. those constraints in V mentioning some component of c'); $L\_Constrs(c')$ is the set of local constraints for c', namely those ones associated with $class(c')$ in CM, plus the constraints expressing the user's requirements for c'. $CONSTRS(c')$ is then partitioned into the set $\{V_1, \ldots, V_n\}$ of equivalence classes w.r.t. the bound relation $\mathcal{B}_{c'}$. Each class V_i induces a subproblem, thus the configuration of the component c' w.r.t. the constraints $CONSTRS(c')$ is decomposed into the set of subproblems $\{\langle T, c', V_i \rangle\}_{i=1}^n$ and this set of configuration requests is sent to the pool $\mathcal{P}$ of configurators. The results of these configurations is collected in $\{T_1, \ldots, T_n\}$. If one (or more) configuration request $\langle T, c', V_i \rangle$ leaded to a failure, it means that, given the tentative configuration T, there is no way to configure the component c' by respecting the constraints $CONSTRS(c')$. In this case, if there are some open choices in the configuration of c, a backtracking mechanism is activated, otherwise a failure occurs.[1] In case all the subproblems are successfully solved, the partial configurations $\{T_1, \ldots, T_n\}$ are merged and a new tentative configuration T, containing the configuration of c' w.r.t. $CONSTRS(c')$, is produced. As shown in the example reported below, the merge operation is fairly simple since it only consists in "summing up" the partial solutions. In fact, the partition of the constraints induces a partition of the partonomic slots associated with $class(c)$.

The configuration of c w.r.t. the constraints in V is completed when all the direct complex components of c in $dirC\_comps(c)$ are successfully configured.

It is worth saying that when a configurator $\mathcal{C}_i \in \mathcal{P}$ sends a set of configuration requests to $\mathcal{P}$, it becomes immediately available, thus the mechanism is deadlock-free.

Let us suppose that the user asks for a configuration of a complex object c_0 of type C and imposes a set of requirements $REQS$. A *main* module computes the set of constraints $CONSTRS(c_0)$ containing the constraints derived from the user's requirements as well as those associated with C in CM. The main decomposes this problem into the requests

$$\{\langle CM, T_0, c_0, V_i \rangle\}_{i=1}^l (l \geq 1) \text{ (where } T_0 \text{ contains only the component } c_0) \text{ and sends}$$
them to $\mathcal{P}$.

5   An Example

Figure 3 reports eight snapshots of the configuration process of an object of type C w.r.t. the constraints $co1$-$co5$, where $co4$ is a user requirement (see figure 1). In figure 3, each x_1 identifies a component of type X, while any partonomic slot p is identified by an arc labelled p; an arrow indicates the last component that has been expanded or the component that will be expanded next. At the beginning, the partial configuration T_a contains only the component c_1 representing the target object. The *main* module partitions the

---

[1] The backtracking mechanism is not described here, since it is out of the scope of this paper. A description of this mechanism can be found in [8].

constraints for c_1 into the two classes $V_1 = \{co1, co2, co3, co4\}$ and $V_2 = \{co5\}$ and sends the two correspondent configuration requests to the pool of configurators. The configuration of c_1 w.r.t. the constraints V_2 leads to the partial configuration T_g; in parallel, the configuration request relevant to V_1 is taken into consideration. Since only the partonomic slots $p1$ and $p2$ of C occur in the constraints belonging to V_1, only the *complex* components $c1\_1$ and $c2\_1$, playing these partonomic roles, are inserted into the partial configuration (T_b). To complete the configuration of c_1 w.r.t. V_1, its direct complex components $c1\_1$ and $c2\_1$ have to be configured too. The constraints for $c1\_1$ (those inherited from c_1 and the local one $co6$) are split into the two classes $V_3 = \{co1, co4, co6\}$ and $V_4 = \{co2\}$; the solutions of the two correspondent sub-problems lead to the partial configurations T_c and T_d, respectively. These two partial configurations are merged and T_e is produced. The configuration of the component $c2\_1$ is decomposed into two subproblems corresponding to the two classes of constraints $V_5 = \{co1\}$ and $V_6 = \{co2, co3\}$; after merging the solutions to these two subproblems, T_f, representing a partial configuration of c_1 w.r.t. V_1 is produced. A final merge between T_g and T_f produces a complete configuration of the target object (T_h).

6   Preliminary Results

In order to test the impact of the decomposition strategy on the configuration process, we have performed an experiment in a real domain of PC configuration. In this domain

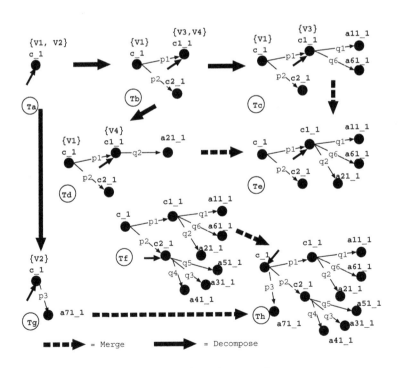

Fig. 3. A configuration example

a set of *atomic* components, such as CPUs, memory slots, monitors, etc., can be used for configuring *complex* objects, such as different kinds of PCs, motherboards etc. according to the user requirements. We have generated a test set of 153 configuration problems: for each of them we have specified the type of the target object (e.g. a PC for graphical applications) and the requirements that it must satisfy (e.g. it must have a CD writer of a certain kind, it must be *fast enough* and so on). In this experiment, we used only one configurator, in order to test the impact of the decomposition technique on a sequential approach to the resolution of configuration problems. A configuration problem is considered solved iff the configurator either provides a configuration or detects that no configuration satisfying the user's requirements can be produced, *within the timeout of 360 sec.*

It came out that the strategy *no_dec* that did not attempt any decomposition was able to solve 150 out of the 153 configuration problems (i.e. its competence was of 98.0%); whereas the strategy *dec* making use of decomposition solved all the problems (i.e. its competence was of 100%). The average CPU time computed on the 150 problems solved by both strategies was 7735.4 msec. for *no_dec* and 2257.4 for *dec* (i.e. −70.8% w.r.t. *no_dec*). Moreover, the average CPU time computed on the 153 problems solved by *dec* was 4502.3 msec. This means that *dec* was able to solve the 3 difficult problems that *no_dec* did not solve with an average cost still less than that relevant to the 150 problems solved by *no_dec*[2].

7 Discussion

The present paper addresses the issue of decomposing a configuration problem into simpler subproblems by exploiting as much as possible the implicit decomposition provided by the partonomic relations of complex components. The adoption of a structured framework for modeling the configuration domains as well as for expressing the configuration problems plays a major role since the criterion for singling out the classes of *bound* constraints is based on an analysis of the partonomic slots mentioned in the constraints. The problem decomposition is induced by this partitioning of the constraints into classes.

Since a set of constraints is associated with each complex component, the configuration process can try to recursively decompose the problem each time it has to configure a component or a subcomponent of the target object. The set of mutually independent subproblems the main problem has been decomposed into can be solved in parallel by a pool of configurators. Our main motivation for decomposing configuration problems is saving in computational effort. However, there are domains in which the configuration problems are distributed by their nature [2]. This is the case, for example, of those domains in which the main components of a complex product are provided by different suppliers. In these cases the capability of decomposing at least the main configuration problem (i.e. the capability of attempting a decomposition at the target object level) can be quite useful, since it would single out the possible interactions among the main components.

---

[2] It is worth noting that if we computed the average CPU time spent by *no_dec* on all the 153 problems (i.e. including the 3 unsolved problems), we would obtain 14642.5 msec.

Preliminary experimental results demonstrate the effectiveness of the decomposition technique in a sequential approach to configuration. Further experiments are planned in order to test the impact of the distribution of the subproblems to a pool of configurators.

References

1. R. Dechter. Enhancement schemes for constraint processing: backjumping, learning, and cutset decomposition. *Artificial Intelligence*, 41:273–312, 1990.
2. A. Felfernig, G. Friedrich, D. Jannach, and M. Zanker. Distributed configuring. In *Proc. IJCAI-01 Configuration WS*, pages 18–24, 2001.
3. G. Fleischanderl, G. E. Friedrich, A. Haselböck, H. Schreiner, and M. Stumptner. Configuring large systems using generative constraint satisfaction. *IEEE Intelligent Systems*, (July/August 1998):59–68, 1998.
4. G. Friedrich and M. Stumptner. Consistency-based configuration. In *AAAI-99, Workshop on Configuration*, 1999.
5. G. Gottlob, N. Leone, and F. Scarcello. A comparison of structural csp decomposition methods. *Artificial Intelligence*, 124:243–282, 2000.
6. D. Magro and P. Torasso. Description and configuration of complex technical products in a virtual store. In *Proc. ECAI 2000 Configuration WS*, pages 50–55, 2000.
7. D. Magro and P. Torasso. Supporting product configuration in a virtual store. *LNAI*, 2175:176–188, 2001.
8. D. Magro and P. Torasso. Problem decomposition in configuration. In *Proc. ECAI 2002 Configuration WS (to appear)*, 2002.
9. D. L. McGuinness and J. R. Wright. An industrial-strength description logic-based configurator platform. *IEEE Intelligent Systems*, (July/August 1998):69–77, 1998.
10. S. Mittal and B. Falkenhainer. Dynamic constraint satisfaction problems. In *Proc. of the AAAI 90*, pages 25–32, 1990.
11. D. Sabin and E.C. Freuder. Configuration as composite constraint satisfaction. In *Proc. Artificial Intelligence and Manufacturing. Research Planning Workshop*, pages 153–161, 1996.
12. D. Sabin and R. Weigel. Product configuration frameworks - a survey. *IEEE Intelligent Systems*, (July/August 1998):42–49, 1998.
13. T. Soininen, I. Niemelä, J. Tiihonen, and R. Sulonen. Unified configuration knowledge representation using weight constraint rules. In *Proc. ECAI 2000 Configuration WS*, pages 79–84, 2000.
14. M. Veron and M. Aldanondo. Yet another approach to ccsp for configuration problem. In *Proc. ECAI 2000 Configuration WS*, pages 59–62, 2000.

Direct Adaptive Neural Control with Integral-Plus-State Action

Ieroham Baruch[1], Alfredo del Carmen Martinez Q.[1],
Ruben Garrido[1], and Boyka Nenkova[2]

[1]CINVESTAV-IPN, Ave. IPN No 2508,
A.P. 14-470 Mexico D.F., C.P. 07360 MEXICO
E-mail: baruch@ctrl.cinvestav.mx
[2] IIT-BAS, Sofia 1113, BULGARIA

Abstract. The paper applied a *Recurrent Neural Network (RNN)* model in two *Integral-Plus-State (IPS)* schemes of real-time adaptive neural control. The proposed control modify and extend a previously published direct adaptive neural control scheme with one or two *I-control* terms, so to obtain a neural, *IPS* adaptive, offset compensational and trajectory tracking control. The control scheme contains only two *RNN* models (systems identificator and *IPS* feedback controller) and not need a third feedforward *RNN* control model. The good performance of the adaptive neural *IPS* control is confirmed by comparative simulation results, obtained using a nonlinear *multi-input multi-output* plant, corrupted by noise. The results exhibits good convergence and noise resistance which not depend on the magnitude of the offset.

1 Introduction

Intelligent control using *Neural Networks (NN)* has been applied to various control problems, [8]. It is known to be effective in many situations, especially when the controlled plant exhibits nonlinearity, and the plant parameters are unknown and time-varying, especially for mechanical systems. On the other hand, the unavoidable effects of identification and control errors, due to model uncertainties, together with a slow load variations, caused a steady-state offset that needs to be removed. In this case, an integral action, added to the control, compensates the plant uncertainties and load effects, and help the system to track the reference signal.

Within the context of the servomechanism problem, integral action is a fundamental technique in the control repertoire and the *I-PD (or PID)* controllers have been the most utilised controllers in the industry, because of their simple structure and robust performance in wide range of operating conditions, [4]. Here the *PD* mode is used to speed up response, whereas the *PI* mode is applied to eliminate the steady state offset. In last years, the classical *PID* scheme has been completed by auto-tuning devices like *Neural Networks*, [5], [6], (*Multi-Layer Perceptron*, learned by *Genetic Algorithms*; *Radial Basis Functions NN*), and *Fuzzy Systems*, [2], to adjust on-line its parameters. To resolve some specific control problems in mechanical systems, some extensions to the classical *PID* scheme, have been added. So, for regulator tasks on mechanical systems that exhibit friction, the *PID*-controller is combined with mass and friction *feedforward*, [2]. The state *PD*-controller plus

D. Scott (Ed.): AIMSA 2002, LNAI 2443, pp. 91-100, 2002.

gravity compensation terms is widely used in robot manipulators control. However, this linear state feedback controllers could not compensate inertial and Corriolis forces and cannot render asymptotic stability for path tracking tasks. To overcome this, in [9], a nonlinear *PID* controller, is proposed. The major disadvantage of this controllers is that they could be applied only for *Single-Input-Single-Output (SISO)* and not for *Multi-Input-Multi-Output (MIMO)* systems. Also, in the case of high order systems, the *PD* action is not sufficient to assure systems stability. The use of *RNN* for systems control could overcome these problems. In [3], *Baruch et all.*, proposed a new *RNN* and a dynamic *Backpropagation (BP)*-like algorithm of its learning, which could resolve identification and control problems in an universal way. The applied direct adaptive neural control system contains three *RNNs* (one for identification and two - for *feedback* and *feedforward* control, respectively), which offers a good performance and flexibility. The aim of this paper is to apply this *RNN* model in two *Integral-Plus-State (IPS)* schemes of real-time identification and control of nonlinear *MIMO* plants with unknown parameters. This objective could be reached modifying and extending the given in [3] control scheme with one or two I-control terms, so to obtain an *IPS* adaptive, offset compensational and trajectory tracking control. The performed study shows that the introduction of *I-actions* gives the possibility to remove the *feedforward* part of the control scheme, given in [3], without to damage the tracking abilities of the proposed control in noise conditions.

2 Recurrent Neural Network Topology and Learning

In [3], a discrete-time model of *Recurrent Trainable Neural Network (RTNN)*, and a dynamic *Backpropagation* weight updating rule, are given. The *RTNN* model is described by the following equations:

$$X(k+1) = JX(k)+BU(k) \tag{1}$$
$$Z(k)=S[X(k)] \tag{2}$$
$$Y(k) = S[CZ(k)] \tag{3}$$
$$J = \text{block-diag } (J_i); \ |J_i| < 0 \tag{4}$$

Where: $X(k)$ is a N - state vector of the system; $U(k)$ is a M- input vector; $Y(k)$ is a L-output vector; $Z(k)$ is an auxiliary vector variable with dimension L , $S(.)$ is a vector-valued activation function with appropriate dimension; J is a (NxN) weight-state diagonal matrix with elements J_i; B and C are weight input and output matrices with appropriate dimensions and block structure, corresponding to the block structure of J. As it can be seen, the given *RTNN* model is a completely parallel parametric one, so it is useful for identification and control purposes. The *controllability* and *observability* of this model is proven in [1], [10]. Parameters of that model are the weight matrices *J,* B, C and the state vector $X(k)$. The equation (4) is a stability preserving condition. The general *BP* learning algorithm is given as:

$$W_{ij}(k+1) = W_{ij}(k) +\eta \ \Delta W_{ij}(k) +\alpha \ \Delta W_{ij}(k-1) \tag{5}$$

Where: W_{ij} (C, J, B) is the ij-th weight element of each weight matrix (given in parenthesis) of the *RTNN* model to be updated; ΔW_{ij} (ΔC_{ij} , ΔJ_{ij}, ΔB_{ij}) is the ij-th weight correction of W_{ij} of each weight matrix (given in parenthesis); η, α are learning rate parameters. The weight updates ΔC_{ij}, ΔJ_{ij}, ΔB_{ij} of model weights C_{ij}, J_{ij}, B_{ij}, are given by:

$$\Delta C_{ij}(k) = [T_j(k) - Y_j(k)] \, S_j'(Y_j(k)) \, Z_i(k) \tag{6}$$
$$\Delta J_{ij}(k) = R \, X_i(k-1) \tag{7}$$
$$R_1 = C_i(k) \, [T(k)-Y(k)] \, S_j'(Z_j(k)) \tag{8}$$
$$\Delta B_{ij}(k) = R \, U_i(k) \tag{9}$$

Where: T is a target vector with dimension L and [T-Y] is an output error vector also with the same dimension; R_1 is an auxiliary variable; S'(x) is the derivative of the activation function, which for the hyperbolic tangent is $S_j'(x) = 1-x^2$.

The next part of the paper incorporates the *RTNN* model in two *IPS* schemes of real-time adaptive control. The block diagrams of that controls are described bellow.

3   A Direct Adaptive Neural Control with IPS Action

Let us suppose that the studied nonlinear plant possess the following structure:

$$X_p(k+1) = F(X_p(k), U(k)) \tag{10}$$
$$Y_p(k) = \varphi(X_p(k)) \tag{11}$$

Where: $X_p(k)$, $Y_p(k)$ are plant state and output vector variables; F and φ are smooth, odd, bounded, unknown nonlinear functions. Two control schemes are considered – with one and with two integral terms in the control part.

3.1   A Direct Adaptive Control Scheme with One Integral Block

The block diagram of the first control scheme, containing one integral block is shown on *Fig.1*. It contains one identification and state estimation *RTNN-1*, which generates states, to the control *RTNN-2* which is a *feedback stabilizing systems controller* with *IPS action*.

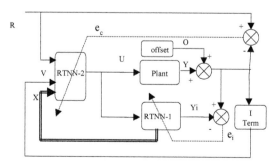

Fig. 1.. Block-diagram of a direct adaptive trajectory tracking control system with IPS action.

From *Fig.1* it is seen that the control *RTNN* have as inputs the state vector, the integral action vector V(k) and the systems reference vector R. Let us define the measurement vector of the control system as:

$$Y^*(k) = Y_p(k) + O(k) \tag{12}$$

Where O(k) is a L-vector offset *(measurement and load disturbance)*. The discrete integral term equation, of the integral block, which integrates the plant measurement output, is written as:

$$V(k+1)=V(k)+T_o Y^*(k) \tag{13}$$

Where V(k) is a L-vector integral action variable and T_o is a period of discretization. The control law is given by the following equation:

$$U(k) = - NS[X^e(k), R(k)] \tag{14}$$

Where: NS is a *RTNN* function; $X^e(k)$ is a (N+L) extended state vector, defined as:

$$X^e(k) = [X(k), V(k)]^T \tag{15}$$

Now, it is easy to add another integral block to this control system.

3.2   A Direct Adaptive Control Scheme with Two Integral Blocks

The block diagram of the second control scheme, containing two successive integral blocks is shown on *Fig.2*. It contains one identification and state estimation *RTNN-1*, which generates states, to the *feedback stabilizing systems controller* with *2I-PS action (the RTNN-2)*. From *Fig.1* it is seen that the control *RTNN* have as inputs the state vector, the first and the second integral action vectors V(k), Z(k) and the systems reference vector R. The discrete integral term equation of the second integral block, which integrates the output of the first integrator, is written as:

$$Z(k+1)=Z(k)+T_oV(k) \tag{16}$$

Where Z(k) is a L-vector integral action variable. The control law of this control scheme, is given by the following equation:

$$U(k) = - NS[X^{ee}(k), R(k)] \tag{17}$$

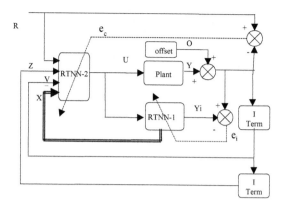

Fig. 2.. Block-diagram of a direct adaptive trajectory tracking control system with double integral terms (2I-PS action).

Where: $X^{ee}(k)$ is a (N+2*L) extended state vector, defined as:

$$X^{ee}(k) = [X(k), V(k), Z(k)]^T \qquad (18)$$

In the next part, simulation result, obtained with a *MIMO* plant, are given.

4 Simulation Results

The plant, considered here, is a third-order nonlinear *MIMO* system whit two inputs, two outputs, three states, and it is described by the following nonlinear state-space equations, [7]:

$$x_1(k+1) = 0.9x_1(k)\sin[x_2(k)] + \left[2 + 1.5\frac{x_1(k)u_1(k)}{1 + x_1^2(k)u_1^2(k)}\right]u_1$$
$$+ \left[x_1(k) + \frac{2x_1(k)}{1 + x_1^2(k)}\right]u_2 \qquad (19)$$

$$x_2(k+1) = x_3(k)\{1 + \sin[4x_3(k)]\} + \frac{x_3(k)}{1 + x_3^2} \qquad (20)$$

$$x_3(k+1) = \{3 + \sin[2x_1(k)]\}u_2(k) \qquad (21)$$

$$y_1(k) = x_1(k); \qquad (22)$$

$$y_1(k) = x_2(k); \qquad (23)$$

Where: $x(k)=[x_1(k), x_2(k), x_3(k)]^T$ is a 3-state vector; $u(k) =[u_1(k), u_2(k)]^T$ is a 2-dimensional input vector; $y(k) =[y_1(k), y_2(k))]^T$ is a 2-dimensional output vector, all at the instant k. The reference signal is a sum of two sinusoids with different amplitudes and frequencies.

Results of simulation experiments with duration of 40 seconds, are shown in 10-second-graphics. The results, obtained using the first control scheme (Fig.1), are given on Fig. 3 and that – by the second control scheme (Fig.2) - are given on Fig. 4, 5, respectively. Comparative results, obtained by control scheme without integral terms, are given on Fig. 6. The graphics, given on Fig. 3, a to m, show simulation results, using the first control scheme with one integral block and constant offset signal with magnitude of 40%, corrupting the systems output signal. The first two graphics (Fig.3,a,b) compare both reference signals with both plant outputs in the first 10 seconds of the plant control simulation. The following two graphics give both control signals, obtained for the last 10 seconds of the control simulation (Fig. 3,c,d). The next two graphics compare both plant outputs with corresponding outputs of the identification *RTNN* during the first 10 seconds of the plant identification (Fig. 3,e,f). The following two graphics give the same results, obtained for the last 10 seconds of the identification (Fig.3, g, h). The control and identification results exhibits good fast convergence to the desired values. Next two graphics represents both control signals (Fig. 3, i, j). The following two graphics represent the total *Mean Squared Error* (*MSE%*) of control and the total *MSE%* of identification (Fig. 3, k, l), both decreasing rapidly to small values. The last graphics, (Fig. 3,m), represents the four states of the system, issued by the identification *RTNN* (architecture 1, 4, 1, $\eta = 0.01$, $\alpha = 0.001$, for both control schemes), which are entry to the control *RTNN*. Similar results, obtained with the second control scheme (Fig. 2), where the plant output is corrupted by 40% linear (triangular) load disturbance, are given on Fig. 4, a to m. The comparison of these results show that the introduction of second integral gives the opportunity to compensate not only constant offsets, but also linear offsets. The price, paid for this, is that the *RTNNs* converges more slowly, which could be seen comparing the graphics, given on Fig. 3, a, b with that, given on Fig. 4, a, b, respectively. For sake of comparison, on Fig. 5 a, b; c, d; e, f, are shown the graphical results, corresponding to that- given on Fig. 4, c, d; g, h; k, l, but for an linear offset of 100%. The graphics show good performance of the systems identification and control in the last 10 seconds of the simulation, in spite of the bigger offset. Results, obtained with a control system without integral blocks and a linear offset of 40%, are shown on Fig. 6, a, b; c, d; e, f; g, h which could be compared with that of Fig. 4 a, b; c, d;, e, f; g, h. As it could be seen, the system without integral action is sensitive to linear load disturbances, especially in the first 10 seconds of the identification and control simulations. The on-line simulation results, for both control schemes, show that an overshoot of the *MSE%* occurs due to improper identification in the beginning (see Fig. 3, e; Fig. 6, e, respectively), but this *MSE%* rapidly decreased.

5 Conclusions

A comparative study of various control systems with I-action, is done. The paper propose to use two direct adaptive feedback control schemes with *Integral-Plus-State* action, applied for discrete-time *MIMO* system, [7]. The control scheme contain one identification and state estimation *RTNN*, one or two integral blocks and one control *RTNN*. The good tracking abilities of this adaptive *IPS* control, for both control schemes, is confirmed by comparative simulation results, obtained with a *MIMO* plant model. The results show that the first control scheme could compensate constant offsets, and the second control scheme could compensate linear offsets.

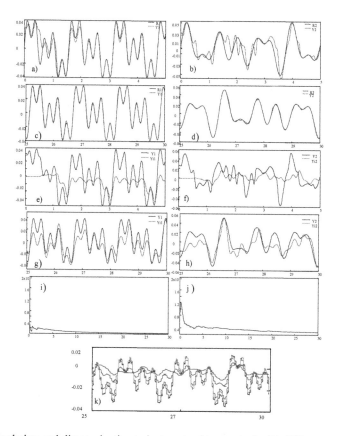

Fig. 3.. A single integral direct adaptive trajectory tracking control with 40% constant offset; a) comparison between the first plant output Y1 and the reference signal R in the first 5 seconds of the simulation; b) comparison between the second plant output Y2 and the reference signal R in the first 5 seconds of the simulation; c) comparison Y1 and R in the last 5 seconds of the simulation; d) comparison between Y2 and R in the last 5 seconds of the simulation; e) comparison between the first plant output Y1 and the first output Yi1 of the identification *RTNN* in the first 5 seconds of the simulation; f) comparison between the second plant output Y2 and the second output Yi2 of the identification *RTNN* in the first 10 seconds of the simulation; g) comparison between Y1 and Yi1 of the identification *RTNN* in the last 5 seconds of the simulation; h) comparison Y2 and Yi2 of the identification *RTNN* in the last 5 seconds of the simulation; i) first control signal U1; j) second control signal U2; k) mean squared error of control (*MSE%*); l) mean squared error of identification (*MSE%*); m) systems state variables, estimated by *RTNN*.

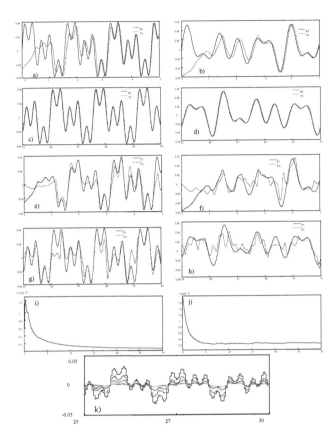

Fig. 4.. A double integral direct adaptive trajectory tracking control with 40% linear offset; a) comparison between the first plant output Y1 and the reference signal R in the first 5 seconds of the simulation; b) comparison between the second plant output Y2 and the reference signal R in the first 5 seconds of the simulation; c) comparison Y1 and R in the last 5 seconds of the simulation; d) comparison between Y2 and R in the last 5 seconds of the simulation; e) comparison between the first plant output Y1 and the first output Yi1 of the identification *RTNN* in the first 5 seconds of the simulation; f) comparison between the second plant output Y2 and the second output Yi2 of the identification *RTNN* in the first 10 seconds of the simulation; g) comparison between Y1 and Yi1 of the identification *RTNN* in the last 5 seconds of the simulation; h) comparison Y2 and Yi2 of the identification *RTNN* in the last 5 seconds of the simulation; i) first control signal U1; j) second control signal U2; k) mean squared error of control (*MSE%*); l) mean squared error of identification (*MSE%*); m) systems state variables, estimated by *RTNN*.

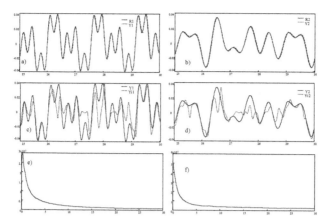

Fig. 5.. A double integral direct adaptive trajectory tracking control with 100% linear offset; a) comparison between the first plant output Y1 and the reference signal R in the last 5 seconds of the simulation; b) comparison between the second plant output Y2 and the reference signal R in the last 5 seconds of the simulation; c) comparison between the first plant output Y1 and the first output Yi1 of the identification *RTNN* in the last 5 seconds of the simulation; d) comparison between the second plant output Y2 and the second output Yi2 of the identification *RTNN* in the last 5 seconds of the simulation; e) mean squared error of control (*MSE%*); f) mean squared error of identification (*MSE%*).

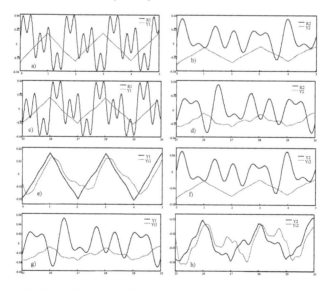

Fig. 6.. A direct adaptive trajectory tracking control without integral action and with 40% linear offset; a) comparison between Y1 and R in the first 5 seconds; b) comparison between Y2 and R in the first 5 seconds; c) comparison between Y1 and R in the last 5 seconds; d) comparison between Y2 and R in the last 5 seconds; e) comparison between Y1 and Yi1 of the identification *RTNN* in the first 5 seconds of the simulation; f) comparison between Y2 and Yi2 in the first 5 seconds; g) comparison between Y1 and Yi1 in the last 5 seconds of the simulation; h) comparison betweenY2 and Yi2 in the last 5 seconds.

The proposed control schemes does not need *feedforward* control part, as the scheme, given in [3], does. The comparison with simulation results, obtained using a system without integral terms confirm that the system with *I-terms* performs better in noise conditions.

References

1. Albertini, F., Sontag, E.: State Observability in Recurrent Neural Networks. System and Control Letters, **22** (1994), 235-244.
2. Almutairi, N.B., Chow, M.Y.: A Modified PI Control Action with a Robust Adaptive Fuzzy Controller Applied to DC Motor. Proceedings of the IEEE-INNS-ENNS International Joint Conference on Neural Networks, Washington D.C., USA, July 15-19, (2001), 503-508.
3. Baruch, I., Flores, J.-M., Thomas, F., Garrido, R.: Adaptive Neural control of Nonlinear Systems. In: Dorfner, G., Bischof, H., Hornik, K. (eds.): Artificial Neural Networks – ICANN 2001. Lecture Notes in Computer Science, Vol. 2130. Springer-Verlag, Berlin Heidelberg New York (2001), 930-936.
4. Cervantes, I., Alvarez-Ramirez, J.: On the PID Tracking of Robot-Manipulators. Systems Control Letters, **42** (2001), 37-46.
5. Hensen, R.H.A., van den Molengraft, M.J.G., Steinbuch, M.: High Performance Regulator Control for Mechanical Systems Subject to Friction. Proceedings. of the 2001 IEEE International Conference on Control Applications, Mexico City, Mexico, September 5-7, (2001), 200-205.
6. Lima, J.M., Azevedo, A.B., Duarte, N., Fonseca, C.M., Ruano, A.E., Fleming, P.J.: Neuro-Genetic PID Auto-tuning. Proceedings of the European Control Conference, Porto, Portugal, September 4-7, (2001), 3899-3904.
7. Narendra, Kumpati S., Mukhopadhyay, Shehasis: Adaptive Control of Nonlinear Multivariable Systems Using Neural Networks. Neural Networks, **7** (1994), 737-752
8. Omatu. S., Khalil, M., Yusof, R: Neuro-Control and Their Applications. Springer-Verlag, Berlin, Heidelberg (1995).
9. Parra-Vega, V., Arimoto, S.: Non-linear PID Control with Sliding Modes for Tracking of Robot Manipulators. Proceedings of the 2001 IEEE Internatrional Conference on Control Applications, Mexico City, Mexico, September 5-7, (2001), 351-356.
10. Sontag, E., Sussmann, H.: Complete Controllability of Continuous Time Recurrent Neural Networks. System and Control Letters, **30** (1997), 177-183.

ILP Techniques for Free-Text Input Processing

Svetla Boytcheva

Department of Information Technology,
Faculty of Mathematics and Informatics,
Sofia University "St. Kliment Ohridski",
5 J. Bauchier Blvd., 1164 Sofia, Bulgaria,
svetla@fmi.uni-sofia.bg

Abstract. This paper presents an application of some Inductive logic programming (ILP) techniques for checking user's answer correctness in a Computer-Aided Language Learning (CALL) system STyLE (Scientific Terminology Learning Environment). STyLE supports adaptive learning of English terminology with a target user group of non-native English speakers. In STyLE are implemented many original features that make this system intelligent and adaptive, but we will focus only on one of them: supporting learner-system communication in Natural Language (NL). The proposed ILP system RICH is used for generation of least generalization(LG) and greatest specialization(GS) of the set of possible correct answers of a given question to the user from the system. The user's answer is correct if it is between LG and GS of the correct answers' set.

Keywords: *Inductive Logic Programming, Natural Language Processing, Free-text input*

1 Introduction

Supporting free NL input requires integration of complex NLP techniques, esp. parsing and checking the correctness of the learner's NL answer. A number of prototypes try to cope with the (almost free) NL input but according to [4] "so few of these systems have passed the concept demonstration phase". The prototypes in [4] contain mostly modules for checking students' competence in vocabulary, morphology, and correct syntax usage (parsers). The most sophisticated semantic analysis is embedded in `BRIDGE/MILT` which matches the learner's utterance (a lexical conceptual structure) against the prestored expected lexical conceptual structures. More recent systems (`CASTLE` in `RECALL` [5] and `SLALOM` [6]) still focus on spelling, morphological, and syntactic errors. Another example is `CIRCSIM-Tutor` [7], which expects quite short answers, permissively extracts whatever is needed and ignores the rest. To conclude, every CALL system pretending for some intelligence has to decide how to analyse learners' NL inputs and check their correctness but the present solutions especially for semantic analysis are far from being perfect.

D. Scott (Ed.): AIMSA 2002, LNAI 2443, pp. 101–110, 2002.

This paper presents an application of some ILP techniques for checking user's answer correctness in a CALL system STyLE [3]. STyLE supports adaptive learning of English terminology with a target user group of non-native English speakers. In STyLE are implemented many original features that make this system intelligent and adaptive, but we will focus only on one of them: supporting learner-system communication in NL. This type of communication in STyLE is supported by its module STyLE-Parasite, which provides a mechanism for checking the correctness of learner's NL utterances. On the other hand STyLE-Parasite uses the system Parasite as an NLU machine.

Section 2 describes the system Parasite. Section 3 deals with the mechanism for checking the correctness of the learner's NL utterances. Section 4 describes application of ILP techniques. In Section 5 are given some examples. Section 6 gives the conclusion.

2 System Parasite

The system Parasite, developed at UMIST by Allan Ramsay, see e.g. [8] and [9], is already integrated in STyLE as an NLU machine for analysing learners' free utterances.

Parasite works using a lexicon, syntax grammar rules and a knowledge base of type (word) hierarchy and meaning postulates. The lexicon contains the morphological description of the words recognised in the input text. The grammar currently covers most of the English syntax, including complex embedded sentences. The hierarchy is a DAG (directed acyclic graph). The meaning postulates define in logical format the word semantics. It is not obligatory to define in advance the semantics of each word to be processed; the designer only has to keep in mind that the prover of the semantic correctness works with the available postulates. Parasite is an open system and allows for the insertion of new words, grammar rules and meaning postulates. When started Parasite checks the KB consistency (contradictions, loop definitions).

As a typical NLU artefact (in contrast to some prototypes for automatic KA),Parasite analyses every input string. It processes separate sentences as well as extended discourse of several sentences. Given a text paragraph, the user might choose analysis type: either independent analysis sentence by sentence, or analysis of all sentences as coherent discourse.

The analysis is performed step by step, starting by morphological and syntactic analysis. Diagnostics is available in cases of unknown or non-correctly derived words, as well as for wrong or ambiguous sentence structure. Soft parsing techniques provide correct analysis of sentences with "small" syntax errors (e.g. wrong subject-verb agreement). Some ambiguity types are resolved by heuristically predefined preference scores; currently the PP-attachment problems are tackled. Syntax analysis fails in case of unknown input words and unresolvable ambiguities.

After correct syntax analysis `Parasite` performs semantic analysis (see [1, 11,12]). Meaning postulates are encoded in a language which is a dynamic, constructive version of Ray Turner's 'property theory' [11].

For instance, the definition of "capital market":*"The capital market is an institutional mechanism which deals with capital goods."* can be translated as following Meaning postulate:

```
lexicalMP(
forall(X :: {capital_market(X)}, institutional_mechanism(X) &
        exists(Z::{deal(Z)}, theta(X,$agent,Z) &
        exists(Y::{capital_goods(Y)}, theta(Y,$object,Z))))).
```

3 Mechanism for Checking the Correctness of the Learner's NL Utterances

Answers in free English are linguistically analysed by the NL Understanding component `Parasite`. An especially implemented prover `STyLE-Parasite` checks whether the linguistically correct student's answer is correct as an answer to the particular exercise performed at the moment.

An especially performed user study [10] investigated how erroneous answers appear in terminology learning. Errors are usually caused by the following reasons:

- Language errors (spelling, morphological, syntax errors);
- Question misunderstanding, which causes wrong answer;
- Correct question understanding, but absent knowledge of the correct term, which implies usage of paraphrases and generalisation instead of the expected answer;
- Correct question understanding, but absent domain knowledge, which implies specialisation, partially correct answers, incomplete answers and wrong answers.

In principle `Parasite` covers errors due to the first two cases while the prover `STyLE-Parasite` discovers errors due to the two later cases. Parasite provides advanced NL understanding in cases when the learner is given the opportunity to type in freely. The expected answers are simple declarative sentences although `Parasite` handles complex sentences as well as simple discourse consisting of several sentences. Analysing the English input and its linguistic consistency, `Parasite` returns a model of the correct answers or indications of four kinds of errors: (i) unknown word, (ii) morpho, (iii) syntax and (iv) wrong. However, to know that an input utterance is linguistically correct is not enough in CALL, for instance "John loves Mary" is linguistically correct but does not answer the question "who does trade stocks on the primary market". Therefore a second step is necessary, to find out whether the given utterance is reasonable as an answer to the exercise being performed. `STyLE-Parasite` checks the answers' correctness against the available domain knowledge and the expected answer. Most generally, STyLE-Parasite takes the logical form built by Parasite , "compares" it to the logical forms of the predefined expected minimal and maximal answers and makes the necessary inferences [2,3]. Figure 1 presents the eight possible cases of intersections of the terms in the three logical forms and shows how STyLE-Parasite decides about the correctness of the input logical form (which strongly depends on the lexical choices and the syntactic structure of the concrete input). Since there might be many correct answers and their language expression varies considerably, it is not practical to compare the input to a single predefined correct logical form. Rather, STyLE-Parasite uses pre-stored maximal and minimal logical forms. Adding new terms to the maximal answer might be redundant or wrong. STyLE-Parasite inference is sound [2] but not complete, because the conclusion "(partially) correct learner utterances" is indicated after the first correct binding of variables. STyLE-Parasite returns the following indications of semantic mistakes: (i) correct, (ii) more general, (iii) more specific, (iv) paraphrase (usage of concept definition instead of the proper term), (v) incomplete, (vi) partially correct, (vii) wrong and (viii) combination of several mistakes.

4 Application of ILP Techniques

Let create clauses from the logical models generated after Parasite analyses, where this model is used as a body of the clause and all clauses have one and same predicate symbol "answer" with arity 1.

To generate sets of minimal and maximal correct answers we will use some ILP Techniques. First we will give some preliminary definitions and results.

Definition 1: (subsumption). Let C and D be clauses. We sat that *C subsumes D*, denoted as $C \geq D$ if there exists a substitution θ such as $C\theta \subseteq D$.

In order subsumption we will say that the clause C is more general than the clause D (or dually D is more specific than C) if C subsumes D.

Definition 2: (implication). Let C and D be clauses. We sat that *C logically implies D*, denoted as $C \models D$ if every model of C is also a model of D.

In order implication we will say that the clause C is more general than the clause D (or equivalently D is more specific than C) if C logically implies D.

Corollary 1. If $C \geq D$ then $C \models D$. The converted does not hold.

Lemma (Gottlob). Let C and D be clauses, which are non-tautologous. If $C \models D$ than $C^+ \geq D^+$ and $C^- \geq D^-$, where by C^+ are denoted positive literals in C and C^- denotes negative literals in C.

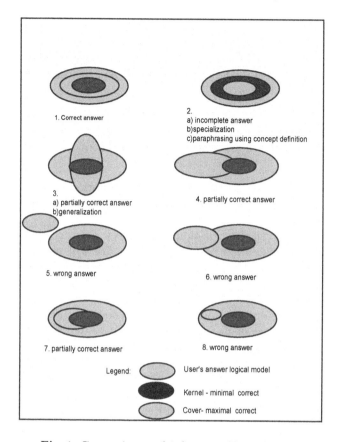

Fig. 1. Comparison and inference of logical forms

Following arguments mentioned in section 3 we can formulate the following theorem:

Theorem. Let C be the clause representing the minimal correct answer of a question, D be a clause representing the maximal correct answer of the same question and U be a clause representing user's answer on this question. Then U is a correct answer iff $K \models U$ and $U \models C$.

Proof: 1. Let U be a correct answer, hence there exists a substitution θ such as $\theta K \subseteq U$, because U as a correct answer contains the logical model of minimal correct answer. Form Definition 1 follows that $K \geq U$. From Corollary 1 follows that $K \models U$. Dually U as a correct answer includes in the logical model of the maximal correct answer, hence there exists a substitution σ such as $U\sigma \subseteq C$. Form Definition 1 follows that $U \geq C$. From Corollary 1 follows that $U \models C$.

2. Let $K \models U$ and $U \models C$. From Lemma (Gettlob) follows that $K^- \geq U^-$ and $U^- \geq C^-$. Hence there exists substitutions θ and σ such as $K^- \theta \subseteq U^-$ and $U^- \sigma \subseteq C^-$. But negative literals in U represents the logical model of the user's answer. Hence the logical model of U contains K and includes in C. Hence U is a correct answer.

Corollary 2. The minimal correct answer of a question is a least generalization under implication (LGI) of all correct answers of this question.

Corollary 3. The maximal correct answer of a question is a greatest specialization under implication(GSI) of all correct answers of this question.

Hence for generating the set of minimal correct answer we can use some ILP algorithms for generation of LGI and GSI. We will use a system RICH (Relative Implication of Clauses of Horn) [13]. In RICH are implemented algorithms for specialization and generalization under relative implication. Both the set of clauses and background knowledge (BK) sets processed by RICH are finite sets of function-free Horn clauses with some restrictions. RICH is an empirical non-interactive single predicate learning system. RICH can generate new predicates. RICH uses direct constructing of hypothese approach, instead of seraching the hypotheses space. The main methods for constructing hypothesis is covering approach, unification algorithm, anti-unification algorithm and resolution. The main idea of the algorithm for inducing least generalization under relative implication is sketched on Fig. 2:

Where S is the set that to be generalized, BK represents the background knowledge set. Head contains head of the hypothesis generated by anti-unification algorithm. Common is a greatest subset of S for which exists most general unifier and DSet is its corresponding disagreement set resulted of unification algorithm. RCommon is a greatest subset of the set of all resolvents of BK and DSet for which exists most general unifier and S' is its corresponding disagreement set resulted of unification algorithm. NewPredicates is a set of autimatically generated new predicates from S'. S" contains literals from S' that to be dropped.

The final hypothesis is constructed from literals in sets Head, Common, RCommon and head literals from the set NewPRedicates. In more details algorithm is presented in [13].

In application of RICH in STyLE-Parasite we do not have background knowledge set.

5   Example

In these section we will show an example for generation of minimal and maximal correct answers' sets using ILP system RICH.

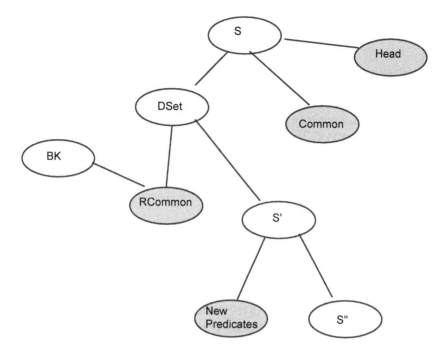

Fig. 2. LGRI algorithm of system RICH

Question (1):
Each of the statements below describe a characteristic of one major type of market. Which? Supports the building of homes, factories, shopping centres.
Some possible correct answers:

(2.1) This situation describes capital market.
(2.2) This is capital market.
(2.3) This characteristics describe capital market

The corresponding clauses created from **Parasite**'s logical model for each of these answers are:

```
(3.1)
answer(N152):-theta(N144152,Object3,N143152),
              capital_goods(N144152),
              deal(N143152),situation(N153),
              theta(N152,Agent3,N143152),
              institutional_mechanism(N152),
              capital_market(N152),market(N152),
              associated_capital(N152),
              theta(N150,Object4,N152),
```

```
                 theta(N150,Agent4,N153),
                 describe(N150).
(3.2)
answer(N149):-theta(N144149,Object5,N143149),
                 capital_goods(N144149),deal(N143149),
                 theta(N149,Agent5,N143149),
                 institutional_mechanism(N149),
                 capital_market(N149),market(N149),
                 associated_capital(N149),
                 theta(N147,Pred1,N149),
                 theta(N147,Topic1,N1475072),
                 predication(N147).
(3.3)
answer(N159):-theta(N144159,Object1,N143159),
                 capital_goods(N144159),deal(N143159),
                 characteristic(N160),
                 theta(N159,Agent1,N143159),
                 institutional_mechanism(N159),
                 capital_market(N159),market(N159),
                 associated_capital(N159),
                 theta(N157,Object2,N159),
                 theta(N157,Agent2,N160),
                 describe(N157).
```

The genreated LGI (minimal set) of these correct answers' set from RICH system will be the following hypothesis:

```
(4)
answer(N5569):-institutional_mechanism(N5569),
                 capital_market(N5569),market(N5569),
                 associated_capital(N5569),
                 capital_goods(N5601), deal(N5633),
                 theta(N5569,Agent9,N5633),
                 theta(N5601,Object9,N5633).
```

The generated GSI (maximal set) of these correct answers' set from RICH system will be the following hypothesis:

```
(5)
answer(N152):-theta(N144152,Object3,N143152),
                 capital_goods(N144152),
                 deal(N143152),situation(N153),
                 theta(N152,Agent3,N143152),
                 institutional_mechanism(N152),
                 capital_market(N152), market(N152),
                 associated_capital(N152),
                 theta(N150,Object4,N152),
```

```
theta(N150,Agent4,N153),
describe(N150),
theta(N147,Pred1,N152),
theta(N147,Topic1,N1475072),
predication(N147),
characteristic(N153).
```

For instance, let we have the following users' answers of this question: (6a) *This is an institutional mechanism which deals with capital goods.* (6b) *This is a financial market that operates with debt instruments.*

The logical model created from `Parasite` of (6a) is:

```
answer(N140):- theta(N144140,Object6,N143140),
               capital_goods(N144140),deal(N143140),
               theta(N140,Agent6,N143140),
               institutional_mechanism(N140),
               capital_market(N140),market(N140),
               associated_capital(N140),
               theta(N141,Pred1,N140),
               theta(N141,Topic1,N1475072),
               predication(N141).
```

STyLE-Parasite will classifies (6a) as "paraphrase of the correct answer", because LGI (4) is not a logical implication from (6a), but GSI(5) logically implies (6a).

STyLE-Parasite will classifies (6b) as "wrong answer", because neither LGI (4) is a logical implication from (6b), nor GSI(5) logically implies (6b).

6   Conclusion

One of the crucial points in implementation of complex learning systems is knowledge base building. Non-automatic generation of minimal and maximal correct answers' sets is rather hard and requires extended knowledge about the system. Presented approach allows automatic generation of minimal and maximal correct answers' sets and avoids necessity knowledge expert to be familiar with rather complex internal data representation. This approach is independent of knowledge domain of the learning system as far as `Parasite`'s lexicon and meaning postulates base have to include this domain concepts. Generation of minimal and maximal correct answers' sets is a pre-process and STyLE-Parasite's efficiency does not depends of it during the learning sessions. Presented approach is a step toward in free-text input processing.

References

1. Cryan, M and A M Ramsay, A Normal Form for Property Theory, 14th Conference on Automated Deduction, 1997, Springer Lecture Notes in Computer Science 1249, pp. 237-251
2. Boytcheva, Sv., O. Kalaydjiev, A. Strupchanska, G. Angelova, Between Language Correctness and Domain Knowledge in CALL, Proc. of European Conference Recent Advances in Natural Language Processing (RANLP-2001), Bulgaria, pp. 40-46, 2001.
3. Angelova G., S. Boytcheva, O. Kalaydjiev, S. Trausan-Matu, P. Nakov and A. Strupchanska, Adaptivity in Web-Based CALL, Proc. of the 15th European conference on Artificial Intelligence (ECAI - 2002), 21-26 July 2002, Lyon, France, 2002 (to appear).
4. Holland, V. M., Kaplan, J. and M. Sams (eds.) Intelligent Language Tutors: Theory Shaping Technology. Lawrence Erlbaum Associates, UK, 1995.
5. RECALL, a Telematics Language Engineering project (1997), http://iserve1.infj.ulst.ac.uk/~recall.
6. McCoy, K., Pennington, C.A., and Suri, L.Z. English error correction: A syntactic user model based on principled "mal-rule" scoring. In Proc. 5th User Modelling, 1996, pp. 59-66.
7. Glass, M. Processing Language Input in the CIRCSIM-Tutor Intelligent System. AAAI 2000 Fall Symposium on Building Dialogue Systems for Tutorial Applications. http://www.csam.iit.edu/ circsim/index.html
8. Ramsay, A. Meaning as Constraints on Information States, in Rupp, Rosner, Johnson (eds.) Constraints, Language and Computation, 1994, Academic Press, London: 249-276.
9. Ramsay, A. and H. Seville. What did he mean by that? Proc. AIMSA-2000, Bulgaria, Sept. 2000, LNAI 1904, Springer, pp. 199-209.
10. Vitanova, I. Learning Foreign Language Terminology: the User Perspective. Larflast report 8.1, August 1999, submitted to the European Commission.
11. Ramsay, A. , Theorem Proving for Intensional Logic, Journal of Automated Reasoning 14, 1995, pp. 237-255
12. Ramsay A., Does It Make Any Sense? Update Semantics as Epistemic Reasoning, see http://www.co.umist.ac.uk/staff/ramsay.htm
13. Boytcheva, S., Z. Markov, An Algorithm for inducing least generalization under relative implication, In Proc. of the 15th International conference of Florida Artificial Intelligence Research Society (FLAIRS-2002), AAAI Press, 13-16 May 2002, Pensacola, Florida, USA, pp. 322-326, 2002.

A Dempster-Shafer Approach to Physical Database Design

Sunil Choenni[1,2] and Henk Blanken[2]

[1] University Nyenrode, Straatweg 25, 3621 BG Breukelen, the Netherlands
[2] Univ. of Twente, P.O. Box 217, 7500 AE Enschede, The Netherlands
s.choenni@nyenrode.nl

Abstract. The selection of an efficient physical schema is an NP-complete problem. In this paper, we show that crucial parts of physical database design can be smoothly modelled as a Dempster-Shafer application. We exploit the properties of the Dempster-Shafer theory to model explicitly a rich set of heuristics —used for the selection of an efficient physical schema— into knowledge rules. These rules may be loaded into a knowledge base, which, in turn, can be embedded in database design tools.

1 Introduction

The design of databases takes place on several levels. One of these levels is the so-called physical level, and the design of databases at this level is called *physical database design*. Physical database design aims to achieve efficient physical schemas by organizing data in such way that the operations defined on the data can be quickly processed and with low cost. Typical problems at the physical level are the assignment of efficient storage structures to certain amounts of data and the allocation of secondary indices to attributes. A storage structure may be considered as a file arrangement, whether or not clustered on a certain attribute, providing a way to access data. The clustering attribute is known as the primary index. Secondary indices, also known as access structures, can be regarded as auxiliary files that allow to retrieve parts of the data satisfying a certain selection predicate without having to examine all available data. Updating the database, causes an index to be updated to remain consistent with the new database state. So, an index speeds up retrieval and slows down maintenance.

The number of physical schemas among which database designers have to select a schema is enormous. The evaluation of a physical schema is a tedious and error-prone process. One should understand the workings of a particular database management system. Therefore, there is a practical need to develop tools that assist database designers in the selection of physical schemas. A significant number of efforts has been reported to develop such tools [1,2,3,4,5,8]. Most of the efforts *implicitly* apply a limited number of heuristics to avoid the evaluation of all schemas. Uncertainty and ignorance, which appear to characterize many of these heuristics, are hardly taken into account.

D. Scott (Ed.): AIMSA 2002, LNAI 2443, pp. 111–121, 2002.
© Springer-Verlag Berlin Heidelberg 2002

In this paper, we show that the selection of crucial parts of a physical schema can be smoothly modelled as a Dempster-Shafer application. As a consequence, the properties of the Dempster-Shafer theory [9] can be used to support the selection process. Based on this theory, we present an approach that *explicitly* models a rich set of heuristics —used for the selection of an efficient schema— into production rules to which a measure of uncertainty is attached. These heuristics can be loaded in a knowledge base that might be used in physical database design tools.

We note that previous work in this field either apply (a limited number of) heuristics in an implicit way and do not take the uncertainty and ignorance into account, which apparently characterize many of these heuristics. We are aware of only one effort [4] that has attempted to take the uncertainty of heuristics into account. This effort captured uncertainty by the well known concept of certainty factors [10]. Unfortunately, this concept does not have a theoretical foundation. Furthermore, [4] is focussed towards network databases, while we focus on relational databases. Perhaps unnecessarily, we note that network and relational databases fundamentally differ from each other.

2   Physical Database Design

As already noticed, the outcome of physical database design is a physical schema. In the selection of a physical schema, the operations defined on the data, called the *workload*, play a crucial role. A physical schema that may be good or optimal for a certain workload, may be bad for another workload.

Basically, we may distinguish four kinds of database operations on a relational schema[1] namely, insertions, deletions, updates, and queries. In general, a number of operations of each type are defined on a relational schema. To each operation a weight is assigned, which is based on the frequency and the importance of the operation.

Based on the relational schema, the workload, and some other database characteristics, such as the cardinality of a relation, length of a tuple, number of pages to store a relation, etc., a storage structure and a set of indices should be selected for each relation. A storage structure determines the order of the tuples of a relation on disk. If this order is determined by an attribute, this attribute is called the *ordering* attribute. An index is a set of pairs (key value, TID-list). The key values are a subset of the domain of the indexed attribute, and a tuple identifier (TID) in the TID-list identifies a tuple possessing the key value.

An index on an ordering attribute is called a *clustering* index and an index on a non-ordering attribute is called a *secondary* index. We note that a storage structure is also associated with each index.

In Figure 1, we depict how the notions storage structure, ordering attribute, and clustering index are related. Furthermore, for a number of storage structures,

---

[1] A relational schema is a set of relations. A relation R is defined over some attributes $\alpha_1, \alpha_2, ..., \alpha_n$, and is a subset of the Cartesian product $dom(\alpha_1) \times dom(\alpha_2) \times ... \times dom(\alpha_n)$, in which $dom(\alpha_j)$ is the domain of attribute α_j.

we have indicated between brackets whether they have an ordering attribute or not. If a storage structure has an ordering attribute, we have indicated whether the ordering attribute is indexed or not. For example, the storage structure *Heap*

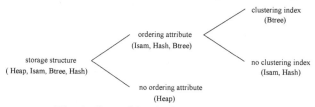

Fig. 1. Several kind of storage structures

does not have an ordering attribute, and, therefore, it is unordered. Storage structures that have an ordering attribute are Isam, Btree, and Hashing [7].

In general, the way a clustering index is organized depends on the storage structure to which the clustering index is related. For example, the storage structure Btree in Ingres allocates an index to the ordering attribute (resulting into a clustering index), and to this clustering index a pre-defined storage structure is assigned.

We focus on the selection of a storage structure and a set of indices for each relation, and refer to it as physical database design. Although our description does not cover the overall problem of physical design, it covers the most difficult and crucial parts [3].

3   Physical Schema

Before formalizing the notion of physical schema, we outline the assumptions on which the definition of a physical schema is based.

We assume that either a secondary index or a clustering index can be allocated on an attribute (but not both). The way a clustering index is stored is assumed to be fixed. Exactly one storage structure can be assigned to a relation. The storage structures that are considered are Heap, Isam, Btree, and Hashing. Since these storage structures are concerned with the arrangement of tuples of a *single* relation on disk, we do *not* consider the possibility to absorb a relation in another relation. As a consequence, we assume that a page contains tuples of exactly one relation. A last assumption is that indices and ordering attributes concern *single* attributes. A physical schema for a single relation is now defined as follows.

Def. 1 Let R be a relation with attributes $\alpha_1, \alpha_2, ..., \alpha_n$. A *physical schema* p^R corresponding to R is an element of P^R, in which

$P^R = \{(x_0(A_0), \{x_i(A_i) \mid i = 1, 2, .., m\}) \mid m \in I\!N;$
$\quad \forall i, j \in \{0, 1, 2, ...m\} : i \neq j \Rightarrow A_i \cap A_j = \emptyset; |A_0| \leq 1;$
$\quad \forall i > 0 : |A_i| = 1; \forall i \geq 0 : A_i \subset \{\alpha_1, \alpha_2, ..., \alpha_n\};$
$\quad x_0, x_i$ are storage structures; $|A_0| = 0 \Rightarrow x_0 = \text{Heap}\}$

The expression $x_0(A_0)$ means that a relation is stored as x_0 and ordered on the set of attributes A_0. We note that if a relation is stored as Heap, then A_0 is the empty set, else A_0 contains exactly one element. The expression $x_i(A_i)$ represents that a secondary index is allocated to the set of attributes A_i and is stored as x_i. Note, A_i consists of exactly one element, since we restrict ourselves to single attribute indices. So, extension of Def. 1 by multi-attribute indices is straightforward.

An (overall) physical schema for a set of relations is defined as the union of the selected physical schema for each relation.

We note that the selection of physical schemas per relation is justified in [11].

The following example illustrates the notion of physical schemas. Since the number of elements of a set $A_i, i \geq 0$, is zero or one, we write $x_i()$ and $x_i(\alpha_i)$ instead of $x_i(\{\})$ and $x_i(\{\alpha_i\})$ respectively. For convenience's sake, the set brackets are omitted.

Example 1 Consider the following relational schema:
Person(per#, first_name, last_name, birth_date, city),
Vehicle(veh#, model, color, doors, body, manufacturer)
Owns(per#, veh#, money_paid)
Two overall physical schemas for the above-mentioned relational schema are given below.
1. ((Heap(),{Btree(*city*), Btree(*last_name*)}), (Hash(*veh#*), {}), (Heap(),{}))
2. ((Heap(),{}), (Heap(),{}), (Btree(*per#*), {Btree(*money_paid*)}))
In the first schema, the relation *Person* is stored as Heap and two secondary indices, both stored as Btrees, to the attributes *city* and *last_name* respectively are allocated. The relation *Vehicle* is hashed on the attribute *veh#*. The relation *Owns* is stored as Heap. □

In the second schema, the relations *Person* and *Vehicle* are stored as Heap. The relation *Owns* is stored as Btree, ordered on attribute *per#*, and a secondary index, stored as Btree, to *money_paid* is allocated.

4   Heuristics

After analysing about 60 heuristics used by experts for physical database design, we observed the following. First, the heuristics consist of a condition and conclusion part (see Figure 2). Second, experts have apparently no difficulties to translate qualitative notions into quantitative measures. In general this is a tough task. In Heuristic 1 of Figure 2, a quantification of the notion small is given between brackets. Third, heuristics have an uncertain character. A heuristic works well in many cases but not in all cases. Database administrators are able to estimate in how many percent of the cases a heuristic may be successfully applied. For example, applying Heuristic 1 of Figure 2 results in 90% of the cases into Heap as storage structure. The heuristic says nothing about the remaining 10% implying *ignorance* in these cases. We note that the latter information is not explicitly captured in Heuristic 1. Fourth, we may distinguish two types of heuristics.

<u>Heuristic 1:</u>
IF   *a relation is small (< 6 pages)*
THEN   *Heap is often (90%) an adequate storage structure*

<u>Heuristic 2:</u>
IF   *the more the percentage of operations that changes*
        the value of an attribute in a workload exceeds 10%
THEN   *the more this attribute is not an index candidate*

Fig. 2. Examples of some heuristics

1. The belief in the conclusion(s) is based on the fact whether the condition part is true or not. For example, in Heuristic 1 of Figure 2, the belief that a Heap storage structure is chosen for a small relation is independent of how small the relation is.
2. The belief in the conclusion(s) is dependent of the extent to which a condition part is satisfied. For example, the idea behind Heuristic 2 of Figure 2 is that if the number of operations in a workload that changes an attribute α_h increases, then the belief that α_h is not an index candidate grows. To represent this uncertain character, it is not sufficient to represent heuristics only with a condition and conclusion part.

For the time being, we represent the heuristics of type 2, thus for which holds that the belief in the conclusion increases (or decreases) if the extent to which the conditions are satisfied increases (decreases), as follows.
<u>IF</u> $(conditions(y\%)) \wedge (y \geq y_0)$ <u>THEN</u> $conclusion$ with belief $f(y - y_0)$
We note that y is the actual percentage to which the conditions are satisfied, y_0 is the minimal required percentage in order to draw *conclusion*, and $f(y)$ is a function of y. The belief in *conclusion* increases (or decreases) if the value of $y - y_0$ becomes higher (smaller).

5   A Dempster-Shafer Approach

We feel that the Dempster-Shafer theory, as a theory of evidence [6], is a suitable theory to capture the uncertainty contained in the heuristics used by database designers. Before illustrating this, we give a brief description of the theory in the context of physical database design. We start with defining what should be understood by all permitted overall physical schemas for a relational schema in which r relations are involved.

Def. 2 Let P^R (see Def. 1)be the set of all permitted physical schemas corresponding to a relation R having attributes $\alpha_1, \alpha_2, ..., \alpha_n$. The *set of permitted overall physical schemas* for a relational schema in which r relations, $R_1, R_2, ..., R_r$, are involved, called the frame of discernment, is $P^{R_1, R_2, ..., R_r} = P^{R_1} \times P^{R_2} \times ... \times P^{R_r}$. In the following, $P^{R_1, R_2, ..., R_r}$ is abbreviated as P^{DB}.

The following example lists all physical schemas corresponding to a relation.

Example 2 Consider the relation *Owner(per#, veh#, money_paid)*, which has been introduced in Example 1. We assume that a relation is either stored as a Heap or hashed on a single attribute. A secondary index is stored as a Btree.

In the following, we write p_i for the i-th physical schema of relation *Owner* instead of p_i^{Owner}. The set of all permitted physical schemas for *Owner*, is $P^{Owner} = \{p_1, p_2, p_3, ..., p_{20}\}$. The schemas $p_1, p_2, p_3, ..., p_{20}$ are listed in Table 1. The physical schema p_1 means that *Owner* is stored as Heap and no

Table 1. Permitted physical schemas for *Owner*

$p_1 =$ (Heap(), {})
$p_2 =$ (Heap(), {Btree(per#)})
$p_3 =$ (Heap(), {Btree(veh#)})
$p_4 =$ (Heap(), {Btree(money_paid)})
$p_5 =$ (Heap(), {Btree(per#), Btree(veh#)})
$p_6 =$ (Heap(), {Btree(per#), Btree(money_paid)})
$p_7 =$ (Heap(), {Btree(veh#), Btree(money_paid)})
$p_8 =$ (Heap(), {Btree(per#), Btree(veh#), Btree(money_paid)})
$p_9 =$ (Hash(per#), {})
$p_{10} =$ (Hash(per#), {Btree(veh#)})
$p_{11} =$ (Hash(per#), {Btree(money_paid)})
$p_{12} =$ (Hash(per#), {Btree(veh#), Btree(money_paid) })
$p_{13} =$ (Hash(veh#), {})
$p_{14} =$ (Hash(veh#), {Btree(per#)})
$p_{15} =$ (Hash(veh#), {Btree(money_paid)})
$p_{16} =$ (Hash(veh#), {Btree(per#), Btree(money_paid) })
$p_{17} =$ (Hash(money_paid), {})
$p_{18} =$ (Hash(money_paid), {Btree(veh#)})
$p_{19} =$ (Hash(money_paid), {Btree(money_paid)})
$p_{20} =$ (Hash(money_paid), {Btree(per#), Btree(veh#)})

secondary indices are allocated, while p_{12} means that *Owner* is hashed on the attribute *per#* and secondary indices —both stored as Btrees— are allocated to attributes *veh#* and *money_paid*. □

Def. 3 Let P^{DB} be the set of all permitted overall physical schemas for a relational schema. Let $I\!P(P^{DB})$ be the power set of P^{DB}, then a function $m : I\!P(P^{DB}) \to [0, 1]$ is called a *basic probability assignment (bpa)* whenever

$$m(\emptyset) = 0 \text{ and } \sum_{P \subseteq P^{DB}} m(P) = 1$$

The quantity $m(P)$ is called P's *basic probability number* and it is understood to be the measure of *belief* that is exactly committed to the set of overall physical schemas P. The *total* belief in P, $(Bel(P))$, is the sum of the basic probability numbers of all subsets PP of P. The relation between belief and bpa is defined as follows.

Def. 4 A function *Bel* is called a *belief function* over P^{DB} if it is given by the following equation for some bpa $m : I\!\!P(P^{\text{DB}}) \rightarrow [0, 1]$.

$$Bel(P) = \sum_{PP \subseteq P \subseteq I\!\!P(P^{\text{DB}})} m(PP) \tag{1}$$

A basic probability assignment induces a belief function and conversely. Two other notions that are related with a belief function are plausibility and ignorance. The plausibility in a set of physical schemas P expresses the maximal belief in this set, and is defined as $Pl(P) = 1 - Bel(P^C)$, in which P^C is the complement of P relative to P^{DB}. The ignorance with regard to a set of overall physical schemas P, is defined as $Ig(P) = Pl(P) - Bel(P)$.

5.1 Knowledge Rules

We continue by illustrating how to model the heuristics into knowledge rules. A knowledge rule has an antecedent and a consequent. With the consequent, a bpa is associated that expresses the belief that is committed to the consequent.

Since the conclusion(s) of both types of heuristics of Section 4 actually support a number of overall physical schemas, the consequent part of a knowledge rule should support this property. In the following, we derive the knowledge rule corresponding to Heuristic 1 of Figure 2.

Heuristic 1 Let the belief in a Heap storage structure for small tables be 0.9 and $P^{R_l}_{\text{Heap}}$ be the set of all permitted physical schemas storing relation R_l as Heap, whatever the set of secondary indices —and their storage structures— is. We note that $P^{R_l}_{\text{Heap}}$ formally means:

$$\{(\text{Heap}(), \{x_i(A_i) \mid i = 1, 2, .., m\}) \mid m \in I\!\!N; \forall i, j \in \{0, 1, 2, ...m\} :$$
$$i \neq j \Rightarrow A_i \cap A_j = \emptyset; \forall i \geq 1 : (A_i \in \{\alpha_1, \alpha_2, ..., \alpha_n\} \wedge |A_i| = 1);$$
$$x_i \text{ is a storage structure}\}$$

We note that $\alpha_1, \alpha_2, ..., \alpha_n$ are attributes of relation R_l.

The knowledge rule (k_1) corresponding to Heuristic 1 is given below. In this rule $n^{R_l}_{pag}$ represents the number of pages required to store relation R_l.

IF $n^{R_l}_{pag} < 6$ pages

THEN

$\quad P^{R_l}_{\text{Heap}} \times P^{\text{DB} \backslash R_l}; m(P^{R_l}_{\text{Heap}} \times P^{\text{DB} \backslash R_l}) = 0.9$

$\quad P^{\text{DB}}; \qquad\qquad m(P^{\text{DB}}) = 0.1$

We note that $P^{R_l}_{\text{Heap}} \times P^{\text{DB} \backslash R_l}$ is an abbreviation for:

$P^{R_1} \times P^{R_2} \times ... \times P^{R_{l-1}} \times P^{R_l}_{\text{Heap}} \times P^{R_{l+1}} \times ... \times P^{R_r}$

Let us explain the belief value committed to P^{DB}. Heuristic 1 of Figure 2 tells us that if a physical table is small we choose to store relation R_l as Heap with a belief of 0.9. However, no statement is made for the remaining belief of 0.1. In this case, no preference is given to any overall physical schema. Therefore, this belief is committed to the whole frame of discernment. In this way *ignorance* is modelled. □

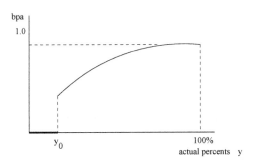

Fig. 3. A possible function between the fraction satisfying a condition and the bpa

Let us recall the meaning of the heuristic of type 2 in Section 4, before giving the corresponding knowledge rule. Suppose that y is the actual percentage that satisfies the condition and y_0 the required percentage that has to be satisfied for committing a non-zero belief to a set of overall physical schemas. Then, the heuristic of this type implies that the belief in a set of overall physical schemas depends on y. In general, the larger $y - y_0$, the stronger the belief in this set of overall physical schemas. Thus, the bpa in modelling heuristics of type 2 will be a function of y, which generally have the form of Figure 3. In the following, we model Heuristic 2 of Figure 2.

Heuristic 2 Let $Ch_W(\alpha_h)$ be the percentage of changes on an attribute α_h of relation R_l by workload W and $f(Ch_W(\alpha_h))$ is a function like the one in Figure 3. Then, Heuristic 2 can be modelled as knowledge rule k_2:

IF $Ch_W(\alpha_h) > 10\%$
THEN
$$P^{R_l}_{\neg\alpha_h} \times P^{\mathrm{DB}\backslash R_l}; m(P^{R_l}_{\neg\alpha_h} \times P^{\mathrm{DB}\backslash R_l}) = f(Ch_W(\alpha_h))$$

$$P^{\mathrm{DB}}; \qquad\qquad m(P^{\mathrm{DB}}) = 1 - f(Ch_W(\alpha_h))$$

The expression $P^{R_l}_{\neg\alpha_h}$ is a shorthand for:

$\{(x_0(A_0), \{x_i(A_i) \mid i = 1, 2, .., m\}) \mid m \in \mathbb{N}; \forall i, j \in \{0, 1, 2, ...m\} :$
$i \neq j \Rightarrow A_i \cap A_j = \emptyset; |A_0| \leq 1; \forall i > 0 : |A_i| = 1; \forall i \geq 0 :$
$A_i \subset \{\alpha_1, \alpha_2, ..., \alpha_n\} \setminus \{\alpha_h\}; x_0, x_i$ are storage structures; $|A_0| = 0 \Rightarrow x_0 = \mathrm{Heap}\}$

We note that the expression $P^{R_l}_{\neg\alpha_h} \times P^{\mathrm{DB}\backslash R_l}$ represents the set of physical schemas storing relation R_l in such a way that R_l is neither ordered on attribute α_h nor a secondary index is allocated on α_h. □

We assume that experts are able to give a reliable belief function for a knowledge rule. If experts are not able to estimate a belief function for a knowledge rule corresponding to a heuristic that is used by them, then the heuristic probably has not taken shape yet. Such a rule might be better omitted from a knowledge base. Consequences of variations in belief functions is a topic for further research.

5.2   Combining Knowledge Rules

Each knowledge rule supports or rejects a set of overall physical schemas with a certain belief. Intuitively, if two rules support the same set of overall physical schemas P, then the combination of these rules should result into a higher belief for P, while if one of the rules supports P and the other rule rejects P, then this should result into a lower belief for P. The combination rule of Dempster possesses these properties and looks as follows:

$$m_1 \oplus m_2(P) = K^{-1} \sum_{\substack{i,j \\ P_i^1 \cap P_j^2 = P}} m_1(P_i^1) m_2(P_j^2)$$

in which P is a non empty set and

$$K = \sum_{\substack{i,j \\ P_i^1 \cap P_j^2 \neq \emptyset}} m_1(P_i^1) m_2(P_j^2)$$

$Bel_1 \oplus Bel_2$ is the belief function induced by $m_1 \oplus m_2$. The following example illustrates the use of the combination rule.

Example 3 Consider a relational schema consisting of the relation $Owner(per\#, veh\#, money\_paid)$ (introduced in Example 1). All physical schemas for $Owner$, $P^{Owner} = \{p_1, p_2, p_3, ..., p_{20}\}$ are listed in Table 1.

Let us assume that the workload W defined on the schema is such that the percentage of modifications on $veh\#$, $Ch_W(veh\#)$, is 15%. This fact induces the execution of rule k_2 (see Section 5), which neither supports a secondary index on $veh\#$ nor an ordering on $veh\#$. Suppose this results in the following bpa: $m_2(\{p_1, p_2, p_4, p_6, p_9, p_{11}, p_{17}, p_{19}\}) = m_2(P_1^2) = 0.6$ and $m_2(P^{Owner}) = 0.4$.

Suppose that another rule k_3, results in (a secondary index on $veh\#$): $m_3(\{p_3, p_5, p_7, p_8, p_{10}, p_{12}, p_{18}, p_{20}\}) = m_3(P_1^3) = 0.9$ and $m_3(P^{Owner}) = 0.1$. And, a third rule k_4, supports hashing on the attributes $veh\#$ and $per\#$ with the following bpa: $m_4(\{p_9, p_{10}, p_{11}, p_{12}\}) = m_4(P_1^4) = 0.6$, $m_4(\{p_{13}, p_{14}, p_{15}, p_{16}\}) = m_4(P_2^4) = 0.3$, and $m_4(P^{Owner}) = 0.1$.

Combining rules k_2 and k_3, which are conflicting, results in a combined bpa: $m_2 \oplus m_3(P_1^3) = 0.36/0.46 = 0.78$ $m_2 \oplus m_3(P_1^2) = 0.06/0.46 = 0.13$ $m_2 \oplus m_3(P^{Owner}) = 0.04/0.46 = 0.09$ We note that the K is 0.46.

The combination of $m_2 \oplus m_3$ with m_4, written as m_{2-4}, can be carried out in the same way, and the results are: For the set $\{p_{10}, p_{12}\}$ the m_{2-4}, Bel, and Pl are 0.64, 0.64 and 0.83 respectively. For $\{p_9, p_{11}\}$ m_{2-4}, Bel, and Pl are 0.11, 0.11, and 0.20 respectively. For P_1^3 we obtain the values 0.11, 0.75, and 0.83 for m_{2-4}, Bel and Pl respectively. For P_1^4 we obtain the values 0.07, 0.71, and 0.95

, for P_2^4, we obtain 0.04, 0.04, and 0.05, for P_1^2 we obtain 0.01, 0.12, and 0.20 for m_{2-4}, Bel, and Pl respectively. For P^{Owner} these values are 0.01, 0.99, and 0.99 We note that the K is 0.73 and due to roundings $Bel(P^{Owner})$ and $Pl(P^{Owner})$ take the value 0.99 in stead of 1.0.

The highest belief, after combining the three rules, is assigned to the set of schemas $\{p_{10}, p_{12}\}$. We note that the high *total* belief in the sets P_1^3, P_1^4 and P^{Owner} is due to the fact that these sets contain the schemas p_{10} and p_{12}. $\square$

The combination of three rules has resulted into the support of several physical schemas with different belief values. If the bpa's assigned to the three knowledge rules are the real bpa values, there is a high belief that a good physical schema is among the schemas p_{10} and p_{12}. By passing both schemas to the optimizer, we may decide which physical schema of two is the best one.

6   Conclusions & Further Research

Since the selection of efficient physical schemas is a tough process, there is a practical need for tools that assist database administrators in this process. A significant number of research has been reported to develop such tools. Most of the efforts implicitly apply a few heuristics to avoid the evaluation of all schemas, while database administrators in real-life apply a rich set of heuristics to select physical schemas. Our goal is to exploit this rich set of heuristics in tools for physical database design. Therefore, we have analysed about 60 heuristics used by database administrators in real-life. These heuristics contain a degree of uncertainty and ignorance. We have proposed an approach to model *explicitly* these heuristics into knowledge rules by using the Dempster-Shafer theory, which appeared to be a suitable theory for our purposes. These knowledge rules may be loaded in a knowledge base, which, in turn, can be embedded in physical database design tools.

References

[1]   F. Bonfatti, D. Maio, P. Tiberio, A Separability-Based Method for Secondary Index Selection in Physical Database Design. *Methodology and Tools for Data Base Design*, North-Holland Publishing Company, the Netherlands, 149-160.

[2]   S. Chaudhuri, V. Narasayya, AutoAdmin 'What-if' Index Analysis Utility. In: *Proc. ACM/SIGMOD Int. Conf. on Management of Data*, 1998, 367-378

[3]   S. Choenni, H. Wagterveld, H. Blanken, T. Chang, ToPhyDe: A Tool for Physical Database Design. In: *Proc. DEXA, Int. Conf. on Databases, Expert Systems, and Applications*, 1995, LNCS 978, 502-511.

[4]   C.E. Dabrowski, K.J. Jefferson, A Knowledge-Based System for Physical Database Design. NBS Special Publication 500-151, Gaithersburg, USA, February 1988.

[5]   S. Finkelstein, M. Schkolnick, P. Tiberio, Physical Database Design for Relational Databases. *ACM Trans. on Database Systems 13(1)*, 91-128.

[6]   J.Y. Halpern, R.Fagin, Two Views of Belief: Belief as Generalized Probability and Belief as Evidence. *Artificial Intelligence 54(3)*, 275-317.

[7]   D.E. Knuth, *The Art of Computer Programming Vol. 3, Sorting and Searching.* Addison Wesley Publishing Company, Kent, Great Britain, 1973.

[8]   S. Rozen, D. Shasha, A Framework for Automating Database Design, In: *Proc. of the 17th Int. Conf. on Very Large Database, 1991,* 401-411.

[9]   G. Shafer, *A Mathematical Theory of Evidence,* Princeton University Press, Princeton, USA, 1976.

[10] E. Shortliffe, *Computer-Based Medical Consultations: MYCIN.* Elsevier Publications, New York, 1976.

[11] Whang, K., Wiederhold, G., Sagalowicz, D., Separability - An approach to physical database design, *Proc. Int. Conf. on Very Large Databases, 1981.* 487-500.

Technical Documentation: An Integrated Architecture for Supporting the Author in Generation and Resource Editing

Nestor Miliaev, Alison Cawsey, and Greg Michaelson

Department of Computing and Electrical Engineering, Heriot-Watt University,
Edinburgh, EH14 4AS, UK
{ceenym, alison, greg}@cee.hw.ac.uk

Abstract. This paper presents an architecture for generating online and written technical documentation. Action plans are generated from an underlying model of the system being documented, which may be post-edited to refine the output. An NLG system is built based on this architecture allowing the generation of documentation in Russian and English. A range of built-in tools enable editing of linguistic and domain knowledge at any point in document processing. This architecture is intended to help an author select the right balance between automatic and controlled generation for a specific application.

1   Introduction

Natural Language Generation (NLG) provides several advantages over other methods of creating technical documentation. It allows consistent versions of a document to be produced possessing various properties, with explanations and layout depending on the user's expertise and requirements. NLG is particularly advantageous for producing multi-lingual documents. Compared with Machine Translation (MT) NLG systems can produce better quality text, less likely to require post-processing. In addition, using NLG ensures that versions generated in different languages are consistent with a domain being documented and between each other [3]. Employing NLG should result in less cost in document maintenance, especially when the documented domain changes often, requiring documentation updates. The use of NLG is particularly justified when [4]:

- The data to be communicated is already present in an existing database;
- The domain data changes frequently and there is a requirement for consistency between a document and the domain described;
- There is a need for producing different versions of a document depending on the user requirements, level of expertise and the desired layout of a document;
- There is a need for producing multi-lingual versions of a document and there is no possibility for post-editing a document, for example, in on-line systems.

However, the output of an NLG system is still unlikely to be as good as that of a competent human author, who might be able to improve the structure, content and language used in a document [3].

D. Scott (Ed.): AIMSA 2002, LNAI 2443, pp. 122–131, 2002.

There is therefore a need to ensure that a documentation system allows the task of creating high quality documentation to be shared appropriately between the system and human. While a fully automated system may be appropriate in some contexts, in others the author (henceforth referred to as user) should be allowed to intervene.

Another important consideration is the feasibility of editing the linguistic and domain resources. This is important in order to provide flexibility for the description of other systems/domains and to ensure that the documentation is up-to-date with the actual system specification.

2 Background

2.1 Limitations of Existing Approaches

Existing systems tend to fall into two groups, which can be referred to as "automatic" or "user-assisted". Automatic systems produce text directly from the domain knowledge representation, with the technical author having no role (e.g., ILEX[9], IDAS[5], and HyperDoc[6]). ILEX and IDAS are hypertext-based tools for exploring electronic catalogues and complex technical systems respectively. They automatically produce textual descriptions in response to the user clicking on a hyperlink corresponding a topic to be explored. HyperDoc is a system for producing instructions that could be incorporated in manuals for home appliances, like VCRs. These instructions represent a sequence of actions which the user should carry out in order to perform some task. The system generates instructions given the initial state of a system and the desired state (i.e. the user's goal).

However useful automatic text generation is, the output of most of these systems is non-optimal as the text lacks rhetorical cohesion and the variety of sentence patterns is small [6]. Attempts have therefore been made to enable a human technical author to support the text production process in order to improve text quality [3,1]. We refer to this approach as user-assisted.

The most usual scenario for user-assisted generation is that the user creates a plan in some form, and this plan is then passed to the generation subsystem to produce an output text [2,3]. Text in several languages may be produced from a single plan. In contrast with automatic systems, user-assisted systems are normally used to generate printable documentation (e.g., Drafter [3], AGILE [1], TechDoc [2]). Text generated by these three systems is similar to that of HyperDoc and consists of a set of operating procedures. Each procedure is a sequence of actions the user should perform to achieve some goal.

The quality of output text of user-assisted NLG systems is normally better than that of automatic systems [3]. However, the user has to perform a great deal of work to create the initial procedure plans. This is clearly not ideal where we want to create new forms of documentation quickly, given new tasks and contexts, as might occur in an online system. The relationship between the user and system in these latter systems is also fairly rigid, with the author given a specific role of procedure plan editor. We aim to provide the author with a wide range of roles, from a passive one, simply making use of existing tools and knowledge base, to an active one, modifying and editing resources, plans and texts as required.

The second practical problem with existing systems is the difficulty in editing knowledge resources. This is important in order to modify the system:

- Given revised specifications and designs;
- For the description of a new device/domain.

While existing systems provide some facilities for knowledge editing, these do not always allow for the easy editing of all parts of a knowledge base, or they are poorly integrated. For example, Drafter's domain knowledge base consists of the two levels – T-box and A-box. T-box contains concepts, actions, relations that are relevant in the software domain. A-box contains a set of assertions modelling a procedure for performing some task. T-box is a static resource which is provided with the system so the user can not easily change it [3]. This makes Drafter difficult to use for documenting new systems and domains. The AGILE system, largely based on Drafter, has similar functionality and the same restrictions.

HyperDoc supports extensive domain knowledge engineering, providing a tool for graphical modelling the user interface of a system being documented. However, domain engineering is only possible within a pre-defined set of linguistic and domain primitives. Changing this set at the system run-time is difficult [6].

3   A New Solution

We have developed an NLG system that allows the user to choose an appropriate balance between automatic and user-assisted generation. Our system provides various means for domain and linguistic knowledge modelling and editing. The system may be adapted for production texts pertinent to different technical systems and domains. The user defines whether to use the system to produce text automatically to obtain a moderate quality text or put more emphasis on editing the text representation to improve its quality.

Our system, called FlexyCAT (flexible computer-aided technical writer), consists of five main parts: knowledge representation module, plan generation module, plan post-editing module, the generator and linguistic knowledge representation/editing module. The FlexyCAT's architecture is depicted in figure 1.

3.1   Linguistic Knowledge Base and Editing Tools and Text Generator

The goal of our project is to produce instructional texts in Russian and English. Because Russian has a rich morphology requiring complicated lexical agreement, it was strongly desirable to avoid the use of canned text. We have tried to keep both the implementation of the linguistic subsystem and its interface with the

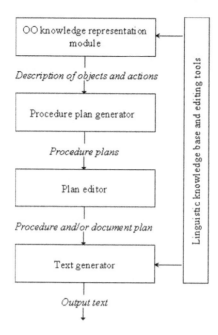

Fig. 1. The proposed NLG system architecture

user and other subsystems as simple as possible. To enable the non-specialist user to edit linguistic knowledge, it was desirable to avoid using relatively complex tools such as KPML. Fortunately, the restricted domain of technical documentation we are working with encompasses a restricted set of possible sentence patterns, enabling us to use fairly simple means for text generation.

The most effective way to generate multilingual text involves the production of text in each language independently, based on a common semantic representation [4]. In this case it is possible to ensure that the generated versions of the text are semantically equivalent, and thus consistent one with another.

To implement this, we had to create a transparent system of encoding the linguistic knowledge, allowing for storing counterparts of linguistic entries in both languages and using them in a unified manner, capturing both universal and language-specific features for generation purposes. This is relevant both for linguistic primitives and more complex structures, up to a text.

We have implemented our linguistic processing subsystem making use of the principles of Role and Reference Grammar [10] and Meaning-Text Theory [8].

Texts generated in our system, like in Drafter or HyperDoc, comprise a set of procedures containing steps (actions) the user is to perform. Each action is described in a single sentence. Each sentence constituent clause contains a verb (head of a clause) and noun phrases representing a subject, object and a complement. A clause consistency structure represents its semantic structure. The semantic structure of a clause is mapped onto a template defining such syntactic features as linear word order, mood and tense. The information on word agreement is defined largely at the semantic level and is partially stored in the lexicon. See a simplified example in figure 2.

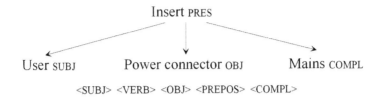

<SUBJ> <VERB> <OBJ> <PREPOS> <COMPL>

Fig. 2. A semantic structure and template of the clause "User inserts power connector into the mains"

This approach enables us to map the same semantic structure onto different syntactic ones. For example, a clause *"Insert power connector into the mains"* may be expressed as a purpose *"To insert power connector into the mains"*, means *"By inserting power connector into the mains"* or condition *"If power connector is inserted into the mains"*, etc.

We employed an object-oriented representation for the description of all linguistic components, from parts of speech through to clauses and sentences, so that the bigger structures are built from more elementary ones and all of them have information relevant for generation in both languages. This enabled us to create an interface for construction, editing and maintenance of linguistic knowledge using a convenient GUI: see figure 3. The user is not required to have any specific expertise except for the basic knowledge of the languages involved.

Sentences are subsequently built using permitted clause combinations, allowing the production of about 20 different sentence structures in two languages. The versions generated in each language have the same syntactic features, like the mood and tense. The following example illustrates how the same meaning may be expressed using different sentence structures:

Press menu button to show TV menu
Show TV menu by pressing menu button

Corresponding Russian versions:

Нажмите кнопку "Меню" чтобы вызвать меню телевизора
Вызовите меню телевизора нажав кнопку "Меню"

The sentence structure can be assigned either heuristically by the planner or explicitly by the user.

Although our linguistic module allows for text generation in two languages, it is likely that the methods used will enable generation in other languages, including the dependent-marking accusative languages [10] (most Slavic languages, German etc.)

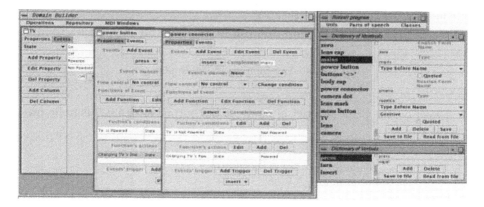

Fig. 3. Screenshot of the system

3.2 OO Knowledge Representation Module

We employ an Object-Oriented (OO) approach for the specification of the domain model. An entity to be described is represented as a set of all its elementary components. The description of each elementary component includes the specification of events, properties and actions.

We have created a GUI that allows for visual manipulation of an object structure. Figure 3 shows a part of the system GUI with the domain knowledge representation module and a part of the linguistic knowledge representation subsystem.

This GUI enables a technical author to change the object dependencies, actions and properties to ensure that object specification is up-to-date with the system design. New objects can be created either from scratch or based on existing ones.

For example, we can adapt the specification of a TV to create a description of a VCR. We re-use many of the existing objects (for example, *"power button"* and *"power connector"*), slightly amending their functionality if needed to take into account the VCR's properties. This allows multilingual documentation for a new device to be developed fairly quickly.

3.3 Procedure Plan Generator and Plan Editor

From the specification of the system being documented the STRIPS-like planner [7] generates procedure plans. The user chooses the initial and final states of the system, and the planner automatically builds a sequence of steps which fulfils the user goal given the search conditions. The description of each step contains its semantic representation, desired mood and rhetorical information. The mood and type of rhetorical relation between sentences is generated using default heuristics. An example plan of a typical procedure for turning on a TV (corresponding to the specification given in figure 3) is shown in figure 4.

▷ Insert power connector → Power TV
▷ Press power button → Turn on TV

Fig. 4. An example procedure plan

Based on the plan depicted in figure 4, the output in figure 5 may be produced.

1. *Insert power connector into the mains to power TV*
2. *Press power button to turn TV on*

Fig. 5. An example of generated text

An automatically generated procedure plan may be non-optimal [3]. Indeed, the text given in figure 5 lacks rhetorical cohesion inherent to a good quality text.

Our system offers the possibility for the user to edit a generated procedure plan to yield a better quality text. This editing includes adding/editing/deleting individual steps of the plan, changing the rhetorical markers denoting their relationships and modifying the structure of sentences expressing individual steps. In our example we may add a header to the procedure and changed the sentence structure of the first step from "Purpose" to "Condition" and from "Purpose" to "Means" for the second step. See figure 6.

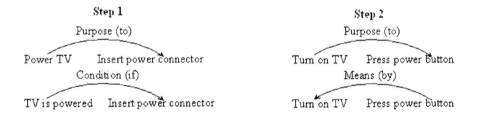

Fig. 6. Example of sentence structure change

The output after the plan refinement is a more coherent and comprehensible text. See figure 7.

Note that the user edits not the output text, but its plan, i.e. its semantic representation. Based on that representation texts may be generated independently in as many languages as needed. If the plan changes in the future (for example, to be up-to-date with the system specification), documentation may be re-generated in every language involved at no extra cost.

To turn on TV:
1. *If TV is not powered, insert power connector to the mains*
2. *Turn TV on by pressing power button*

Fig. 7. An example of text after refining a plan

A manual does not consist of just one procedure, but includes a number of them arranged in some order. Our system provides for the possibility of composing a plan of the entire document from individual procedure plans. An interactive tool has been created that enables the technical author to pick up procedure plans from a collection of previously generated ones and place them in an appropriate order. When necessary, plan grouping and additional plan editing may be performed. Based on a composed document plan it is possible to generate documents with a consistent content in multiple languages.

3.4 An Integrated CATW

All the parts described so far are incorporated into an integrated system with a common user interface. This integration allows the user to control text content and quality at various inter-dependent levels. The common OO approach used at all the levels of system design enabled easy module interfacing.

A common GUI simplifies use of components of the subsystems by other modules. For example, in the KR module the name of every object is represented by the class "nominal" of the linguistic primitives database. When creating a new object, e.g. *"Power Button"*, the user assigns a name to the object by dragging and dropping a linguistic primitive *"Power Button"* from the dictionary of nominals into the corresponding GUI element of the KR. After that, the corresponding slot in the object structure is filled with the nominal *"Power button"*. This nominal already "knows" how to behave, e.g., to get agreement with other lexemes in a clause both in English and Russian, or how to represent itself as a string to display a title of an object in the GUI. Similarly, the planning subsystem can easily access objects of the KR module and their actions.

Our system also provides the user with flexibility to amend linguistic or domain knowledge at any stage of document design. For example, the user can create a new linguistic entry describing an object or an action. Also the user can modify a domain model, e.g., by creating a new object or changing the object properties or actions. After the domain model or linguistic knowledge editing is complete, the changes made will be immediately proliferated though all the relevant parts of the text plan and the resultant text.

3.5 Using the Architecture in Interactive Systems

At the moment our system is only intended for the production of printable documents. We expect that our architecture can be used also for building interactive documenting systems (on-line help systems, interactive tutoring/simulation systems, etc.) We can re-use many resources used for the creation of a printed version. The method for representing the domain knowledge allows us to generate a wide range of explanations and instructions, answering queries like: '*What is it?*', '*What is it used for?*', '*How do I...?*', and context specific questions: '*What should I do next?*', '*What do I do it for?*', etc. It is possible to query a domain model by object, type of object, properties, actions, or events. Below there is a possible scenario of using the architecture in an on-line system.

The user asked the system for TV control '*How do I turn TV on?*'. The system searches among all the available actions for the one having an effect '*TV is turned on*'. The same domain model is used as for the generation of a printed version. The action '*Turn on TV*' is picked up. Then the system looks up in the scope of previously composed and edited plans to see if there are any containing that action. If one is found, it is offered to the user as an answer to his/her query, like the one in figure 7. If no pre-composed procedure plan is found, a new one is generated, like the one in figure 5.

The advantage of this approach to the generation of interactive documents is that it always gives an answer, in a form of a good quality text if the pre-edited plan conforming to the user request exists, and in a form of readable and correct text otherwise.

4   Advantages of the Architecture

Our architecture combines many advantages of other NLG systems, while providing some additional functionality.

Firstly, it provides a facility for automatic text generation, like HyperDoc, alleviating the work of technical author. The time to create a domain model and producing an output text in two languages is in some cases comparable to the time taken to write a version of the text in a single language. At the same time, it enables the user to control what the system produces, like Drafter or TechDoc, when user wants to produce a better quality text.

Secondly, our generation system, while simple, avoids the use of canned text [2,9]. This allows the generation of grammatical texts in Russian and English possessing fairly rich structure and facilitates system maintenance. If canned text is used, when the system specification or context changes, the author has to locate and change all relevant text fragments, in all languages supported.

Thirdly, it allows for knowledge re-use. This is relevant both for the domain and linguistic knowledge. Knowledge reuse is possible at two levels:

- When creating a new object description based on a previously created one, it is possible to reuse many common elements of both the linguistic and domain knowledge bases.
- The architecture enables using the same domain and linguistic knowledge both for the creation of a printable version of document and for building on-line interactive explanatory system. By this, the overhead of using existing resources for the creation of another type of documentation is reduced.

5   Conclusion and Further Work

We present an NLG system for creating printable technical documentation, able to generate documents in multiple languages. The system combines advantages of operating with a simulation model of the documented system, with representations that facilitate post-editing and language generation. The system can currently be used to generate offline printed documentation, but is also suitable for online interactive documentation. In that case, the simulation model can be invoked when needed to answer unusual questions, while the post-edited plans can be retrieved to provide more refined answers to commonly asked queries. We are currently working on the evaluation of the system.

Acknowledgements. This project is being carried out in the scope of the work towards a Ph.D., sponsored by Heriot-Watt University, Edinburgh. We also would like to thank all the people who helped us in the development of our system and preparing this paper by their ideas and feedback.

References

1. A. Hartley, R. Power, D. Scott, S. Varbanov. Design specification of the user interface for the AGILE final prototype. Brighton University, AGILE project, Deliverable INTF-2, 30/11/2000.
2. Dietmar Rosner and Manfred Stede. TECHDOC: a system for the automatic production of multilingual technical documents. In Proceedings of the First German Conference on Natural Language Processing. Springer-Verlag, Heidelberg, 1992.
3. Hartley, A.F. and Paris, C. (1997) 'Multilingual document production: from support for translating to support for authoring', Machine Translation, Special Issue on New Tools for Human Translators, Vol. 12, nos 1-2, pp. 109-129
4. Ehud Reiter and Robert Dale. 'Building Natural Language Generation Systems', Cambridge University Press, 2000
5. Ehud Reiter, Chris Mellish, John Levine. 'Automatic Generation of Technical Documentation', Applied Artificial Intelligence, pp259–289, vol.9, 1995.
6. Harold Thimbleby, 'Combining Systems and Manuals', J. L. Alty et al. eds., People and Computers, VIII, HCI'93, pp. 479-488, Cambridge University Press, 1993.
7. I. Refanidis and I. Vlahavas, 'A Heuristic Based Approach to Planning in Strips Domains', in Advances in Informatics, ed. by D.I. Fotiadis and S.D. Nikolopoulos, World Scientific, April 2000
8. Igor Mel'chuk. Dependency Syntax: Theory and Practice. State University of New York, 1987.
9. John Oberlander, Ehud Reiter. Final report on the ILEX project. Edinburgh University, 1999.
10. R. D. Van Valin and R. J. LaPolla Syntax: structure meaning and syntax, Cambridge University Press, 1997.

Optimistic vs. Pessimistic Interpretation of Linguistic Negation

Daniel Pacholczyk[1], Mohamed Quafafou[2], and Laurent Garcia[1]

[1] LERIA, University of Angers, 2 Bd Lavoisier, 49045, ANGERS Cedex 01, FRANCE
{pacho,garcia}@info.univ-angers.fr
[2] IRIN, University of Nantes, 2 Rue de la Houssiniere, BP 92208, 44322, NANTES Cedex 3, FRANCE
Mohamed.Quafafou@irin.univ-nantes.fr

Abstract. Linguistic negation processing is a challenging problem studied by a large number of researchers from different communities, i.e. logic, linguistics, etc. We are interested in finding the positive interpretations of a negative sentence represented as "x is not A". In this paper, we do not focus on the single set of translations but on two approximation sets. The first one called pessimistic corresponds to the positive translations of the negative sentence that we can consider as sure. The second one called optimistic contains all the sentences that can be viewed as possible translations of the negative sentence. These approximation sets are computed according to the rough sets framework and based on a neighbourhood relation defined on the space of properties. Finally, we apply an original strategy of choice upon the two approximation sets which allows us to select the suitable translations of the initial negative sentence. It appears that we obtain results in good accordance with the ones linguistically expected.

1 Introduction

When dealing with sentences expressed in natural language, it is difficult to define precisely their meaning since they are imprecise, ambiguous, etc. However, a human reasoning with such information is able to find a specific interpretation of these sentences. The methods used to manage these information are based on deep natural language analysis, the notion of context, etc ([6], [2], [8], [7], [21]). Here, the framework we are interested in is the one dealing with information, expressed in natural language, using a negation like "John is not tall" or "John is not really small" ([9], [1], [5], [4]). The issue is then to find a positive interpretation of a such negative sentence. Let us notice that different significances may be associated with this sentence, like "John is extremely tall" or "John is very small" ([10], [12], [11], [13]). The goal of this paper is made of three parts: (1) analyze the problem of linguistic negation, (2) introduce a formalization of linguistic negation approximation using rough set theory, (3) propose a formal framework for selecting automatically the certain and possible interpretations of a linguistic negation. This paper is organized as follows. Section 2 is dedicated to the introduction of the main concepts and notations related to the problem of linguistic negation which is viewed here as a negation of a nuanced property. Section 3 is devoted to the definition of the reference frame from which one can extract (if needed) the affirmative, called also positive, interpretations of a linguistic negation. This approach takes into account some

D. Scott (Ed.): AIMSA 2002, LNAI 2443, pp. 132–141, 2002.

results of linguistic analysis of linguistic negation proposed in ([9], [1], [4], [5]). This new definition of reference frame can be viewed as a generalization of the one proposed in [13]. Section 4 presents a new approach to linguistic negation: the originality results from the fact that we do not search directly all affirmative interpretations of a negative sentence, but we approximate its significance. Our approach is based on two optimistic and pessimistic operators that are defined according to rough set theory ([14], [15], [16]). These operators refer to a specific neighbourhood (or similarity) relation defined in such a way that the pessimistic operator returns certain positive interpretations whereas the result of the optimistic operator contains all possible positive interpretations. We briefly recall the basic notions of rough set theory in Section 4.1. The linguistic negation re-formulation is presented in Section 4.2. Its approximation within rough set theory is developed in Section 4.3. In Section 4.4, we propose tools allowing us to give the affirmative interpretations of linguistic negations, and this, by using previous approximation sets. More precisely, we both propose a standard choice of this relation resulting from the neighbourhood relation of nuance meanings and the reference frame of a denied assertion and show how our method works to define these approximations sets when the neighbourhood relation has been computed. We can point out that all examples lead to results in good accordance with the ones linguistically expected.

2   Universe Description

We suppose that our discourse universe is characterized by a finite set of concepts. For example, the concepts of "height", "wage" and "appearance" should be understood as qualifying individuals of the human type. Moreover, each concept can be characterized by a finite set of basic properties having the same description domain. For example, the basic properties "small", "medium" and "tall" can be associated with the concept "height". Finally, linguistic modifiers bearing on these basic properties permit us to express nuanced knowledge, like "John is really very tall". This work uses the model proposed in [3] to represent affirmative information expressed in the form "x is $f_\alpha m_\beta P_{ik}$" or "x is not $f_\alpha m_\beta P_{ik}$" in the case of negation. In this context, expressing a property like "$f_\alpha m_\beta P_{ik}$" called here nuanced property, requires a list of linguistic terms. Two ordered sets of modifiers are selected depending on their modifying effects. The first one groups translation modifiers resulting somehow in both a translation and a possible precision variation of the basic property: For example, the set of translation modifiers could be $M_7 = \{m_\alpha \mid \alpha \in [1..7]\} = \{$extremely little, very little, rather little, moderately $(\emptyset)$, rather, very, extremely$\}$ totally ordered by the relation: $m_\alpha < m_\beta \Leftrightarrow \alpha < \beta$. Let us notice that the seven terms have been choosen to define a symmetrical scale in the French language. Unfortunately, this could not correspond exactly to usual adverbs used in English language. The second one consists of precision modifiers which make it possible to increase (or decrease) the precision of the previous properties. For example, $F_6 = \{f_\beta \mid \beta \in [1..6]\} = \{$vaguely, neighboring, more or less, moderately $(\emptyset)$, really, exactly$\}$ totally ordered by the relation: $f_\alpha < f_\beta \Leftrightarrow \alpha < \beta$. Within our discourse universe, let us denote as : $\mathfrak{C}$ the set of distinct concepts C_i, $\mathfrak{D}_i$ the domain associated with the concept C_i, $\mathfrak{M}$ the set of modifier combinations, $\mathfrak{N}_{ik}$ the set of all nuances of the basic property P_{ik}, $\mathfrak{N}_i$ the set of all nuanced properties associated with C_i, $\mathfrak{N}$ the set of all nuanced properties, $\mathfrak{P}_i$ the set of all basic properties associated with C_i and $\mathfrak{P}$ the set of all basic properties.

3   The Reference Frame of a Linguistic Negation

The main idea justifying our approach is the fact that the traduction of a negative nuanced property does not correspond to a single positive property due to the vagueness of basic properties and the nuances that are applied. For example, "John is not tall" does not necessary refers to the sentence "John is small" but can correspond to several possible interpretations like "John is very small", "John is small" and "John is medium". It appears clearly that a modelisation implying denied properties cannot be viewed as a one-to-one correspondence but as a one-to-many one, called here multi-set function.

By using linguistic analysis results of linguistic negation ([9] [1], [5], [4]), it has been pointed out in ([10], [11]) that when one asserts that " x is not A " then, (1) one rejects a reference to " x is A ", and (2) if necessary, one refers either to another object y (i. e., "y is A") or the logical negation of A, or to another property P different from A (i. e., "x is P ") but defined in the same domain, or sometimes to a another nuance of A, or finally to a new basic property denoted as not-A. The previous analysis only defines the standard forms of the linguistic negation. The linguistic negation is defined by using one-to-many mappings from E into $\mathcal{P}(E)$ (E parts).

Definition 1. *A multi-set function is a one-to-many function from E into $\mathcal{P}(E)$ (E parts).*

In this paper we propose a new definition of linguistic negation which can be viewed as a generalization of the one proposed in [13]. For any concept C_i, we define the reference frame of a linguistic negation as a *parameterized function* Ref_Neg^t.

Definition 2. *For any concept C_i, the reference frame of a linguistic negation is a function Ref_Neg^t: $\mathfrak{D}_i \times \mathfrak{N}_i \to \mathcal{P}(\mathfrak{D}_i) \times \mathcal{P}(\mathfrak{N}_i)$ defined as follows, knowing that $n_\gamma \in \mathfrak{M}$ and $t \in [0 .. 5]$:*
- *Ref_Neg^0(x , $n_\gamma P_{ik}$) = $(\emptyset, \emptyset)$,*
- *Ref_Neg^1(x, $n_\gamma P_{ik}$) = $(\mathfrak{D}_i \backslash \{x\}, \{n_\gamma P_{ik}\})$,*
- *Ref_Neg^2(x, $n_\gamma P_{ik}$) = $(\{x\}, \mathfrak{N}_i \backslash \{n_\gamma P_{ik}\})$,*
- *Ref_Neg^3(x, $n_\gamma P_{ik}$) = $(\{x\}, \mathfrak{N}_{ik} \backslash \{n_\gamma P_{ik}\})$,*
- *Ref_Neg^4(x, $n_\gamma P_{ik}$) = $(\{x\}, \mathfrak{N}_i \backslash \mathfrak{N}_{ik})$,*
- *Ref_Neg^5(x, $n_\gamma P_{ik}$) = $(\{x\}, \{not\text{-}(n_\gamma P_{ik})\})$, where not-$(n_\gamma P_{ik})$ is a new basic property associated with C_i.*

Each value of the parameter t is associated with a possible scope of the negation operator, this scope characterizes the reference frame which contains the possible intended positive meanings. It is possible to associate a standard form F_t for "x is not A" with each previous Ref_Neg^t(x, A). More precisely, when a speaker says "x is not A", he means that:
- F_0: *For this x, "x is A" is rejected and there is not any corresponding affirmative expression.* For instance, saying "Smith is not guilty" without reference to affirmative property, may occur in a context where the only thing about his culpability is that his alibi is confirmed.
- F_1: *Another object of the same domain satisfies the same nuanced property.* As an example, "Jack is not guilty" since it is John who is guilty.
- F_2: *The same x satisfies another nuance of $\mathfrak{N}_i$, the set of all nuanced properties associated with C_i.* For example, "John is not small" since he is "really medium".

- F_3: *The same x satisfies another nuance of $\mathfrak{N}_{ik}$, the set of all nuances of the basic property P_{ik}.* For instance, the doctor can say "the temperature is not low" because he thinks that "the temperature is really low".

- F_4 : *The same x satisfies a nuance of another basic properties associated with the same concept C_i.* For instance, the doctor can say "cholesterol risk is not low" because he thinks that "cholesterol risk is medium".

- F_5 : *The same x satisfies a nuance of a new affirmative basic property.* In this case, "x is not A" means that "x is not-A", this new property "not-A" is associated with the same concept as A. "The patient is not seriously ill" may introduce a new basic property "not-seriously-ill".

Remark 1. Note that, in this paper, we are not concerned with the form F_0 (which is scarcely used in knowledge base field) or F_5 (which is in fact an affirmative assertion, and can be directly translated). As noted before, when the user says "x is not A", he possibly refers either to another object y (Standard form F_1, "y is A") or to another nuance P ("x is P") (standard forms F_2 to F_4). So, Ref_Neg^t is defined with the aid of two multi-set functions giving the two main scopes of the negation operator: either an object or a nuanced property is denied.

It is obvious that we have:

Proposition 1. *Ref_Neg^4 (x, n_γ P_{ik}) $\subseteq$ Ref_Neg^2 (x, n_γ P_{ik}) and Ref_Neg^3 (x, n_γ P_{ik}) $\subseteq$ Ref_Neg^2 (x, n_γ P_{ik}).*

4   A New Approach to Linguistic Negation

Let us notice that the handling of linguistic negation using the scope proposed in previous section has yet been developped in the framework of fuzzy logic (see [10], [11], [12]). The difference which is made when working with rough set theory is that we do not work on the reference frame but on two approximations of this set (an optimistic one and a pessimistic one).

4.1   Rough Set Theory

The theory of rough sets was introduced by Z. Pawlak in the early 1980's ([14], [15], [16]). It offers a new tool for the study of vagueness and uncertainty in the context of data analysis. This theory is based on two approximation operators that allow the approximation of a concept, represented as a set, by a pair of sets called lower and upper approximation.

Definition 3. *Let R be a binary relation on a universe U, r(x)={y∈U| xRy}, and X a subset of U. A pair of approximation operators, R_* and R^* are defined by :*
- $R_*(X)=\{x \in U \mid r(x) \subseteq X\}$, *called the lower approximation of X,*
- $R^*(X)=\{x \in U \mid r(x) \cap X \neq \emptyset\}$, *called the upper approximation of X.*

Consequently, one may approximate a subset X⊆U by a pair of subsets of U with respect to the binary relation R. The lower approximation of a set X is $R_*(X)$ and contains elements that necessarily belong to X whereas the upper approximation R^* (X) contains those that possibly belong to X. This approximation expresses nuanced notion as elements in the lower approximation are referred to as strong members, while elements in the upper approximation are weak members.

Definition 4. *The system* $(2^U, \cap, \cup, \frown, R_*, R^*)$ *is called a rough set algebra, where* $\cap$, $\cup$ *and* $\frown$ *are the standard set intersection, union and complement.*

Proposition 2. *Let U be a universe and* $R \subseteq U \times U$ *be a reflexive relation. The approximation operators* R_*, R^* *have the following property:* $R_*(X) \subseteq X \subseteq R^*(X)$.

This proposition is a direct deduction from the previous definition of the operators (see Definition 3). In fact, we know that r(x) contains x (reflexivity of R) and r(x) $\subseteq$ X implies that $R_*(X) \subseteq X$. Similarly, X is contained in its upper approximation $R^*(X)$ because r(x)$\cap$X$\neq \emptyset$ for all x$\in$X.

Definition 5. *A set X is said to be a rough set iff its boundary is not empty* $R^*(X) \setminus R_*(X) \neq \emptyset$.

In this situation, the elements that belong to the boundary can not be classified correctly to belong to X nor to its complement $\frown$X. More details on foundations, methodology and applications of rough set theory are developed in [18]. Different generalizations of rough set theory have been suggested in ([20], [17], [19]).

4.2   Linguistic Negation Reformulation

The goal of this section is to reformalize the process we have introduce previously to deal with negation (see Section 3). The input of this process is a sentence with negation that have the following general form "x is not A", whereas its output is a set of "positive" sentences "x is Q". Any positive sentence that belongs to the output of the process is a possible interpretation of the negative sentence given as input. Thus, the general goal of the method is to found the set of positive sentences corresponding to an input negative sentence. Let E+ (resp. E-) represents a set of admissible positive (resp. negative) sentences:

- E+=$\{(x$ is $n_\delta P_{ik}) \mid x \in \mathfrak{D}_i, n_\delta \in \mathfrak{M}, P_{ik} \in \mathfrak{P}_i \}$, and
- E-=$\{ (x$ is not $n_\gamma P_{ik}) \mid x \in \mathfrak{D}_i, n_\gamma \in \mathfrak{M}, P_{ik} \in \mathfrak{P}_i\}$

The main question is what is the significance of a given negative sentence? The answer is represented as a subset of E+. How to determine this subset? We have introduced our method and process to answer this question. Our approach starts by a first step that rewrite the input negative sentence as a set of nuanced properties. The main problem is next to search a subset of $\mathfrak{N}_i$ that represents the semantic of this negation. Finally we instantiate the subset of nuanced properties to determine the corresponding subset of E+. This subset contains positive sentences that are possible interpretations of a given negative sentence.

More formally we can view our process that deals with the linguistic negation as a general function of sets transformation. In fact, we can rewrite, in the case where t = 2, 3, 4, the reference frame of the linguistic negation (see Definition 2) Ref_Neg^t(x, A) as follows:

Ref_Neg^t(x, A) = ($\{x\}$, [Ref_Neg^t(x,A)])$\in \{x\} \times \mathcal{P}(\mathfrak{N}_i)$.

This approach is characterized by a global view of negation processing as the ultimate goal is to determine the set $\{$"x is Q"$\mid Q \in$[Ref_Neg^t(x, A)]$\}$ that gives a global interpretation of the sentence "x is not A".

This output set may be vague and difficult to compute. For this reason we refine our method and modify the goal of negation processing. In fact, we only search for an approximation of linguistic negation and not the set of its global interpretation, as it is the case in the approach using fuzzy context. For this reason, we use the rough set framework ([14], [15], [16]) to formalize the notion of linguistic approximation.

4.3   Linguistic Negation Approximation

This section presents an operationalization of the basic concepts of rough sets in the context of linguistic negation. Let us consider λ a binary relation that defines the neighborhood of each basic property P_{ik} or each nuanced property $m_\alpha of_\beta(P_{ik})$. Now, given a standard form F_t (with $t \in \{2, 3, 4\}$) we consider a subset denoted as X^t of properties that can be nuanced or not. We define then the two main operators, named lower and upper approximations, and denoted respectively R_* and R^*, considering a binary relation λ.

Definition 6. *Knowing that λ is a binary relation defined on $\mathfrak{N}_i$, the set of all nuances associated with the concept C_i, we denote $[p]_\lambda = \{q \in \mathfrak{N}_i \mid p\lambda q \}$.*

Definition 7. *For any standard form F_t with $t \in \{2, 3, 4\}$, let us suppose that λ is a binary relation (at least reflexive) defined on $\mathfrak{N}_i$, and X^t, Y^t and T^t are subsets of $\mathfrak{N}_i$ such that $X^t = Y^t \backslash T^t$. Then, a pair of approximation operators, R_* and R^* are defined by :*
- $R_*(X^t) = \{p \in \mathfrak{N}_i \mid [p]_\lambda \subseteq X^t\}$, and
- $R^*(X^t) = \{p \in \mathfrak{N}_i \mid [p]_\lambda \cap X^t \neq \emptyset\} \backslash T^t$.

Remark 2. The particular set T^t contains nuanced properties to be rejected according to the standard form F^t of the linguistic negation. For this reason we exclude this set from the solution computed by the upper approximation. This operation is not necessary for the lower operator since we have: $R_*(X^t) \subseteq X^t$ and $T^t \cap X^t = \emptyset$.

Example 1. In the following, for any standard form F_t with $t \in \{2, 3, 4\}$, previous sets refer to the definition of $[Ref\_Neg^t (x, A)]$ resulting from the reference frame of the linguistic negation. More precisely, the sets X^t and T^t are defined as follows: $X^2 = \mathfrak{N}_i \backslash \{n_\gamma P_{ik}\}$, $X^3 = \mathfrak{N}_{ik} \backslash \{n_\gamma P_{ik}\}$, $X^4 = \mathfrak{N}_i \backslash \mathfrak{N}_{ik}$, and $T^2 = T^3 = \{n_\gamma P_{ik}\}$, $T^4 = \mathfrak{N}_{ik}$.

These two operators allow us to introduce two main approximations of the negation. Let us now prove the main result giving us the link between each reference frame of a linguistic negation and two precise approximation sets based on rough set theory.

Proposition 3. $R_*([Ref\_Neg^t(x, A)]) \subseteq [Ref\_Neg^t(x, A)] \subseteq R^*([Ref\_Neg^t(x, A)])$, for any standard form F_t knowing that $t \in \{2, 3, 4\}$.

The inclusion of the lower approximation in $[Ref\_Neg^t(x, A)]$ results from Proposition 2. The inclusion of $[Ref\_Neg^t(x, A)]$ in the upper approximation results also from Propoposition 2 by taking into account the fact that $X^t \cap T^t = [Ref\_Neg^t(x, A)] \cap T^t = \emptyset$.

Consequently, we have a more flexible interpretation of the negation with a pessimistic operator (R_*) which reduces the interpretation of "x is not A" to only certain nuanced properties when the optimistic one (R^*) extends the result to more possible nuanced properties.

4.4 Dealing with Linguistic Negation

The goal of this Section is to show the interest of our approach to deal with linguistic negation. More particularly, we point out the relationship between the standard form of negation and the results of the approximation. First, we more emphasize the choice of the binary neighbourhood relation associated with expected linguistic negations. Then, we propose some focusing examples allowing to explain the process of determination of the positive interpretation(s) associated with a negative sentence from its reference frame.

Let us propose some tools allowing us to propose a binary relation λ defining the approximation sets R_* and R^* leading to the intended meanings of linguitic negations. We search the approximation sets associated with the precise negative assertion "x is not $n_\gamma P_{ik}$" for a given standard form F_{t0} with $t0\in\{2, 3, 4\}$, knowing also that the other negative assertions "x is not $n_\delta P_{ij}$" are defined for a standard form F_t with $t\in\{2, 3, 4\}$. In our context of linguistic negation problem, it is necessary to propose an extension of rough sets by using a neighbourhood (or similarity) relation as model for indiscernibility instead of an equivalence one ([18]): intuitively, knowing (x, $n_\gamma P_{ik}$) and the standard form F_{t0} with $t0\in\{2, 3, 4\}$ of linguistic negation of "$n_\gamma P_{ik}$", $n_\gamma P_{ik}$ and some other nuances rather close to $n_\gamma P_{ik}$ should be viewed as indiscernible. First of all, we suppose that we know, for each nuance $n_\gamma P_{ik}$, the set of nuances having a *meaning rather close to the one of* $n_\gamma P_{ik}$ (it results from a linguistic analysis of nuance meaning). So, we obtain a first binary *neighbourhood relation ϑ related to the nuance meaning* and defined on $\mathfrak{N}_i$: $[p]_\vartheta=\{q\in \mathfrak{N}_i \mid p\vartheta q\}=\{$nuances q having a meaning rather close to the one of p$\}$. Indeed, this relation should be reflexive, certainly symmetrical, but never transitive. This being so, we have to define another relation λ as *model of indiscernibility related now to the process of linguistic negation* of $n_\gamma P_{ik}$ *for a standard form* F_{t0} *with* $t0\in\{2, 3, 4\}$. For previous standard form F_{t0}, this relation defines the reference frame X^{t0} of the linguistic negation, and the approximation sets $R_*(X^{t0})$ and $R^*(X^{t0})$ for the nuance $n_\gamma P_{ik}$. So, we propose to put in this case $[p]_\lambda=[p]_\vartheta$. For other F_t, we have to avoid as neighbour of $n_\delta P_{ij}$, a nuance which can belongs to X^t and $R_*(X^t)$, but being not a certain intended meaning of the linguistic negation. This can be done by choosing in these cases $[p]_\lambda$ equal to p or $\mathfrak{N}_i$. As a result, λ *will also be a neighbourhood relation*, since λ will be reflexive, possibly symmetrical, but never be transitive. In the following, knowing previous neighbourhood relation ϑ, we propose a standard neighbourhood relation λ as model of indiscernibility allowing us to define, in all cases, the previous approximation sets R_* and R^*.

Proposition 4. *The neighbourhood relation ϑ related to nuance meaning is supposed well-known. Then, we search R_* and R^* the approximation sets associated with the negative assertion "x is not $n_\gamma P_{ik}$" for a given standard form F_{t0} with $t0\in\{2, 3, 4\}$ knowing that the other negative assertions "x is not $n_\delta P_{ij}$" being defined for a precise standard form F_t with $t\in\{2, 3, 4\}$. Then, in order to obtain approximations sets in good accordance with linguistic analysis, a new neighbourhood relation λ, dealing with all cases of linguistic negation, can be build as follows:*
- Case t0=3. For any $t\neq3$ we put $[n_\delta P_{ij}]_\lambda=\{n_\delta P_{ij}\}$. For t0=3 and t=3, $[n_\gamma P_{ik}]_\lambda$ (resp. $[n_\delta P_{ij}]_\lambda$) contains the nuance $n_\gamma P_{ik}$ (resp. $n_\delta P_{ij}$) and none or several other neighbours[1] *(if they exist) of $n_\gamma P_{ik}$ (resp. $n_\delta P_{ij}$) related to ϑ.*

---

[1] In this paper, we will always choose all neighbours of $n_\gamma P_{ik}$ (resp. $n_\delta P_{ij}$) related to ϑ.

- Case t0=2 (resp.t0=4). For any t≠2 (resp. t≠4) we put $[n_\delta P_{ij}]_\lambda = \mathfrak{N}_i$. For t0=2 (resp. t0=4) and t=2 (resp. t=4), $[n_\gamma P_{ik}]_\lambda$ (resp. $[n_\delta P_{ij}]_\lambda$) contains the nuance $n_\gamma P_{ik}$ (resp. $n_\delta P_{ij}$) and none or several other neighbours, if any, of $n_\gamma P_{ik}$ (resp. $n_\delta P_{ij}$) related to ϑ.

In the first case, the $X^{t0}=X^3$, the set associated with "x is not $n_\gamma P_{ik}$", contains only all nuances of P_{ik} except P_{ik}. So, no nuance of an other basic property belongs to $R_*(X^{t0})$, but can belong to $R^*(X^{t0})$. In other words, the certain affirmative interpretation are nuances of P_{ik}. In the second case, knowing that X^{t0} cannot be a strict subset of $\mathfrak{N}_i$, $R_*(X^{t0})$ cannot contains nuances associated with a standard form F^t different from F^{t0}. In other words, the certain interpretations refer only to nuances belonging to X^{t0}, the reference frame of "x is not $n_\gamma P_{ik}$". It appears that this relation leads, in all cases, to results in good accordance with the intended meanings of the linguistic negations. The following examples illustrate the use of the relation λ.

Example 2. Let us suppose that the set $\mathfrak{D}_i=\{John, Jack\}$ and $\mathfrak{P}_i=\{P_{i1}, P_{i2}\}=\{visible$ (in the crowd), invisible (in the crowd)$\}$. We do not use modifiers. The relation υ is defined as follows : $[visible]_\vartheta=\{visible\}$, $[invisible]_\upsilon = \{invisible\}$. We suppose that F_4 is associated with "x is not visible" and "x is not invisible". So, we have: $[visible]_\lambda=\{visible\}$, $[invisible]_\lambda = \{invisible\}$. Then, the approximation of "John is not visible" gives us: $X^4=\{invisible\}$, $R_*(X^4) = R^*(X^4) = \{invisible\}$ and the approximation of "Jack is not invisible": $X^4=\{visible\}$, $R_*(X^4) = R^*(X^4) = \{visible\}$. So, "John is invisible" and "Jack is visible" are certain interpretations of previous linguistic negations.

Example 3. In this example, we consider the sets $\mathfrak{D}_i=\{John, Jack, Tom\}$ and $\mathfrak{P}_i=\{P_{i1}, P_{i2}, P_{i3}\}=\{small, medium, tall\}$. We consider only one modifier called "very" applied to the basic properties "small" and "tall". So, $\mathfrak{N}_i=\{very\ P_{i1}, P_{i1}, P_{i2}, P_{i3}, very\ P_{i3}\}$. We suppose now that we know the standard form F_t associated with the linguistic negation. So, "x is not very P_{i1}", "x is not P_{i1}", "x is not P_{i2}", "x is not P_{i3}", "x is not very P_{i3}" are respectively connected with standard forms F_3, F_4, F_2, F_4 and F_3. The natutal neighbourhood relation υ is defined as follows: in all cases, $[p]_\vartheta = \{p\}$. We can now define explicitly the binary relation λ, by using previous results about particular cases of linguistic negation.

- Approximation of "x is not very P_{i1}". We obtain: for any p, $[p]_\lambda=\{p\}$. Then, $X^3=\{P_{i1}\}$ leads to $R_*(X^3)=\{P_{i1}\}$ and $R^*(X^3)=\{P_{i1}\}$. So, "x is small" is the certain linguistic negation of "x is not very small".

- Approximation of "x is not very P_{i3}". This symmetrical case gives us: $X^3=\{P_{i3}\}$ leads to $R_*(X^3)=\{P_{i3}\}$ and $R^*(X^3)=\{P_{i3}\}$. So, "x is tall" is the certain linguistic negation of "x is not tall".

- Approximation of "x is not P_{i1}". We can have: $[very\ P_{i1}]_\lambda=\mathfrak{N}_i$, $[P_{i1}]_\lambda=\{P_{i1}\}$, $[P_{i2}]_\lambda=\mathfrak{N}_i$, $[P_{i3}]_\lambda=\{P_{i3}\}$, $[very\ P_{i3}]_\lambda=\mathfrak{N}_i$. So, $X^4=\{P_{i2}, P_{i3}, very\ P_{i3}\}$ leads to $R_*(X^4)=\{P_{i3}\}$ and $R^*(X^4)=\{P_{i2}, P_{i3}, very\ P_{i3}\}$. So, "x is tall" is a certain linguistic negation of "x is not small". Moreover, "x is medium" and "x is very tall" are possible but not certain interpretations.

- Approximation of "x is not P_{i3}". This symmetrical case gives us: $X^4=\{P_{i2}, P_{i1}, very\ P_{i1}\}$ leads to $R_*(X^4)=\{P_{i1}\}$ and $R^*(X^4)=\{P_{i1}, P_{i2}, very\ P_{i1}\}$. So, "x is small" is a certain linguistic negation of "x is not tall", and "x is medium" or "x is very small" are possible but not certain interpretations.

- Approximation of "x is not P_{i2}". We obtain: $[very\ P_{i1}]_\lambda=\mathfrak{N}_i$, $[P_{i1}]_\lambda=\mathfrak{N}_i$, $[P_{i2}]_\lambda=\{P_{i2}\}$, $[P_{i3}]_\lambda=\mathfrak{N}_i$, $[very\ P_{i3}]_\lambda=\mathfrak{N}_i$. Then, $X^2=\{very\ P_{i1}, P_{i1}, P_{i3}, very\ P_{i3}\}$ leads to $R_*(X^2)=\emptyset$

and $R^*(X^2)=\{$very $P_{i1}, P_{i1}, P_{i3},$ very $P_{i3}\}$. It appears that no certain interpertation of "x is not medium" exists, but four affirmative interpretations are possible.

It appears clearly that this standard neighbourhood relation λ leads to results in good accordance with the ones linguistically expected. Note that we are currently studying other plausible relations λ and its basic properties, like the ones proposed in ([17], [18]). The examples presented in this Section give an idea on the quality of the results computed by the approximation according to each standard form of negation (due to lack of space, we do not present more examples). More refined relations can be used to analyze the behavior of the approximations.

We can point out the fact that the upper approximation R^* contains all possible interpretations of each linguistic negation, but can also contain some neighbours very close to these expected solutions. Moreover, the lower approximation R_* only contains nuances acceptable for the standard form associated with this linguistic negation. So, among the elements of the approximation sets, several of them are certain or possible interpretations, and others are neighbours of them but not plausible. Then, it is necessary to propose a default strategy of choice of suitable affirmative interpretations. Unfortunately, due to the lack of space, we do not present these several strategies.

5   Conclusion

This paper deals with a new approach of the problem of linguistic negation. Clearly, it consists in finding, for a given negative sentence, the suitable positive translations that are linguistically expected. The originality of the work is that we do not compute the reference frame of positive translations associated with the negative sentence but we work on two approximation sets of the reference frame: a pessimistic one gives the translations which are sure and an optimistic one gives all the possible translations. These sets being computed, we propose a standard choice of the relation of neighbourhood. The last step, which is not studied here, is the choice strategy of one (or several) affirmative interpretation(s) associated with a negative sentence from its reference frame. These strategies leads to select positive translations that are in good accordance with the ones linguistically expected.

References

1. Culioli, A.: Pour une linguistique de l'énonciation : Opérations et Représentations, Tome 1, Ophrys 2ds., Paris, 1991.
2. Dermott D., "Tarskian Semantics, or no Notation Without denotation", Cognitive Science 2(3), 277-282, 1978.
3. Desmontils, E., Pacholczyk, D.: Towards a linguistic processing of properties in declarative modelling, Int. Jour. CADCAM and Computer Graphics, 12:4, 351-371, 1997
4. Ducrot, O., Schaeffer J. -M.et al.: Nouveau dictionnaire encyclopédique des sciences du langage. Eds. du Seuil, Paris, 1995
5. Horn, L.R.: A Natural History of Negation. The University of Chicago Press, 1989
6. McCawley J. D., Everything That linguists Have always Wanted to Know about Logic (2nd ed.), Chicago Univ. Press, 1993.

7. Mel'cuk I. A., Dependency Syntax: Theory and Practice, Univ. of New York Press, 1988.
8. Moore R. C., "Problems in logical Form" Proc. of the 19th Annual Meeting of Association for Computational Linguistics, Standford, California, 117-124, 1981.
9. Muller, C.: La négation en français, Publications romanes et françaises, Genève, 1991
10. Pacholczyk, D.: An Intelligent System Dealing with Negative Information". LNAI, 1325, 467-476, 1997
11. Pacholczyk, D.: A New Approach to the Intended Meaning of Negative Information", Proc. of ECAI'98, Brighton, UK, Pub. by J. Wiley&Sons, 114-118, 1998
12. Pacholczyk D.: A Fuzzy Analysis of Linguistic Negation of Nuanced Property in Knowledge-based Systems. Proc. of Int. Conf. ECSQARU-FAPR'97, LNAI. 1244, 451-465, 1997.
13. Pacholczyk, D., Levrat, B.: Coping with Linguistically Denied Nuanced Properties: a Matter of Fuzziness and Scope, Proc. of 1998 IEEE ISIC/CIRA/ISAS joint Conf., Gaithersburg, MD, 1998, 753-758, 1998
14. Pawlak, Z.: Rough Sets. Int. J. Comput. Inf. Sci. 11 (1982), 341-356
15. Pawlak, Z.: Rough sets. Theoretical Aspects of Reasoning about Data. Kluwer, Netherlands, 1991.
16. Pawlak, Z., et al: Rough Sets. Communication of the ACM, Vol. 38, No 11, 89-94, 1995.
17. Pawlak, et al.: Rough sets : probabilistic versus deterministic. In B.R. Gaines and J.H. Boose Eds, Machine Learning and Uncertain Reasoning, 227-241. Academic Press, 1990.
18. Polkowski, L., Skowron, A. : Rough sets in Knowledge Discovery 1, 2. Physica-Verlag, 1998.
19. Quafafou, M.: Alpha-Rough set: A generalization of rough set theory, Information Sciences 124, 301-316., 2000.
20. Ziarko W, Variable precision rough sets model, Journal of Computer and Systems Sciences, Vol 46, n° 1, 35 - 59, 1993.
21. Zubert R., Implications sémantiques dans les langues naturelles, Ed. du CNRS, Paris, France, 1989.

Left Corner Parser for Tree Insertion Grammars

Vicente Carrillo and Víctor J. Díaz

Department of Computer Languages and Systems
University of Seville
Avda. Reina Mercedes s/n, Seville 41012, Spain
{carrillo,vjdiaz}@lsi.us.es

Abstract. *Tree Adjoining Grammar* (TAG) is a grammar formalism that has become very popular for the description of natural languages, however, this context-sensitive formalism entails important computation costs ($O(n^6)$-time). *Tree Insertion Grammar* (TIG) is a compromise between *Context Free Grammar* (CFG) and TAG that can be parsed in $O(n^3) - time$. In the literature, just two Earley-like parsers for TIGs have been defined. In this paper, we define a new variant of Earley-like parser for TIGs. In order to improve the performance of this parser, we show how the *left corner relation* for CFG can be generalized to the case of TIG and we present an efficient parser for TIG that uses this relation.

Keywords: natural language processing, parsing, TIG, TAG, left corner

1 Introduction

Tree Insertion Grammar (TIG) [6] is a compromise between Context Free Grammar (CFG) and Tree Adjoining Grammar (TAG) [4] that combines the efficiency of the former with the strong lexicalizing power of the latter. TIGs are characterized by the following: like CFG, TIG can be parsed in $O(n^3) - time$, instead of $O(n^6) - time$ for TAG; TIGs are a subclass of TAGs, therefore, TIG is naturally lexicalized.

Most parsers for TAGs and TIGs are extensions of well-known parsers for CFGs. Several parsers for TAGs have been defined on the basis of the Earley's algorithm ([4],[5],[1]), however, just two Earley-like parsers for TIGs have been defined ([6],[3]).

Parsing algorithms can be defined as deduction systems ([8],[9]) where formulas, called items, are sets of complete or incomplete constituents. Parsing schemata were introduced in [9] as a framework for high-level description of parsing algorithms. A parsing schema abstracts from implementation details of an algorithm like data control structures. This framework allows us to establish relations between two parsers in a formal way. The *filters* are very interesting relations because they can be used to improve the performance of parsers in practical cases. An example of filter is the relation between Earley and Left Corner (LC) parsers for CFGs.

D. Scott (Ed.): AIMSA 2002, LNAI 2443, pp. 142–151, 2002.

A LC parser, like an Earley parser, proceeds through the sentence from left to right, but differs in the way in which top-down predictions are used to guide the bottom-up recognition. A LC parser reduces the number of predictions applied by an Earley's parser by using a *left corner relation*. A LC parser for TAGs has been defined in [2], but to the best of our knowledge, no attempt has been made to improve the practical performance of Earley-like parsers for TIGs by using an *left corner relation*.

2   Tree Insertion Grammars

A TIG is a five-tuple (V_N, V_T, S, I, A), where V_N is a set of nonterminal symbols, V_T is a set of terminal symbols, $S \in V_N$ is the axiom, I is a finite set of finite *initial trees* and A is a finite set of finite *auxiliary trees*. The set $I \cup A$ is referred to as the *elementary trees*. Internal nodes in an elementary tree are labeled by nonterminal symbols. We refer to the root of an elementary tree γ as $\mathbf{R}^\gamma$. In each elementary tree the nodes on the frontier are labeled by terminal symbols, the empty string (ε) or nonterminal symbols marked for substitution, except that exactly one node in each auxiliary tree which is marked as the foot and whose label is the same as the root. We refer to the foot of an auxiliary tree β as $\mathbf{F}^\beta$. The path from the root to the foot is called the *spine*. We use $label(M^\gamma)$ to denote the label of node M^γ.

Auxiliary trees in which every frontier node is to the left (right) of the foot are called *left (right) auxiliary trees*. Other auxiliary trees are called *wrapping auxiliary trees*. We use A_L and A_R to denote the sets of left auxiliary trees and right auxiliary trees, respectively.

A TIG derivation starts with an initial tree rooted at S. This tree is repeatedly extended using *substitution* and *adjunction*. The *adjunction* inserts an auxiliary tree β into another tree γ on a node M^γ that has the same label as $\mathbf{R}^\beta$. In concrete, M^γ is replaced by β and $\mathbf{F}^\beta$ is replaced by the subtree rooted at M^γ. We use $\beta \in adj(M^\gamma)$ to denote that a tree $\beta \in A$ may be adjoined on node M^γ, i.e. M^γ is an adjunction node. If adjunction is not mandatory on M^γ then $\mathbf{nil} \in adj(M^\gamma)$, where $\mathbf{nil}$ is a dummy symbol. The adjunction of a left (right) auxiliary tree is referred to as *left (right) adjunction*. We use $\beta \in ladj(M^\gamma)$ ($\beta \in radj(M^\gamma)$) to denote that a tree $\beta \in A_L$ ($\beta \in A_R$) may be adjoined on node M^γ, i.e. M^γ is a left (right) adjunction node. If left (right) adjunction is not mandatory on M^γ then $\mathbf{nil} \in ladj(M^\gamma)$ ($\mathbf{nil} \in radj(M^\gamma)$). The *substitution* is mandatory and replaces a node marked for substitution M^γ with a copy of an initial tree α whose root has the same label as M^γ. We use $\alpha \in subst(M^\gamma)$ to denote that node M^γ may be substituted by a tree $\alpha \in I$.

TIG does not allow wrapping auxiliary trees and an left (right) auxiliary tree to be adjoined on any node that is in the spine of a right (left) auxiliary tree. To increase the trees that can be generated, TIG allows arbitrarily simultaneous adjunctions on a single node (look up details in [6]). Simultaneous adjunction is fundamentally ambiguous in nature and typically results in the creation of several different trees. One can easily imagine variants of TIG where simultaneous adjunction is more limited. In order to preserve the trees that can be generated without increasing the ambiguity of derivations, we have chosen the variant of TIG presented in [7] that allows right and left adjunction on a node, but at most once each.

In order to represente partial parse trees, we define a production $N^\gamma \to N_1^\gamma...N_g^\gamma$ for every node N^γ and its ordered g children $N_1^\gamma...N_g^\gamma$ in an elementary tree. We refer to the set of productions related to an elementary tree γ as $\mathcal{P}(\gamma)$. For technical reasons, we consider additional productions $\top \to \mathbf{R}^\alpha$, $\top \to \mathbf{R}^\beta$ and $\mathbf{F}^\beta \to \bot$ for every initial tree α and auxiliary tree β. To preserve the generative capability of the grammar, the nodes $\top$ and $\bot$ can not be adjoined.

3   Earley-Like Parser for TIGs

We present a new efficient left-to-right parsing algorithm for TIG that maintains the valid prefix property [5] and requires $O(n^3)$ time in the worst case, by combining top-down predictions as in Earley's algorithm for parsing CFGs with bottom-up recognition.

We define a parsing system $\mathbb{P}_{\text{Earley}}$ for an arbitrary tree insertion grammar $G \in TIG$ and an input string $a_1...a_n$ with $n \geq 0$. The domain $\mathcal{I}_{\text{Earley}}$ is given by

$$\mathcal{I}_{\text{Earley}} = \mathcal{I}_{\text{Earley}}^{(i)} \cup \mathcal{I}_{\text{Earley}}^{(ii)}$$

$$\mathcal{I}_{\text{Earley}}^{(i)} = \{[M^\gamma \to \delta \bullet \nu, i, j, code]\}$$

such that $M^\gamma \to \delta\nu \in \mathcal{P}(\gamma)$, $\gamma \in I \cup A$, $0 \leq i \leq j$, $\nu \neq \varepsilon$, $code = \emptyset$ if no adjunction was completed on M^γ and $code = \{L\}$ if a left adjunction was completed on M^γ. The purpose of the $code$ is to insure that left and right adjunction can each be applied at most once on the node M^γ.

$$\mathcal{I}_{\text{Earley}}^{(ii)} = \{[M^\gamma \to \nu\bullet, i, j, code]\}$$

such that $M^\gamma \to \nu \in \mathcal{P}(\gamma)$, $\gamma \in I \cup A$, $0 \leq i \leq j$, $code = \emptyset$ if no adjunction was completed on M^γ, $code = \{L\}$ if a left adjunction was completed on M^γ, $code = \{R\}$ if a right adjunction was completed on M^γ and $code = \{L, R\}$ if a left adjunction and a right adjunction were completed on M^γ.

For the set of deduction steps, we define subsets for *initialize*, *scan* and *complete* similar to the Earley parser for CFGs. The set $\mathcal{D}_{\text{Earley}}$ is defined by:

$$\mathcal{D}_{\text{Earley}} = \mathcal{D}_{\text{Earley}}^{\text{Ini}} \cup \mathcal{D}_{\text{Earley}}^{\text{Sc}} \cup \mathcal{D}_{\text{Earley}}^{\varepsilon} \cup \mathcal{D}_{\text{Earley}}^{\text{Pred}} \cup \mathcal{D}_{\text{Earley}}^{\text{Cmp}} \cup \mathcal{D}_{\text{Earley}}^{\text{Foot}} \cup \mathcal{D}_{\text{Earley}}^{\text{LAdjPred}} \cup$$

$$\mathcal{D}_{\text{Earley}}^{\text{LAdjCmp}} \cup \mathcal{D}_{\text{Earley}}^{\text{RAdjPred}} \cup \mathcal{D}_{\text{Earley}}^{\text{RAdjCmp}} \cup \mathcal{D}_{\text{Earley}}^{\text{SubsPred}} \cup \mathcal{D}_{\text{Earley}}^{\text{SubsCmp}}$$

The recognition starts by predicting every initial tree $\alpha \in I$ whose root is labeled with the axiom $(label(\mathbf{R}^\alpha) = S)$:

$$\mathcal{D}_{\text{Earley}}^{\text{Ini}} = \frac{}{[\top \to \bullet\mathbf{R}^\alpha, 0, 0, \emptyset]}$$

The scanning steps recognize terminal symbols and match fringe nodes against the input string. $\mathcal{D}_{\text{Earley}}^{\text{Sc}}$ recognizes the presence of a terminal symbol in the input string. $\mathcal{D}_{\text{Earley}}^{\varepsilon}$ and $\mathcal{D}_{\text{Earley}}^{\text{Foot}}$ encode the fact that one can skip over nodes labeled with ε and foot nodes without having to match anything:

$$\mathcal{D}_{\text{Earley}}^{\text{Sc}} = \frac{[a, j, j+1]}{[N^{\gamma} \to \delta \bullet M^{\gamma}\nu, i, j, code]} \quad label(M^{\gamma}) = a$$

$$\mathcal{D}_{\text{Earley}}^{\varepsilon} = \frac{[N^{\gamma} \to \delta \bullet M^{\gamma}\nu, i, j, code]}{[N^{\gamma} \to \delta M^{\gamma} \bullet \nu, i, j, code]} \quad label(M^{\gamma}) = \varepsilon$$

$$\mathcal{D}_{\text{Earley}}^{\text{Foot}} = \frac{[\mathbf{F}^{\beta} \to \bullet \bot, j, j, \emptyset]}{[\mathbf{F}^{\beta} \to \bot \bullet, j, j, \emptyset]} \quad \beta \in A$$

In the case of TIGs, we have four kinds of predictions with their associated completion steps: subtree, left adjunction, right adjunction and substitution. The subtree traversal steps control the recognition of subtrees. $\mathcal{D}_{\text{Earley}}^{\text{Pred}}$ predicts a subtree rooted at M^{γ} if the previous siblings have already been recognized and M^{γ} has not mandatory left adjunction ($\mathbf{nil} \in \text{ladj}(M^{\gamma})$):

$$\mathcal{D}_{\text{Earley}}^{\text{Pred}} = \frac{[N^{\gamma} \to \delta \bullet M^{\gamma}\nu, i, j, code]}{[M^{\gamma} \to \bullet\omega, j, j, \emptyset]}$$

$\mathcal{D}_{\text{Earley}}^{\text{Cmp}}$ completes the recognition of a subtree rooted at M^{γ} if and only if M^{γ} has not mandatory adjunction ($\mathbf{nil} \in \text{adj}(M^{\gamma})$) and $code = \emptyset$ or M^{γ} is a adjunction node and $code \neq \emptyset$:

$$\mathcal{D}_{\text{Earley}}^{\text{Cmp}} = \frac{[M^{\gamma} \to \omega\bullet, j, k, code]}{[N^{\gamma} \to \delta \bullet M^{\gamma}\nu, i, j, code']} {[N^{\gamma} \to \delta M^{\gamma} \bullet \nu, i, k, code']}$$

The left and right adjunction steps recognize the adjunction of left and right auxiliary trees. When the recognition reaches a left adjunction node M^{γ}, $\mathcal{D}_{\text{Earley}}^{\text{LAdjPred}}$ triggers the recognition of every left auxiliary tree β that may be adjoined on M^{γ} ($\beta \in \text{ladj}(M^{\gamma})$):

$$\mathcal{D}_{\text{Earley}}^{\text{LAdjPred}} = \frac{[N^{\gamma} \to \delta \bullet M^{\gamma}\nu, i, j, code]}{[\top \to \bullet \mathbf{R}^{\beta}, j, j, \emptyset]}$$

$\mathcal{D}_{\text{Earley}}^{\text{LAdjCmp}}$ supports the bottom-up recognition of the adjunction of a left auxiliary tree. In order to avoid other left adjunction we set $\{L\}$ the $code$ of the consequent:

$$\mathcal{D}_{\text{Earley}}^{\text{LAdjCmp}} = \frac{[\top \to \mathbf{R}^{\beta}\bullet, j, k, \emptyset]}{[N^{\gamma} \to \delta \bullet M^{\gamma}\nu, i, j, code]} {[M^{\gamma} \to \bullet\omega, j, k, \{L\}]}$$

The right adjunction steps, $\mathcal{D}_{\text{Earley}}^{\text{RAdjPred}}$ and $\mathcal{D}_{\text{Earley}}^{\text{RAdjCmp}}$, are analogous to the left adjunction steps, but are triggered by items of the form $[M^\gamma \to \nu\bullet, i, j, code]$ where $R \notin code$:

$$\mathcal{D}_{\text{Earley}}^{\text{RAdjPred}} = \frac{[M^\gamma \to \nu\bullet, i, j, code]}{[\top \to \bullet\mathbf{R}^\beta, j, j, \emptyset]}$$

$$\mathcal{D}_{\text{Earley}}^{\text{RAdjCmp}} = \frac{[\top \to \mathbf{R}^\beta\bullet, j, k, \emptyset]}{[M^\gamma \to \nu\bullet, i, j, code]}{[M^\gamma \to \nu\bullet, i, k, \{R\} \cup code]}$$

$\mathcal{D}_{\text{Earley}}^{\text{SubsPred}}$ predicts a substitution of an initial tree α on a node M^γ if $\alpha \in subst(M^\gamma)$, whereas $\mathcal{D}_{\text{Earley}}^{\text{SubsCmp}}$ completes the substitution:

$$\mathcal{D}_{\text{Earley}}^{\text{SubsPred}} = \frac{[N^\gamma \to \delta \bullet M^\gamma\nu, i, j, code]}{[\top \to \bullet\mathbf{R}^\alpha, j, j, \emptyset]}$$

$$\mathcal{D}_{\text{Earley}}^{\text{SubsCmp}} = \frac{[\top \to \mathbf{R}^\alpha\bullet, j, k, \emptyset]}{[N^\gamma \to \delta \bullet M^\gamma\nu, i, j, code]}{[N^\gamma \to \delta M^\gamma \bullet \nu, i, k, code]}$$

The set of final items is defined by:

$$\mathcal{F}_{\text{Earley}} = \{[\top \to \mathbf{R}^\alpha\bullet, 0, n, \emptyset] \mid \alpha \in I, label(\mathbf{R}^\alpha) = S\}$$

4   Left Corner Parser for TIGs

In this section we present a parser that uses left corner relation to filter the predictions on Earley-like parser for TIGs. The time complexity of the algorithm is $O(n^3)$ but improves the performance by the reduction in the size of chart. Before describing the new parser, we need define the left corner relation for TIGs.

Definition 1. *Left corner relation on elementary trees of TIGs*
The left corner of a node O^γ is her leftmost daughter P^γ if and only if ladj$(P^\gamma) = \{$**nil**$\}$. *The relation $>_\ell$ on $V_N \times (V_N \cup V_T \cup \{\varepsilon, \bot\})$ is defined by*
$O^\gamma >_\ell P^\gamma$ *if there is a production $O^\gamma \to P^\gamma\nu \in \mathcal{P}(\gamma)$ and* ladj$(P^\gamma) = \{$**nil**$\}$.
The transitive and reflexive closure of $>_\ell$ is denoted by $>_\ell^*$.

It is worth noting that left corner relation for TIGs starts on a node labeled with a nonterminal symbol and ends on a left adjunction node, a node marked for substitution, a node labeled with a terminal symbol or a node ε.

We define a parsing system $\mathbb{P}_{\text{LC}}$ for an arbitrary tree insertion grammar $G \in TIG$ and an input string $a_1...a_n$ with $n \geq 0$. The set of items $\mathcal{I}_{\text{LC}}$ is given by

$$\mathcal{I}_{\text{LC}} = \mathcal{I}_{\text{LC}}^{(i)} \cup \mathcal{I}_{\text{LC}}^{(ii)} \cup \mathcal{I}_{\text{Earley}}^{(ii)}$$

$$\mathcal{I}_{\text{LC}}^{(i)} = \{[M^\gamma \to \delta \bullet \nu, i, j, code]\}$$

such that $M^\gamma \rightarrow \delta\nu \in \mathcal{P}(\gamma)$, $\gamma \in I \cup A$, $0 \leq i \leq j$, $\delta \neq \varepsilon$, $\nu \neq \varepsilon$, $code = \emptyset$ if no adjunction was completed on M^γ and $code = \{L\}$ if a left adjunction was completed on M^γ;

$$\mathcal{I}_{LC}^{(ii)} = \{[M^\gamma \rightarrow \bullet P^\gamma\nu, i, j, code]\}$$

such that $M^\gamma \rightarrow \nu \in \mathcal{P}(\gamma)$, $\gamma \in I \cup A$, $0 \leq i \leq j$, $code = \{L\}$ if a left adjunction was completed on M^γ and $code = \emptyset$ if P^γ is a left adjunction or substitution node and no adjunction was completed on M^γ.

For the set of deduction steps, we define subsets for *initialize*, *scan* and *complete* similar to the Earley-like parser. The left corner relation will be applied for the six cases of prediction: initial, subtree, foot, left adjunction, right adjunction and substitution. The left corner steps come in four varieties of left corners: terminal, empty, foot and nonterminal. The latter is presented when the left corner is a left adjunction or substitution node, because the auxiliary tree or the initial tree must be recognized. The set $\mathcal{D}_{LC}$ is defined by:

$$\mathcal{D}_{LC} = \mathcal{D}_{LC}^{LI_t} \cup \mathcal{D}_{LC}^{LI_\varepsilon} \cup \mathcal{D}_{LC}^{LI_{pre}} \cup \mathcal{D}_{Earley}^{Sc} \cup \mathcal{D}_{Earley}^{\varepsilon} \cup \mathcal{D}_{LC}^{LC_t} \cup \mathcal{D}_{LC}^{LC_\varepsilon} \cup \mathcal{D}_{LC}^{LC_{pre}} \cup \mathcal{D}_{LC}^{LC_{foot}} \cup$$

$$\mathcal{D}_{LC}^{LC_n} \cup \mathcal{D}_{LC}^{LA_n} \cup \mathcal{D}_{LC}^{LF_n} \cup \mathcal{D}_{LC}^{LA_t} \cup \mathcal{D}_{LC}^{LA_\varepsilon} \cup \mathcal{D}_{LC}^{LA_{pre}} \cup \mathcal{D}_{LC}^{LF_t} \cup \mathcal{D}_{LC}^{LF_\varepsilon} \cup \mathcal{D}_{LC}^{LF_{pre}} \cup$$

$$\mathcal{D}_{LC}^{LF_{foot}} \cup \mathcal{D}_{LC}^{LACmp} \cup \mathcal{D}_{LC}^{RA_{foot}} \cup \mathcal{D}_{Earley}^{RACmp} \cup \mathcal{D}_{LC}^{LS_t} \cup \mathcal{D}_{LC}^{LS_\varepsilon} \cup \mathcal{D}_{LC}^{LS_{pre}} \cup \mathcal{D}_{Earley}^{SubsCmp}$$

The recognition starts by predicting every initial tree α whose root is labeled with the axiom S. If $\top >_\ell^* O^\alpha$ we can apply LC filter and obtain:

$$\mathcal{D}_{LC}^{LI_t} = \frac{[a, 0, 1]}{[O^\alpha \rightarrow P^\alpha \bullet \nu, 0, 1, \emptyset]} \quad label(P^\alpha) = a$$

$$\mathcal{D}_{LC}^{LI_\varepsilon} = \frac{}{[O^\alpha \rightarrow P^\alpha \bullet \nu, 0, 0, \emptyset]} \quad label(P^\alpha) = \varepsilon$$

$$\mathcal{D}_{LC}^{LI_{pre}} = \frac{}{[O^\alpha \rightarrow \bullet P^\alpha\nu, 0, 0, \emptyset]} \quad \exists\beta \in \text{ladj}(P^\alpha) \text{ or } \exists\alpha' \in subst(P^\alpha)$$

When the recognition reaches a node M^γ that dominates O^γ by a LC relation $(M^\gamma >_\ell^* O^\gamma)$ and M^γ has not mandatory left adjunction (**nil** $\in$ ladj(M^γ)), we apply LC filter and obtain:

$$\mathcal{D}_{LC}^{LC_t} = \frac{[N^\gamma \rightarrow \delta \bullet M^\gamma\nu, i, j, code]}{[a, j, j+1]}{[O^\gamma \rightarrow P^\gamma \bullet \omega, j, j+1, \emptyset]} \quad label(P^\gamma) = a$$

$$\mathcal{D}_{LC}^{LC_\varepsilon} = \frac{[N^\gamma \rightarrow \delta \bullet M^\gamma\nu, i, j, code]}{[O^\gamma \rightarrow P^\gamma \bullet \omega, j, j, \emptyset]} \quad label(P^\gamma) = \varepsilon$$

$$\mathcal{D}_{LC}^{LC_{pre}} = \frac{[N^\gamma \rightarrow \delta \bullet M^\gamma\nu, i, j, code]}{[O^\gamma \rightarrow \bullet P^\gamma\omega, j, j, \emptyset]} \quad \exists\beta \in \text{ladj}(P^\gamma) \text{ or } \exists\alpha \in subst(P^\gamma)$$

$\mathcal{D}_{LC}^{LC_{foot}}$ is applied when the recognition reaches a node M^β that has not mandatory adjunction and dominates the foot node of a left auxiliary tree

$(M^\beta >_\ell^* \mathbf{F}^\beta)$. This step encodes the fact that one can skip over nodes labeled with $\perp$ of left auxiliary trees without having to match anything:

$$\mathcal{D}_{\mathrm{LC}}^{\mathrm{LC_{foot}}} = \frac{[N^\beta \to \delta \bullet M^\beta \nu, i, j, code]}{[\mathbf{F}^\beta \to \perp \bullet, j, j, \emptyset]}$$

The following steps perform the bottom-up recognition trough the nodes in a LC relation. In order to set an accurate value of $code$, we distinguish three cases:

$$\mathcal{D}_{\mathrm{LC}}^{\mathrm{LC_n}} = \frac{\begin{array}{c}[N^\gamma \to \delta \bullet M^\gamma \nu, i, j, code']\\ [O^\gamma \to \omega \bullet, j, k, code]\end{array}}{[Q^\gamma \to O^\gamma \bullet v, j, k, \emptyset]}$$

such that $M^\gamma >_\ell^* O^\gamma$, $M^\gamma \neq O^\gamma$, $\mathbf{nil} \in \mathrm{ladj}(M^\gamma)$, O^γ has not mandatory right adjunction and $code = \emptyset$ or O^γ is a right adjunction node and $code = \{R\}$;

$$\mathcal{D}_{\mathrm{LC}}^{\mathrm{LA_n}} = \frac{[O^\gamma \to \omega \bullet, j, k, code]}{[Q^\gamma \to O^\gamma \bullet v, j, k, \emptyset]}$$

such that $\top >_\ell^* O^\gamma$, O^γ has not mandatory right adjunction and $code = \emptyset$ or O^γ is a right adjunction node and $code = \{R\}$;

$$\mathcal{D}_{\mathrm{LC}}^{\mathrm{LF_n}} = \frac{\begin{array}{c}[N^\gamma \to \delta \bullet M^\gamma \nu, i, j, code'']\\ [\top \to \mathbf{R}^\beta \bullet, j, k, \emptyset]\\ [O^\gamma \to \omega \bullet, k, l, code']\end{array}}{[Q^\gamma \to O^\gamma \bullet v, k, l, code]}$$

such that $M^\gamma >_\ell^* O^\gamma$, $M^\gamma \neq O^\gamma$, $\beta \in \mathrm{ladj}(M^\gamma)$, O^γ has not mandatory right adjunction and $code' = \emptyset$ or O^γ is a right adjunction node and $code' = \{R\}$, $code = \{L\}$ if $Q^\gamma = M^\gamma$ and $code = \emptyset$ if $Q^\gamma \neq M^\gamma$.

$\mathcal{D}_{\mathrm{LC}}^{\mathrm{Cmp}}$ completes the recognition of a subtree dominated by a node M^γ if this node has not right adjunction mandatory and $code = \emptyset$ or M^γ is a right adjunction node and $code = \{R\}$:

$$\mathcal{D}_{\mathrm{LC}}^{\mathrm{Cmp}} = \frac{\begin{array}{c}[M^\gamma \to \omega \bullet, j, k, code]\\ [N^\gamma \to \delta \bullet M^\gamma \nu, i, j, code']\end{array}}{[N^\gamma \to \delta M^\gamma \bullet \nu, i, k, code']}$$

When a left adjunction node M^γ is predicted, we must trigger the recognition of every left auxiliary tree β that may be adjoined on this node ($\beta \in \mathrm{ladj}(M^\gamma)$). If $\top >_\ell^* O^\beta$ we apply again a LC filter and obtain:

$$\mathcal{D}_{\mathrm{LC}}^{\mathrm{LA_t}} = \frac{\begin{array}{c}[N^\gamma \to \delta \bullet M^\gamma \nu, i, j, code]\\ [a, j, j+1]\end{array}}{[O^\beta \to P^\beta \bullet \omega, j, j+1, \emptyset]} \quad label(P^\beta) = a$$

$$\mathcal{D}_{\mathrm{LC}}^{\mathrm{LA_\varepsilon}} = \frac{[N^\gamma \to \delta \bullet M^\gamma \nu, i, j, code]}{[O^\beta \to P^\beta \bullet \omega, j, j, \emptyset]} \quad label(P^\beta) = \varepsilon$$

$$\mathcal{D}_{\mathrm{LC}}^{\mathrm{LA_{pre}}} = \frac{[N^\gamma \to \delta \bullet M^\gamma \nu, i, j, code]}{[O^\beta \to \bullet P^\beta \omega, j, j, \emptyset]} \quad \exists \beta' \in \mathrm{ladj}(P^\beta) \text{ or } \exists \alpha \in subst(P^\beta)$$

When a left auxiliary tree β that may be adjoined on a node M^γ is exhausted ($\beta \in \mathrm{ladj}(M^\gamma)$), the recognition of the excised subtree must be started. If $M^\gamma >_\ell^* O^\gamma$ we can apply LC filter, but in order to insure the accurate value of $code$, we must add a condition defined by $code = \emptyset$ if $M^\gamma \neq O^\gamma$ and $code = \{L\}$ if $M^\gamma = O^\gamma$:

$$\mathcal{D}_{\mathrm{LC}}^{\mathrm{LF_t}} = \frac{\begin{array}{c}[a, k, k+1]\\ [\top \to \mathbf{R}^\beta \bullet, j, k, \emptyset]\\ [N^\gamma \to \delta \bullet M^\gamma \nu, i, j, code']\end{array}}{[O^\gamma \to P^\gamma \bullet \omega, k, k+1, code]} \quad label(P^\gamma) = a$$

$$\mathcal{D}_{\mathrm{LC}}^{\mathrm{LF_\varepsilon}} = \frac{\begin{array}{c}[\top \to \mathbf{R}^\beta \bullet, j, k, \emptyset]\\ [N^\gamma \to \delta \bullet M^\gamma \nu, i, j, code']\end{array}}{[O^\gamma \to P^\gamma \bullet \omega, k, k, code]} \quad label(P^\gamma) = \varepsilon$$

$$\mathcal{D}_{\mathrm{LC}}^{\mathrm{LF_{pre}}} = \frac{\begin{array}{c}[\top \to \mathbf{R}^\beta \bullet, j, k, \emptyset]\\ [N^\gamma \to \delta \bullet M^\gamma \nu, i, j, code']\end{array}}{[O^\gamma \to \bullet P^\gamma \omega, k, k, code]} \quad \exists \beta \in \mathrm{ladj}(P^\gamma) \text{ or } \exists \alpha \in subst(P^\gamma)$$

$$\mathcal{D}_{\mathrm{LC}}^{\mathrm{LF_{foot}}} = \frac{\begin{array}{c}[\top \to \mathbf{R}^\beta \bullet, j, k, \emptyset]\\ [N^\gamma \to \delta \bullet M^\gamma \nu, i, j, code']\end{array}}{[\mathbf{F}^\gamma \to \bot \bullet, k, k, \emptyset]} \quad \gamma \in A_L$$

$\mathcal{D}_{\mathrm{LC}}^{\mathrm{LACmp}}$ completes a left adjunction:

$$\mathcal{D}_{\mathrm{LC}}^{\mathrm{LACmp}} = \frac{\begin{array}{c}[\top \to \mathbf{R}^\beta \bullet, j, k, \emptyset]\\ [M^\gamma \to \omega \bullet, k, l, code]\\ [N^\gamma \to \delta \bullet M^\gamma \nu, i, j, code']\end{array}}{[N^\gamma \to \delta M^\gamma \bullet \nu, i, l, code']} \quad \beta \in \mathrm{ladj}(M^\gamma), L \in code$$

$\mathcal{D}_{\mathrm{LC}}^{\mathrm{RA_{foot}}}$ go down on an right auxiliary tree up to the node $\bot$:

$$\mathcal{D}_{\mathrm{LC}}^{\mathrm{RA_{foot}}} = \frac{[M^\gamma \to \nu \bullet, k, l, code]}{[\mathbf{F}^\beta \to \bot \bullet, l, l, \emptyset]} \quad \beta \in \mathrm{radj}(M^\gamma), R \notin code$$

When the recognition reaches a substitution node M^γ ($\alpha \in subst(M^\gamma)$) we apply LC filter to the prediction of the initial tree α and obtain:

$$\mathcal{D}_{\mathrm{LC}}^{\mathrm{LS_t}} = \frac{\begin{array}{c}[N^\gamma \to \delta \bullet M^\gamma \nu, i, j, code]\\ [a, j, j+1]\end{array}}{[O^\alpha \to P^\alpha \bullet \omega, j, j+1, \emptyset]} \quad label(P^\alpha) = a$$

$$\mathcal{D}_{\mathrm{LC}}^{\mathrm{LS_\varepsilon}} = \frac{[N^\gamma \to \delta \bullet M^\gamma \nu, i, j, code]}{[O^\alpha \to P^\alpha \bullet \omega, j, j, \emptyset]} \quad label(P^\alpha) = \varepsilon$$

$$\mathcal{D}_{\mathrm{LC}}^{\mathrm{LS_{pre}}} = \frac{[N^\gamma \to \delta \bullet M^\gamma \nu, i, j, code]}{[O^\alpha \to \bullet P^\alpha \omega, j, j, \emptyset]} \quad \exists \beta \in \mathrm{ladj}(P^\alpha) \text{ or } \exists \alpha' \in subst(P^\alpha)$$

The set of final items is defined by:

$$\mathcal{F}_{\mathrm{LC}} = \{[\top \to \mathbf{R}^\alpha \bullet, 0, n, \emptyset] \mid \alpha \in I, label(\mathbf{R}^\alpha) = S\}$$

5   Experimental Results

The time complexity of the algorithm with respect to the length n of the input string is $O(n^3)$ for both parsers (look up details about the calculation of the complexity in [5]). The improvement in the performance of Left Corner parsers comes from the reduction in the size of the chart (the set of deduced items). It is clear that this reduction depends on the grammar and the input string considered. We have made a preliminary study where we have tested and compared the behavior of the LC parser and the Earley-like parser explained before.

We have incorporated both parsers into a naive implementation in Prolog of the deductive parsing machine presented in [8]. We have taken a subset of elementary tree of the XTAG grammar [10] that cover a variety of English constructions: relative clauses, auxiliary verbs, unbounded dependencies, extraction, etc. In order to eliminate the time spent by unification, we have not considered the feature structures of elementary trees. Instead, we have simulated the features using local constraints. Every sentence has been parsed without previous filtering of elementary trees. Briefly, we can remark that LC parser shows on average a time reduction of 11% and a chart size reduction of 50%.

6   Conclusion

We have defined two new parsers for TIGs, an Earley-like parser and a Left Corner parser, both of them are extensions of parsers for Context Free Grammars. The LC parser can be view as a filter on an Earley-like parser for TIGs, where the number of predictions is reduced due to the generalized left corner relation that we have established on the nodes of elementary trees. The worst-case complexity with respect to space and time is the standard one for TIG parsing, but preliminary experiments have shown a better performance than classical Earley-like parsers for TIGs.

References

1. Alonso, M.A., Cabrero, D., de la Clergerie, E., Vilares, M.: Tabular algorithms for TAG parsing. In Proc. of EACL'99 (1999) 150–157
2. Diaz, V., Carrillo, V., Alonso, M.A.: A left corner parser for tree adjoining grammars. In Proc. of TAG+6 (2002) 90–95
3. Diaz, V., Carrillo, V., Toro, M.: A review of Earley-based parser for TIG. Lecture Notes in Artificial Intelligence. Subseries of LNCS **1415** (1998) 732–738
4. Joshi, A.K., Schabes, Y.: Tree-adjoining grammars. Handbook of Formal Languages **3** (1997) 69–123
5. Nederhof, M.: The computational complexity of the correct-prefix property for TAGs. Computational Linguistics **25(3)** (1999) 345–360
6. Schabes, Y., Waters, R.C.: Tree insertion grammar: A cubic-time parsable formalism that lexicalizes context-free grammar without changing the trees produced. Computational Linguistics **21(4)** (1995) 479–513

7. Schabes, Y., Waters, R.C.: Stochastic lexicalized tree-insertion grammar. Recent Advances in Parsing Technology (1996) 281–294
8. Shieber, S.M., Schabes, Y., Pereira, F.C.N.: Principles and implementation of deductive parsing. Journal of Logic Programming **24(1–2)** (1995) 3–36
9. Sikkel, K.: Parsing Schemata — A Framework for Specification and Analysis of Parsing Algorithms (1997)
10. XTAG Research Group: A Lexicalized Tree Adjoining Grammar for English. Technical Report IRCS-01-03, University of Pennsylvania, USA (2001)

Bulgarian Noun – Definite Article in DATR

Velislava Stoykova

Institute of the Bulgarian Language, Bulgarian Academy of Sciences
52, Shipchensky proh. str., bl. 17, 1113 Sofia, Bulgaria
vili1@bas.bg

Abstract. The paper is focused on a DATR-theory of Bulgarian noun inflectional morphology. It takes into account the morphosyntactic nature of the grammar feature of definiteness in Bulgarian, and argues for a specific computational approach of interpretation. The constructed semantic network is explained in details, supported by a particular linguistic motivation. The grammar feature of gender is accepted as a starting point of the encoding, and a possible query to be evaluated is given as a result.

Keywords: DATR formal language for lexical knowledge presentation, Bulgarian definite article, computational morphology, definiteness.

1   Introduction

The standard Bulgarian language does not use cases for syntactic representation, and at the same time, it has very rich inflectional system - both for word-formation and for inflectional morphology [7]. Also, it uses prepositions and a base noun form instead of a case declination, which is a result of its development over the centuries. Another important grammar feature of Bulgarian, in which it differs with all the Slavic languages, is the feature of a definite article.

Concerning its syntax, Bulgarian language is considered to be a language using relatively free word order [7]. Practically, the subject can take every syntactic position in the sentence (including the last one) and the definite article is the only marker of it. Thus, modeling inflectional morphology of the definite article is a most important stage of a successful part-of-speech parsing of Bulgarian.

2   The Definite Article – A Grammar Feature Standing between the Morphology and the Syntax

The syntactic function of definiteness in Bulgarian is expressed by a formal morphological marker which is an ending morpheme [8]. It differs with respect to gender, however, for the masculine gender a two types of definite morpheme exist – to determine a full and a partly defined entity, which have two phonetic variants, respectively. For the feminine and for the neuter gender only definite morphemes exist, respectively. For the plural, two definite morphemes are used depending on the ending vocal of the main plural form.

D. Scott (Ed.): AIMSA 2002, LNAI 2443, pp. 152–161, 2002.

The following part-of-speech in Bulgarian take a definite article [8]: nouns, adjectives, numerals (both cardinals and ordinals), possessive pronouns, and reflexive-possessive pronoun.

With respect to its semantics, the definite article can assign an individual, a quantity or a part-of-whole definiteness, and it has a generic use as well. The formal morphological marker (definite article) is one and the same for all part-of-speech but it has different forms to account for the feature of number and gender. Therefore, our task is to model it using specific approaches to computational morphology, and at the same time, the proposed analysis should be interpreted syntactically.

Following these preliminary requirements, we are going to present the starting point of our morphological interpretation.

3   Some Approaches to Computational Morphology and Suitable Formal Models

The standard computational approach to both word-formation and inflectional morphology is to represent words as a rule-based concatenation of morphemes, and the main task is to construct relevant rules for their combinations. However, different approaches exist depending on whether the stem or the concatenating morpheme stays stable or varies. With respect to the number and the types of morphemes, the different theories offer different approaches depending on the variations of either stems or suffixes as follows:

(i)   conjugational solution offers an invariant stem and variant suffixes;
(ii) variant stem solution offers variant stems and invariant suffix.

Both these approaches are suitable for languages, which use inflection rather rarely to express syntactic structures, whereas for those using rich inflection some cases where phonological alternations appear both in stem and in concatenating morpheme a "mixed" approach is used to account for the complexity. We considered such approach as a most appropriate for our task. Thus, to reduce the size of our morphological lexicon, to make it more computationally tractable, and to account for the specific phonetic alternations, we are considering both stems and suffixes as invariable.

With respect to the existing formal models, we have found the HPSG as not a suitable because of the fact, that in its framework the lexicon is generated on the fly, and thus it limits us to the use of lexical rules which produce only one type of inflecting forms.

We considered the DATR language for lexical knowledge presentation as being suitable formal framework for modeling inflectional morphology of Bulgarian definite article.

4   The DATR Language

The DATR language is a non-monotonic language for defining the inheritance networks through path/value equations [6]. It has both an explicit declarative semantics and an explicit theory of inference allowing efficient implementation, and at the same time, it has the necessary expressive power to encode the lexical entries presupposed by the work in the unification grammar tradition [3,4,5].

In DATR, information is organized as a network of nodes, where a node is a collection of related information. Each node has associated with it a set of equations that define partial functions from paths to values where paths and values are both sequences of atoms. Atoms in paths are sometimes referred to as attributes.

DATR is functional, it defines a mapping which assigns unique values to node attribute-path pair, and the recovery of this values is deterministic. It can account for such language phenomena like regularity, irregularity, and subregularity, and allows the use of deterministic parsing. The DATR language has a lot of implementations, however, our application was made by using QDATR 2.0 (consult URL http://www.cogs.susx.ac.uk/lab/nlp/datr/datrnode49.html for a related file bul_det.dtr). This PROLOG encoding uses Sussex DATR notation [9].

DATR allows construction of various types of language models (language theories), however, our model is presented as a rule-based formal grammar and a lexical database. The particular query to be evaluated is a related inflecting word form, and the implementation allows to process words in Cirillic alphabet.

5   DATR Account of Bulgarian Noun Inflectional Morphology – The Overall Architecture

We are not committed to a particular morphological theory, and we accept a rather traditional view of the paradigm as an underlying basic idea of our analysis.

Concerning word, we shall follow an old and well-known lexicographic notion of the lexeme. The structure we use to present a lexeme remains very much that of a dictionary's lexical entry, however, we use different roots to account for the particular morphophonological phenomena instead of presenting different meanings of the word. So, the difference is semantic rather than syntactic.

Also, we consider morphemes as a semantic realization of a particular morphosyntactic phenomenon (note part (i) of the following description, which represents inflecting morphemes for definite article, and part (ii) representing plural morphemes).

In general, the approach we use to account for Bulgarian noun inflection is closely related and is indebted to those of Cahill&Gazdar [1] developed for German noun inflection, except their account of morphophonology.

Our model represents an inheritance network consisting of various nodes which allows us to account for all related inflecting forms within the framework of one grammar theory. Using this strategy, we propose the following architecture (see Fig. 1.):

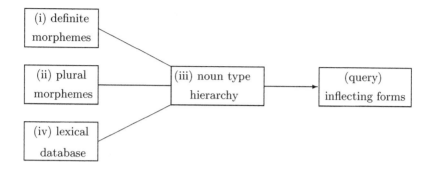

Fig. 1. The overall architecture of Bulgarian noun inflection.

(i)   all definite inflecting morphemes for all forms of definite article attached to node DET, and given by their values through the paths <masc>, <masc_1>, <femn>, <neut>, and <plur>.

(ii)   12 inflecting morphemes for generating plural forms (they origin from Old Bulgarian, and represent old case morphemes for the different declinational types) defined at node Suff.

(iii) the inflectional types are defined as a rule-based concatenation of morphemes at the related nodes.

(iv)   The words, themselves, are given as a lexical database attached to their inflectional nodes, respectively. They are defined by giving information for the lexical entries through paths <root> [2] and <root plur>, so to account for the different phonological alternations. It is important to note that our interpretation of Bulgarian nominal inflection is made for text processing, not for speech processing.

5.1   DATR Account of Bulgarian Noun Inflectional Morphology – The Inheritance Hierarchy

The Bulgarian noun, as it is described traditionally [7,8], has three grammar features: gender, number, and definiteness. Among them only number and definiteness are inflectional, whereas gender is not an inflectional one but is constant for every noun. Thus, we can consider the gender as a specific trigger in our formal interpretation. It is assigned by the path <gender>, which takes the following values: masc_1, masc, femn, and neut. With respect to its gender, Bulgarian nouns are divided into three groups: (1) of masculine gender (assigned by masc_1 and masc); (2) of feminine gender (assigned by femn); (3) of neuter gender (assigned by neut). Within these groups, there are different types of nouns depending of their suffix for forming plural, so that, the next triggering factor is the feature of number, assigned by path `<sing>` – for singular, and `<plur>` – for plural. The Bulgarian noun type hierarchy is presented in Fig. 2.

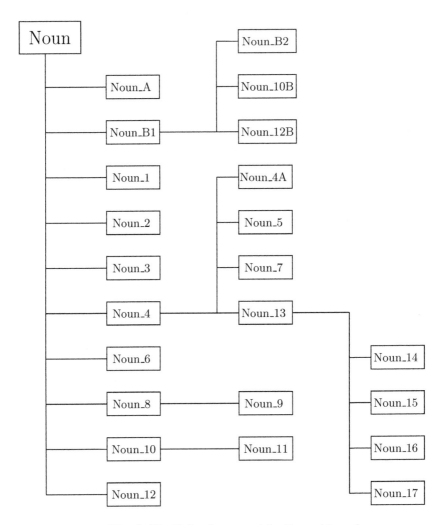

Fig. 2. The Bulgarian noun inheritance hierarchy.

With respect to the above assumptions, we are starting our encoding with the definition of node DET consisted of inflecting morphemes for articles as follows:[1]

```
DET:     <sing undef>   ==
         <sing def_2 masc> == _ja
```

---

[1] Here and elsewhere in the description we use Latin alphabet to present morphemes, instead of Cirillic used normally. Because of the mismatching between both, some of the typically Bulgarian phonological alternations are assigned by two letters, whereas in Cirillic alphabet they are marked by one.

```
<sing def_2 masc_1> == _a
<sing def_1 masc>   == _jat
<sing def_1 masc _1> == _ut
<sing def_1 femn> == _ta
<sing def_1 neut> == _to
<plur undef>   ==
<plur def_1> == _te.
```

Also, we define node Suff as consisting of 12 endings for plural.

```
Suff:   <suff_11> == _i
        <suff_111> == _ovci
        <suff_12> == _e
        <suff_121> == _ove
        <suff_122> == _eve
        <suff_123> == _ovce
        <suff_21> == _a
        <suff_22> == _ja
        <suff_211> == _ishta
        <suff_212> == _ta
        <suff_213> == _ena
        <suff_214> == _esa.
```

Every node in our network, which starts with Noun... represents a noun inflectional type. It consists of grammar rules for generating a related inflecting form using the information given through paths <root> and <root plur> for the stem, and <masc>, <masc_1>, <femn>, <neut>, and <plur> for the particular inflecting morpheme. The different inflectional types were defined both according to their lexical semantic constraints to generate an inflecting form (like nouns of type pluralia or singularia tantum), and according to their grammar feature constraints (like gender or related plural form morphemes).

The node Noun is a basic in our semantic network, and consists of grammar rules generating a related inflecting forms for number and definiteness. It, basically, describes nouns of masculine gender forming their plural forms in -i, full definite form in -ut, and short definite form in -a.

```
Noun:   <suff> == suff_11
        <gender> == masc_1
        <> == <stem> DET:<Idem "<gender>">
        <stem sing> == "<root sing>"
        <stem plur> == "<root plur>" Suff:<"<suff>">.
```

Node Noun_A describes nouns, so-called, pluralia tantum assigned to masculine gender, ending in -i, and forming their definite plural form using -te.

```
Noun_A:  <> == Noun
         <sing> == "<plur>"
         <sing def_2> == "<plur def_1>".
```

Node Noun_B1 defines rules for inflectional morphology of nouns, which are of type singularia tantum, forming their full definite form using -ut, and short definite form with -a.

```
Noun_B1: <> == Noun
        <plur> == "<sing>"
        <plur def_2> == Noun.
```

Node Noun_B2 describes group of nouns singularia tantum of masculine gender, ending in -a, forming their full definite form using -jat, and short definite form using -ja.

```
Noun_B2: <> == Noun_B1
        <gender> == masc.
```

Node Noun_1 describes nouns, which are of masculine gender forming their plural form in -e, full definite form in -ut, short definite form in -a, and definite plural form in -te.

```
Noun_1: <> == Noun
        <suff> == suff_12.
```

Node Noun_2 describes a class of nouns, which are of masculine gender forming plural in -ove, full definite form in -ut, short definite form in -a, and definite plural form in -te.

```
Noun_2: <> == Noun
        <suff> == suff_121.
```

Node Noun_3 defines group of nouns of masculine gender forming plural in -eve, full definite form in -jat, short definite form in -ja, and definite plural form in -te.

```
Noun_3: <> == Noun
        <gender> == masc
        <suff> == suff_122.
```

Node Noun_4 describes nouns of masculine gender forming their plural form in -a, full definite form in -ut, short definite form in -a, and definite plural form in -ta.

```
Noun_4: <> == Noun
        <plur def_1> == <stem plur> DET:<sing def_1 femn>
        <suff> == suff_21.
```

Node Noun_4A defines group of nouns pluralia tantum assigned to masculine gender ending in -a, and forming their (plural) definite form in -ta.

```
Noun_4A: <> == Noun_4
         <sing> == Noun_A.
```

Node Noun_5 defines nouns of masculine gender having their plural form in -ja, full definite form in -ut, short definite form in -a, and definite plural form in -ta.

```
Noun_5: <> == Noun_4
        <suff> == suff_22.
```

Node Noun_6 describes group of nouns of masculine gender, forming their plural form in -i, full definite form in -jat, short definite form in -ja, and definite plural form in -te.

```
Noun_6: <> == Noun
        <gender> == masc.
```

Node Noun_7 defines nouns of masculine gender forming their plural form in -ishta, full definite form in -jat, short definite form in -ja, and plural definite form in -ta.

```
Noun_7: <> == Noun_4
        <gender> == masc
        <suff> == suff_211.
```

Node Noun_8 describes group of nouns of masculine gender forming their plural form in -i, definite form in -ta, and plural definite form in -te.

```
Noun_8: <> == Noun
        <sing def_1> == "<stem sing>" DET:<sing def_1 femn>
        <sing def_2> == "<sing def_1>".
```

Node Noun_9 defines nouns of masculine gender forming their plural form in -ovci, definite form in -to, and definite plural form in -te.

```
Noun_9: <> == Noun_8
        <sing def_1> == "<stem sing>" DET:<sing def_1 neut>
        <suff> == suff_111.
```

Node Noun_10 describes group of nouns of feminine gender forming plural form in -i, definite form in -ta, and plural definite form in -te.

```
Noun_10: <> == Noun
         <gender> == femn.
```

Node Noun_10B defines nouns singularia tantum of feminine gender forming definite form in -ta.

```
Noun_10B: <> == Noun_B1
          <gender> == femn.
```

Node Noun_11 describes nouns of feminine gender forming their plural form in -e, definite form in -ta, and plural definite form in -te.

```
Noun_11: <> == Noun_10
         <suff> == suff_12.
```

Node Noun_12 defines group of nouns of neuter gender forming their plural form in -i, definite form in -to, and plural definite form in -te.

```
Noun_12: <> == Noun
         <gender> == neut.
```

Node Noun_12B describes nouns singularia tantum of neuter gender forming their definite form in -to.

```
Noun_12B: <> == Noun_B1
          <gender> == neut.
```

Node Noun_13 defines group of nouns of neuter gender forming their plural form in -a, and (plural) definite form in -ta.

```
Noun_13: <> == Noun_4
         <gender> == neut.
```

Node Noun_14 describes nouns of neuter gender forming their plural form in -ja, definite form in -to, and plural definite form in -ta.

```
Noun_14:  <> == Noun_13
          <suff> == suff_22.
```

Node Noun_15 defines group of nouns of neuter gender forming their plural form
in -ta, definite form in -to, and plural definite form in -ta.

```
Noun_15:  <> == Noun_13
          <suff> == suff_212.
```

Node Noun_16 describes group of nouns of neuter gender forming their plural
form in -ena, definite form in -to, and plural definite form in -ta.

```
Noun_16:  <> == Noun_13
          <suff> == suff_213.
```

Node Noun_17 defines nouns of neuter gender forming their plural form in -esa,
definite form in -to, and plural definite form in -ta.

```
Noun_17:  <> == Noun_13
          <suff> == suff_214.
```

5.2   Given Knowledge and Evaluating Query

The above formal description forms a DATR-theory which describes inflectional
morphology of Bulgarian noun. The lexemes are given as different nodes. Every-
one is attached to a related inflectional type, and consists of lexical information
given by the paths <root>, and <root plur>, so to account for the different
phonological alternations. An example lexeme for bulgarian word for *newspaper*
(vestnik), which uses inflectional rules defined at node Noun is as follows:

```
Vestnik:  <> == Noun
          <root> == vestnik
          <root plur> == vestnic.
```

Following the consequence of the given axioms, we can generate the queries
which are all possible inflecting forms by asking the system using following paths:
<gender> – to evaluate for the gender, it takes one and the same value for all gen-
erated inflecting forms; <sing undef> – to evaluate for the singular uninflecting
form; <plur undef> – to evaluate for the plural uninflecting form; <sing def_1>
and <sing def_2> – to evaluate for the definite singular form; <plur def_1> –
to evaluate for the definite plural form. For the example word *vestnik* the queries
are:

```
Vestnik: <gender> == masc_1.
Vestnik: <sing undef> == vestnik.
Vestnik: <plur undef> == vestnic_i.
Vestnik: <sing def_1> == vestnik_ut.
Vestnik: <sing def_2> == vestnik_a.
Vestnik: <plur def_1> == vestnic_i_te.
```

6   Conclusions and Future Work

The proposed network is linguistically motivated, and it uses the feature of gender and of number for triggering a given morphological information to evaluate inflecting forms. In general, the architecture of the model is based on our belief that the best strategy to interpret inflectional morphology is to start with a non-inflectional grammar feature (like gender, for example), and to use it as a trigger to change different values of the inflecting morphemes directing in that way the process of morphemes concatenation. An inflectional grammar feature is possible to be used as well, however, the structure becomes more complicated, and the application is limited. For our model, the grammar feature of number has been used as a trigger.

The proposed inheritance hierarchy is based only on a morphological account of the grammar feature of definiteness in Bulgarian. An account from the point of view of the syntax is possible as well. However, it might be given either in the DATR framework or as a separate formal semantic interpretation.

We are planning to expand our DATR application of definite article for all part-of-speech, and to define the definiteness in Bulgarian within the framework of one common DATR theory.

References

1. Cahill, L. and Gazdar, G. (1999a). German noun inflection. *Journal of Linguistics* 35.1, 1-42.
2. Cahill, L. and Gazdar, G. (1999b). The Polylex architecture: multilingual lexicons for related languages. *Traitment automatique des langues*, vol. 40.1.
3. Evans, R. and Gazdar, G. (1989a). Inference in DATR. *Fourth Conference of the European Chapter of the Association for Computational Linguistics*, 66-71.
4. Evans, R. and Gazdar, G. (1989b). The semantics of DATR. In Anthony G. Cohn ed. *Proceedings of the Seventh Conference of the Society for the Study of Artificial Intelligence and Simulation of Behaviour*. London: Pitman/Morgan Kaufmann, 79-87.
5. Evans, R. and Gazdar, G. (1990.) The DATR papers. *CSRP 139, vol. 1, Research Report*, University of Sussex, Brighton.
6. Evans, R., and Gazdar, G. (1996.) DATR: A language for lexical knowledge representation. *Computational Linguistics* 22.2, 167-216.
7. Gramatika na suvremennia bulgarski knizoven ezik, tom. 2, Morphologia. 1983.
8. Stojanov, S. (1959). Emploi et signification de l'article defini dans la langue Bulgare litteraire. I parte - Les noun (substantifs). *Annuaire de l'Universite de Sofia, Faculte philologique*, LIII, 2, 1-137.
9. The DATR Web Pages at Sussex URL
   http://www.cogs.susx.ac.uk/lab/nlp/datr/datrnode49.html

A Methodology to Solve Optimisation Problems with MAS Application to the Graph Colouring Problem

Gaële Simon, Marianne Flouret, and Bruno Mermet

LIH, Université du Havre, 76058 Le Havre Cedex, France
{Gaele.Simon, Marianne.Flouret, Bruno.Mermet}@univ-lehavre.fr

Abstract. Developing multi-agent systems may be a rather difficult task. Having confidence in the result is still more difficult. In this article, we describe a methodology that helps in this task. This methodology is dedicated to global optimization problems that can be solved combining local constraints. We developed CASE tools to support this methodology which are also presented. Finally, we show how this methodology has been successfully used to develop a multi-agent system for the graph colouring problem.

Keywords: multi-agent system, methodology, graph colouring

1 Introduction

Many methods already exist to build multi-agent systems (MAS) [12,15]. Theses methods are composed of a set of models, but there is often a lack of methodology to help to transform real system specifications into a modelization provided by the method. [18,1]. In this paper, we introduce the bases of a methodology associated to a method to develop multi-agent systems that are dedicated to optimization problems. The first part of the article presents essentially the *methodology*. In the second part, we introduce a *system* made of java classes we developed to help us to write agents derived from our methodology. Finally, in the third part, we present an *application* of our methodology to a particular problem : the graph colouring problem. Using the methodology and the system presented before, we developed a MAS for the graph colouring problem.

2 Methodology

The goal of our research is to have a method, a methodology and also tools to help the analysis and design of distributed problem solving by MAS.

An important aspect of our methodology is that :

- at *any time*, the system can be stopped ;
- as time goes by, the solution proposed by our system gets better and better.

As presented in the sequel, the methodology is based on a top-down approach which guaranty the progress of our system towards a *satisfying* solution.

D. Scott (Ed.): AIMSA 2002, LNAI 2443, pp. 162–172, 2002.
© Springer-Verlag Berlin Heidelberg 2002

2.1   Usage Conditions

The methodology defined here must be used to solve global problems which can be specified by a set of local constraints (LC). A more restrictive usage condition is that this methodology is dedicated to optimisation problems for which a trivial (but bad) solution exists.

Of course, for non NP-hard and non distributed problems for which a sequential algorithm is known, using agents (and so our methodology) is rarely a good solution because communications and synchronisations introduced by MAS make the program less efficient [17].

An example of a target problem for our methodology is the graph colouring problem which consists in colouring a graph with a minimal number of colours in such a way that two connected nodes do not have the same colour. This application is presented in section 4.

2.2   The Methodology

Global variant. The first thing to do is to define a variant : a notion often used to prove termination of algorithms. A variant is a variable defined on a totally ordered structure that must decrease at each iteration and that has a lower bound. These two properties imply the termination of the iterations.

Local decomposition. The second step is perhaps the hardest one : the global problem has to be expressed in terms of local sub-problems. This consists in dividing the solution of the problem into several parts. These parts are not necessarily disjunctive. Each part is associated to a local sub-problem. The resolution of each of these sub-problems must help to solve the global problem. The ideal case is a sub-problem whose resolution is a necessary condition for solving the global problem. However, this is not always the case. An other possibility is a sub-problem whose resolution makes the global variant decrease.

Agentification. Once the global problem has been decomposed, we still do not have agents. Of course, a first idea could be to assign each local problem to an agent, but this is not always possible for the following reason.

To agentify a problem, two types of constraints must be considered :

– each sub-problem must be assigned to an agent ;
– each property (piece of data) must be assigned to an agent.

Each agent perceives only a local part of the environment. Moreover, an agent being autonomous, no other agent can modify directly its properties. These two constraints are called *the locality principle*. So, if the resolution of two sub-problems needs to modify the same property, assigning two problems to two different agents is impossible. A first solution could be to assign properties to the environment. This is an easy solution, but this makes the environment a central resource for our MAS, limiting the benefit of the distribution.

A better solution is to change the structure of the local-problems so that the modification of a property occurs only in the resolution of one sub-problem. So, each property modification is controlled by one and only one agent. Other agents that need to get the value of this property must have the agent owning the property in their accointance set and can know its value by message passing. Sub-problems resulting from this restructuring are called Property Oriented Sub-Problems (POSP) in the sequel.

This step is necessary (it provides the agents and the accointance relations of the MAS) and not so difficult to realize as it is shown in this article for the graph-colouring problem.

Agents behaviour. We consider the agents as reactive and social ones, that is they can react to changes of their environment and communicate with other agents.

General behaviour. Each POSP is assigned to an agent. So, the general behaviour of each agent is very simple :

- if its problem is solved, it does nothing (it could also help other agents). The agent is *satisfied* ;
- otherwise, it tries to find a solution to its problem.

Solving a problem. For the global problem, we introduced a variant. We have to do the same for each POSP in such a way that each time a local variant decrease, the global variant does not increase.

Each POSP can be divided into sub-goals whose resolution makes the local variant decrease. Then, an unsatisfied agent chooses a sub-goal and must solve it.

When a sub-goal has to be solved, there are two cases :

- either it can be solved by the agent : the agent can then choose a new goal ;
- or the agent cannot solve it.

There are two reasons making a subgoal unable to be reached :

- either there is a blocking situation : an other agent prevent the acting agent to apply one of its stategies ;
- or the agent doesn't know what to do to solve the subgoal in the given situation.

In the second case, the agent chooses an other goal or waits for a modification of the situation. In the first case, the agent attacks the obstructing agent. This behaviour follows the eco-agent's one [7]. The attack mecanism is simulated by sending an agression message. An agent under attack has to flee so that the blocking situation disappears, but preserving the local constraints LC. Note that the fleeing behaviour can increase the local variant. If the agent cannot flee, it ignores the attack.

In order to help us specifying agents behaviours, we used the formalism of automata with multiplicities [2]. This formalism can also be used to specify

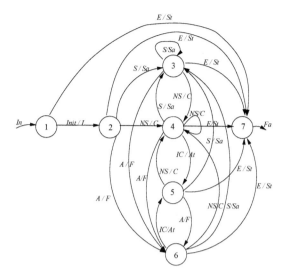

Fig. 1. Eco-agent : general behaviour

behaviours of other kinds of agents [13]. Thus, we defined the general behaviour of an eco-agent by the automaton shown in figure 1.

$\Sigma = \{Init, S, NS, A, IC, E\}$ is the set of the following perceptions :

$Init$: Synchronization signal,

S :   goal is satisfied,

NS :   goal is unsatisfied,

A :   attacked by an other agent,

IC :   main action impossible,

E :   stop signal.

The set of elementary actions (behaviour primitives), performed when a state is reached, is defined by {In,L,C,Sa,At,St,F,Fa} with

In :   initialization of agent parameters,

L :   lauching agent functionalities,

C :   main action itself,

Sa :   satisfied message,

At :   agression,

St :   stop process,

F :   flee,

Fa :   final message.

To help us developing MAS whose agents are specified by automata with multiplicities, we developed Java classes that are described in the next section.

3   System : CASE Tools Dedicated to Our Agents

3.1   Presentation of the System

In order to help developers in coding agents specified by automata with multiplicities, Java classes have been developed by our team. These classes give to the programmer an upper level to the MAS platform Madkit on which they rely [14]. These classes can however be easily adapted to other contexts because their concepts are general.

The Madkit plateform is based on a multi-agent model (agent, group, role) proposed in the Aalaadin method [8].

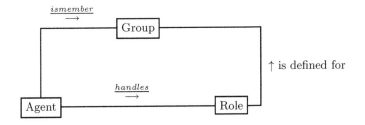

Fig. 2. AALAADIN concepts

In this model, an agent is defined as an autonomous and communicating entity that can play a given number of roles in one or more groups. A group is a set of agents. A semantic is given to groups at the design step, depending of the application. Roles are functionnalities (or services) performed by the agents in a given group. There is no other constraint in this model. Moreover, the inner structure of each agent is unspecified.

Madkit provides an **Agent** class based on three main methods :
- **activate** : describes actions to perfom when the agent is initialized ;
- **live** : specifies the general behaviour of the agent ;
- **end** : lists actions to be executed when the agent dies.

To develop its application, the developer must create its own classes extending the **Agent** class. The three methods described above must be written using primitives provided by Madkit, helping to manage groups, roles, communications, etc.

The classes we developed, and we present in this section, specialize the **Agent** class of Madkit to help to describe the agent's behaviour. According to the first part of this article, here are the concepts our system helps to manage :
- description of the general behaviour of the agent by an automaton with multiplicities ;
- description of the set of perceptions of the agent;
- description of actions associated to perceptions ;
- description of the behaviour of the agent according to its inner state.

These four concepts are available thanks to two main classes : the **Automate** and **AgentAuto** classes.

The *Automate* (automaton) class. The goal of this class is to provide functionnalities to built and use automata with multiplicities. In this class, each state is caracterized by :

- a number n ;
- a method $etat_n$ describing the behaviour of this agent in state n. This method must be written in the class representing the agent (presented below).

Following the definition given in [2], each transition of the automaton is specified by a 4-tuple (initial state, final state, perception, action). Initial and final states are represented by their number n. The *perception* is identified by a method that is executed to determine wether the perception is valid or not. If it is valid, the transition may be fired. The *action* is identified by a method that is executed if the corresponding transition is activated. Both methods representing the perception and the action must be defined in the class describing the agent.

The Automaton class provides to the user the two following main methods :

- *setTransition* : a method to add a transition to the automaton. The four parameters correspond to the four characteristics of a transition ;
- *transiter* : this method determines valid transitions in the current state by dynamic invocation of perception methods. If many perceptions are valid, a method *choix_perception* (choose perception), defined in the class associated to the agent, is executed to determine the transition to fire. The associated action is executed (by dynamic invocation). Finally, the method associated to the final state is executed.

AgentAuto **class.** This class inheritates from the *Agent* class of Madkit. It allows to implement an agent whose behaviour is described by an automaton with multiplicities. The characteristics of this class are the following :

- definition of the *live* method : the standard algorithm looks like this :

```
current_state = initial_state;
execute the initial_state method
while (current_state != final_state)
        current_state = transiter(current_state);
```

- definition of the *choix_perception* method : this method tells to the *Automate* class which perception must be chosen when several are valid at the same time. A default version, written in the *AgentAuto* class, chooses a perception randomly.

Using classes described above. To define an agent, a developer has to write a class *MyAgent* inheritating from the *AgentAuto* class defining at least the *activate, etat_i, perception and action* methods as shown in the following example.

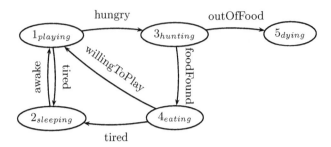

Fig. 3. Behaviour of a simple agent

3.2   A Toy Example

We want to write an agent with the behaviour described in figure 3.

This behaviour can be built on 4 properties :

```
private int food_storage;
private int tiredness;
private boolean hasFood;
private boolean isNoMoreTired;
```

The automaton is defined using the *setTransition* method in the constructor. Here are three examples of methods :

– a method associated to a *state*, the *playing* state :

```
public void etat1() {// I play
    foodStorage-=2;
    tiredness++;
}
```

– a *perception* method, the *tired* perception :

```
public boolean isTired() {return (tireness > 5);}
```

– an action to perform when a state change is performed, the *tiredAction* method :

```
public void tiredAction()
    {System.out.println("I am tired");isNoMoreTired=false;}
```

4   Application to Graph Colouring

4.1   The Graph Colouring Problem

We give in this part the application of the methodology presented before to a graph colouring problem. The *general problem* is to colour the nodes of a graph with a minimal number of colours (*optimisation*) without two neighbour nodes having the same colour (*local constraint*).

The problem of graph colouring being NP-hard, algorithms looking for optimal solutions are numerous [5] but rarely usefull for real-size problems. We can refer to [6,9,10,11] for various methods trying to solve this problem, and more precisely to [3,16] for ants algorithms.

The essential characteristic of our solution is that it starts with a correctly coloured graph but not optimal as far as the number of colours is concerned. For instance, a trivial initial solution is to assign a different colour for each node. As the time goes, our algorithm tries to suppress colours, keeping a correct coloration of the graph, and, at any time, we can stop our algorithm and obtain a correctly coloured graph. Obviously, the more our algorithm will work, the more pertinent the proposed solution will be.

4.2   Some Coloured Graph Properties

For details about graph definitions and properties, it can be refered to [4] for example. Here are given the main ones used in the sequel. We denote $G = (N, E)$ an oriented (resp. non oriented) *graph* with N and E two sets such that elements of E are ordered (resp. unordered) couples $(u, v) \in N^2$, and $N \cap E = \emptyset$. The elements of N are *nodes*, those of E are the *edges*. Two nodes u, v of G are *neighbours* if $(u, v) \in E$. $V(u)$ will denote the set of all neighbours of u.

Let $C(u)$ the colour associated to a node u, and $C(V(u))$ the set of colours of u neighbours. The *k-colouring* of a graph $G = (N, E)$ is the attribution, to each node, of a colour among k such that, for each edge (u, v) of E, $C(u) \neq C(v)$. A graph is *k-colourable* if a *k*-colouring can be applied[1]. The smallest k such that G is *k*-colourable is the *chromatic number* of G and denoted $\chi(G)$. In the sequel, we will consider a *k*-coloured graph.

For this application, we have to define two new specific notions concerning nodes. The *local chromatic number* of a node u is $lcn(u) = max\{|C|, \forall C$ clique of G $/u \in C\}$. The *current chromatic number* of u is $ccn(u) = |\{c(u)\} \cup \{c(v)/v \in V(u)\}|$. Then, a node u *satisfies its lcn* if and only if $lcn(u) = ccn(u)$. The following properties are used to implement our solution.

Theorem 1. *Let $G = (N, E)$ be a graph. For all node $u \in N$, if G is correctly coloured, then $ccn(u) \leq lcn(u)$.*

Theorem 2. *Let $G = (N, E)$ a graph, and let $\chi(G) = n$. For each node $u \in N$, we have $lcn(u) \leq n$.*

Remark 1. Let us notice that, despite these two theorems, even if all the nodes of a graph satisfy their *lcn*, the chromatic number of the graph can not always be reached. There are also some graphs which can not be coloured such that each node satisfies its *lcn*.

---

[1] For $k \geq 3$, decide wether a graph is *k*-colourable or not is NP-hard.

4.3   Application

Global variant. Our goal is to make decrease the number of colours of the nodes of a graph (the chosen global variant), trying to reach the graph chromatic number.

Local decomposition. The previous property is decomposed into subproblems for each node. Each node tries to change the colours of its neighbours in order to make the local variant decrease. This variant corresponds to the node *ccn* whose lower bound is the node *lcn*.

Agentification. The previous decomposition does not follow the locality principle (indeed an agent should modify the colour of another agent). So, the *POSP* of our general problem, is, for a node u, to change its own colour. The new associated local variant is the tuple of the *ccn* of its neighbours. Then, each *POSP* is assigned to an agent called a *node agent*. It can be reached by solving a set of subgoals (decreasing the *ccn* of a given neighbour). Notice that as each node agent has at least one neighbour, its neighbours will make its *ccn* decrease.

Agents Behaviour. When the *POSP* assigned to an agent is not satisfied (that is one of its neighbours has a *ccn* greater than its *lcn*), it has to choose a colour:

- existing in the graph ;
- making the *ccn* of the neighbour n decrease ;
- being different from the colours of its neighbours.

As a node agent can only see (and communicate with) its neighbours, to find a colour verifying the two first items enumerated above, it asks to its neighbour u the colours of its neighbours, which gives a first set $C(V(u))$, the colours set of the neighbours of u.

To verify the third point, the acting agent a first asks to its neighbours their colours and constructs the set $C(V(a))$ of these colours. Then it chooses a colour among the new set $S = C(V(u)) \backslash \{C(V(a)) \cup C(a)\}^2$.

If a node agent u can not change its colour, necessarily, the set $C(V(u))$ is a member of the set $C(V(a))$. In such a case, the node agent u attacks one of its neighbours whose colour is in the set $C(V(u))$. If it is attacked, it flees, trying to take another colour. It chooses a colour among the neighbours' ones of its neighbours, which is not a colour in its neighbours' colours.

Two other agents have to be created for coordination and implementation reasons. The topological agent creates the initial graph, node agents with their characteristics (e.g. list of neighbours, initial colours), and a drawer agent giving a graphic view of the graph updated when colours change.

---

[2] The new colour must be different from the previous one, that is why $C(a)$ is removed from possible colours.

Now we can precise the structure of the automaton with multiplicities which defines the node agents behaviour. It has been given in figure 1 of paragraph 2.2 under its general form. With the notations of figure 1, we associate the IC perception to the impossibility to change its own colour, and the C action to the fact of recolouring itself.

5 Conclusion and Future Work

The last part presented an application of our methodology to a graph colouring problem. It allowed to illustrate that the methodology presented in this paper can be applied to real problems.

Our research now leads in adding to the methodology a fully specified method with formal or semi-formal models (like, for instance, automata with multiplicities presented here) to help designers of MAS.

CASE-Tools will also have to be enriched to support both the methodology and the method.

References

1. F. M. T. Brazier, B. M. Dunin-Keplicz, N. R. Jennings, and J. Treur. DESIRE: Modelling multi-agent systems in a compositional formal framework. *Int Journal of Cooperative Information Systems*, 6(1):67–94, 1997.
2. V. Jay D. Olivier C. Bertelle, M. Flouret and J.-L. Ponty. Automata with multiplicities as behaviour model in multi-agent simulations.
3. F. Comellas. An ant algorithm for the graph colouring problem. http://citeseer.nj.nec.com/112038.html.
4. R. Diestel. *Graph Theory*. Springer-Verlag, New-York, 2000.
5. dimacs92. Clique and coloring problems, a brief introduction, with project ideas, 1992. ftp://dimacs.rutgers.edu/pub/challenge.
6. Raphaël Dorne and Jim-Kao Hao. A new genetic local search algorithm for graph coloring. In Agoston E. Eiben, Thomas Bäck, Marc Schoenauer, and Hans-Paul Schwefel, editors, *Parallel Problem Solving from Nature – PPSN V*, pages 745–754, Berlin, 1998. Springer. http://citeseer.nj.nec.com/dorne98new.html.
7. A. Drogoul. *De la simulation multi-agents à la résolution collective de problèmes: une étude de l'émergence de structure d'organisation dans les systèmes multi-agents*. PhD thesis, Univ. Paris VI, 1993.
8. J. Ferber and O. Gutknecht. Aalaadin: a meta-model for the analysis and design of organizations in multi-agent systems, 1998.
9. G. Ribeiro Filho. Improvements on constructive genetic approaches to graph coloring. http://citeseer.nj.nec.com/242708.html.
10. G. Ribeiro Filho and G. Lorena. A constructive genetic algorithm for graph coloring, 1997. http://citeseer.nj.nec.com/filho97constructive.html.
11. G. Ribeiro Filho and G. Lorena. Constructive genetic algorithm and column generation: an application to graph coloring, 2000. http://citeseer.nj.nec.com/filho00constructive.html.

12. Carlos Iglesias, Mercedes Garrijo, and José Gonzalez. A survey of agent-oriented methodologies. In Jörg Müller, Munindar P. Singh, and Anand S. Rao, editors, *Proceedings of the 5th International Workshop on Intelligent Agents V : Agent Theories, Architectures, and Languages (ATAL-98)*, volume 1555, pages 317–330. Springer-Verlag: Heidelberg, Germany, 1999.

13. Bruno Mermet. Formal model of a multiagent system. In Robert Trappl, editor, *Cybernetics and Systems*, pages 653–658. Austrian Society for Cybernetics Studies, 2002.

14. J. Ferber O. Gutknecht and F. Michel. Madkit : une expérience d'architecture de plateforme multi-agent générique. 2000.

15. Arsène Sabas, Sylvain Delisle, and Mourad Badri. A comparative analysis of multi-agent system development methodologies : Towards a unified approach. In Robert Trappl, editor, *Cybernetics and Systems*, pages 599–604. Austrian Society for Cybernetics Studies, 2002.

16. A. Vesel and J. Zerovnik. How good can ants color graphs? *Journal of computing and Information Technology - CIT*, 8:131–136, 2000.
    http://citeseer.nj.nec.com/443529.html.

17. Michael Wooldridge and Nicholas R. Jennings. Pitfalls of agent-oriented development. In Katia P. Sycara and Michael Wooldridge, editors, *Proceedings of the 2nd International Conference on Autonomous Agents (Agents'98)*, pages 385–391, New York, 9–13, 1998. ACM Press.

18. Michael Wooldridge, Nicholas R. Jennings, and David Kinny. The gaia methodology for agent-oriented analysis and design. *Autonomous Agents and Multi-Agent Systems*, 3(3):285–312, 2000.

OCOA: An Open, Modular, Ontology Based Autonomous Robotic Agent Architecture

Feliciano Manzano Casas and L.A. García

Intelligent Control Systems research group,
manzano@guest.uji.es, garcial@icc.uji.es, Universitat Jaume I,
Campus de Riu Sec s/n, 12071 Castellón (Spain)

Abstract. Ontology based Component Oriented Architecture (OCOA)[1] is an open software architecture designed for autonomous robotic agents. It is comprised of four kinds of objects that manage and interchange information with each other on a distributed peer to peer basis. The central architectural information service in the agent is the Agent Information Manager (AIM), which is notified and notifies any capability added, updated, substracted, or failed in the agent. These capabilities are managed ontologically. The architectural knowledge base is built dynamically by the components of the agent, and all of them can be searched and found using ontology as resource and information retrieval mechanism. High level logical data processing services are performed by Common Framework objects (CFo). CFos also offer the infrastructure needed to interchange raw and ontological architectural information. The interface to physical devices is provided by Devide object Drivers (DoD). DoDs extend CFo features by incorporating device and platform dependent code wrapped in Device Input Output Drivers (DIOD). DIODs are Java Native Interface objects, which operate directly with physical devices. Therefore, OCOA uses these four kinds of objects (AIM, CFo, DoD and DIOD), giving (by replacing only DIODs) a scalable, modular, open, platform neutral, dynamic, ontology based agent architecture.

1 Introduction

The most succeful robotic software architectures developed can be classified into three categories [1]: hierarchical, deliverative and hybrid. The main feature of a hierarchical architecture [2] is to be guided to reach a high level plan by restricting low-level horizontal communications. This architecture has poor flexibility, so it is difficult to adapt to modern robots, which have to manage many sensors in reactive and reflex loops. The deliverative architecture [3] adopts the opposite approach. It comprises several modules known as behaviours which run concurrently through communication and through the environment. The design of high level goals is usually difficult to achieve. Hybrid architectures [4] are the most recent. They try to combine hierarchical and deliberative control. However, the connection between these two levels is generally a difficult task [1]. There are

---

[1] This work is partly supported by the Spanish CICYT project TAP1999-0590-c02-02.

D. Scott (Ed.): AIMSA 2002, LNAI 2443, pp. 173–182, 2002.

several trends in the development of software that can help to the development of new and powerful robotic architectures.

From Software Engineering there is a recent approach for building software architectures that reuse off-the-shelf components. This approach is called component based architectures [5]. Also, there is a growing interest in using ontologies[2] as the main tool for the development of new and powerful knowledge based systems [9]. OCOA architecture follows these trends by integrating ontology into the core of the architecture. As far as we know, this is a new approach for designing autonomous robotic software architectures that may perform dynamic reconfiguration of robotic system software components. OCOA, writen in Java, is a hybrid robotic software architecture that uses component based features. This architecture proposes approaches to:

- Total portability of components among different robotic platforms (openess).
- Dynamic plug/unplug of interdependent behavioral reactive, deliverative and physical-driver components, even among different physical agents, without loss of control over the agent.
- Ability to perform, structure and coordinate complex interdependent reactive and deliverative behaviors.

In order to be able to coordinate behaviors and manage the dynamic adding and removing of components, OCOA architecture uses an architectural knowledge base. This knowledge base is dynamically built by the components of the OCOA architecture. All its components manages the same ontology, which is stored in the AIM, and provides the OCOA with a yellow and white pages server, thus any request for information about services available in OCOA is answered by the AIM. Logical data processing services are performed by Common Framework objects (CFo) whilst the interface to physical devices is provided by Device object Drivers (DoD). DoDs extend CFo features by incorporating device and platform dependent code wrapped in Device Input Output Drivers (DIOD). DIODs are Java Native Interface [6] objects, which operate directly with physical devices. Therefore, OCOA is a scalable (components can be added or removed), modular (component based), open and platform neutral (by replacing only DIOD components the rest of the OCOA architecture can be used in different robotic hardware architectures), dynamic and ontology based software agent architecture. Moreover, due to the use of Java Remote Method Invocation (Java/RMI) [7] [8], each component may be located in a different Java Virtual Machine, therefore it also has distributed characteristics.

This paper describes OCOA architecture and it is organized as follows: section 2 sets out the robotic architecture ontology used by the OCOA architecture. Section 3 describes the components of OCOA: AIM, CFo and DoD. Section 4 shows an overview of the coordination resources that OCOA provides. Section 5 shows. an example of a robotic agent that uses OCOA. Section 6 describes some details of OCOA implementation. Finally, the conclusions are drawn.

---

[2] In this context, an ontology is a description (like a formal specification of a program) of the concepts and relationships that can exists for an agent or a community of agents [13].

2   OCOA Robotic Ontology

In this section it is set out the ontological representation of the architectural knowledge base of OCOA. The description includes the properties, features, attributes and restrictions of each concept. Figure (1) shows the class tree used for representing the architectural knowledge base.

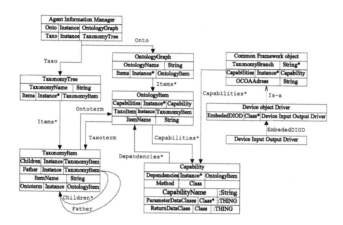

Fig. 1. OCOA architectural ontology.

The root of the class tree is the Agent Information Manager, which has an instance of the OntologyGraph and an instance of the TaxonomyTree. The TaxonomyTree contains the name of the taxonomy, and a collection of TaxonomyItems. Each TaxonomyItem contains the name of the item, the Children that the item owns (which are instances of TaxonomyItem), the Father of the item itself (which is, again, an instance of TaxonomyItem), and a link to OntologyItem (which is the ontological correspondence of the TaxonomyItem in the knowledge base).

The OntologyGraph contains the name of the Ontology and a collection of OntologyItems. Each OntologyItem contains the name of the item, a link to TaxonomyItem (which is its taxonomical hierarchy correspondence), and a collection of instances of Capabilities. Each Capability contains the CapabilityName, a collection of Dependencies (which are instances of OntologyItem), and information related to the concrete capability implementation made by the part of a concrete CFo (Method, ParameterClass and ReturnDataClass). The CFo is comprised of a collection of Capabilities, an OCOAAddress (which univocally identifies the component in the OCOA agent), and a series of strings related to the taxonomy branch kept by this CFo in the TaxonomyTree. Device object Driver has is-a relationship with a Common Framework object. This relationship represents that a DoD is a kind of CFo. Device object Driver contains an EmbebedDIOD, which links DoD to the system library that can be used to manage physical devices.

3   The Structural Components of OCOA Architecture

In this section the main structural components of the OCOA architecture are explained.

3.1   The Agent Information Manager (AIM)

The Agent Information Manager provides the agent with a white and yellow pages server. It manages available information about components of the agent by using the architectural knowledge base. Through the registration process, a component anounces its existence, capabilities, goals and dependencies to the AIM. Thus, the AIM incorpotes the component in its architectural knowledge base. Capabilities, goals and dependencies are specified by the component being registered using the common ontology of the architecture. The taxonomical information provided by the component can be non existent. Thus, the AIM must include this information as a new branch of the taxonomical tree.

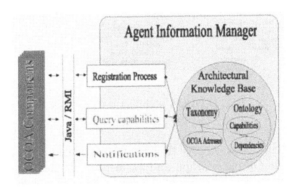

Fig. 2. Modular description of the Agent Information Manager (AIM).

As a result of this registration process, the component receives its own OCOA address and all the addresses of its dependent components. If any of the component dependences are not available (i.e. not yet registered), the dependence addresses will be not provided. These addresses will be sent when the related components that provide these capabilities are registered in the AIM. The modular structural description of the AIM is shown in Figure 2. It includes the architectural knowledge base (which includes taxo-ontological information and component addresses) and facilities to communicate with other components by providing methods for performing registration, notifications and requests of capability explanations.

3.2   Common Framework Object (CFo)

Common Framework object provides facilities to interchange information with other agent components: methods to register and unregister to the AIM and methods to attach listeners and triggers to other OCOA components. Also, the CFo includes its own timers and watchdogs.

The CFo implements a *Listener Manager* which accepts and processes new listener registrations from other components and requests listener registrations to other components. This *Listener Manager* processing involves a complete ontological knowledge of the component to be registered. This knowledge is used to deal with conflicting external requests. CFo also implements a *Dependence Manager* which manages all dependency information that this CFo has with other components in the agent.

The *Capability Manager* performs several tasks in the CFo: 1) informs the *Listener Manager* about new registrations to be made to other components; 2) provides all necesary information to perform the registration to the AIM; 3) manages all communications needed by any capability method; and 4) it is informed of dependency modifications by the *Dependence Manager*.

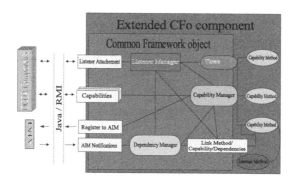

Fig. 3. Modular description of an Extended Common Framework object (ECFo).

The CFo must be extended with capability methods to perform the desired tasks and, afterwards, must be linked to an onto-taxonomical description of the capabilities that these methods perform. Figure 3 shows the modular structural description of an extended CFo component (ECFo).

When a CFo is incorporated into the architecture, the CFo communicates with the AIM in order to provide its capabilities and dependencies. The AIM incorporates the CFo into the general ontology and, as result, the AIM sends the CFo OCOA address, and the addresses of the CFo dependence components to the CFo. With this information, the CFo determines how and when to use the dependences relating to the tasks to be executed. If any of its core dependences are not available, the CFo states inactive until the AIM notifies it of the availability of those dependences.

3.3 Device Object Driver (DoD)

The Device object Driver can be shown as an abstraction layer to hide platform dependant device implementation issues. DoD, besides inheriting all the
functionalities of its superclass (the CFo), adds a new object, the Device Input
Output Driver (DIOD). This new object wraps a link to a plattform dependant
driver (a system library program, usually written in C), which allows access
to physical, plattform dependant devices. The DIOD links platform dependant
code through Java Native Interface.

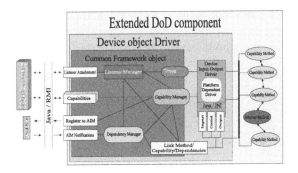

Fig. 4. Modular description of an Extended Device object Driver(EDoD).

The possibilities offered by its superclass (the CFo) enable preprocessing of
input data signals and revision of the execution of commands that interact with
the external world environment. As a result, DoD can carry out explicit trap-
ping of errors that occur within primitive action/sense tasks and the subsequent
activation of an alternative or error-correction activity. These reactive control
possibilities that DoD offers, allow prewired patterns of behavior. DoD may have
either eager sensing (i.e. senses often to update the system's view of the world)
or lazy sensing (i.e. senses by request of any other component of the agent). Both
ways can be chosen. This gives OCOA agents the ability to selectively focus their
attention on specific aspects of their environment. These considerations allow an
OCOA agent to operate in real-time dynamic environments, due to the possibility of executing simple reaction strategies, the lack of an explicit external world
representation, and the reactive response to stimuli.

The DoD must be extended with: 1) a platform dependant driver linked to
the DIOD, 2) capability methods to develop the desired tasks; and 3) linkage
of these methods to a taxo-ontological description of the capabilities. Figure
4 shows the modular structural description of an Extended DoD component
(EDoD).

4   Component Coordination

In OCOA architecture coexists several components[3]. All of them try to accomplish their job, and ocassionally will race to obtain necessary resources. These resources can be, i.e. complying with DoD sensors, efectors, CFos that express different levels of behavior, etc. Coordination among them is reached by getting semantic knowledge of the tasks and goals asigned to each component. This knowledge is expressed at an ontological level, and it is stored in the AIM when the component is registered. Details of tasks to be accomplished are expressed by:

- Precondition(s) to activate the behavior. These preconditions can be, i.e. a definite state of the environment.
- Postcondition: State of the agent after the execution of a behavior. This can imply the interchange of messages among different components.
- Execution priority: It has to be set off-line. Some behaviors will require a higher priority over remainder behaviors(obstale avoidance, panic behavior, etc...). Remainder behaviors may have an standard priority, and given a punctual situation, race for resources.
- Execution deadline: It can be an absolute or relative temporal definition, and in terms of available resources or state of the agent.

5   OCOA for Example

In figure (5) an example of use of OCOA in an autonomous robotic agent can be seen. In the lower side of the figure, we can see three physical devices managed by DIODs, which are embebed in Extended DoD (EDoD) components. Each EDoD manages a DIOD. All EDoDs are interconnected to allow data interchange needed to perform reactive behaviors. Above the EDoDs, a series of Extended CFos (ECFos) can be seen. These ECFos perform logical processing of data provided by the EDoDs; one of the ECFos uses an EDoD to deal with the movement of the robot. All ECFos perform deliverative processing of data (i.e.: map building, spatial and temporal reasoning, and navigational processing). The AIM manages architectural knowledge data and, as a future work to be done, will perform communication with external agents.

Figure (6) shows a cronogram representing event registrations, notifications and capability requests during the execution of the OCOA implementation shown in figure (5). The first action each component performs is to register itself to the AIM; after providing their capabilities and dependences, the AIM provides each component with its own OCOAAddress and the OCOAAddresses of their dependence components (if available).

Next, the components mutually perform a series of registration processes, in order to append listeners to achieve automatic event notification. The last series

---

[3] The term "component" (structural), can be freely interchanged by the term "behaviour" (functional).

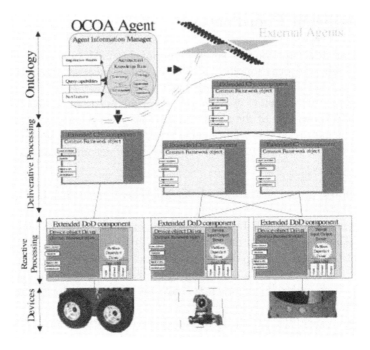

Fig. 5. Software components and hierarchical relationships in an example agent.

of processes shown in figure (6) evidences the interaction between the active components in the agent.

6   OCOA Implementation. Ongoing Efforts

OCOA implementation is being done using JADE [14] and its framework. According with JADE philosophy, every agent runs an unique execution thread. By this reason, every OCOA component will be compound by several JADE agents. Every manager of OCOA components (Listener, Dependence and Capability managers), is being implemented using a different and separate execution thread; and every manager will be a different JADE agent. Also, every OCOA capability will be implemented by a JADE agent. All OCOA components will have common methods for initialize, register and cleanly exit from the system.

Implementation of service requests will be done using Service Request broker model (SRB). This will be done exchanging JADE pure ACL text messages between OCOA components. This makes needless to know the exact API of the server component and types/clases of parameter objects. Also, this will provide loose coupling between OCOA components. Aside of exchange ACL text messages, the possibility of direct calling to remote methods of the components will be provided.

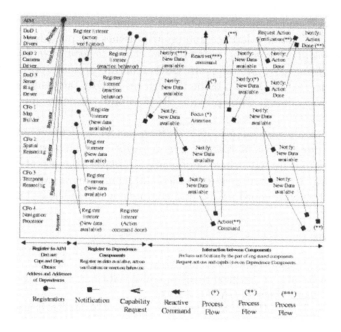

Fig. 6. Cronogram of the execution of OCOA implementation shown in figure 5.

There is a need of more flexibility regarding to the ontology framework provided by JADE. Its current implementation, makes necessary to known exactly the kind of Java class that houses an ontology item. This lack of flexibility will be overcomed supossing a previous agreement about the idea that a determinate ontology item (identified by its tokens(s)) means the same concept among all components. As further work, an analisys and comparation with the most relevant robotic software architectures will be done.

7   Conclusions

Several recently published architectures for robotic autonomous agents use component based theories (i.e. the works of [10] [11] [12]). OCOA main advantages among other architectures are:

- *Openess and Portability*: the choice of Java as the language to use in this architecture allows the implementation on a wide variety of target platforms, and OCOA is not tied to any specific operating system.
- *Modularity and Reusability*: The definition of OCOA architecture is inherently modular. CFos and DoDs (but no DIODs) can be reused off-the-shelf in different robotic platforms.
- *Scalability, Fault Tolerance and Security*: through the Java/RMI distributed computation model, nodes can be attached to the system to add more com-

pute power, and thanks to OCOA this is done transparently. Due to the use of Java/RMI, fault tolerance and security issues are provided.

- *Reactive control behaviour patterns and ability to focus attention on specific aspects of the robot environment*: DoD structure provides prewired patterns of behavior. Also, DoDs provide to perform lazy or eager sensing.
- *High level planning*: CFos provide the possibility of performing deliverative processing.
- *Dynamic component plug-in and ability to perform, structure and coordinate complex interdependent reactive and deliverative behaviors*: The ontology is built dynamically with the components. Moreover, the use of ontology provides a way to perform real dynamic component plugin and resolution of all possible behavior coordination and component dependences in the agent.

References

1. Eve Coste-Maniere, Reid Simmons: Architecture, the Backbone of Robotic Systems. Proceedings of the 2000 IEEE International Conference on Robotics & Automation. San Francisco, CA, April 2000.
2. J. Albus, R. Lumia, H. McCain: Hierarchical control of intelligent machines applied to space station telerobots. Transactions on Aerospace and Electronic Systems. September 1988.
3. R.A. Brooks: A robust layered control system for mobile robot. IEEE Journal of Robotics and Automation. March 1986.
4. A. Stoytchev, R. C. Arkin: Combining Deliberation, Reactivity, and Motivation in the Context of a Behavior-Based Robot Architecture.
   http://www.cc.gatech.edu/ai/robot-lab/publications.html. 2000.
5. Jean-Guy Schneider, Oscar Nierstrasz: Components, Scripts and Glue. Software Architectures - Advances and Applications. Springer-Verlag 1999.
6. Sun Corporation: JNI-Java Native Interface. Sun Microsystems 1999.
   http://www.javasoft.com/products/jdk/1.1/~docs/guide/jni/index.html
7. The Java Virtual Machine Specification: Release 1.1. Sun Microsystems white paper. Sun Microsystems 1997.
8. Sun Microsystems. User's Manual: Java Remote Method Invocation Specification, Revision 1.4, JDK 1.1. Sun Microsystems. Sun Microsystems 1997.
9. A. Gomez Perez, V. R. Benjamins: Overview of Knowledge Sharing and Reuse Components: Ontologies and Problem-Solving Methods. Proceedings of the IJCAI-99 workshop on Ontologies and Problem-Solving Methods (KRR5). Stockholm, Sweden, August 2, 1999.
10. R. Volpe et al.: The CLARAty Architecture for Robotic Autonomy. Proceedings of the 2001 IEEE Aerospace Conference. Big Sky, Montana, March 2001.
11. K. Konolige et al.: The Saphira Architecture: A Design for Autonomy. Journal of Experimental and Theoretical Artificial Intelligence, 9(1): 215-235. 1997.
12. R. Alami et al.: An Architecture for Autonomy. International Journal of Robotics Research, 17(4). April 1998.
13. T.R. Gruber: A Translation Approach to Portable Ontologies. Knowledge Acquisition, 5(2):199-220. 1993.
14. Fabio Bellifemine, Agostino Poggi, Giovanni Rimassa: JADE –A FIPA-compliant agent framework. Proceedings of PAAM'99, pg.97-108. London, April 1999.

A Replanning Algorithm for a Reactive Agent Architecture

Guido Boella and Rossana Damiano

Dipartimento di Informatica
Cso Svizzera 185 Torino ITALY
guido@di.unito.it

Abstract. We present an algorithm for replanning in a reactive agent architecture which incorporates decision-theoretic notions to drive the planning and meta-deliberation process. The deliberation component relies on a refinement planner which produces plans with optimal expected utility. The replanning algorithm we propose exploits the planner's ability to provide an approximate evaluation of partial plans: it starts from a fully refined plan and makes it more partial until it finds a more partial plan which subsumes more promising refinements; at that point, the planning process is restarted from the current partial plan.

1 Introduction

In this paper we present a replanning algorithm developed for a reactive agent architecture which incorporates decision-theoretic notions to determine the agent's commitment. The agent architecture is based on the planning paradigm proposed by [3], which combines decision-theoretic refinement planning with a sound notion of action abstraction ([2]): given a goal and a state of the world, the planner is invoked on a partial plan (i.e. a plan in which some actions are abstract) and iteratively refines it by returning one or more plans which maximize the expected utility according to the agent's preferences, modelled by a multi-attribute utility function.

The decision-theoretic planning paradigm extends the classical goal satisfaction paradigm by allowing partial goal satisfaction and the trade-off of goal satisfaction against resource consumption. Moreover, it accounts for uncertainty and non determinism, which provide the conceptual instruments for dealing with uncertain world knowledge and actions having non-deterministic effects. These features make decision-theoretic planning especially suitable for modelling agents who are situated in dynamically changing, non deterministic environments, and have incomplete knowledge about the environment.

However, decision-theoretic planning frameworks based on plan refinement ([3]) do not lend themselves to reactive agent architectures, as they do not include any support for reactive replanning. In this paper, we try to overcome this gap, by proposing an algorithm for replanning for a reactive agent architecture based on decision-theoretic notions.

Since optimal plans are computed with reference to a certain world state, if the world state changes, the selected plan may not be appropriate anymore. Instead of planning an alternative solution from the scratch, by re-starting the planning process from the goal, the agent tries to perform replanning on its current plan.

D. Scott (Ed.): AIMSA 2002, LNAI 2443, pp. 183–192, 2002.

The replanning algorithm is based on a *partialization process*: it proceeds by making the current solution more partial and then starting the refinement process again. This process is repeated until a new feasible plan is found or the partialization process reaches the topmost action in the plan library (in this case, it coincides with the standard planning process).

We take advantage of the decision-theoretic approach on which the planner is based not only for improving the quality of the replanned solution, but also for guiding the replanning process. In particular, the planner ability to evaluate the expected utility of partial plans provides a way to decide whether to continue the partialization process or to re-start refinement: for each partial plan produced in the partialization step, it is possible to make an approximate estimate of whether and with what utility the primitive plans it subsumes achieve the agent's goal.

Then, the pruning heuristic used during the standard planning process to discard sub-optimal plans can be used in the same way during the replanning process to reduce its complexity.

2   The Agent Architecture

The architecture is composed of a *deliberation module*, an *execution module*, and a *sensing module*, and relies on a *meta-deliberation* module to evaluate the need for re-deliberation, following [9]. The agent is a BDI agent ([7]), i.e. its internal state is defined by its beliefs about the current world, its goals, and the intentions (plans) it has formed in order to achieve a subset of these goals . The agent's deliberation and redeliberation are based on decision-theoretic notions: the agent is driven by the overall goal of maximizing its utility based on a set of preferences which are encoded in a utility function.

The agent is situated in a dynamic environment, i.e. the world can change independently from the agent's actions, and actions can have non-deterministic effects, i.e., an action can result in a set of alternative effects. Moreover, there is no perfect correspondence between the environment actual state and the agent's representation of it.

In this architecture, intentions are not static, and can be modified as a result of re-deliberation: if the agent detects a significant mismatch between the initially expected and the currently expected utility brought about by a plan, the agent revises its intentions by performing re-deliberation. As a result, the agent is likely to become committed to different plans along time, each constituted of a different sequence of actions. However, while the intention to execute a certain plan remains the same until it is dropped or satisfied, the commitment to execute single actions evolves continuously as a consequence of both execution and re-deliberation.

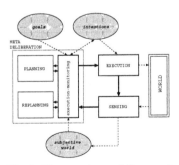

Fig. 1. The structure of the agent architecture. Dashed lines represent data flow, solid lines represent control flow.

In order to represent dynamic intentions, separate structures for representing plan-level commitment and action-level commitment have been introduced in the architecture. So, intentions are stored in two kind of structures: *plans*, representing goal-level commitment, and *action-executions*, representing action-level commitment. New instances of the *plan* structure follow one another in time as a consequence of the agent's re-deliberation; on the contrary, the action-level commitment of an agent is recorded in a unitary instance of the *action-execution* structure, called *execution record*, whose temporal extent coincides with the agent's commitment to a goal and which is updated at every cycle.

The behavior of the agent is controlled by an execution-sensing loop with a meta-level deliberation step (see figure 1). When this loop is first entered, the deliberation module is invoked on the initial goal; the goal is matched against the plan schemata contained in the library, and when a plan schema is found, it is passed to the planner for refinement. This plan becomes the agent's current intention, and the agent starts executing it. After executing each action in the plan, the sensing module monitors the effects of the action execution, and updates the agent's representation of the world. Then, the meta-deliberation module evaluates the updated representation by means of an execution-monitoring function: if the world meets the agent's expectations, there is no need for re-deliberation, and the execution is resumed; otherwise, if the agent's intentions are not adequate anymore to the new environment, then the deliberation module is assigned the task of modifying them.

Due to the agent's uncertainty about the outcome of the plan, the initial plan is associated to an expected utility interval, but this interval may vary as the execution of the plan proceeds. More specifically, after the execution of a non-deterministic action (or a conditional action, if the agent did not know at deliberation time what conditional effect would apply), the new expected utility interval is either the same as the one that preceded the execution, or a different one. If it is different, the new upper bound of the expected utility can be the same as the previous one, or it can be higher or lower - that is, an effect which is more or less advantageous than expected has taken place.

The execution-monitoring function, which constitutes the core of the meta-deliberation module, relies on the agent's subjective expectations about the utility of a certain plan: this function computes the expected utility of the course of action constituted by the remaining plan steps in the updated representation of the world. The new expected utility is compared to the previously expected one, and the difference is calculated: replanning is performed only if there is a significant difference.

If new deliberation is not necessary, the meta-deliberation module simply updates the execution record and releases the control to the execution module, which executes the next action. On the contrary, if new deliberation is necessary, the deliberation module is given the control and invokes its *replanning component* on the current plan with the task of finding a better plan; the functioning of the replanning component is inspired to the notion of persistence of intentions ([1]), in that it tries to perform the most local re-planning which allows the expected utility to be brought back to an acceptable difference with the previously expected one.

3 The Planning Algorithm

The action library is organised along two *abstraction* hierarchies. The *sequential abstraction* hierarchy is a task decomposition hierarchy: an action type in this hierarchy is a macro-operator which the planner can substitute with a sequence of (primitive or non-primitive) action types. The *specification hierarchy* is composed of abstract action types which subsume more specific ones.

The specification hierarchy is obtained by *inheritance abstraction*, a technique for grouping together conditional probabilistic action operators in abstract classes based on their outcomes which is characterized by the common features of all elements of the class ([4]), while the decomposition hierarchy is obtained by sequential abstraction, i.e., by gathering stereotypical sequences of action types into complex action types ([8]). In the following, for simplicity, we will refer to *sequentially abstract* actions as *complex* actions and to actions in the specification hierarchy as *abstract* actions.

A plan (see section 2) is a sequence of action instances and has associated the goal the plan has been planned to achieve. A plan can be partial both in the sense that some steps are complex actions and in the sense that some are abstract actions. Each plan is associated with the derivation tree (including both abstract and complex actions) which has been built during the planning process and that will be used for driving the replanning phase.

Before refining a partial plan, the agent does not know which plan (or plans) - among those subsumed by that partial plan - is the most advantageous according to its preferences. Hence, the expected utility of the abstract action is *uncertain*: it is expressed as an interval having as upper and lower bounds the expected utility of the best and the worst outcomes produced by substituting in the plan the abstract action with all the more specific actions it subsumes. This property is a key one for the planning process as it makes it possible to compare partial plans which contain abstract actions.

The planning process starts from the topmost action in the hierarchy which achieves the given goal. If there is no time bound, it proceeds refining the current plan(s) by substituting complex actions with the associated decomposition and abstract actions with all the more specific actions they subsume, until it obtains a set of plans which are composed of primitive actions.

At each cycle the planning algorithm re-starts from a less partial plan: at the beginning this plan coincides with the topmost action which achieves the goal, in the subsequent refinement phases it is constituted by a sequence of actions; this feature is relevant for replanning, as it make it possible to use the planner for refining any partial plan, no matter how it has been generated.

At each refinement step, the expected utility of each plan is computed by projecting it from the current world state. Then, a *pruning* heuristic is applied by discarding the plans identified as suboptimal, i.e., plans whose expected utility upper bound is lower than the lower bound of some other plan p. The suboptimality of a plan p' with respect to p means that all possible refinements of p have an expected utility which dominates the utility of p', and, as a consequence, dominates the utility of all refinements of p': consequently, suboptimal plans can be discarded without further refining them. On the contrary, plans which have overlapping utilities need further refinement before the agent makes any choice. At each step of refinement the *expected utility interval* of a plan tends

```
procedure plan replan(plan p, world w){
/* find the first action which will fail */
 action a := find-focused-action(p,w);
 mark a; //set a as the FA
 plan p' := p;
 plan p'' := p;
/* while a solution or the root are not found */
 while (not(achieve(p'',w, goal(p''))))
            and has-father(a)){
/* look for a partial plan with better utility */
  while (not (promising(p', w, p))
          and has-father(a)){
    p' := partialize(p');
    project(p',w); } //evaluate the action in w
/* restart planning on the partial plan */
 p'' := refine(p',w);}
 return p'';}
```

Fig. 2. The main procedure of the replanning algorithm, *replan*

to become narrower, since it subsumes a reduced number of plans (in fact, the plan appears deeper in the hierarchy of plans).

4   The Replanning Algorithm

If a replanning phase is entered, then it means that the current plan does not reach the agent's goal, or that it reaches it with a very low utility compared with the initial expectations. But it is possible that the current plan is 'close' to a similar feasible solution, where closeness is represented by the fact that both the current solution and a new feasible one are subsumed by a common partial plan at some level of the action abstraction hierarchy.

The key idea of the replanning algorithm is then to make the current plan more partial by traversing the abstraction hierarchies in a upsidedown manner, until a more promising abstract plan is found. The abstraction and the decomposition hierarchy play complementary roles in the algorithm: the abstraction hierarchy determines the alternatives for substituting the actions in the plan, while the decomposition hierarchy is exploited to focus the substitution process on a portion of the plan.

A partial plan can be identified as promising by observing its expected utility interval, since this interval includes not only the utility of the (unfeasible) current plan but also the utility of the new solution. So, during the replanning process, it is possible to use this estimate in order to compare the new plan with the expected utility of the more specific plan from which it has been obtained: if it is not promising it is discarded.

The starting point of the partialization process inside the plan is the first plan step whose *preconditions* do not hold, due to some event which changed the world or to some failure of the preceding actions. In [4]'s planning framework the Strips-like precondition/effect relation is not accounted for: instead, an action is described as a set of conditional effects. The representation of an action includes both the action intended

```
function plan partialize(plan p){
action a := marked-action(p); /* a is the FA of p */
/* if it is subsumed by a partial action */
if (abstract(father(a))){
  delete(a, p); /* delete a from the tree */
  return p;}
/* no more abstract parents: we are in a decomposition */
 else if (complex(father(a))){
        a1 := find-sibling(a,p);
        if (null(a1)){
/* there is no FA in the decomposition */
          mark(father(a)) //set the FA
      //delete the decomposition
          delete(descendant(father(a)),p);
          return p;}
   else { //change the current FA
          unmark(a);
          mark(a1);}}}
```

Fig. 3. The procedure for making a plan more abstract, *partialize*.

effects, which are obtained when its 'preconditions' hold, and the effects obtained when its 'preconditions' do not hold. For this reason, the notation of the action has been augmented with the information about the action intended effect, which makes it possible to identify its preconditions.[1]

The task of identifying the next action whose preconditions do not hold (the 'focused action') is accomplished by the *Find-focused-action* function (see the main procedure in Figure 2); *mark* is the function which sets the current focused action of the plan. Then, starting from the focused action (FA), the replanning algorithm partializes the plan, following the derivation tree associated with the plan (see the *partializes* function in Figure 3).

If the action type of the FA is directly subsumed by an abstract action type in the derivation tree, the focused action is deleted and the abstract action substitutes it in the tree frontier which constitutes the plan. On the contrary, if FA appears in a decomposition (i.e., its father in the derivation tree is a sequentially abstract action) then two cases are possible (see the find-sibling function in 4):

1. There is some action in the plan which is a descendant of a sibling of FA in the decomposition and which has not been examined yet: this descendant of the sibling becomes the current FA. The order according to which siblings are considered reflects the assumption that it is better to replan non-executed actions, when possible: so, right siblings (from the focused action on) are given priority on left siblings.
2. All siblings in the decomposition have been already refined (i.e., no one has any descendant): all the siblings of FA and FA itself are removed from the derivation

---

[1] Since it is possible that more than one condition-effect branch lead to the goal (maybe with different satisfaction degrees), different sets of preconditions can be identified by selecting the condition associated to successful effects.

```
function action find-sibling(a,p){
/* get the next action  to be refined (in the same decomposition as a) */
  action a0 := right-sibling(a,p);
  action a1 := leftmost(descendant(a0,p));
  while(not (null (a1))){
/* if it can be partialized */
    if (not complex(father(a1))){
      unmark(a); //change FA
      mark(a1)
      return a1;}
/* move to next action */
    a0 := right-sibling(a0,p);
    a1 := leftmost(descendant(a0,p));}
/* do the same on the left side of the plan */
  action a1 := left-sibling(a,p);
  action a1 := rightmost(descendant(a0,p));
  while(not (null (a1))){
    if (not complex(father(a1))){
      unmark(a);
      mark(a1)
      return a1;}
  action a1 := left-sibling(a,p);}
```

Fig. 4. The procedure for finding the new focused action.

tree and replaced in the plan by the complex sequential action, which becomes the current FA (see Figure 4).[2]

As discussed in the Introduction, the pruning process of the planner is applied in the refinement process executed during the replanning phase. In this way, the difficulty of finding a new solution from the current partial plan is alleviated by the fact that suboptimal alternatives are discarded before their refinement.

Beside allowing the pruning heuristic, however, the abstraction mechanism has another advantage. Remember that, by the definition of abstraction discussed in Section 2, it appears that, given a world state, the outcome of an abstract action includes the outcomes of all the actions it subsumes.

Each time a plan p is partialized, the resulting plan p' has an expected utility interval that includes the utility interval of p. However p' subsumes also other plans whose outcomes are possibly different from the outcome of p. At this point, two cases are possible: either the other plans are better than p or not. In the first case, the utility of p' will have an higher higher bound with respect to p, since it includes all the outcomes of the subsumed plans. In the second case, the utility of p' will not have a higher upper bound than p. Hence, p' is not more promising than the less partial plan p.

The algorithm exploits this property (see the *promising* condition in the procedure *replan*) to decide when the iteration of the partialization step must be stopped: when a

---

[2] Since an action type may occur in multiple decompositions[3], in order to understand which decomposition the action instance appears into, it is not sufficient to use the action type library, but it is necessary to use the derivation tree).

promising partial plan (i.e., a plan which subsumes better alternatives than the previous one) is reached, the partialization process ends and the refinement process is restarted on the current partial plan.

The abstraction hierarchy has also a further role. The assumption underlying our strategy is that a plan failure can often be resolved *locally*, within the subtree the focused action appears into. Not all failures, however, can be resolved locally, but these cases are taken into account by the algorithm as well: after the current subtree has been completely partialized, a wider subtree in the derivation tree will be considered, until the topmost root action is reached: in this case, the root of the derivation tree becomes the FA and the planning process is restarted from scratch.

In case of non-local causal dependencies among actions (i.e., a precondition of the FA is enabled by the effect of an action which does not appear in the local context of FA), the algorithm takes advantage from the fact that the current partial plan is *projected* onto its final state and its expected utility is computed: provided that the definition of abstract action operators is sufficiently accurate to make casual dependencies explicit, it is likely that invalid dependencies will be reflected in the expected utility of the current partial plan, and, as a consequence, it will be pruned during refinement without being further expanded.

Finally, the movement of the FA is a critical point of the algorithm. Here we presented *find-sibling* as a simple process which follows the local structure of the tree. However, some improvements are possible to take advantage from the cases in which non local dependencies are known. Hence, the *find-sibling* procedure should be modified in order to use in deeper way the structure of the plans and, in particular, the implicit enablement links among actions for choosing the next FA.

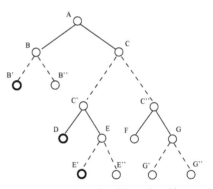

Fig. 5. A generic action hierarchy. Abstraction relations are represented by dashed lines.

For the sake of brevity, in order to illustrate how the replanning algorithm works, we will resort to a generic action hierarchy (see fig. 5), which abstracts out the details of the domains we used to test the implementation.

In the following, we will examine the replanning process that the algorithm would perform, given the initial plan composed of the steps B' - D - E' (see fig. 6).

1. Assume that, at the beginning of the replanning process, the focused step is action D (1). D is examined first, but an alternative instantiation of it cannot be found (as its immediate parent is not an abstract action). The find-siblings function returns the right sibling of D, E.

2. The planner is given as input the partial plan B' - D - E. Assuming that a feasible plan is not found (i.e., B' - D - E'', the only possible alternative to the original plan,

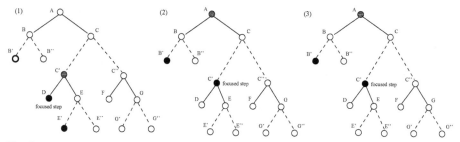

Fig. 6. A graphical representation of the plan replanning process on the generic action library introduced in 5. Black nodes represent the siblings of the focused action node, while the grey nodes represent the local decomposition context. (1)-(2)-(3) represent the phases of the replanning process.

does not work), the replanning process is started again after collapsing the sub-plan $(D - E)$ on its father, the complex node C' (no siblings left).

3. Given the new input plan $B' - C'$, the focused step now is C' (2). The focused step is examined first, and the more abstract father node C is found; C' is replaced by C in the plan and the planner is invoked on the new partial plan B'-C.

4. Again, assuming that a new feasible plan has not been found by refining B'-C, the replanning process continues by examining B, the only sibling of the focused action C (3). Before the candidate plan is collapsed on its root (A), the replanning process gives the planner as input the plan obtained by substituting the more abstract node B for B' in the current partial plan, obtaining B - C.

5. Finally, if the refinement of the partial plan B - C does not yield a feasible plan, the plan is collapsed on the its father A. If a feasible plan is not found by refining the plan constituted by the root alone, the plan replanning algorithm fails.

In the previous version of the algorithm, the *find-sibling* step proceeds not only from left to right (towards actions yet to be executed), but also in a backward manner: at a certain point it is possible that the focused point is shifted to an already executed actions. In order to overcome this problem, we propose that the projection rule should is changed to include in the projection the actions that must be executed again (possibly in an alternative way). In this case, the FA would be moved incrementally to the left, and would become the reference point for starting the projection of the current partial plan.

5   Related Work and Conclusions

[5] has proposed a similar algorithm for an SNLP planner. The algorithm searches for a plan similar to known ones first by retracting refinements: i.e., actions, constraints and causal links. In order to remove the refinements in the right order, [5] add to the plan an history of 'reasons' explaining why each new element has been inserted.

In a similar way, our algorithm adapts the failed plan to the new situation by retracting refinements, even if in the sense of more specific actions and decompositions. The same role played by 'reasons' is embodied in the derivation tree associated to the plan which explains the structure of the current plan and guides the partialization process.

As it has been remarked on by ([6]), reusing existing plans raises complexity issues. They show that modifying existing plans is advantageous only under some conditions: in particular, when, as in our proposal, it is employed in a replanning context (instead of a general plan-reuse approach to planning) in which it is crucial to retain as many steps as possible of the plan the agent is committed to. Second, when the complexity of generating plans from the scratch is hard, as in the case of our decision-theoretic planner.

For what concerns the complexity issues, it must be noticed that the replanning algorithm works in a similar way as the *iterative deepening* algorithm. At each stage, the height of the tree of the state space examined increases. The difference with the standard search algorithm is that, instead of starting the search from the tree root and stopping at a certain depth, we start from a leaf of the plan space and, at each step, we select a higher tree which rooted by one of the ancestors of the leaf.

In the worst case, the order of complexity of the replanning algorithm is the same as the standard planning algorithm. However, two facts that reduce the actual work performed by the replanning algorithm must be taken into account: first, if the assumption that a feasible solution is "close" to the current plan is true, then the height of the tree which includes both plans is lower than the height of root of the whole state space. Second, the pruning heuristics is used to prevent the refinement of some of the intermediate plans in the search space, reducing the number of refinement runs performed.

Finally, it is worth mentioning that the replanning algorithm we propose is complete, in that it finds the solution if one exists, but it does not necessarily finds the optimal solution: the desirability of an optimal solution, in fact, is subordinated to the notions of resource-boundedness and to the persistence of intentions, which tend to privilege conservative options.

References

1. M. E. Bratman, D. J. Israel, and M. E. Pollack. Plans and resource-bounded practical reasoning. *Computational Intelligence*, 4:349–355, 1988.
2. Vu Ha and Peter Haddawy. Theoretical foundations for abstraction-based probabilistic planning. In *12th Conf. on Uncertainty in Artificial Intelligence*, pages 291–298, Portland, 1996.
3. P. Haddawy and S. Hanks. Utility models for goal-directed, decision-theoretic planners. *Computational Intelligence*, 14:392–429, 1998.
4. P. Haddawy and M. Suwandi. Decision-theoretic refinement planning using inheritance abstraction. In *Proc. of 2nd AIPS Int. Conf.*, pages 266–271, Menlo Park, CA, 1994.
5. Steve Hanks and Daniel S. Weld. A domain-independent algorithm for plan adaptation. *Journal of Artificial Intelligence Research*, 2:319–360, 1995.
6. B. Nebel and J. Koehler. Plan modification versus plan generation: A complexity-theoretic perspective. In *Proceedings of of the 13th International Joint Conference on Artificial Intelligence*, pages 1436–1441, Chambery, France, 1993.
7. A. Rao and M. P. Georgeff. Modeling rational agents within a BDI-architecture. In *Proc. 2th Int. Conf. Principles of Knowledge Representation and Reasoning (KR:91)*, pages 473–484, Cambridge, MA, 1991.
8. E. D. Sacerdoti. *A Structure for Plans and Behavior*. American Elsevier, New York, 1977.
9. Mike Wooldridge and Simon Parsons. Intention reconsideration reconsidered. In Jörg Müller, Munindar P. Singh, and Anand S. Rao, editors, *Proc. of ATAL-98)*, volume 1555, pages 63–80. Springer-Verlag, 1999.

A Broker Approach for Multi-agent Scheduling

S.L.M. Lin

IC-Parc, William Penney Laboratory, Imperial College, London SW7 2AZ, U.K.
`slm@icparc.ic.ac.uk`

Abstract. We propose an iterative broker approach for solving a multi-agent scheduling problem in an inherently distributed environment. The agents have incomplete information about the environment and incomplete models of other agents, and are reluctant to disclose any information to other agents. The algorithm allows the agents to reach a solution close to the global optimum found in the centralised approach. The algorithm is demonstrated through two scenarios. We have applied the algorithm to a case study and the result is as good as in the centralised approach. Experimental results on random data are also provided.

Keywords: distributed AI, multi-agent systems, planning

1 Introduction

A number of studies in multi-agent systems focus on co-operative problem solving. There are two types of situations in which agents co-operate. In the first situation, the agents have a common objective but individual agents cannot solve the problem alone, thus the task requires agents to co-ordinate their plans and share resources. In this case, co-operation is mandatory. In the second situation, each agent can solve its own problem independently, but co-operation with other agents helps to reduce the cost of operation. In this case, co-operation is desirable but not mandatory and usually involves the exchange of tasks, resources and goals.

However, in an environment where each agent has incomplete information of what the other agents need and agents are unwilling to disclose all their requirements and resources to the other agents, co-operation could be difficult, if not impossible.

Richards *et al.* [6] presents the Teaching Space Utilisation (TSU) problem in such an environment. The TSU is a course scheduling problem involving a number of departments. Each department has many courses to schedule and rooms available. Each department schedules its own courses using its own resources. However, these solutions when combined together are unlikely to be optimal in terms of the overall number of resources used throughout the university. Alternatively the departments can let the problem be solved centrally, which can result in a better solution than when each department solves the problem itself.

In practice there are good reasons to use a multi-agent approach. Each department has its own local constraints, preferences and perhaps even confidential requirements and optimisation criteria. It is desirable to respect these and still obtain a solution better than independent departmental scheduling.

D. Scott (Ed.): AIMSA 2002, LNAI 2443, pp. 193–202, 2002.

The goal of this paper is to use an iterative broker approach to achieve the global optimum with respect to one optimisation criterion. The rest of the paper is organised as follows. Section 2 presents the related works. Section 3 presents the formalities and Section 4 the algorithm. Section 5 presents two scenarios and Section 6 the results using TSU as a case study. Finally, Section 7 discusses the approach and Section 8 concludes.

2   Related Work

Both [5] and [1] use broker approach to manage resource. [5] develops a resource management system which supports a de-centralised approach using three types of agents: the application agents, the broker agents and resource agents. However, neither of them are concerned with optimisation.

A number of works point out that co-operative planning can improve costs. However, mostly they are either seeking a feasible solution or a better solution without seeking further for a global optimum. In some case, without rescheduling [3,7], the global optimum is unlikely to be found.

While [2] investigates a cooperative planning using complete information, in this paper, we propose a multi-agent cooperative scheduling problem under incomplete information. Both their approach and ours require agents to construct their plans or schedules first before the agent interaction phase starts. Although [2] develops methods to reason about free resources, in our case, free resources are much easier to compute. Unlike their approach in which the agents pass complete plans with solutions to a planner, in our case, the agents pass only the non-optimised problem to the broker.

3   Formalities

In this section we present the notion of activities, resources, constraints and optimisation criteria. Details of the problem descriptions can be found in [4].

3.1   Variables

Activities. Activities have properties: resource requirement, room type, student group, teacher, and duration. Two decision variables are associated with each activity: Room (Rm) and Time (T).

Resources. The set of resources will be denoted by R which is $Rm \cup T$. Resources can have different attributes and different capacities. If two resources are of the same type and same capacities, they may be used for the same type of activities.

Each activity requires exclusive access to a resource throughout its duration. If a resource is used by an activity, the resource constraint has to be updated to indicate that it is no longer available.

3.2 Constraints

There are two main types of constraints: the temporal constraints and the capacity constraints. The temporal constraints are imposed mainly by the group of students attending the activities and the teacher lecturing the activity. Resource must be exclusive, so no students will be assigned to the same room at the same time. This is the same for the teachers. For each activity, the size of the student group determines the capacity of the room required and the activity type must match that of the room.

3.3 Optimisation Criteria

The optimisation criterion is based on a cost function of resource usage. Without loss of generality, the objective is to minimise the resource cost. The task is to schedule the activities into resources without violating the constraints with the goal to optimise on resource usage.

Depending on the optimisation criterion, the cost function varies. [6] used two optimisation criteria: the room usage and the seat usage where the objective function is to minimise the number of rooms used and the number of overall empty seats respectively.

Each agent produces a schedule with cost function $Cost : \mathbb{R} \to \mathbb{N}^{+}$.

$$Cost = \sum_{i=1}^{k} R_i \tag{1}$$

where k is the total number of activities.

In the room usage case, R_i is 100 if a new room is needed during allocation; otherwise, it is 0. In the seat usage case, R_i is the number of empty seats of the activity.

4   Algorithm

The architecture consists of two types of agents: an optimising agent who owns a number of resources and a broker which acts as an intermediary to assist agents in locating resources for optimisation.

The iterative broker algorithm extends from the simple broker approach proposed by [6]. In the simple broker approach, only the agent can deallocate resources and can communicate to the broker. In the iterative broker approach, the broker can deallocate resources, negotiate and reschedule. Communication among the agents and the broker is bidirectional.

The simple approach is as follows:

- Each agent solves its local problem to create a schedule from its own resources. The schedule stipulates the resources needed, and the cost of the schedule.
- The agents then deallocate requests, and send them with unallocated resources to the broker.
- The broker gathers the requests from the agents and optimises the problems using the aggregated free resources.

The iterative broker approach continues from the simple broker approach as follows:

- The broker deallocates requests and sends the deallocated requests and some resources to the agents.
- The agents may need to revise their schedules, whether partially or completely, to accommodate these requests. The agents then send bids to request resources for local activities using external requests.
- The broker awards the bids with minimal cost and rejects otherwise.
- The agent receives the answer from the broker and the rejected bids form the deallocated requests which the agent then sends to the broker together with the associated constraints.
- The broker reschedules the deallocated requests.

The broker and the agents interact until no more deallocation is done or no improvement on the solution is achieved or until the global optimal is reached. The global solution of the broker approach is found by aggregating the partial solutions of the agents and the solution of the broker.

4.1   Deallocation Procedure

The deallocation procedure is at the heart of the broker model. It has two parameters: the deallocation criterion and the deallocation factor.

Deallocation Criterion. The choice of a deallocation criterion follows from the optimisation criterion. If the optimisation criterion is on room usage, then the deallocation criterion is also on room usage.

Deallocation Factor. A deallocation criterion has a variable deallocation factor, f, which affects the number of events to be deallocated. f is the percentage of the resources not used per resource, therefore, f is from 0 to 100. For a resource with fixed capacity, the percentage can be replaced by a number between 0 and the maximum capacity.

Algorithm 1 shows the deallocation procedure using the deallocation factor f.

Algorithm 1 Deallocation

Deallocation
   for each used optimising resource R **do**
     let c be $f \times$ max usage
     if number of times R is used $\leq c$ **then**
       for each activity using R **do**
         deallocate the activity
       end for
     end if
   end for

According to the deallocation criterion, an agent creates a new subproblem by partitioning the solution into two parts: an *optimised* part and a *suboptimal* part. For the optimised part, the agent keeps the solution unchanged. For the suboptimal part, the agent creates an unsolved subproblem by unassigning values for the variables.

The agents then bundle all the deallocated events with the associated constraints into a request. All the agents send the deallocated requests with the associated constraints, and all the free resources, to the broker.

4.2   Rescheduling

The broker aggregates all the deallocated requests and free resources from all the agents as a new subproblem and solves the new subproblem to optimality.

We propose two strategies for broker rescheduling:

1. The broker deallocates the activities using the same deallocation factor as the agents. Afterwards, the broker sends the deallocated requests to all the agents. At the same time, the broker also sends back the unallocated resources to the original agents. The broker waits for the reply from the agents. Bidding may be needed if more than one agent can solve the external requests from the broker.
2. The broker requests the agent to increase the deallocation factor, and sends these deallocated activities and resources. Then the broker continues optimisation and deallocation.

Note that when the broker sends back the unallocated resources to the agents for rescheduling, it may be necessary to consider what these unallocated resources are: should the broker send the resource previously owned by the agents, or resources of the other agents. In this paper, for the room usage, the broker sends only those free resources that belong to the agents previously. However, the free resources sent are those that are used by at least one activity; in other words, those resources that are currently in use after broker deallocation.

4.3   Convergence

Remember that all the deallocated activities belong to the non-optimised activities; each activity after broker scheduling can be either better off as optimised or remain as non-optimised.

Cost can be reduced in two ways. First, when activities are assigned to a resource currently in use; second, when non-optimised activities of two agents are combined to use the same resources. If an agent reschedules the activities successfully, the resources will incur no additional cost because all the resources returned to the agents are currently in use. Additionally the broker could save the cost from deallocated activities. In this regard, there is an improvement in cost. But if agent rescheduling fails, the deallocated activities of the broker have to make use of the previous schedule and this will result in no cost improvement. Therefore, in the worst case, the cost of the resource usage would be as before broker deallocation. However, due to the labelling strategy being incomplete since it is order-dependent, it is possible that the results may not converge.

5   Scenario

In this section, we consider two scenarios. The first has a co-operative objective; the second has a competitive objective.

5.1   Scenario 1

In the first scenario, the deallocation criterion is

Room Usage: Minimise the number of rooms used in scheduling lectures. A room is considered as used if a lecture is scheduled in it for at least one time slot in a week.

Suppose agent A has one room with 8 seats, and agent B has one room with 25 seats and one room with 30 seats. Suppose after deallocation, the agents both deallocate activities and send the requests and resource to the broker.

Fig. 1 shows the broker view of the schedule before broker scheduling.

Rooms	Agent	Capacities	Time-units(1..5)
r1	A	8	UUU--
r2	B	25	U-U-U
r3	B	30	-----

Fig. 1. Broker before scheduling (room usage)

where U represents rooms used by the agents and therefore *unavailable* for scheduling and – represents free time-units, so the broker can schedule into these time-units.

Suppose that the broker has two external requests, from agent A and B, with seating requirements of 6 and 8 to be scheduled at time 2 only. The broker has limited knowledge about the time-domain of the activities of the scheduled activities of the agents, so it is unable to make a better schedule. Therefore, without interacting with the agents, the broker may require three rooms instead of two rooms (see Fig. 2).

Rooms	Agent	Capacities	Time-units(1..5)
r1	A	8	UUU--
r2	B	25	U6U-U
r3	B	30	-8---

Fig. 2. Broker original schedule

The broker deallocates the room which is used less than two times, and so the activity requesting 8 seats is deallocated and sent to agent A. Agent A can accommodate the requests of the broker by rescheduling its activities, so the broker can schedule the activities into two rooms (see Fig. 3).

Rooms	Agent	Capacities	Time-units(1..5)
r1	A	8	U8UU–
r2	B	25	U6U–U
r3	B	30	– – – – –

Fig. 3. Broker final schedule

As a result of the algorithm, the total number of rooms needed is 2, which is the same as that in the centralised approach.

We have only presented the first strategy in rescheduling. The second strategy will have similar effects when the broker requests agent A to deallocate more resources. The reason why agent A is requested instead of agent B is because r1 is used 3 times while r2 is used 4 times. The broker chooses the one with the lower usage.

5.2 Scenario 2

In the second scenario, we use seat usage as the deallocation and optimisation criteria. The scenario is more complicated than scenario 1, since the agents actually compete to use the rooms with the least empty seats. One time-unit used by one agent may not be re-used by another agent.

The Deallocation criterion is:

Seat Usage: Minimise the number of empty seats in the scheduled rooms. The total number of empty seats in a schedule is obtained by summing all the empty seats in all the rooms used in that schedule.

Fig. 4 shows the broker view of the schedule before broker scheduling.

Rooms	Agent	Capacities	Time-units			
r1	A	8	5	6	7	–
r2	B	25	18	–	20	21
r3	B	30	–	–	–	–

Fig. 4. Broker before scheduling (seat usage)

Again, suppose there are two external requests, one requires 6 seats and one requires 8 seats, both at time 2 only.

If the broker only schedules to the time-slots available, without requiring the agents to reschedule, the result would be as in Fig. 5, which yields 63 empty seats.

Suppose the broker deallocates any activities with more than 10 empty seats, so the external activities are deallocated again. The broker sends these deallocated activities and asks the agents to reconsider their schedule taking into account of the external requests.

Rooms	Agent	Capacities	Time-units			
r1	A	8	5	6	7	-
r2	B	25	18	8	20	21
r3	B	30	-	6	-	-

Fig. 5. Broker original schedule

Rooms	Agent	Capacities	Time-units			
r1	A	8	5	8	6	7
r2	B	25	18	6	20	21
r3	B	30	-	-	-	-

Fig. 6. Broker final schedule

Rescheduling from the part of the agents is required, because the broker cannot reschedule the schedule made by the agents. Both agents A and B may bid the resource for external requests. These resources could be the same or different. Fig. 6 shows a final schedule of 41 empty seats.

6   Experimental Results

In order to study the algorithm, as a case study, we have used Teaching Space Utilisation (TSU) problem [6]. The TSU problem schedules a number of lectures in a number of rooms with 36 time-slots per week such that no constraints are violated. In this section, the results of using the broker approach on the TSU problem [6] are presented. There are four agents and altogether 519 activities, 45 rooms and 22286 seat available.

6.1   TSU – Room Usage

Fig. 7 shows the TSU results using the centralised approach, the distributed approach, the simple broker approach and the iterative broker approach, using room usage as the optimisation criterion such that the number of rooms used is minimised. In the distributed approach, the agent solves the problem independently without communicating with the broker.

	Centralised	Distributed	Simple Broker	Iterative Broker
Optimal	16	19	17	16
Time	65	2	2	17

Fig. 7. TSU problems - Centralised vs. Distributed vs. Broker

The experiments are run using ECL^{i}PS^e version 4.2 under a Pentium III at 933 Mhz with 512MB RAM of main memory. The optimal is the number of rooms needed.

The time is the total of the execution time for constraint propagation, labelling and optimisation in seconds. In [6], the simple broker approach has tried deallocation factor from 0 to 20 time-slots in intervals of 5; the best solution found is 17 rooms, which is still greater than the centralised approach. Instead, our iterative broker approach can find the optimum of 16 rooms using either the strategies described in Section 4.2.

6.2 Random Data

We generate two sets of random problem by modelling them on the TSU problems. Each problem has 4 agents, each with 90 activities and 10 rooms. Set A and Set B differ in the way using p_o, where p_o represents the probability that two groups of students cannot occur at the same time. Each set has 50 instances for each p_o. We only compare instances that are solvable by both the agents and the broker. The problems are tried using the centralised approach, the simple broker approach and the iterative approach.

Problem Set	p_o	Centralised	Simple	Iterative	Better	Solvable
A1	0.2	20	6	22	12	34
B1	0.2	24	5	40	24	49
B2	0.3	13	3	42	34	48

Fig. 8. Random solution (room)

Fig. 8 shows the number of instances with which each algorithm can reach the global optimum, a solution which has the lowest resource usage among the three; it also shows that the simple broker model performs the most unsatisfactory. For problem set A1, in 22 instances of the iterative approach, 12 of them find solutions better than the centralised approach, which shows that the broker models can produce results better than the centralised approach. In all the instances, the iterative broker model can always achieve better results than the simple broker model. For problem set B2 with 0.3 p_o, the number of instances in the iterative broker approach reaching a global optimum even outnumber the centralised approach.

7 Discussion

Experimental results show that the iterative broker approach can do better than the simple broker approach. We can identify three reasons. First, in the simple approach, each agent uses a fixed deallocation factor. However, the problem of each agent may be different: some may have rooms better utilised than the other. Second, in the iterative approach, rescheduling provides the opportunities that allow some of the activities release resources for other agents' need. In addition, the agent may be able to find non-local resources to accommodate the needs of the current already activities. Third, in the iterative approach, the overall number of deallocated activities is in fact greater than that in the simple approach. When the number is small, the simple approach is closer to the distributed approach than the centralised approach.

The effectiveness of the iterative broker approach can be affected by two factors. First, increase in the probably of conflict in the problem makes the problem less densely scheduled which may increase the number of activities deallocated. Second, the sequence of agent communication affects the order of the activities to be labelled. To ease the comparison, this sequence is fixed in our implementation; otherwise, the results would be non-deterministic. For a 4-agent scenario, there would be 24 of ways to read the messages.

We have also tried the seat usage on the TSU problem. However, the strategies mentioned in Section 4.2 are limited since the broker has less information to reason about seat usage in other agents. The seat usage is more complicated than the room usage and details of experimental results on seat usage will be reported later.

Though in the room usage, the result of improvement does not look significant: only by one unit. However, we need to understand that the solution of TSU problem are densely allocated. Remember that it takes 36 activities to reduce further the cost, since one room can allocate 36 activities. However, as seen in Scenario 2, the resource cost can be reduced by more than one unit.

8   Conclusion and Future Work

We have presented an iterative broker-based approach to global optimisation. We have proposed two strategies for rescheduling, and we have found that the iterative broker approach can produce result better than the simple approach. Sometimes, the broker approach can even outperform the centralised approach. To reach the ultimate goal of achieving multi-criteria optimisation as addressed by [6], further work will be necessary.

References

1. A. Asvanund, K. Bhargava, D. Fernandes, R. Krishnan, and R. Padman. Brokering decision support resources for supply chain management. In *Workshop on Agents for Electronic Commerce and Managing the Internet-Enabled Supply Chain*, Seattle, Washington, May 1999.
2. M. M. de Weerdt, A. Bos, H. Tonino, and C. Witteveen. A plan fusion algorithm for multi-agent systems. In K. Satoh and F. Sadri, editors, *Proceedings of the Workshop on Computational Logic in Multi-Agent Systems (CLIMA-00)*, pages 56–65. Imperial College, 2000.
3. F. Kokkoras and S. Gregory. D-WMS: Distributed workforce management using CLP. In *Proceedings of the 4th International Conference on the Practical Application of Constraint Technology*, pages 129–146. Practical Application Company Ltd., March 1998.
4. V. Listsos. An environment for a resource allocation problem in CLP. MSc thesis, IC-Parc, Imperial College, London, 1995.
5. O. F. Rana, M. Winikoff, L. Padgham, and J. Harland. Applying conflict management strategies in BDI agents for resource management in computational grids. In *25th Australasian Computer Science Conference (ASCS2002)*, Melbourne, Australia, 2002.
6. E. B. Richards, S. Das, H. J. Choi, A. El-Kholy, V. Liatsos, and C. Harrison. Distributed optimisation: A case study of utilising teaching space in a college. In *Proceedings of the Expert Systems 96 Conference*, pages 153–161, 1996.
7. K. Sycara, S. Roth, N. Sadeh, and M. S. Fox. Distributed constrained heuristic search. *IEEE Transactions on Systems, Man, and Cybernetics*, 21(6):1446–1461, 1991.

Recognition of Common Areas in a Web Page Using a Visualization Approach

Miloš Kovačević [1], Michelangelo Dilligenti [2], Marco Gori [2], and
Veljko Milutinović [3]

[1]School of Civil Engineering, University of Belgrade, Serbia
milos@grf.bg.ac.yu
[2]Dipartimento di Ingegneria dell'Informazione, University of Siena, Italy
{diligmic, marco}@dii.unisi.it
[3]School of Electrical Engineering, University of Belgrade, Serbia
vm@etf.bg.ac.yu

Abstract. Extracting and processing information from web pages is an important task in many areas like constructing search engines, information retrieval, and data mining from the Web. Common approach in the extraction process is to represent a page as a "bag of words" and then to perform an additional processing on such a flat representation. In this paper we propose a new, hierarchical representation that includes the browser screen coordinates for every HTML object in a page. Using a spatial information one is able to define heuristics for recognition of common page areas such as a header, left and right menu, footer and the center of a page. We show in initial experiments that using our heuristics, defined objects are recognized properly in 73% of cases.

1. Introduction

Web pages are designed for humans! While the previous sentence is more than obvious, still many machine learning and information retrieval techniques for processing web pages do not utilize implicit spatial information contained in the HTML source. By spatial information we assume positions of HTML objects in the browser window. For example, one can say that a certain image is on the top left corner of the screen or that the most informative paragraph is in the center of the page and it occupies the area of 100x200 pixels. Where can this kind of information be useful?

Consider the problem of feature selection in a document (web page) classification. There are several methods to perform the feature selection process. We will mention just the two of them. The first one is based on finding the expected information gain that the presence or absence of a word w gives toward the classification of a document D [1]. Using this approach D is represented as a vector of k most informative words. The other approach is to represent D as a vector relative to some collection of words that define vocabulary V. Every coordinate has a value – frequency of the corresponding word in the document, weighted by the factor that identifies the inverse frequency of the word in the whole reference corpus to which D belongs to. This

D. Scott (Ed.): AIMSA 2002, LNAI 2443, pp. 203-212, 2002.
© Springer-Verlag Berlin Heidelberg 2002

measure is called TF-IDF (term frequency – inverse document frequency)[2]. In both cases we try to estimate what are the most relevant words that describe D i.e. the best vector representation of D that will be used in the classification process. Assuming that web pages are designed for visual sense, we can argue that some words represent noise with respect to the page topic if they belong to menu, banner link or perhaps page footer. That noise can be misleading for classifiers. We can also suppose that the words which belong to the central part of the page (screen) carry more information than the words from the bottom right corner. Hence there should be a way to weight differently words from different layout contexts. Presently, in classical algorithms positions of words and their spanning areas are not considered at all!

Let us mention another problem – designing an efficient crawling strategy for a focused search engine. Given a specific topic T and the starting set of pages S, it is necessary to find as much T on-topic pages as possible in a predefined number of steps. By step means visiting (and downloading and indexing) a page reachable from S following the hyperlinks from the pages in S. In other words it is important to estimate whether an outgoing link is promising or not. In [3][4] and [5] different techniques are described. In any case when a crawler decides to take into account a page for link expansion, all the links from the page are inserted into the crawl frontier (links that are to be visited). But many of them are not interesting at all (i.e. "*this page is designed by XYZ*"). Sometimes, the links that belong to menus or to the footer are also misleading. Can we measure the importance of a link according to its position in a page (on the browser screen). Links in the center of the page are probably more important than the links in the bottom left corner. We can also calculate link density in some area of the page (screen) and weight links taking into account that density factor. The links that are surrounded by "more" text are probably more important for the topic than the links positioned in groups. On the other hand groups of links can signify we are on the hub page that can also be important for our focused crawler. Can we learn the positions of interesting links for some topics? In any case, we believe information about the position of a link can help to infer if it is promising or not!

To give a final example, let's consider the problem of cheating search engines by inserting irrelevant keywords into the HTML source. This is a widely used technique in order to raise the probability of indexing a page by a search engine and representing it with higher rank among search results. While it is relatively easy to detect and reject false keywords where their foreground color is the same as the background color, there is no way to detect keywords of regular color covered with images. If the coordinates of objects in a page representation are known, then search engines could filter the false keywords hidden by other objects and users would get better answers on their queries!

The outline of the paper is as follows: In Section 2 we define the M-$Tree$ format of a page used to render the page on the virtual screen, i.e. to obtain coordinates for every HTML object. Section 3 describes heuristics for recognition of a header, footer, left and right menu, and the "center" of a page. In Section 4, experimental results on a predefined dataset are shown. Finally, conclusions and remarks about the future work are given in Section 5.

2. Extraction of Spatial Information from an HTML Source

We introduce a virtual screen (VS) that defines a coordinate system for specifying the positions of HTML objects (in further text - objects) inside Web pages (in further text - pages). VS is a half strip with a predefined width and an infinite height both measured in pixels. It is set to correspond to the page display area in a maximized browser window on a standard monitor with the resolution of 1024x768 pixels. Of course one can set any desirable resolution. The width of VS is set to 1000 (when the vertical scroll bars are removed that quantity is usually left for rendering the page). Obviously pages are of different length and therefore height can be theoretically infinite. The top left corner of VS represents the origin of the referent coordinate system.

The process of the spatial information extraction consists of three steps. In the first step a page is parsed using an HTML parser that extracts two different types of elements – tags and data. Tag elements (TE) are delimited with "<>" while data elements (DE) are contained between the two consecutive tags. Each TE includes the name of the corresponding tag and a list of attribute-value pairs. DE is represented as a list of tokens, which taken all together form a data string between the consecutive tags. In the second step, as soon as <TE,DE> pair is extracted from the input HTML stream, it is injected into the tree builder. Tree builder applies a stack machine and a set of predefined rules to build the tree that represents the HTML structure of the page. We named the output of this component *m-Tree*. There are many papers that describe the construction of the parsing tree of an HTML page [6][7]. In our approach a technique is adopted which constructs the *m-Tree* in one single pass through the given page. Rules used to properly nest TEs into the hierarchy conform to the HTML 4.01 specification [8]. Additional efforts were made to design a tree builder that will be immune to the bad HTML source.

Definition 1: *m-Tree* (in further text *mT*) is directed n-ary tree defined with a set of nodes N and a set of edges E with the following characteristics:

1. $N = N_{desc} \cup N_{cont} \cup N_{data}$ where:

☐ N_{desc} (description nodes) is a set of nodes, which correspond to TEs of the following HTML tags: {*<TITLE>*, *<META>*}

☐ N_{cont} (container nodes) is a set of nodes, which correspond to TEs of the following HTML tags: {*<TABLE>*, *<CAPTION>*, *<TH>*, *<TD>*, *<TR>*, *<P>*, *<CENTER>*, *<DIV>*, *<BLOCKQUOTE>*, *<ADDRESS>*, *<PRE>*, *<H1>*, *<H2>*, *<H3>*, *<H4>*, *<H5>*, *<H6>*, *<OL>*, *<UL>*, *<LI>*, *<MENU>*, *<DIR>*, *<DL>*, *<DT>*, *<DD>*, *<A>*, *<IMG>*,*
,<HR>*}

☐ N_{data} (data nodes) is a set of nodes, which correspond to DEs.

Each $n \in N$ has the following attributes: *name* equals the name of the corresponding tag except for N_{data} nodes where *name = "TEXT"*, *attval* is a list of attribute-value pairs extracted from the corresponding tag and can be null (i.e. nodes from N_{data} have this attribute set to null). Additionally, each N_{data} node has four more attributes: *value*, *fsize*, *emph*, and *align*. The first contains tokens from the corresponding DE, the second describes font size of these tokens, the third caries information whether the tokens belong to the scope of validity of one or more of the following HTML tags: $\{<B>,<I>,<U>, <STRONG>, <EM>, <SMALL>, <BIG>\}$. The last one describes the alignment of the text (left, right or centered). In further text if n corresponds to tag X we write $n_{<X>}$ (n has the attribute $name = X$).

2. The root of mT, $n_{ROOT} \in N_{cont}$ represents a page as a whole and its name is set to *"ROOT"* while *attval* contains only one pair (*URL : source url of the page itself*).

3. $E = \{(n_x , n_y) \mid n_x , n_y \in N \}$.

There can be only the following types of edges:

- (n_{ROOT}, n_{desc}), $n_{desc} \in N_{desc}$
- (n_{cont1}, n_{cont2}), $n_{cont1} \in N_{cont} \setminus \{n_{<IMG>}\}$, $n_{cont2} \in N_{cont} \setminus \{n_{ROOT}\}$ iff n_{cont2} belongs to the context of n_{cont1} according to the nesting rules of the HTML 4.01 specification
- (n_{cont}, n_{data}), $n_{cont} \in N_{cont} \setminus \{n_{<IMG>}\}$, $n_{data} \in N_{data}$ iff n_{data} belongs to the context of n_{cont} •

From definition 1 it is clear that image and text nodes can be only the leafs in an mT. After mT is obtained from the input page and when the context of every object of interest is known, it is possible to apply the algorithm for coordinate calculation. In fact, it is nearly the same algorithm that browsers perform when rendering a page. The coordinates of objects are calculated in the third step using the rendering module and constructed mT as its input. We did not find any specific algorithm for page rendering except some recommendations from W3C [8] and therefore it was necessary to design our own. We decided to imitate the visual behavior of *Internet Explorer* because of the popularity of this product. It is clear how difficult it could be if all aspects of the rendering process would be taken into account. Hence some simplifications were made, which in our opinion do not influence significantly the final task – recognition of common areas in a page. The simplifications are as follows:

1. Rendering module (RM) calculates only coordinates for nodes in mT, i.e. the HTML tags out of mT are skipped.

2. RM does not support layered HTML documents.

3. RM does not support frames.

4. RM does not support style sheets.

Rendering module produces the final, desirable representation of a page – *M-Tree* (in further text *MT*). *MT* extends the concept of mT by incorporating coordinates for each $n \in N \setminus N_{desc}$.

Definition 2: *MT* is the extension of *mT* with the following characteristics:

1. For $\forall n \in N \setminus N_{desc}$, there are two additional attributes: X and Y. These are arrays which contain x and y coordinates of the corresponding object polygon on VS.

2. If $n \in N_{cont} \setminus \{n_{<A>}\}$ then X and Y have dimension 4 and it is assumed that the object represented with n occupies rectangle area on VS. The margins of this n's rectangle are:

- The bottom margin is equal to the top margin of the left neighbor node if it exists. If n does not have a left neighbor or $n = n_{<TD>}$ then the bottom margin is equal to the bottom margin of

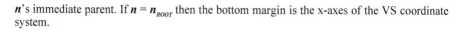

n's immediate parent. If $n = n_{ROOT}$ then the bottom margin is the x-axes of the VS coordinate system.

☐ The top margin is equal to the top margin of the rightmost leaf node in the subtree in which n is the root node.

☐ The left margin is equal to the left margin of n's immediate parent, shifted to the right for the correction factor. This factor depends on the name of the node (i.e. if *name* = "*LI*" this factor is set to 5 times current font width because of the indentation of list items). If $n = n_{<TD>}$ and n has a left neighbor then the left margin is equal to the right margin of n's left neighbor. If $n = n_{ROOT}$ then the left margin is the y-axes of the VS coordinate system.

☐ The right margin is equal to the right margin of n's immediate parent. If $n = n_{<TABLE>}$ or $n = n_{<TD>}$ then the right margin is set to correspond to table/cell width.

3. If $n \in N_{data}$ or $n = n_{<A>}$ then X and Y can have dimension from 4 to 8 depending on the area on VS occupied by the corresponding text/link (see Figure 1-B). Coordinates are calculated using the number of characters contained in the *value* attribute and the current font width. Text flow is restricted to the right margin of the parent node and then the new line is started. Heights of lines are determined by the current font height. •

The previous definition covers most aspects of the rendering process, but not all because of the complexity of the process. For example if the page contains tables then RM implements modified auto-layout algorithm [8] for calculating table/column/cell widths. If $n_{<TABLE>}$ is encountered, RM makes one more pass from that node down the *mT* to calculate cell/column/table widths. Hence the first pass is dedicated to table width calculations, and in the second pass RM calculates the final coordinates for the nodes that belong to the observed subtree. If there are other $n_{<TABLE>}$ nodes down on the path (nesting of the tables in a page) the process of calculating widths is recursively performed, but with no additional passes. Before resolving a table, artificial cells (nodes) are inserted in order to simplify calculus in cases where cell spanning is present (*colspan* and *rowspan* attributes in a *<TD>*).

Let us consider the complexity of the *MT* extraction process. The first and the second step (extracting *<TE,DE>* pairs and building the *mT*) are performed in a single pass through the page. Hence the complexity so far is *O(s)*, where *s* represents the size of the file. In the third step RM transforms *mT* into *MT* while passing through *mT* and calculating coordinates for every non-descriptive node. If *mT* does not contain the nodes that represent table TEs (tables in a page) then one single pass in the third step is needed and the complexity remains linear. If the page contains tables then in the worst case RM performs an additional pass. Hence the complexity of the RM phase is *O(2s)* and the resulting complexity of the *MT* extraction process is *O(3s)*, which is satisfactory for most applications.

3. Defining Heuristics for Recognition of Common Areas of Interest

Given the *MT* of a page and assuming the common web design patterns [9], it is possible to define a set of heuristics for recognition of standard areas in a page such as a menu or footer. First, we choose the areas of interest to be: a header (H), footer (F), left menu (LM), right menu (RM), and the center of a page (C). Presently there are no exact definitions in the open literature for these page areas (one can think of these areas as groups of objects). Therefore we adopted intuitive definitions of these areas, which rely exclusively upon VS coordinates of logical groups of objects in a page. It is helpful to understand these groups of objects as frequently found areas in pages regardless of a page topic. They are tightly related to the presentational concept of a page. Naturally, heuristics based on spatial information are used to recognize them, instead of exact algorithms. After careful examination of many different pages on the Web, we restricted the areas in which H, F, LM, RM, and C can be found. Before we describe what is recognized to be H, F, LM, RM, and C, we will introduce the specific partition of a page as it is shown in figure 1-A.

We set $W_1 = W_2$ to be 30% of the page width in pixels determined by the rightmost margin among nodes from MT. W_1 and W_2 define $\mathcal{LM}$ and $\mathcal{RM}$ respectively which are the locations where LM and RM can be exclusively found. We set $H_1 = 200$ pixels and $H_2 = 150$ pixels. H_1 and H_2 define $\mathcal{H}$ and $\mathcal{F}$ respectively which are the locations where H and F can be exclusively found. Of course one can set different values, but the initial experiments showed that the previous values are appropriate (see Section 4). Now we define the following heuristics:

Heuristic 1: H consists of all nodes from MT that satisfy one or more of the following conditions:

1. Subtree S of MT with its root r_s belongs to H iff r_s is of type $n_{<TABLE>}$ and completely belongs to $\mathcal{H}$ (i.e. the upper bound of the table is less than or equal to H_1).

2. Subtree S of MT with its root r_s belongs to H iff the upper bound of r_s is less than or equal to m and does not belong to the subtrees found in 1. Number m is the maximum upper bound of all $n_{<TABLE>}$ nodes found in 1. •

Heuristic 2: LM consists of all nodes from MT that are not contained in H and satisfy one or more of the following conditions:

1. Subtree S of MT with its root r_s belongs to LM iff r_s is of type $n_{<TABLE>}$ and completely belongs to $\mathcal{LM}$ (i.e. the right bound of the table is less than or equal to W_1).
2. Subtree S of MT with its root r_s belongs to LM iff r_s is of type $n_{<TD>}$, and completely belongs to $\mathcal{LM}$, and $n_{<TABLE>}$ which this r_s belongs to has the lower bound less than or equal to H_1, and the upper bound greater then or equal to H_2. •

Heuristic 3: RM consists of all nodes from MT that are not contained in H, LM and satisfy one or more of the following conditions:

(Analogously as heuristic 2 except $\mathcal{RM}$ and W_2 instead of $\mathcal{LM}$ and W_1) •

Heuristic 4: F consists of all nodes from MT that are not contained in H, LM, RM, and satisfy one or more of the following conditions:

1. Subtree S of MT with its root r_s belongs to F iff r_s is of type $n_{<TABLE>}$ and completely belongs to $\mathcal{F}$ (i.e. the lower bound of the table is greater than or equal to H_2).

2. Subtree S of MT with its root r_s belongs to F iff the lower bound of r_s is greater than or equal to m and r_s does not belong to the subtrees found in 1. Number m is the maximum lower bound of all $n_{<TABLE>}$ nodes found in 1.

3. Let $n \in \{n_{
}, n_{<HR>}\}$ or n is in the scope of the central text alignment. Further, assume n is the lowest of all nodes in MT completely contained in $\mathcal{7}$. Subtree S of MT with its root r_s belongs to F iff lower bound of r_s is greater than or equal to the upper bound of n, and r_s does not belong to the subtrees found in 1 and 2. •

Heuristic 5: C consists of all nodes from MT that are not in H, LM, RM, and F. •

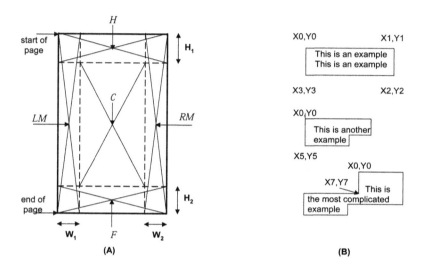

Fig. 1. Position of areas of interest in a page (A) and some possible text polygons (B)

From previous definitions of heuristics one can understand the importance of the $<TABLE>$ tag and its related tags $<TR>$ and $<TD>$. These tags are commonly used ($\approx 88\%$) for the purposes not originally intended by inventors of HTML [10]. Web designers usually organize the layout of a page and the alignment of objects by including a lot of tables in the page. Therefore every table cell often represents a smallest amount of the logically grouped information, visually presented to the user in a browser window (in our case on the VS). The same stands for tables that often group menu objects, footers, search and input forms, and other common page objects. Realization of the previous heuristics is done in at most 2 additional passes through the given MT. Hence the resulting complexity of the whole recognition process is nearly $O(5s)$, allowing us to apply it in different applications mentioned in Section 1.

4. Experimental Results

An experiment is performed to show how efficient the recognition process can be using only the spatial information given through *MT*. The setup of the experiment was as follows:

Step 1: Construct the dataset *D* that contains sufficient number of different pages from different sites.

Step 2: Walk through *D* manually and label areas that can be considered as H, F, LM, RM, and C.

Step 3: Perform automatic extraction of *MT* for each page in *D*. Perform automatic recognition of the areas of interest using defined heuristics on *MT*. Make the new automatically labeled dataset D_I from each previously processed *MT*.

Step 4: Walk through D_I manually and estimate how well the areas are recognized using manually labeled *D* as a reference point.

Step 1 is conducted by downloading nearly 16000 pages from the open source directory *www.dmoz.org* as a starting point for our crawler. We downloaded nearly 1000 files from the first level of every root category. *D* is constructed from the downloaded set by randomly choosing 515 files, uniformly distributed among categories and also by size. Two persons performed step 2 once. The second person was a kind of control and an ultimate judge for labeling. Step 3 is performed using a tool that includes *MT* builder and the logic for applying the recognition heuristics. This tool can be used to visualize objects of interest from a web page. For example one can see in a scrolling window where the paragraphs and line breaks are placed. One can also enter any sequence of HTML tags to obtain the picture (visualization) of their positions. In step 4, two persons make the judgment of recognizer performance by entering into each labeled file and comparing the automatic labels with the hand made labels from step 2. After step 4 we obtained the results shown in table 1.

In order to discuss results, notions of "bad" or "good" in recognition process have to be clarified. If area *X* exists but is not labeled at all, or if *X* does not exist but something is labeled as *X*, then mark "not recognized" is evidenced. If less than 50% of objects that belong to *X* are labeled, or if some objects out of *X* are labeled too, then mark "bad" is evidenced. Mark "good" is evidenced if more than 50% but less than 90% of objects from *X* are labeled and no objects out of *X* are labeled. Mark "excellent" is evidenced if more than 90% of objects from *X* and no objects out of *X* are labeled. The verification process was very tedious and it lasted a whole week!

We stress that mark "bad" is given in cases where something is wrongly recognized. That is because we intend to use our tool to filter the noise for the text classification purposes. Therefore if some text from the center of a page is wrongly removed we could lose important information. Also, the recognition of C is, according to heuristic 5, complementary to the recognition of other areas. So we did not include it in the performance measurements.

Results from Table 1 (column "overall") are obtained by introducing the total score *S* for the page *P* as a sum of all marks for recognition of all areas of interest. If $X \in \{H, F, LM, RM\}$ is "not recognized" then the corresponding mark is 0. Marks "bad", "good", and "excellent" are mapped into 1, 2, and 3 respectively. Now, if $S = 12$ we assume that recognition process for a particular file (page) is "excellent". Similar "good" stands for $8 \leq S < 12$, "bad" stands for $4 \leq S < 8$, and "not recognized" stands for $S < 4$. Analyzing pages that produced "bad" or "not recognized" we found that in nearly 20% **MT** was not quite correct but **mT** was correct i.e. the rendering process was not good enough. The typical error is that portions of a page are internally rendered well but they are scrambled as a whole.

Table 1. Success in the recognition process (in %). Shaded rows represent successful recognition.

	Header %	Footer %	Left Menu %	Right Menu %	Overall %
Not recognized	25	13	6	5	3
Bad	16	17	15	14	24
Good	10	15	3	2	50
Excellent	49	55	76	79	23

For the rest of 80% of "not recognized" and "bad" recognized pages we suppose that defined heuristics are not sufficient enough. Finally we selected values for margins H_1, H_2, W_1, and W_2 according to the statistics from [9]. In further research other values have to be considered as well.

5. Conclusion

This paper describes a possible representation for a web page in which objects are placed into the well-defined tree hierarchy according to where they belong in an HTML structure of a page. We named this representation **M-Tree**. Further, each object (node from **M-Tree**) carries information about its position in a browser window. This spatial information enables us to define heuristics for the recognition of common areas such as a header, footer, left and right menus, and the center of a page. The crucial difficulty was to develop sufficiently good rendering algorithm i.e. to imitate behavior of the popular user agents such as *Internet Explorer*. We concluded from analyzed pages that an HTML source was often far away from the proposed standard and it posed additional problems in the rendering process. After applying some techniques for the error recovery in the construction of the parsing tree and introducing some rendering simplifications (we do not deal with frames, layers and style sheets) we defined recognition heuristics based only on spatial information. We could have included other types of information into the recognition process, but we wanted to observe the percentage of successfully recognized areas based only on a page layout structure and common design patterns. The overall success in recognizing targeted areas yields 73% ("good+excellent"). From Table 1 one can see that menus are either recognized or not. On the other hand recognition of header and footer is more complex and heuristics other than just spatial have to be considered. In further research we plan to improve the rendering process and the recognition heuristics. We plan to apply the *MT* format in a page classification task by grouping features from similar contexts and learning these newly created structures using Hidden-Tree Markov Models. We also hope that we can improve the crawling strategy for the focused crawler described in [4] by estimating the importance of a link based on its position and neighborhood. We believe that *MT* can find its application in many other areas related to search engines, information retrieval and data mining from the Web.

References

1. Quinlan, J.R., "Induction of decision trees", *Machine Learning*, 1986, pp. 81-106.
2. Salton, G., McGill, M.J., *An Introduction to Modern Information Retrieval*, McGraw-Hill, 1983.
3. Chakrabarti S., van den Berg M., Dom B., "Focused crawling: A new approach to topic-specific web resource discovery", *Proceedings of the 8ᵗʰ Int. World Wide Web Conference*, Toronto, Canada, 1999.
4. Diligenti M., Coetzee F., Lawrence S., Giles C., Gori M., "Focused crawling using context graphs", *Proceedings of the 26ᵗʰ Int. Conf. On Very Large Databases*, Cairo, Egypt, 2000.
5. Rennie J., McCallum A., "Using reinforcement learning to spider the web efficiently", *Proceedings of the Int. Conf. On Machine Learning*, Bled, Slovenia, 1999.
6. Embley D.W., Jiang Y.S., Ng Y.K., "Record-Boundary Discovery in Web Documents", *Proceedings of SIGMOD*, Philadelphia, USA, 1999.
7. Lim S. J., Ng Y. K., "Extracting Structures of HTML Documents Using a High-Level Stack Machine", Proceedings of the 12ᵗʰ *International Conference on Information Networking ICOIN*, Tokyo, Japan, 1998
8. World Wide Web Consortium (**W3C**), "HTML 4.01 Specification", http://www.w3c.org/TR/html401/ , December 1999.
9. Bernard L.M., "Criteria for optimal web design (designing for usability)", *http://psychology.wichita.edu/optimalweb/position.htm,* 2001
10. James F., "Representing Structured Information in Audio Interfaces: A Framework for Selecting Audio Marking Techniques to Represent Document Structures", Ph.D. thesis, Stanford University, available online at http://www-pcd.stanford.edu/frankie/thesis/, 2001.

A Neural Approach to Abductive Multi-adjoint Reasoning

Jesús Medina, Enrique Mérida-Casermeiro, and Manuel Ojeda-Aciego

Dept. Matemática Aplicada. Universidad de Málaga*
{jmedina,merida,aciego}@ctima.uma.es

Abstract. A neural approach to propositional multi-adjoint logic programming was recently introduced. In this paper we extend the neural approach to multi-adjoint deduction and, furthermore, modify it to cope with abductive multi-adjoint reasoning, where adaptations of the uncertainty factor in a knowledge base are carried out automatically so that a number of given observations can be adequately explained.

1 Introduction

Uncertainty, incompleteness, and/or inconsistency have to be faced, sooner or later, when dealing with complex applications of knowledge representation. As a result, several frameworks for manipulating data and knowledge have been proposed in the form of extensions to classical logic programming and deductive databases. The underlying uncertainty formalism in the proposed frameworks includes probability theory, fuzzy set theory, many-valued logic, or possibilistic logic. Our approach to modelling uncertainty in human cognition and real world applications is based on the multi-adjoint logic programming paradigm.

In this paper we introduce and study a model of abduction problem. Abductive reasoning is widely recognized as an important form of reasoning with uncertain information that is appropriate for many problems in Artificial Intelligence. Broadly speaking, abduction aims at finding explanations for, or causes of, observed phenomena or facts; it is inference to the best explanation, a pattern of reasoning that occurs in such diverse places as medical diagnosis, scientific theory formation, accident investigation, language understanding, and jury deliberation. More formally, abduction is an inference mechanism where given a knowledge base and some observations, the reasoner tries to find hypotheses which together with the knowledge base explain the observations. Reasoning based on such an inference mechanism is referred to as abductive reasoning.

Abduction methods can be characterised within different frameworks, such as logical, neural, data analysis, etc. We will use the logical and the neural approach in this paper, in order to present our model of abduction reasoning. In general, as pointed out in [1], a neural network is assumed to support complex patterns of interaction between effects and causes; however, it is very difficult to model relationships such as competition between two causes when a common effect shows up and cooperation between them otherwise.

---

* Partially supported by Spanish DGI project BFM2000-1054-C02-02.

D. Scott (Ed.): AIMSA 2002, LNAI 2443, pp. 213–222, 2002.

This is why we have chosen a hybrid approach, in which all these relationships are expressed in the rich language of multi-adjoint logic. The purpose of this work is to link, following ideas from [3,9], the theoretical framework for abductive multi-adjoint reasoning presented in [7], and its neural net implementation [6].

Transformation rules carry multi-adjoint logic programs into corresponding neural networks, where the confidence values of rules relate to output of neurons in the net, confidence values of facts represent input values for the net, and network functions are determined by a set of conjunctors, implications and aggregation operators; the output of the net being the values of the propositional variables in the program under its minimal model. Also, some examples from a first prototype are reported.

2 Preliminary Definitions

In order to make this paper as self-contained as possible, we give here the essentials of multi-adjoint logic programming, and its neural implementation framework. Due to space limitations, neither comments nor motivations are presented, the interested reader is referred to [8] where multi-adjoint logic programs are formally introduced and its procedural semantics is given, to [7] where the framework for abductive reasoning is set, and to [6] in which a neural approach to multi-adjoint logic programming is given.

Originally, the multi-adjoint paradigm was developed for multi-adjoint lattices (a much more general structure for the set of truth-values than the unit real interval $[0, 1]$), however, for the sake of simplicity, in this specific application we will restrict our attention to $[0, 1]$. However, the other special feature of multi-adjoint logic programs, that a number of different implications are allowed in the bodies of the rules, will remain in force. Formally,

Definition 1. *A* multi-adjoint program *is a set of rules* $\langle A \leftarrow_i B, \vartheta \rangle$ *satisfying:*

1. *The* head *of the rule A is a propositional symbol.*
2. *The* body *formula B is a formula of $\mathfrak{F}$ built from propositional symbols $B_1, \ldots, B_n$ ($n \geq 0$) by the use of conjunction ($\&_j$) operators.*
3. *The* confidence factor *ϑ is an element (a truth-value) of $[0, 1]$.*

Facts *are rules with body* $\top$ *(which usually will not be written), and a* query *(or* goal*) is a propositional symbol intended as a question* $?A$ *prompting the system.*

Regarding the implementation as a neural network, it will be useful to give a name to a specially simple type of rule: the *homogeneous rules*.

Definition 2. *A rule* $\langle A \leftarrow_i B, \vartheta \rangle$ *is said to be* homogeneous *if its body is either a propositional symbol or a $\&_i$-conjunction of variables.*

As usual, an *interpretation* is a mapping $I : \Pi \to L$. Note that each of these interpretations can be uniquely extended to the whole set of formulas. The ordering $\preceq$ of the truth-values L can be easily extended to the set of interpretations, which also inherits the structure of complete lattice.

Definition 3.

1. *An interpretation I satisfies* $\langle A \leftarrow_i B, \vartheta \rangle$ *if and only if* $\vartheta \preceq \hat{I}(A \leftarrow_i B)$.
2. *An interpretation I is a* model *of a multi-adjoint logic program* $\mathbb{P}$ *iff all weighted rules in* $\mathbb{P}$ *are satisfied by I.*
3. *An element* $\lambda \in L$ *is a* correct answer *for a program* $\mathbb{P}$ *and a query* $?A$ *if for any interpretation I which is a model of* $\mathbb{P}$ *we have* $\lambda \preceq I(A)$.

The immediate consequences operator, given by van Emden and Kowalski, can be easily generalised to the framework of multi-adjoint logic programs.

Definition 4. *Let* $\mathbb{P}$ *be a multi-adjoint program. The* immediate consequences operator $T_{\mathbb{P}}$ *maps interpretations to interpretations, and is defined by*

$$T_{\mathbb{P}}(I)(A) = \sup \left\{ \vartheta \mathbin{\dot{\&}_i} \hat{I}(B) \mid \langle A \leftarrow_i B, \vartheta \rangle \in \mathbb{P} \right\}$$

The semantics of a multi-adjoint logic program can be characterised, as usual, by the post-fixpoints of $T_{\mathbb{P}}$; that is, an interpretation I is a model of a multi-adjoint logic program $\mathbb{P}$ iff $T_{\mathbb{P}}(I) \sqsubseteq I$. The $T_{\mathbb{P}}$ operator is proved to be monotonic and continuous under very general hypotheses, see [8], and it is remarkable that these results are true even for non-commutative and non-associative conjunctors. In particular, by continuity, the least model can be reached in at most countably many iterations of $T_{\mathbb{P}}$ on the least interpretation.

3   Model of Neural Network

In this section we briefly describe the model of neural net chosen to implement the immediate consequences operator $T_{\mathbb{P}}$ for multi-adjoint logic programming.

Before describing the model, some considerations are needed: The set of operators to be implemented will consist of the three most important adjoint pairs: product ($\&_P, \leftarrow_P$), Gödel ($\&_G, \leftarrow_G$) and Lukasiewicz ($\&_L, \leftarrow_L$). Regarding the selection of operators implemented, just recall that every t-norm, the type of conjunctor more commonly used in the context of fuzzy reasoning, is expressible as a direct sum of these three basic conjunctors [5]. Regarding the aggregation operators, we will implement a family of weighted sums, which are denoted $@_{(n_1,\dots,n_m)}$ and defined as follows:

$$@_{(n_1,\dots,n_m)}(p_1,\dots,p_m) = \frac{n_1 p_1 + \cdots + n_m p_m}{n_1 + \cdots + n_m}$$

A neural net is considered in which each process unit is associated to either a propositional symbol or an homogeneous rule. The state of the i-th neuron in the instant t is expressed by its output $I_i(t)$. Thus, the state of the network can be expressed by means of a state vector $\mathbf{I}(p)$, whose components are the output of the neurons in the net, and its initial state is the null vector.

Regarding the user interface, there are two layers, a visible one, whose output is part of the overall output of the net, and a hidden layer, whose outputs are only used as input values for other neurons.

The connection between neurons is denoted by a matrix of weights $\mathbf{W}$, in which w_{kj} indicates the existence or absence of connection from unit k to unit j; if the neuron represents a weighted sum, then the matrix of weights also represents the weights associated to any of the inputs. The weights of the connections related to neuron i (that is, the i-th row of the matrix $\mathbf{W}$) are represented by $\boldsymbol{w}_{i\bullet}$, and are allocated in an internal vector register of the neuron.

We will work with two vectors in the internal register: the first one stores the confidence values $\boldsymbol{v}$ of atoms and homogeneous rules, the second vector, $\boldsymbol{m}$, stores the functioning mode of each neuron in the net as a signal m_i. The different functioning modes are described below:

If $m_i = 1$ the neuron is assumed to be associated to a propositional symbol, and its next state is the maximum value among all its input, its previous state, and the initial confidence values v_i. More precisely:

Case p, $m_i = 1$: $I_i(t+1) = \max \left\{ \max_{k|w_{ik}>0} \{I_k(t)\}, I_i(t), v_i \right\}$

When a neuron is associated to the product, Gödel, or Lukasiewicz implication, then the signal m_i is set to 2, 3, and 4, respectively. Its input is formed by the external value v_i of the rule, and the outputs of the neurons associated to the body of the implication. The output of the neuron somehow mimics the behaviour of the procedural semantics when a rule of type m_i has been used; specifically, the output in the next instant will be:

Case $\leftarrow_P$, $m_i = 2$: $I_i(t+1) = \max \left\{ I_i(t), v_i \cdot \prod_{k|w_{ik}>0} I_k(t) \right\}$

Case $\leftarrow_G$, $m_i = 3$: $I_i(t+1) = \max \left\{ I_i(t), \min \left\{ v_i, \min_{k|w_{ik}>0} \{I_k(t)\} \right\} \right\}$

Case $\leftarrow_L$, $m_i = 4$: $I_i(t+1) = \max \left\{ I_i(t), v_i + \sum_{k|w_{ik}>0} I_k(t) - N_i \right\}$,

where N_i indicates the number of arguments of the body of the rule.
Case @, $m_i = 5$: the aggregators considered as weighted sums, therefore

$$I_i(t+1) = \sum_{k|w_{ik}>0} w'_{ik} \cdot I_k(t) \qquad \text{where} \qquad w'_{ik} = \frac{w_{ik}}{\displaystyle\sum_{r|w_{ir}>0} w_{ir}}$$

Finally, neurons associated to the adjoint conjunctors have signals $m_i = 6, 7, 8$, for product, Gödel, or Lukasiewicz conjunctions, respectively. Its output is:

Case $\&_P$, $m_i = 6$: $I_i(t+1) = \prod_{k|w_{ik}>0} I_k(t)$

Case $\&_G$, $m_i = 7$: $I_i(t+1) = \min_{k|w_{ik}>0} I_k(t)$

Case $\&_L$, $m_i = 8$: $I_i(t+1) = \max \left\{ 0, \sum_{k|w_{ik}>0} I_k(t) - N_i + 1 \right\}$

Note that the output of the neurons is never decreasing.

By means of an external reset signal r, common to all the neurons, one can modify both the values of the internal registers of the neurons and their state vector $I(t)$.

- $r = 1$. The initial truth-value v_i, the type of formula m_i, and the i-th row of the matrix of weights $w_{i\bullet}$ are set in the internal registers. This allows to reinitialise the network for working with a new problem.
- $r = 0$. The neurons evolve with the usual dynamics, and it is only affected by the state vector of the net $I(t)$. The value m_i, set in their internal register, selects the function which is activated in the neuron. By using a delay, the output of the activated function is compared with the previous value of the neuron.

Once the corresponding values for both the registers and the initial state of the net have been loaded, the signal r is set to 0, and each neuron will only be affected by the neurons given by $I(t)$, its state vector at step t.

A number of programs have been carried out with the implementation. Here we present two toy examples:

Example 1. Consider the program with rules

$$\langle h \leftarrow_G (r \& _P o), 0.9 \rangle \qquad \langle v \leftarrow_G @_{(1,2)}(o, w), 0.8 \rangle$$
$$\langle n \leftarrow_P r, 0.8 \rangle \qquad \langle n \leftarrow_P w, 0.9 \rangle \qquad \langle w \leftarrow_P v, 0.75 \rangle$$

and facts $\langle o, 0.2 \rangle$, $\langle w, 0.2 \rangle$, $\langle r, 0.5 \rangle$.

As there are non-homogeneous rules, the rules of the program are transformed as follows

$$\langle i \leftarrow_P r \& _P o, 1 \rangle \qquad \langle j \leftarrow_P @_{(1,2)}(o, w), 1 \rangle$$
$$\langle h \leftarrow_G i, 0.9 \rangle \qquad \langle v \leftarrow_G j, 0.8 \rangle \qquad \langle n \leftarrow_P r, 0.8 \rangle$$
$$\langle n \leftarrow_P w, 0.9 \rangle \qquad \langle w \leftarrow_P v, 0.75 \rangle$$

Therefore, we will need 13 neurons (7 in the hidden layer) associated to variables h, n, o, r, v, w, i, j and to the last five rules.

The initial values of the registers are:

- The vector $v = (0, 0, 0.2, 0.5, 0, 0.2, 1, 1, 0.9, 0.8, 0.8, 0.9, 0.75)$
- The vector $m = (1, 1, 1, 1, 1, 1, 6, 5, 3, 3, 2, 2, 2)$
- The matrix W_1 is given in Figure 1 (left).

After five iterations, the net gets a stable state:

$$I = (0.1, 0.4, 0.2, 0.5, 0.2, 0.2, 0.1, 0.2, 0.1, 0.2, 0.4, 0.18, 0.15)$$

with the following values for the variables: $v_h = 0.1$; $v_n = 0.4$; $v_o = 0.2$; $v_r = 0.5$; $v_v = 0.2$; $v_w = 0.2$.

Example 2. Consider the program with rules

$$\langle p \leftarrow_G @_{(1,2,3)}(q, r, s), 0.8 \rangle \qquad \langle q \leftarrow_P (t \& _L u), 0.6 \rangle$$
$$\langle t \leftarrow_P (v \& _G u), 0.5 \rangle \qquad \langle v \leftarrow_P u, 0.8 \rangle$$

and facts $\langle u, 0.75 \rangle$, $\langle r, 0.7 \rangle$, $\langle s, 0.6 \rangle$.

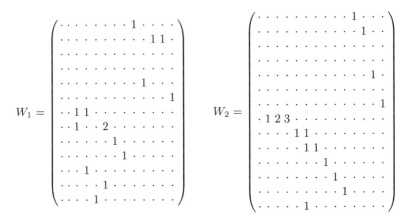

Fig. 1. Matrices for Examples 1 and 2.

Firstly, the rules of the program are homogenised as follows

$$\langle h \leftarrow_P @_{(1,2,3)}(q,r,s),1\rangle \quad \langle i \leftarrow_P t\&_L u,1\rangle \quad \langle j \leftarrow_P v\&_G u,1\rangle$$
$$\langle p \leftarrow_G h,0.8\rangle \quad \langle q \leftarrow_P i,0.6\rangle$$
$$\langle t \leftarrow_P j,0.5\rangle \quad \langle v \leftarrow_P u,0.8\rangle$$

The net will consist of 14 neurons, to represent variables $p, q, r, s, t, u, v, h, i, j$ together with the last four (homogeneous) rules in the program.

The initial values of the net are:

- The vector $v = (0,0,0.7,0.6,0,0.75,0,1,1,1,0.8,0.6,0.5,0.8)$.
- The vector $m = (1,1,1,1,1,1,1,5,8,7,3,2,2,2)$.
- The matrix W_2 is given in Figure 1 (right).

After running the net, its state vector get stabilised at

$$I = (0.5383,0.03,0.7,0.6,0.3,0.75,0.6,0.5383,0.05,0.6.0.5383,0.03,0.3,0.6)$$

where the first nine components correspond to the visible layer, which are interpreted as the obtained truth-value for p, q, etc.

4   Abduction in Multi-adjoint Logic Programs

In this section we introduce the basics of abductive reasoning in a multi-adjoint context; specifically, we will define the concept of (multi-adjoint) abduction problem and correct explanation for an abduction problem. Later, we will make the necessary adaptations to the neural model to cope with abductive reasoning.

Definition 5. *An* abduction problem *is a tuple* $\mathcal{A} = \langle \mathbb{P}, OBS, H \rangle$, *where*

1. $\mathbb{P}$ *is a multi-adjoint logic program.*
2. H *is a (finite) subset of the set of propositional symbols, the set of hypotheses.*
3. $OBS: OV \rightarrow [0, 1]$ *is the theory of observations (where OV is a set of observation variables such that $OV \cap H = \varnothing$).*

The intended meaning of $OV \cap H = \varnothing$ is that observation variables should not be explained by themselves.

Definition 6. *A theory $E: H \rightarrow [0, 1]$ is a* correct explanation *to $\langle \mathbb{P}, OBS, H \rangle$ if*

1. $\mathbb{P} \cup E$ *is satisfiable.*
2. *Every model of $\mathbb{P} \cup E$ is also a model of OBS.*

In [7] it was given a the procedural semantics based on the $T_{\mathbb{P}}$ operator which is sound and complete and, furthermore, it was proved that the surface corresponding to all the solutions for particular observations has the shape of a convex body and the set of all solutions is the union of such surfaces.

4.1 Neural Model for Multi-adjoint Abduction

Our main goal here is to adapt the neural model above to the abductive framework for multi-adjoint logic programming. The general approach to abduction is, given a program $\mathbb{P}$ and a set of observations, to obtain a set of explanations for these observations, as a number of *abduced* facts. In addition, we are also interested in allowing the possibility of changing the confidence values of the rules in the given program for a number of reasons; for instance, it could happen that no explanation exists simply because the confidence values of the rules have not been suitably assigned although, obviously, it might also happen that no explanation can be obtained for a given problem, for instance, in the case of badly posed problems.

Our neural model for abductive reasoning will allow to divide the set of rules as rules with 'hard' confidence value and rules with 'soft' confidence value; the former assumed to have a fixed confidence value throughout all the computation and the latter whose confidence value could be modified if necessary.

Once the parameters v, m and $\mathbf{W}$ have been set in the initial registers of the net, the program can be run in order to obtain the minimal model, which may or may not explain all the observed values (loaded in a vector of observed values ov). Obviously, the interesting case from an abductive point of view is when the minimal model does not explain all the observed values.

The neural model for abduction will be a modification on that given in the previous section which includes, apart from the vector of observed values ov, another vector for setting the rules whose confidence values will remain unmodified u. Now, our goal will be to find either an explanation based solely on the set of hypotheses or set new confidence values to rules (determined by vector u) so that the observed values are attained. The search for these new confidence values v is obtained by training the net.

If there are n neurons, and we have b observed values and h rules have hard confidence values then the net implements a function $f: [0, 1]^{n-b-h} \rightarrow [0, 1]^b$, since the b

components of the observations and the h components of the hard rules will remain fixed. Therefore we can consider the space $[0, 1]^{n-b-h}$ as the search space and, given $v \in [0, 1]^n$ we will denote its projection on the search space as $\pi_v \in [0, 1]^n$.

Given the observations $ov \in [0, 1]^b$, we define the **feasible region** as the set $\mathcal{F} \subset [0, 1]^{n-b-h}$ such that if $\pi_v \in \mathcal{F}$ then $\pi_{v_j} \geq ov_j$ for all $j = 1, \dots, b$.

The function implemented by the net has the following properties:

1. It is non-decreasing in all its components.
2. If there is some correct explanation, then $f(\mathbf{1}) \in \mathcal{F}$.
3. If every interpretation is a correct explanation, then $f(\mathbf{0}) \in \mathcal{F}$.

4.2   Training the Net

Given an abduction problem, firstly, we have to check whether there is at least a model for the program and the observations. This is done by checking that the vector $\pi_v = \mathbf{1}$, changed by including the observed values, is a point of the feasible region. If we get affirmative answer, then the effective training of the net begins, having in mind that the components of v corresponding to the observations will be fixed for all the training process, as well as m and $\mathbf{W}$.

We have chosen to randomly search for explanations, so that we have chance to obtaining a wide range of possible explanations to a given abduction problem. The training process aims at obtaining a vector of confidence values for hypotheses and soft rules such that the resulting least model (that is, the output of the function implemented by the net) is as close as possible to the frontier of the feasible region.

The training is based on an iterative procedure which begins with the initial vector $v_0 = \pi_v$, where v corresponds to the confidence values of rules and facts in the program $\mathbb{P}$, and zeroes assigned to variables which are not facts. Now, assume that the net gets stable at point $f(v_0)$, and randomly take another vector $v_1 \in [0, 1]^{n-b-h}$, and assume the net stabilises at $f(v_1)$. Then, calculate the values $0 \leq k \leq 1$, such that the point $kf(v_0) + (1 - k)f(v_1)$ is the closest (using euclidean distance) to vector ov. The new initial vector will be $v_2 = kv_0 + (1 - k)v_1$, which by convexity is in the search space.

The procedure is repeated by choosing new random vectors, until the resulting confidence values v_n are such that $f(v_n)$ can be no longer improved, in the sense of getting closer to ov. This occurs if in several trials (in a number greater than the dimension $n - b - h$ of the search space) the obtained point gets fixed. This point is checked to be in the feasible region, if affirmative the training is finished, otherwise, we will find the point in the frontier of the feasible region contained in the segment $[v_n, \mathbf{1}]$.

As a result, after the training process, the net is able to explain the observed facts, in the sense that new confidence values are assigned to rules and facts, and possibly new facts are added to the program, obtaining a modified program $\mathbb{P}'$, so that the observations are logically implied by $\mathbb{P}'$.

4.3   Simulations for Multi-adjoint Abduction

A number of problems have been carried out with the resulting implementation. Here we present some toy examples:

Example 3. Consider the program with rules

$$\langle p \leftarrow_P (q \& _P r), 0.8 \rangle \qquad \text{and} \qquad \langle r \leftarrow_G s, 0.7 \rangle$$

and the observation $\langle p, 0.7 \rangle$.

By assigning neurons with the variables p, q, r, s and with the two rules, the initial registers will be $v = (0,0,0,0,0.8,0.7)$, $m = (1,1,1,1,2,3)$, the matrix W whose entries are all zeros but $w_{15}, w_{36}, w_{52}, w_{53}$ and w_{64} which are 1, and the observed value $p = 0.7$.

After training the net, without considering any hard rule, we get the new vector of confidence values $v = (0, 0.8599, 0.9024, 0.9268, 0.8783, 0.9641)$, which gives the new program with rules

$$\langle p \leftarrow_P (q \& _P r), 0.8783 \rangle \quad \text{and} \quad \langle r \leftarrow_G s, 0.9641 \rangle$$

and facts $\langle q, 0.8599 \rangle$, $\langle r, 0.9268 \rangle, \langle s, 0.9268 \rangle$.

Example 4. Consider the following program

$$hi\_fuel\_comp \overset{0.8}{\leftarrow_G} @_{(2,1)}(ri\_mix, lo\_oil) \tag{1}$$

$$overheating \overset{0.5}{\leftarrow_P} lo\_oil \tag{2}$$

$$overheating \overset{0.9}{\leftarrow_L} lo\_water \tag{3}$$

This program is intended to represent some kind of knowledge about the behaviour of a car.[1] Let us assume that we have two observed facts, namely

$$\langle hi\_fuel\_comp, 0.75 \rangle \qquad \langle overheating, 0.5 \rangle$$

The vector of observed values is $ov = (0.75, 0.5)$

We have trained the net twice: the first one considering no hard rule, and the second one considering no soft rule.

The non-homogeneous rule has been separated by introducing a hidden neuron implementing its body The obtained results in either case are the following:

1. No hard rules: The obtained explanation, regarding the hypotheses, is $ri\_mix = 0.853$, $lo\_oil = 0.5656$, $lo\_water = 0.6214$, and the updated confidence values for the rules are (1)= 0.75, (2)= 0.9519 and (3)=0.8837.

   The values above give the following results to the observed variables is $hi\_fuel\_comp = 0.75$ and $overheating = 0.5384$.
2. No soft rules: The obtained explanation is $ri\_mix = 0.8335$, $lo\_oil = 0.5864$, and $lo\_water = 0.6$.

   The values above give the following results to the observed variables is $hi\_fuel\_comp = 0.7511$ and $overheating = 0.5$.

---

[1] We do not intend that these relationships correspond to an actual case.

5 Conclusions and Related Work

A neural model has been introduced, which implements the procedural semantics recently given to multi-adjoint logic programming, in addition, it has been adapted to model abductive reasoning. As a result, it is possible to adjust the confidence values of the rules and facts of a given program which is supposed to explain a set of given observations. An advantage of the use of multi-adjoint programs is that one has a uniform computational model for a number of fuzzy rules and, thus, the implementation can be easily modified to add new connectives.

Some authors have addressed similar problems as those stated here; for instance [4] introduces a neural implementation of the fixed point of the $T_\mathbb{P}$ operator but only for classical logic. On the other hand [1,2] introduces some neural approaches to the simulation of abductive reasoning, in which the complexity of the relationships between causes and effects is reproduced at the neural level; in our case, this complexity is dealt with by using the great expressive power of multi-adjoint logic, and the neural approach is used to provide a massively parallel computational model.

As future work, we will have to study different training strategies for the net in order to minimise its complexity and improving the approximation to the observed values, in order to apply some criteria for selecting the "best" explanation are used, such as the *parsimony covering* (the best explanation should include a minimal set of causes) or *maximal plausibility* (the best explanation must be the most likely wrt a given belief function).

Acknowledgements. We thank P. Eklund for providing interesting comments on previous versions of this work.

References

1. B.E. Ayeb and S. Wang. Abduction based diagnosis: A competition based neural model simulating abductive reasoning. *J. of Parall. and Distributed Computing*, 24(2):202–212, 1995.
2. B.E. Ayeb, S. Wang, and J. Ge. A unified model for neural based abduction. *IEEE Transactions on Systems, Man and Cybernetics*, 28(4):408–425, 1998.
3. P. Eklund and F. Klawonn. Neural fuzzy logic programming. *IEEE Trans. on Neural Networks*, 3(5):815–818, 1992.
4. S. Hölldobler, Y. Kalinke, and H.-P. Störr. Approximating the semantics of logic programs by recurrent neural networks. *Applied Intelligence*, 11(1):45–58, 1999.
5. E.P. Klement, R. Mesiar, and E. Pap. *Triangular norms*. Kluwer academic, 2000.
6. J. Medina, E. Mérida-Casermeiro, and M. Ojeda-Aciego. Multi-adjoint logic programming: a neural net approach. In *Logic Programming. ICLP'02*. Lect. Notes in Computer Science, 2002. To appear.
7. J. Medina, M. Ojeda-Aciego, and P. Vojtáš. A multi-adjoint logic approach to abductive reasoning. In *Logic Programming, ICLP'01*, pages 269–283. Lect. Notes in Computer Science 2237, 2001.
8. J. Medina, M. Ojeda-Aciego, and P. Vojtáš. A procedural semantics for multi-adjoint logic programming. In *Progress in Artificial Intelligence, EPIA'01*, pages 290–297. Lect. Notes in Artificial Intelligence 2258, 2001.
9. E. Mérida-Casermeiro, G. Galán-Marín, and J. Muñoz Pérez. An efficient multivalued Hopfield network for the traveling salesman problem. *Neural Processing Letters*, 14:203–216, 2001.

Restricted Δ-Trees in Multiple-Valued Logics*

I.P. de Guzmán, M. Ojeda-Aciego, and A. Valverde

Dept. Matemática Aplicada
Universidad de Málaga
{guzman,aciego,a_valverde}@ctima.uma.es

Abstract. This paper generalises the tree-based data structure of Δ-tree to be applied to signed propositional formulas. The Δ-trees allow a compact representation for signed formulas as well as for a number of reduction strategies in order to consider only those occurrences of literals which are relevant for the satisfiability of the input formula. The conversions from signed formulas to Δ-trees and vice versa are described and a notion of restricted form based on this representation is introduced, allowing for a compact representation of formulas in order to consider only those occurrences of literals which are relevant for its satisfiability.

Keywords. Automated Reasoning. Knowledge Representation

1 Introduction

Proof methods for multiple-valued logic have developed alongside the evolution of the notions of *sign* and *signed formula*. The use of signs and signed formulas allows one to apply classical methods in the analysis of multiple-valued logics. Forgetting the set of truth-values associated with a given logic, in the metalanguage one may interpret sentences about the multiple-valued logic as being true-or-false. For example, in a 3-valued logic with truth-values $\{0, 1/2, 1\}$ and with $\{1\}$ as the designated value, the satisfiability of a formula φ can be expressed as: *Is it possible to evaluate φ in $\{1\}$?* In the same way, the unsatisfiability of φ is expressed by: *Is it possible to evaluate φ in $\{1, 1/2\}$?* These questions can be represented by the signed formulas $\{1\}{:}\varphi$ and $\{1/2,1\}{:}\varphi$ which are evaluated on the set $\{0, 1\}$ with the following meaning:

$\{1\}{:}\varphi$ takes the value 1 iff φ can be evaluated in $\{1\}$

$\{1/2,1\}{:}\varphi$ takes the value 1 iff φ can be evaluated in $\{1/2, 1\}$

In other words, the formulas in a signed logic are constructions of the form $S{:}\varphi$, where S is a set of truth-values of the multiple-valued logic, called the *sign*, and φ is a formula of that logic. The interpretations that determine the semantics of the signed logic are defined from the interpretations of the multiple-valued logic as follows:

$$I_\sigma(S{:}\varphi) = 1 \quad \text{if and only if} \quad \sigma(\varphi) \in S$$

The first works to provide a systematic treatment of sets of truth-values as signs were due to Hähnle in [5] and Murray and Rosenthal in [7]. There the notion of *signed formula* is formally introduced. In [5] these tools are used in the framework of truth tables,

---

* Research partially supported by Spanish DGI project BFM2000-1054-C02-02.

D. Scott (Ed.): AIMSA 2002, LNAI 2443, pp. 223–232, 2002.
© Springer-Verlag Berlin Heidelberg 2002

while in [7] they are used to develop another, nonclausal proof method, that of *dissolution*. As a result of these works, the use of signed formulas in the field of automated deduction has been extended, and has lead to significant advances in this method; therefore, efficient representations for signed formulas are necessary in order to describe and implement efficient algorithms on this kind of formulas.

An approach to the efficient handling of signed formulas that one can find in the literature is the clause form [6], which allow the extension of classical techniques such as resolution, or Davis-Putnam procedures. Another representation is the Multiple-Valued Decision Diagrams (MDDs) and its variants [11, 2], but they are not useful for the study of satisfiability because although they make straightforward the testing of satisfiability, the construction of a restricted MDD for a given formula is exponential in the worst case. Some specific representation approaches exist for particular tasks, such as labelled rough partitions [3] to work with multiple-valued relations.

The approach we follow in this paper is that introduced in [4], interpreting signed formulas given means of Δ-trees, that is, trees of clauses and cubes. We will be mainly concerned with the metatheory of multiple-valued Δ-trees, not with implementation issues; however, the results obtained for the classical case are promising. It is interesting to recall the intrinsic parallelism between the usual representation of cnfs as lists of clauses and our representation of signed formulas as lists of Δ-trees.

Clause	$\rightsquigarrow$	List of literals
Cnf	$\rightsquigarrow$	List of clauses
Δ-tree	$\rightsquigarrow$	Tree of clauses/cubes
Signed formula	$\rightsquigarrow$	List of Δ-trees

In this multiple-valued version, we will consider clauses and cubes with *basic* literals: signed literals with singleton signs.

2   Reduced Signed Logics

The notion of *reduced signed logic* was introduced in [8] as a generalisation of previous approaches. It is developed in the general framework of propositional logics, without reference either to an initially given multiple-valued logic or to a specific algorithm, ie. the definition is completely independent of the particular application at hand. The generalisation consists in introducing a *possible truth values function* to restrict the truth values for each variable. These restrictions can be motivated by the specific application and they can be managed dynamically by the algorithms. For example, in [8] these restrictions are used to improve the efficiency of tableaux methods; in [10] are used to characterize non-monotonic reasoning systems.

The formulas in the reduced signed logics are built by using the connectives $\wedge$ and $\vee$ on the atomic formulas. The atomic formulas are the ω-*signed literals*: if $\mathbf{n} = \{1, \dots, n\}$ is a finite set of truth-values, [1] $\mathcal{V}$ is the set of propositional variables and

---

[1] The specific elements of $\mathbf{n}$ are not important, in the examples of this work we will use $\mathbf{n} = \{1, \dots, n\}$ as set of truth values in a n-valued logic.

$\omega : \mathcal{V} \to (2^{\mathbf{n}} \setminus \varnothing)$ is a mapping, called the *possible truth-values function*, then the set of ω-*signed literals* is

$$\text{LIT}_\omega = \{S{:}p \mid S \subseteq \omega(p), p \in \mathcal{V}\} \cup \{\bot, \top\}$$

In a literal $\ell = S{:}p$, the set S is called the *sign of* ℓ and p is the *variable of* ℓ. The opposite of a signed literal $S{:}p$ is $(\omega(p) \setminus S){:}p$ and will be denoted $\overline{S{:}p}$.

The semantics of $\mathbf{S}_\omega$, the *signed logic valued in* $\mathbf{n}$ *by* ω, is defined using the ω-*assignments*. The ω-assignments are mappings from the language into the set $\{0, 1\}$ that interpret $\vee$ as maximum, $\wedge$ as minimum, $\bot$ as falsity, $\top$ as truth and have the following properties:

1. For every p there exists a unique $j \in S$ such that $I(\{j\}{:}p) = 1$
2. $I(S{:}p) = 1$ if and only if there exists $j \in S$ such that $I(\{j\}{:}p) = 1$

These conditions arise from the objective for which signed logics were created: the ω-assignment I over $S{:}p$ is 1 if the variable p is assigned a value in S; this value must be unique for every multiple-valued assignment and thus unique for every ω-assignment. This is why we some times will write $I(\{j\}{:}p) = 1$ as $I(p) = j$.

An important operation in the sequel will be the *reduction* of a signed logic. This operation decreases the possible truth-values set for one or more propositional variables. The reduction will be forced during the application of an algorithm but it can also help us to specify a problem using signed formulas. Specifically, we will use two basic reductions: to prohibit a specific value for a given variable, $[p \neq j]$, and to force a specific value for a given variable, $[p = j]$: If ω is a possible truth-values function, then the possible truth-values functions $\omega[p \neq j]$ and $\omega[p = j]$ are defined as follows:

$$\omega[p \neq j](v) = \begin{cases} \omega(p) \setminus \{j\} & \text{if } v = p \\ \omega(v) & \text{otherwise} \end{cases} \qquad \omega[p = j](v) = \begin{cases} \{j\} & \text{if } v = p \\ \omega(v) & \text{otherwise} \end{cases}$$

If A is a formula in $\mathbf{S}_\omega$, we define the following substitutions:

- $A[p \neq j]$ is a formula in $\mathbf{S}_{\omega[p \neq j]}$ obtained from A by replacing $\{j\}{:}p$ by $\bot$, $\overline{\{j\}{:}p}$ by $\top$ and $S{:}p$ by $(S \setminus \{j\}){:}p$. In addition, the constants are deleted using the 0-1-laws.
- $A[p = j]$ is a formula in $\mathbf{S}_{\omega[p = j]}$ obtained from A by replacing every literal $S{:}p$ satisfying $j \in S$ by $\top$ and every literal $S{:}p$ satisfying $j \notin S$ by $\bot$; in addition, the constants are deleted using the 0-1-laws.

An immediate consequence is the following: if I is a model of A in $\mathbf{S}_\omega$ and $I(p) \neq j$, then (the restriction of) I is also a model of $A[p \neq j]$ in $\mathbf{S}_{\omega[p \neq j]}$; if I is a model of A in $\mathbf{S}_\omega$ and $I(p) = j$, then I is a model of $A[p = j]$ in $\mathbf{S}_{\omega[p = j]}$.

Throughout the rest of the paper, we will use the following standard definitions. A signed formula A in $\mathbf{S}_\omega$ is said to be *satisfiable* if there is an ω-assignment I such that $I(A) = 1$; in this case I is said to be a *model* for A. Two signed formulas A and B are said to be *equisatisfiable*, denoted $A \approx B$, if A is satisfiable iff B is satisfiable.

Two formulas A and B are said to be *equivalent*, denoted $A \equiv B$, if $I(A) = I(B)$ for all ω-assignment I. The symbols $\top$ and $\bot$ denote truth and falsity. We will also use the usual notions of clause (disjunction of literals) and cube (conjunction of literals). A literal ℓ is an *implicant* of a formula A if $\ell \models A$. A literal ℓ is an *implicate* of a formula A if $A \models \ell$.

We will use the standard notions of list and tree. Finite lists are written in juxtaposition, with the standard notation, nil, for the empty list; if λ and λ' are lists, $\ell \in \lambda$ denotes that ℓ is an element of λ; the concatenation of two lists λ and λ' is written as either $\lambda\langle\rangle\lambda'$ or $\lambda \cup \lambda'$; the inclusion and intersection of lists are defined in the usual way.

3 Multiple-Valued Δ-Trees

The satisfiability algorithm we will describe is based on the structure of multiple-valued Δ-trees. In the classical case, nodes in the Δ-trees correspond to lists of literals; in the multiple-valued case we will exploit a duality in the representation of signed literals in terms of basic literals (whose sign is a singleton). To better understand this duality, let us consider the literal $\{1,4\}{:}p$ in the signed logic $\mathbf{S}_\omega$ where $\omega(p) = \{1, 2, 4, 5\}$, then:

$$\{1,4\}{:}p \equiv \{1\}{:}p \vee \{4\}{:}p \qquad \{1,4\}{:}p \equiv \overline{\{2\}{:}p} \wedge \overline{\{5\}{:}p}$$

This way, we have both a disjunctive and a conjunctive representation of signed literals using the literals $\{j\}{:}p$ and $\overline{\{j\}{:}p}$, which are called *basic literals*. In the sequel, we will use a simpler representation for these literals:

$$pj \stackrel{def}{=} \{j\}{:}p \qquad\qquad \overline{pj} \stackrel{def}{=} \overline{\{j\}{:}p}$$

The basic literals pj are the *positive literal* and their opposites, $\overline{pj}$, are the *negative literal*. In the Δ-tree representation we work with lists of positive literals.

Definition 1.

1. *A list/set of positive literals, λ, is* saturated *for the variable p if $pj \in \lambda$ for all $j \in \omega(p)$. (This kind of lists/sets will be interpreted as logical constants.)*
2. *A Δ-list is either the symbol $\natural$ or a list of positive literals such that it does not have repeated literals and it is non-saturated for any propositional variable.*
3. *A Δ-tree T is a tree with labels in the set of Δ-lists.*

In order to define the operator sgf which interprets a Δ-tree as a signed formula, we should keep in mind that:

1. The empty list, nil, has different conjunctive and disjunctive interpretations, since it is well-known the identification of the empty clause with $\bot$ and the empty cube with $\top$; but anyway it corresponds to the neutral element for the corresponding interpretation. Similarly, we will use a unique symbol, $\natural$, to represent the absorbent elements, $\bot$ and $\top$, under the conjunctive and disjunctive interpretation, respectively.

2. A given Δ-tree will always represent a conjunctive signed formula, however, its subtrees are alternatively interpreted as either conjunctive or disjunctive signed formulas, i.e. the immediate subtrees of a conjunctive Δ-tree are disjunctive, and vice versa.

Definition 2. *The operator* sgf *over the set of Δ-trees is defined as follows:*

1. $\mathtt{sgf}(\mathtt{nil}) = \top$, $\mathtt{sgf}(\sharp) = \bot$, $\mathtt{sgf}(\ell_1 \ldots \ell_n) = \overline{\ell_1} \wedge \cdots \wedge \overline{\ell_n}$

2. $\mathtt{sgf}\left(\underset{T_1 \quad \cdots \quad T_m}{\overset{\lambda}{\wedge}}\right) = \mathtt{sgf}(\lambda) \wedge \mathtt{dsgf}(T_1) \wedge \cdots \wedge \mathtt{dsgf}(T_m)$

where the auxiliary operator dsgf *is defined as follow:*

1. $\mathtt{dsgf}(\mathtt{nil}) = \bot$, $\mathtt{dsgf}(\sharp) = \top$, $\mathtt{dsgf}(\ell_1 \ldots \ell_n) = \ell_1 \vee \cdots \vee \ell_n$

2. $\mathtt{dsgf}\left(\underset{T_1 \quad \cdots \quad T_m}{\overset{\lambda}{\wedge}}\right) = \mathtt{dsgf}(\lambda) \vee \mathtt{sgf}(T_1) \vee \cdots \vee \mathtt{sgf}(T_m)$

In short, we will write $\hat{T} = \mathtt{sgf}(T)$ *and* $\check{T} = \mathtt{dsgf}(T)$*; in particular, if $T = \lambda = \ell_1 \ldots \ell_n$ we have:* $\hat{\lambda} = \ell_1 \wedge \cdots \wedge \ell_n$ *and* $\check{\lambda} = \ell_1 \vee \cdots \vee \ell_n$.

The notions of validity, satisfiability, equivalence, equisatisfiability or model are defined by means of the sgf operator; for example, a Δ-tree, T is satisfiable if and only if $\mathtt{sgf}(T)$ is satisfiable and the models of T are the models of $\mathtt{sgf}(T)$.

In the next definition we introduce an operator to make the converse translation, that is, to define the Δ-tree associated to a signed formula. To begin with, we will introduce the representation of clauses and cubes in terms of basic literals.

Definition 3.

1. Given $A = S_1{:}p_1 \vee \cdots \vee S_n{:}p_n$, *consider the following set of positive literals:*

$$\mathcal{A} = \{ps \mid p = p_i \text{ for some } i \text{ and } s \in S_i\}$$

Then the Δ-list $\mathtt{d\Delta List}(A)$ *is $\sharp$ if $\mathcal{A}$ is saturated for some p_i, otherwise it is the list of the elements of $\mathcal{A}$.*

2. Given $A = S_1{:}p_1 \wedge \cdots \wedge S_n{:}p_n$, *consider the following set of positive literals:*

$$\mathcal{B} = \{ps \mid p = p_i \text{ for some } i \text{ and } s \in \omega(p) \smallsetminus S_i\}$$

Then the Δ-list $\mathtt{c\Delta List}(A)$ *is $\sharp$ if $\mathcal{B}$ is saturated for some p_i, and it is the list of the elements of $\mathcal{B}$ otherwise.*

Example 1. In the logic $\mathbf{S}_\omega$ with $\omega(p) = \{1, 2, 4, 5\}$, $\omega(q) = \{1, 2, 3\}$, $\omega(r) = \{2, 5\}$.

- $\mathtt{d\Delta List}(\{1,4\}{:}p \vee \{1,2\}{:}q) = p1\, p4\, q1\, q2$
- $\mathtt{c\Delta List}(\{1,4\}{:}p \wedge \{1,2\}{:}q) = p2\, p5\, q3$
- $\mathtt{d\Delta List}(\{1,4\}{:}p \vee \{2\}{:}r \vee \{2,4,5\}{:}p) = \sharp$, for $\{p1, p2, p4, p5, r2\}$ is saturated for p.
- $\mathtt{d\Delta List}(\{1\}{:}q \wedge \{1,2,4\}{:}p \wedge \{2\}{:}q) = \sharp$, for $\{p5, q1, q2, q3\}$ is saturated for q.

In the following definition, we will work with lists of Δ-trees. To help the reading, we will write these lists with the elements separated by commas and using square brackets as delimiters. This way, for example, $p_1 s_1 \ldots p_n s_n$ is a Δ-list, and $[p_1 s_1, \ldots, p_n s_n]$ is a list of Δ-trees (in which each Δ-tree is a leaf, which turns out to be a singleton Δ-list).

Definition 4. *Let A be a signed formula, $\Delta\mathtt{Tree}(A)$ is a list of Δ-trees defined recursively as follow:*

1. *If A is a disjunctive signed formula, and the disjunction of its literals disjuncts is $A_0 = S_1{:}p_1 \vee \cdots \vee S_k{:}p_k$, and $A_1,\ldots, A_n$ are the non-literal disjuncts of A, then*
   (a) *If $k = 0$ then $\Delta\mathtt{Tree}(A) = [\mathtt{c}\Delta\mathtt{Tree}(A_1), \ldots, \mathtt{c}\Delta\mathtt{Tree}(A_n)]$ (in this case, necessarily $n \neq 0$)*
   (b) *If $\mathtt{d}\Delta\mathtt{List}(A_0) = \natural$, then $\Delta\mathtt{Tree}(A) = [\mathtt{nil}]$ (that is, a list with just one Δ-tree, the leaf $\mathtt{nil}$.)*
   (c) $\Delta\mathtt{Tree}(A) = [\mathtt{c}\Delta\mathtt{List}(S_1{:}p_1), \ldots, \mathtt{c}\Delta\mathtt{List}(S_k{:}p_k),$
   $$\mathtt{c}\Delta\mathtt{Tree}(A_1), \ldots, \mathtt{c}\Delta\mathtt{Tree}(A_n)] \quad \text{otherwise}$$

2. *If A is a conjunctive signed formula, then $\Delta\mathtt{Tree}(A) = [\mathtt{c}\Delta\mathtt{Tree}(A)]$ (that is, a list with just one Δ-tree)*

The auxiliary operators $\mathtt{d}\Delta\mathtt{Tree}$ and $\mathtt{c}\Delta\mathtt{Tree}$ are defined as follows:

- *Let A be a conjunctive signed formula, let $A_0 = S_1{:}p_1 \wedge \cdots \wedge S_k{:}p_k$ be the conjunction of its literal conjuncts, and let $A_1, \ldots, A_n$ be the non-literal conjuncts of A. If $\mathtt{c}\Delta\mathtt{List}(A_0) = \natural$, then $\mathtt{c}\Delta\mathtt{Tree}(A) = \natural$; if $\mathtt{c}\Delta\mathtt{List}(A_0) \neq \natural$, then*

$$\mathtt{c}\Delta\mathtt{Tree}(A) = \frac{\mathtt{c}\Delta\mathtt{List}(A_0)}{\mathtt{d}\Delta\mathtt{Tree}(A_1) \quad \cdots \quad \mathtt{d}\Delta\mathtt{Tree}(A_n)}$$

- *Let A be a disjunctive signed formula, let $A_0 = S_1{:}p_1 \vee \cdots \vee S_k{:}p_k$ be the disjunction of its literals disjuncts, and let $A_1, \ldots, A_n$ be the non-literal disjuncts of A. If $\mathtt{d}\Delta\mathtt{List}(A_0) = \natural$, then $\mathtt{d}\Delta\mathtt{Tree}(A) = \natural$; if $\mathtt{d}\Delta\mathtt{List}(A_0) \neq \natural$, then*

$$\mathtt{d}\Delta\mathtt{Tree}(A) = \frac{\mathtt{d}\Delta\mathtt{List}(A_0)}{\mathtt{c}\Delta\mathtt{Tree}(A_1) \quad \cdots \quad \mathtt{c}\Delta\mathtt{Tree}(A_n)}$$

A Δ-tree will always be interpreted as a conjunctive signed formula. To work with arbitrary signed formulas, we will use lists of Δ-trees; this way, the study of satisfiability can be performed in parallel with the elements of the list.

Example 2. The following examples are from $\mathbf{S}_3$.

$$\Delta\mathtt{Tree}\big(\big(\{1,2\}{:}p \vee \{2\}{:}q\big) \wedge \big(\{2,3\}{:}p \vee \{1,3\}{:}r\big)\big) = \left[\frac{\mathtt{nil}}{p1p2q3 \quad p2p3r1r3} \right]$$

$$\Delta\mathtt{Tree}\big(\{2,3\}{:}q \vee \big(\{1,2\}{:}p \wedge \big(\{1,2\}{:}q \vee \{2,3\}{:}p\big) \wedge \{3\}{:}q \vee \{1\}{:}p\big)\big)$$
$$= \left[q1, \frac{p3}{p2p3q1q2 \quad p1q3} \right]$$

The next theorem shows that the operators $\mathtt{sgf}$ and $\Delta\mathtt{Tree}$ are inverse, up to equivalence.

Theorem 1. *Let A be a signed formula*

1. *If A is disjunctive, then* $\texttt{dsgf}(\texttt{d}\Delta\texttt{Tree}(A)) \equiv A$
2. *If A is conjunctive, then* $\texttt{sgf}(\texttt{c}\Delta\texttt{Tree}(A)) \equiv A$
3. *If* $\Delta\texttt{Tree}(A) = [T_1, \ldots, T_n]$, *then* $A \equiv \hat{T}_1 \vee \cdots \vee \hat{T}_n$. *In particular, if* $n = 0$, *then* $A \equiv \perp$.

From this result we have that, in some sense, the structure of Δ-tree allows to substitute reasoning with literals by reasoning with clauses and cubes. Other important consequence is that the structure of Δ-tree gives us a means to calculate implicants and implicates, which will be used in the reduction transformations below.

Proposition 1. *If T is rooted with* λ *and* $pj \in \lambda$, *then:*

$$\texttt{sgf}(T) \models \overline{pj} \qquad and \qquad pj \models \texttt{dsgf}(T)$$

4 Restricted Δ-Trees

In multiple-valued logic there is not a notion which captures the well-known definition of restricted clauses of classical logic, in which opposite literals and logical constants are not allowed. We can say that restricted Δ-trees are Δ-trees without *trivially* redundant information. The aim of this section is to give a suitable generalisation built on the notion of restricted multiple-valued Δ-tree which is built from its classical counterpart [4].

To begin with, we need the technical definitions given below and in the subsequent sections:

Definition 5. *The operators* Uni *and* Int *are defined on the set of Δ-lists as follows. If* $\lambda_1, \ldots, \lambda_n$ *are Δ-lists then:*

1. $\texttt{Uni}(\lambda_1, \ldots, \lambda_n) = \natural$ *if either there exists i such that* $\lambda_i = \natural$ *or* $\bigcup_{i=1}^{n} \lambda_i$ *is saturated for some variable p. Otherwise,* $\texttt{Uni}(\lambda_1, \ldots, \lambda_n) = \bigcup_{i=1}^{n} \lambda_i$.
2. $\texttt{Int}(\lambda_1, \ldots, \lambda_n) = \natural$ *if* $\lambda_i = \natural$ *for all i.*
   Otherwise, $\texttt{Int}(\lambda_1, \ldots, \lambda_n) = \bigcap_{\lambda_i \neq \natural} \lambda_i$.

The following definition gathers the specific situations that will not be allowed in a restricted form: nodes in the Δ-tree which, in some sense, can be substituted by either $\perp$ or $\top$ without affecting the meaning and leaves with only one propositional variable; in addition, our restricted trees must have explicitly the implicants and implicates of every subtree in order to perform the reductions based in these objects (see [9]).

Definition 6. *Let T be a Δ-tree.*

1. *A node of T is said to be conclusive if it satisfies any of the following conditions:*
   - *It is labelled with* $\natural$, *provided that* $T \neq \natural$.
   - *It is either a leaf or a monary node labelled with* nil, *provided that it is not the root node.*

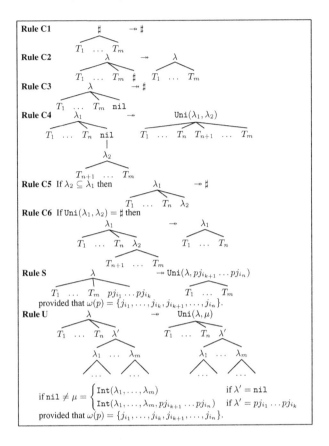

Fig. 1. Rewriting rules to obtain the restricted form

- *It is labelled with λ, it has an immediate successor λ' which is a leaf and $\lambda' \subseteq \lambda$.*
- *It is labelled with λ and $\mathtt{Uni}(\lambda, \lambda') = \sharp$, where λ' is the label of its predecessor.*

2. *A leaf in T is said to be* simple *if the literals in its label share a common propositional variable.*

3. *Let λ be the label of a node of T; let λ' be the label of one immediate successor of λ and let $\lambda_1, \ldots, \lambda_n$ be the labels of the immediate successors of λ'. We say that λ can be updated if it satisfies some of the following conditions:*
   - $\lambda' = \mathtt{nil}$ *and* $\mathtt{Int}(\lambda_1, \ldots, \lambda_m) \not\subseteq \lambda$.
   - $\lambda' = pj_{i_1} \ldots pj_{i_k}$ *and* $\mathtt{Int}(\lambda_1, \ldots, \lambda_m, pj_{i_{k+1}} \ldots pj_{i_n}) \not\subseteq \lambda$, *provided that* $\omega(p) = \{j_{i_1}, \ldots, j_{i_k}, j_{i_{k+1}}, \ldots, j_{i_n}\}$.

   We say that T is updated *if it has no nodes that can be updated.*

4. *If T is updated and it has neither conclusive nodes nor simple leaves, then it is said to be* restricted.

The rewriting rules (up to the order of the successors) in figure 1 allow to delete the conclusive nodes and simple leaves of a Δ-tree and in addition, to update the updatable nodes. Note that the rewriting rules have a double meaning; since they need not apply to the root node, the interpretation can be either conjunctive or disjunctive. This is just another efficiency-related feature of Δ-trees: duality of connectives ∧ and ∨ gets subsumed in the structure and it is not necessary to determine the conjunctive/disjunctive character to decide the transformation to be applied.

Theorem 2. *If T is a Δ-tree, there exists a list of restricted Δ-trees, $[T_1, \ldots, T_n]$, such that* $\texttt{sgf}(T) \equiv \hat{T}_1 \vee \cdots \vee \hat{T}_n$.

The proof of the theorem allows to specify a procedure to obtain $[T_1, \ldots, T_n]$. Let T' be the Δ-tree obtained from T by exhaustively applying the rules C1, C2, C3, C4, C5, C6, S, and U till no one of them can be applied any more, then the list of restricted Δ-trees $[T_1, \ldots, T_n]$, denoted by $\texttt{Restrict}(T)$, is defined as:

1. If $T' = \begin{array}{c}\texttt{nil}\\|\\\texttt{nil}\\ \overbrace{T_1 \ \ldots \ T_n}\end{array}$ then $\texttt{Restrict}(T) = [T_1, \ldots, T_n]$

2. If $T' = \begin{array}{c}\texttt{nil}\\|\\\lambda\\ \overbrace{T_1 \ \ldots \ T_n}\end{array}$, and $\texttt{dsgf}(\lambda) = S_1{:}p_1 \vee \cdots \vee S_k{:}p_k$ with $p_i \neq p_j$ for every $i \neq j$, then $\texttt{Restrict}(T) = [\texttt{cΔList}(S_1{:}p_1), \ldots, \texttt{cΔList}(S_k{:}p_k), T_1, \ldots, T_n]$

3. Otherwise, $\texttt{Restrict}(T) = [T']$.

Example 3. Let us obtain the restricted form of the following Δ-tree in $\mathbf{S}_\omega$ with $\omega(p) = 5$, $\omega(q) = \{1, 3, 5\}$, $\omega(r) = \{1, 2\}$, $\omega(s) = \{1, 4, 5\}$.

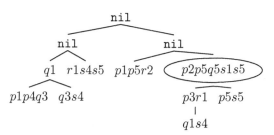

Rule C5 can be applied on the circled node because it contains its right successor: the subtree is substituted by ♯ and it is deleted by rule C2 obtaining the leftmost Δ-tree in the figure below. The restricted form is obtained by applying rules C4 and U on the corresponding circled nodes.

5   Conclusions and Future Work

An extension to a multiple-valued framework of the results obtained for classical logic in [4] has been introduced, which can be seen as the refined version of the results in [9, 1]. As a result it is possible to obtain simpler statements of the theorems and, therefore, reduction transformations are more easily described in terms of rewrite rules.

We have introduced Δ-trees for signed formulas; this allows for a compact representation for well-formed formulas, as well as for a number of reduction strategies, in order to consider only those occurrences of literals which are relevant for the satisfiability of the input formula. Obviously, one cannot hope that just the reduction strategies are enough to prove the (un)satisfiability of any signed formula, this is possible adding a branching strategy based on the substitutions $[p = j]$ and $[p \neq j]$ in a Davis-Putnam flavour.

References

1. G. Aguilera, I. P. de Guzmán, M. Ojeda-Aciego, and A. Valverde. Reductions for non-clausal theorem proving. *Theoretical Computer Science*, 266(1/2):81–112, 2001.
2. C. Files, R. Drechsler, and M. Perkowski. Functional decomposition of MVL functions using multi-valued decision diagrams. In *Proc. ISMVL'97*, pages 7–32, 1997.
3. S. Grugiel and M. Perkowski. Labeled rough partitions—a new general purpose representation for multiple-valued functions and relations. *Journal of Systems Architecture*, 47(1):29–59, 1997.
4. G. Gutiérrez, I. P. de Guzmán, J. Martínez, M. Ojeda-Aciego, and A. Valverde. Satisfiability testing for Boolean formulas using Δ-trees. *Studia Logica*, 2002. Accepted.
5. R. Hähnle. Uniform notation of tableaux rules for multiple-valued logics. In *Proc. Intl Symp on Multiple-Valued Logic*, pages 238–245. IEEE Press, 1991.
6. R. Hähnle. Short conjunctive normal forms in finitely valued logics. *Journal of Logic and Computation*, 4(6):905–927, 1994.
7. N.V. Murray and E. Rosenthal. Improving tableau deductions in multiple-valued logics. In *Proc. 21st Intl Symp on Multiple-Valued Logic*, pages 230–237. IEEE Press, 1991.
8. M. Ojeda-Aciego, I.P. de Guzmán, and A. Valverde. *Multiple-Valued Tableaux with Δ-reductions*. In *Proceedings of IC-AI'99*, pages 177–183, Las Vegas, Nevada, USA, 1999.
9. I.P. de Guzmán, M. Ojeda-Aciego, and A. Valverde. Reducing signed propositional formulas. *Soft Computing*, 2(4):157–166, 1999.
10. D. Pearce, I.P. de Guzmán, and A. Valverde. Computing equilibrium models using signed formulas. In *Proc. 1st Intl Conf on Computational Logic, CL'2000*, Lect. Notes in Artificial Intelligence 1861, pages 688–702, 2000.
11. A. Srinivasan, T. Karn, S. Malik, and R.E. Brayton. Algorithms for discrete function manipulation. In *Proc. Intl. Conf. on CAD*, pages 92–95, 1990.

Knowledge Management in Expert System Creator

Daniel Pop and Viorel Negru

Department of Computer Science, University of the West Timisoara
4 V. Pârvan Street, RO-1900 Timisoara, Romania
{popica, vnegru}@info.uvt.ro

Abstract. Recent explosive growth in data and the availability of large data-sets in multiple disciplines, generates the need for new techniques and tools that can intelligently transform the data into useful information and knowledge. The machine learning algorithms synthesize various knowledge representation forms, most of them equivalent and inter-changeable. A new approach is needed to support and combine the knowledge representation form with various data sources (represented by database management systems). In this paper, a powerful, visual CASE tool for knowledge management is introduced. It supports the integration of high-level knowledge "beans" into host projects. A scalable approach to the problem of data integration from conventional database systems in expert systems is also over-viewed.

Keywords: Expert systems, knowledge management, data integration, integrated development environments.

1 Introduction

An approach towards developing a software engineering tool for knowledge management by merging conventional CASE tool facilities with the expert system technology is introduced. The Expert System Creator assists the human designer by efficient encoding and by reusing the expert knowledge. One of the most well-known tools for the development of rule-based expert systems is CLIPS (C Language Integrated Production System) [2] environment from NASA. In the late 90s, its Java counterpart, the JESS (Java Expert System Shell) [4], received great interest from both commercial and academic environments. More recently, a family of software CREATOR expert systems has been developed [3],[8]. Although an application of these systems is assisting the human designer when using a conventional CASE tool, they do not support the translation between different knowledge representation forms nor the debugging or profiling phases, in contrast to the Expert System Creator suite.

Expert System Creator is a software tool for the development, testing and debugging, profiling and optimization of expert system based applications. Its main facilities include: representing domain knowledge using rules set, decision tables or classification trees; additional representation power, such as using pictorial

D. Scott (Ed.): AIMSA 2002, LNAI 2443, pp. 233–242, 2002.

elements and designers' comments; automatic code generation for declarative, functional or object-oriented programming languages; integration with "native" external programs and with expert systems shells (such as JESS or CLIPS).

After the main facilities are over-viewed, the integration of expert systems with external programs is presented. The next section presents the knowledge representation forms and their equivalence. Section 3 outlines the Expert System Creator architecture and briefly describes its modules. In section 4 aspects related to code generation and integration with host projects are detailed. The database integration issue is addressed in section 5. The last section presents several applications, as well as and future research directions and extensions.

2   Knowledge Representation

For the representation of knowledge in expert systems, a number of forms are used, such as: rules set (production rules, association rules, rules with exceptions), decision tables, classification and regression trees, instance-based representations, and clusters. Each representation has its advantages and drawbacks. Expert System Creator is endowed with advanced graphical manipulation tools for three of the above forms: decision table, classification tree and rules set. While a human expert can build in a straightforward way an expert system based on classification or association rules, the decision table representation allows easy automatic analysis and error and consistency checking. A classification tree can be very easily translated into any common programming language (such as C/C++, Java, Pascal etc.). As these three forms are equivalent [1],[12], an expert system built in one of them can be translated into any other one. The rest of the section will briefly describe the knowledge representation forms (see [1],[16] for a detailed presentation).

Rules set - A rule-based system form is a set of one or more rules. A rule has two parts - an antecedent and a consequent - and has the following form: **if antecedent then consequent**, where the antecedent of a rule is a conjunction of elementary constraints, and the consequent is a sequence of elementary actions. It is worth to mention that important, mature large rule-based systems are already in use (Mycin, Garvan ES1).

Decision table - A decision table consists of a two-dimensional array of cells, where the columns contain the system's constraints and each row makes a classification according to each cell's value (case of condition). Although easy to be visualized and understood, the decision table is a rudimentary form.

Classification tree - A classification tree consists of a set of nodes and a set of arcs [13]. The set of nodes is divided into two classes: decision nodes (associated with a constraint of the system) and classification/action nodes (leaf nodes) that make the classification based on the cases of the constraints from the decision nodes. Each arc has as its source a deciding node, and is associated with a case corresponding to the constraint from the source decision node, and the destination is a decision or classification node. Using data mining and statistical algorithms classification trees can be automatically built from large datasets.

Regression tree - When it comes to predict numeric quantities, the same kind of tree representation as above can be used, but the leaf nodes of the tree would contain a numeric value which is the average of all the training set values that the leaf applies to.

Clusters - In case of clusters, the knowledge takes the form of a diagram that shows how the instances fall into clusters. Instances can be associated probabilistic to more than one cluster. Clustering is often followed by a stage where a classification tree or rule set is inferred. Data visualization techniques are used frequently in clustering process.

2.1   The Equivalence of Representation Forms

When a decision object is transformed from one form into another, the new object can be far larger than the original (it has more parts - rules, rows or nodes - than the original), and far less compact (not all of its parts will be used in practice), caveat named *inflation problem*. For example, applying brute-force algorithms to the well-known medical expert system Garvan ES1 [7] constructed as a set of production rules results in a decision table with only 13% useful rows [1]. These larger objects are side effects of the fact that these decision objects are constructed as total functions on the *attribute space* (the space defined by the distinct possible choices for the variables monitoring of the classification system). This observation suggests that in systems with large attribute spaces the real-world process can be confined to a very small region. The knowledge of the experts is confined to this small region, which is called the *region of experience.* A natural way to represent the characterisation K of the region of experience is by a set of constraints stating that the values of certain variables are determined by the values of others (for example if a pacient is a male, pregnant variable will always be false, although sex and pregnant are independent variables). These constraints are called *partial functional dependencies (PFD)*. PFD could be constructed by the domain experts as part of the process of building a decision object. There are also proposals for estimating this region using algorithms from rough sets theory or algorithms from data mining literature, more specifically association rules discovery.

Colomb and Chung propose an approach for the inflation problem based on partial functional dependencies [1]. The main idea is to represent the knowledge only over the region of experience instead of the entire attribute space. A case is consistent with K if it is consistent with at least one PFD of K (i.e. there is one PFD which verifies the case). The most distinct and representative knowledge representation forms are discussed below: classification tree, rules set and decision table.

Let us suppose that the characterization K of the region of experience was obtained using one of the methods presented above. We present translation algorithms modified so that they use K, the set of PFDs. A good estimate of K would not only control inflation, but would act as a filter detecting cases which are either spurious or perhaps legitimate but outside the experience of the domain experts

2.2   Rules and Decision Table

An acyclic rule system defined on the region of the attribute space covered by
K is equivalent to a decision table defined on the same region of the attribute
space.

Construction Algorithm:

a. **Table ⇒ Rule based system.**

Each row of the table is translated into a rule in rule based system as follows:
the antecedent is the conjunction of all cell's values from one row and the
consequent is represented by the classification performed by the row.

b. **Rule based system ⇒ Table.**

For each rule of the system the antecedent is unfolding so that it is represented as a conjunction of cases. In unfolding process, each case is tested for
consistency with respect to K and inconsistent cases will be removed. The
resulting antecedent will form a new row in decision table. A column in the
decision table will hold the consequent of each rule.

2.3   Decision Table and Classification Tree

A classification tree defined on the region of the attribute space covered by K is
equivalent to an unambiguous decision table defined on the same region of the
attribute space.

Construction Algorithm:

a. **Classification Tree ⇒ Decision Table.**

Each path through the classification tree consistent with K is included in
the decision table. If the path is inconsistent with K, no valid case will
be consistent with it and path will not be included in decision table. As
each classification (leaf) node of the classification tree performs a unique
classification, the resulting decision table is unambiguous.

b. **Decision Table ⇒ Classification Tree.**

(by induction on the number of attributes associated with the table)

Basis step: i) If the number of attributes is zero, then create a leaf node whose
classification is the table's single classification, and whose leaf proposition
is TRUE; ii) If the number of rows is zero, then create a leaf node whose
classification elementary proposition is arbitrary and whose leaf proposition
is FALSE; iii) If the number of distinct classifications is 1, then create a
leaf node whose classification elementary proposition is the table's unique
classification, and whose leaf proposition is the disjunction of propositions
created from each row by the conjunction of the cell propositions.

Induction step: There is at least one attribute, at least one row, and at least
two distinct classifications in the table T. i) Select an attribute A by some
method (this point is discussed below); ii) Create a deciding node associated
with this attribute; iii) For each v in the value set of A such that the path
proposition in the tree down to A (P(A, v)) is consistent with K, create: an
arc whose source is the deciding node created and whose arc proposition is

A = v and a decision table T(A, v) with one row derived from each row r of T in which the cell associated with A is consistent with A = v, and such that P(A, v) & r consistent with K, by removing the cell associated with A.

T(A, v) has one fewer attribute in its associated attribute set than T, so the induction proceeds.

This proves that the tree is equivalent to the table on K, since no branch pruned is consistent with K, nor is any row excluded from the T(A, v). The key to the algorithm developed above is in the method of choosing an attribute in part i of the induction step. Shwayder [15] uses a heuristic based on equalizing the number of rows in the T(A, v) (*maximum dispersion*), giving one of the standard algorithms for translating from a decision table to a classification tree. Quinlan [13] uses a heuristic based on minimizing the maximum number of distinct classifications in the T(A, v) (*maximum entropy gain*). With the maximum entropy gain selection procedure the algorithms gives a variant of the ID3 algorithm.

Table 1. The results of the translation algorithm

Decision Table	MDC	ID3	C4.5
(rows)	(cn/dn/l)	(cn/dn/l)	(cn/dn/l)
37	45/38/8	37/29/7	37/74/16
59	59/52/9	59/52/8	59/139/17
100	100/92/17	100/92/8	100/249/17

In order to compare various heuristics, we implemented three selection procedures based on ID3, C4.5 and MDV (*maximum distinct values*, the attribute with the most distinct values is chosen first). The translation algorithm was implemented based on the construction presented above. The results are presented in table 1, where cn is the number of classification nodes of the tree, dn represents the number of decision nodes of the tree and l is the number of tree levels.

3   Expert System Creator Overview

An overview of the Expert System Creator is shown in Fig. 1. The human expert prepares an initial design using one of the graphic designers: Decision Frame, Decision Table or Classification Tree. This is converted into programming language code by the Code Generator module. The designers can compile the generated code and report any existing errors. In order to use symbols (constants, variables, functions, user types) from other software projects (denoted as *host projects*) a Dictionary is introduced. The code generated by the Code Generator module can be automatically integrated in the host project. The integrated debuggers in Decision Frame/Table/Tree Debugger can be used to debug the generated code in its original form (as a frame, table or tree). The communication mechanism between Expert System Creator and the host project is detailed in the next section.

The Expert System Creator suite supports all the phases of a project's life cycle: analysis and documentation, development and implementation, testing, debugging and profiling.

Three powerful graphic designers support the analysis and development phases: Decision Frame Designer - rule-based expert system development; Decision Table Designer - decision table based expert systems construction; Decision Tree Designer - classification tree based expert systems development.

The graphical elements provided by each designer help the human expert to express his/her knowledge in the most suitable form.

In addition to debugging the generated code with appropriate tools for target programming languages, the integrated debuggers in all three designers support the testing and debugging of constructed systems in their original forms (as rule set, decision table or tree). Their advanced facilities (breakpoints, variables inspection and step-by-step execution) are presented to the user in a visually easy to use way.

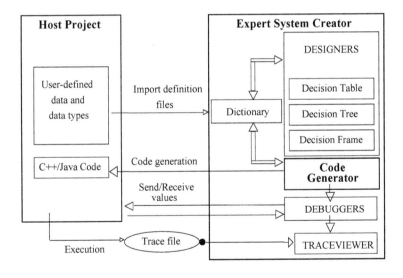

Fig. 1. Expert System Creator architecture

The trace files that record all fired rules or executed branches for a classification tree support the profiling phase. The execution context (formed by the antecedent and the consequent in the case of rule systems, or by variable values for classification tree nodes) is also stored in the trace file. The Trace Viewer visualizes trace files in order to find system bottlenecks or time-consuming rules.

The knowledge base completion and correctness are key issues in designing large knowledge base systems. Expert System Creator includes appropriate mechanisms for testing the correctness of constructed knowledge bases. In the case of rules sets the dependency graph is visualized, offering the user a graphical image of intrinsic relationships inside the knowledge base. For decision tables, the Table Analyzer tool highlights the duplicated and ambiguous rules that exist in the table. In the case of classification trees, encapsulated rules are explicitly shown in a separate window, thus giving the user an overview of tree functionality.

The system is entirely implemented in Java using Java2 SDK 1.3. The Decision Frame module works together with CLIPS [2],[14] or JESS [4] expert system shells that perform the knowledge-based reasoning process. Interfacing with external programs written in C/C++ is carried out using JNI specifications [6]. The Code Generator module supports the following programming languages: C/C++, Java and CLIPS/JESS (for decision frames).

4   Embedding Expert Systems in Host Systems

An important issue in developing knowledge-based systems is their embedding and communication with a host project. The knowledge system is a form of representing the logic of a particular field, a form that is most suitable for the way of perception of the domain for a human expert. Embedding the field's logic with the user interface and database communication modules of a large software application is still an open issue. A new solution, made up of two components - the Code Generator module and the use of dictionaries - is proposed here. In the following two subsections the components are presented in more detail.

4.1   Code Generator Module

After the expert system has been built (as a rules set, decision table or classification tree) it can be translated into a common programming language, such as C/C++, Java or Basic. For the moment, C/C++ and Java code generators for decision tables and classification trees are implemented, while rule-based expert systems are exported in CLIPS/JESS language. Although the generation of programming code for classification trees and rules sets is straightforward, the following two steps are necessary for decision tables:

- Translation of decision tables into classification trees (see [14] for details);
- C++ code generation for the obtained classification trees.

The Code Generator module can be easily customized for any structured, functional or object-oriented programming language, offering an easy way of embedding expert systems into host projects. The generated code can have sections for debugging or tracing purposes. If tracing is enabled when generating the code, then at the execution time of the expert system a trace file will log all the fired rules (branches in classification trees). This file is later used in the Expert System Creator's TraceViewer module in order to discover time-consuming rules, frequent (or spurious) rules or rule-sequences (a set of rules activated in the same order). All this information helps you improve the performances of your expert system.

4.2   Use of Dictionaries

A Dictionary is a collection of external interfaces imported into expert systems from a host project for communication with the project's data and data structures. In order to use the data types, variables or constants defined inside the host project, they have to be imported into the expert system frame. A dictionary contains the following:

- Data and data types imported from the host project: user-defined types (classes or structures), constants and variables, user-defined or system native functions;
- Data defined only in the expert system module denoted as internal variables.

The Code Generator module gets the information about the module in which the constant / variable / function is defined in the host project, and includes the necessary information in the generated files. The internal variables are also exported in the generated code. The Dictionary Builder module is able to read user-defined data types, constants and variables from C/C++ header files and Java files.

5   Database Integration

Large databases of digital information are available in all fields of human activity. Reasoning using information stored in these large warehouses is a demand of our age. Expert System Creator offers direct support for database access for all three forms: rules set, decision table and classification tree.

In the case of decision tables and classification trees, users can use their preferred database access libraries by importing them in the dictionary component. Using database access functions from within the constructed decision table or classification tree is straightforward and requires no specific handling.

In the case of rules set (or decision frames), the problem of reasoning on facts residing in conventional relational database systems requires more attention. A major objective of database integration is to provide independence of both inference engine and database server. The DFDB (Decision Frame DataBase) is an independent subsystem which acts as a communication channel between database server and a decision frame based expert system. The subsystem presents an architecture (see Fig. 2) where an independent subsystem acts as a communication channel between relational DBMSs and KBSs (ESs).

DFDB is composed of a *data dictionary* and three modules: DBWizard, DBEngine and DBMiddleware. The data dictionary collects and stores in CLIPS

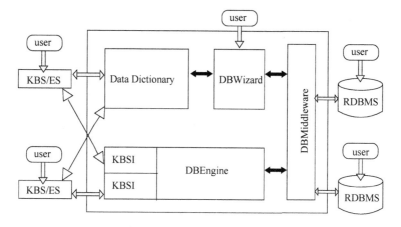

Fig. 2. Database integration in Expert System Creator

files format all the information about the data managed by relational database server (for example: sources of data, relationships to other data and rules assuring the data integrity). The DBMiddleware level ensures a uniform, transparent access to different RDBMSs, being responsible for all database access code. It provides Data Manipulation Language features (retrieving, updating, deleting data from tables or views), automatic data type conversion between the database server data types and the inference engine data types and many other database-specific operations. The DBWizard module is a graphical tool helping the user to build and maintain the data dictionary. The user may select the columns of the table/view or the relationships he/she is interested in, having the ability to reduce the size of data that will be transferred to/from the database server. The DBEngine is responsible for data downloading/uploading from/to database server during the knowledge inference step. It also controls the translation between internal database format and the inference engine's formats.

6   Applications, Future Research, and Extensions

Expert System Creator gives users the opportunity to develop an expert system based decision aid that is geared towards their specific needs (such as accounting, planning or decision-making in various domains). It also assists users who do not possess technical expertise in computers in building powerful expert systems. An effective decision support system must have accurate data, user-friendly interface, reliable knowledge base, and good inference mechanism. Expert System Creator helps you combine these requirements and assists programmers and software engineers in building resource planning systems.

Future research includes the optimization of the decision table to classification tree conversion based on automatic building of the characterization of region of experience.

Expert System Creator has an open architecture for building and testing the decision objects. Further extensions are planned to integrate the rule-based expert systems with fuzzy logic engines such as FuzzyCLIPS [10] or FuzzyJ [11]. The automatic growth of classification trees for classification from large data sets [5] is another important feature to be added in the near future.

Acknowledgements. This work is partially supported by the World Bank and Romanian Government Grant no. 12623/98 and INFOSOC Grant no. 23/01. Special thanks goes to Optimal Solution [9] team for their support and understanding.

References

1. Colomb, R. M., Representation of Propositional Expert Systems as Partial Functions, Artificial Intelligence 1999, 109: 187-209.
2. Culbert, C., Riley, G., Donnell, B., CLIPS Reference Manual, Volume 1-3, Johnson Space Center NASA; 1993.
3. Far, B. H., Takizawa, T., Koono, Z., Software Creation: An SDL-Based Expert System for Automatic Software Design. In Faergemand, O., Sarma, A. editors. Proceedings of SDL '93; Elsevier Publishing Co, North-Holland, 1993; p. 399-410.
4. Friedman-Hill, E., JESS: The Rule Engine for the Java Platform. http://herzberg.ca.sandia.gov/jess [3/11/2002]
5. Gehrke, J., Ganti, V., Ramakrishnan, R., Wei-Yin, Loh., BOAT-Optimistic Decision Tree Construction, Proceedings of SIGMOD Conference 1999, 169-180.
6. Gordon, R., Essential JNI: Java Native Interface, Prentince Hall PTR; 1998.
7. Horn, K.A., Compton, P., Lazarus, L., Quinlan, J. R., An Expert Computer System for the Interpretation of Thyroid Assays in a Clinical Laboratory, Australian Computer Journal 1985, 17:7-11.
8. Koono, Z., Far, B. H., Takizawa, T., Ohmori, M., Hatae, K., Baba, T.,Software Creation: Implementation and Application of Design Process Knowledge in Automatic Software Design, Proceedings of the 5th Int. Conference on Software Eng. and Knowledge Eng., SEKE, 1993 June; CA, USA; p. 332-336.
9. ***, Optimal Solution web site. http://www.optsol.at [3/21/2002]
10. Orchard, R. A., FuzzyCLIPS User's Guide, Integrated Reasoing Institute for Information Technology National Research Council Canada; 1998.
11. Orchard R. A., NRC FuzzyJ Toolkit for the Java^{TM} Platform. User's Guide; 2001. http://www.iit.nrc.ca/IR_public/fuzzy/fuzzyJDocs [3/11/2002]
12. Pop, D., Negru, V. Intertranslability of Representation Forms in Classification, Proceedings of 10th SINTES Conference; 2000 May; Craiova, Romania.
13. Quinlan, J. R., Introduction of Decision Trees, Machine Learning 1; 1984.
14. Riley, G., Donnell, B., CLIPS Arhitecture Manual, Johnson Space Center NASA; 1993.
15. Shwayder, K., Extending the information theory approach to converting limited-entry decision tables to computer programs. Communications of the ACM 17, pp. 532-537, 1974.
16. Witten, I. H., Frank, E., Data Mining. Practical Machine Learning Tools and Techniques with Java Implementations, Morgan Kaufman Publishers; 2000.

Towards Semantic Goal-Directed Forward Reasoning in Resolution

Seungyeob Choi

School of Computer Science
The University of Birmingham
Birmingham B15 2TT, England
S.Choi@cs.bham.ac.uk

Abstract. Semantic goal-directed forward reasoning is a three stage procedure. In the first stage a reference set of models is generated from the negated theorem. In the second stage the assumption clause set is refined to a set which has an as small set of models as possible in common with the negated theorem with respect to the reference set of models. In the last stage a refutation is generated in the space consisting of the original problem along with the refined assumption. In order to form a refined assumption, unlike traditional approaches like set of support, only clauses from assumptions are resolved with each other.

1 Introduction

Resolution [16] is one of the best developed approaches to automated theorem proving, in which the problem is transformed into a clausal form and a proof is searched for on this clausal level. Many powerful systems have been built on this paradigm, e.g. MKRP [5], SETHEO [11], OTTER [12], SPASS [20], and VAMPIRE [15]. On the one hand, these systems show remarkable performance on many problems in particular application areas. Recently a variant of OTTER successfully solved the Robbins problem [13] that had remained as an open problem for several decades. On the other hand, since these methods depend largely on blind search, exponential explosion is unavoidable. The key technique to successful theorem proving consists of efficiently searching through a big search space and making good heuristic choices.

Semantic information seems to be used as a form of heuristic knowledge in human problem solving. It is widely understood that automated theorem provers can also benefit from the use of semantic information. Many semantically guided provers, e.g. SCOTT [17,19], CLIN-S [4], MGTP [6], PTTP+GLiDeS [1,2], and SCG [8], use semantics to guide (or restrict) the proof search. Those techniques are based on the idea that a resolution step between two clauses from the assumption part is not likely to contribute to the generation of the empty clause [21], a clause evaluated to true in a guiding model (or model set) is not likely to lead to an empty clause [17,19,1,2], or similarly a clause evaluated to true in some smaller subset of the guiding model set is more likely to generate an empty clause [8].

D. Scott (Ed.): AIMSA 2002, LNAI 2443, pp. 243–252, 2002.

Typically, models are either generated incrementally during the proof search or supplied by the user.

In this paper a semantic approach is presented that starts with goal-directed forward reasoning, in which – instead of pursuing a refutation by best-first search from the start – initially only clauses from assumptions are allowed to produce resolvents. This way a set of clauses is generated, which is a logical consequence of the original assumptions. We use semantics to guide the procedure so that every generated clause is more likely to be useful with respect to the conclusion. The guiding set of models are generated once at the beginning and reused to check candidate clauses during the rest of the initial transformation procedure. When a refined assumption set is obtained, it is added to the original problem as additional assumption. The modified problem will typically be easier to solve than the original one.

Semantic goal-directed forward reasoning is not a complete theorem prover, but a preprocessor. It does not prove any theorem on its own, but it modifies the problem in a form that can more easily be proved by other theorem provers. The modification procedure is sound and complete to refine the problem. Our prototype implementations were built using KEIM [7] and experimented in combination with SCG [8].

2   Semantic Guidance in Resolution

The semantics of a first-order formula (or formula set) is defined by a pair $\mathcal{M} = (\mathcal{D}, \mathcal{I})$, consisting of a domain and an interpretation. The domain $\mathcal{D}$ is a nonempty set of objects, and the interpretation $\mathcal{I}$ is a mapping from the terms of the language to values in the domain. We say $\mathcal{M}$ is a model of a formula (or formula set) if $\mathcal{M}$ evaluates the formula (or all formulas in the formula set) to true.

Assume we have a first-order problem given by a set Γ and a theorem φ for which we want to show that φ follows from Γ (i.e., $\Gamma \models \varphi$). Furthermore we assume that the formula set Γ is consistent, that is, that it has models. Resolution theorem provers negate φ and prove that $\Gamma \cup \{\neg\varphi\}$ is unsatisfiable, that is, $\Gamma \cup \{\neg\varphi\}$ has no model.

FINDER [18] is a model generator which fixes the domain to a specific number of objects and then performs an exhaustive search in the space of functions and constants which can be satisfied in that domain. We use FINDER as a model generator to generate a set of models from a set of formulas.

3   Goal-Directed Refinement of Assumptions

Let Γ be a set of assumptions $\Gamma = \{A_1, A_2, \ldots, A_n\}$ and φ be the theorem, such that $\Gamma \vdash \varphi$. The sets of clauses Γ^* and $\{\neg\varphi\}^*$ are obtained from normalisation of Γ and $\{\neg\varphi\}$, respectively. The resolution procedure searches for a contradiction (an empty clause) from $\Gamma^* \cup \{\neg\varphi\}^*$.

Let $\{\neg\varphi\}^*$ be the reference clause set. From $\{\neg\varphi\}^*$ the finite model set $\mathcal{M} = \{m_1, m_2, \ldots, m_n \mid m_i \models \{\neg\varphi\}^*\}$ is generated with the interpretation domain fixed to a finite set of objects. We use $\mathcal{I}^m$ to denote the interpretation of a clause c ($c \in \{\neg\varphi\}^*$) using a model m.

$$\mathcal{I}^m : c \rightsquigarrow \{T, F\}$$

$\mathcal{M}^c$ is a subset of $\mathcal{M}$ such that $\mathcal{M}^c = \{m \mid \mathcal{I}^m : c \to T, m \in \mathcal{M}\}$. If $\Gamma \models \varphi$, $\mathcal{M}^\Gamma$ is a subset of $\mathcal{M}^\varphi$.

$$\mathcal{M}^\Gamma = \mathcal{M}^{A_1} \cap \mathcal{M}^{A_2} \cap \ldots \cap \mathcal{M}^{A_n} \subseteq \mathcal{M}^\varphi$$

$$\mathcal{M}^\Gamma \cap \mathcal{M}^{\neg\varphi} = \varnothing$$

Fig. 1 is a semantic diagram of assumptions and the theorem.

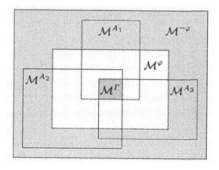

Fig. 1. Semantic diagram of the original assumptions and the theorem

If c_1 and c_2 are clauses, we use R_{c_1,c_2} to denote the set of resolvents produced by the application of binary resolution to c_1 and c_2. If a set of clauses $\mathcal{C}$ consists of R_{c_1,c_2} with $c_1, c_2 \in \Gamma^*$, $\mathcal{C}$ can be used as an additional assumption for φ along with Γ^*.

$$\mathcal{C} = \{r \mid r \in R_{c_1,c_2} \ (c_1, c_2 \in \Gamma^*)\}$$

$$\mathcal{C} \cup \Gamma^* \models \varphi$$

$$\mathcal{M}^{\mathcal{C} \cup \Gamma^*} \subseteq \mathcal{M}^\varphi$$

In order to guide the transformation, the clauses are checked against the reference model set. We use $\{\neg\varphi\}^*$ as reference clause set and, from $\{\neg\varphi\}^*$, generate the reference model set $\mathcal{M}^{\{\neg\varphi\}^*}$ with a model generator. $\mathcal{M}^c$ is the set of models in which c is true ($c \in \{\neg\varphi\}^*$ and $\mathcal{M}^c \subseteq \mathcal{M}^{\{\neg\varphi\}^*}$) and $|\mathcal{M}^c|$ is the number of models in $\mathcal{M}^c$. Let $\mathcal{C} = \{c_1, c_2, \ldots, c_n\}$ be a finite set of clauses, and $\mathcal{N}^\mathcal{C}$ the set of numbers of models that evaluate each clause in $\mathcal{C}$ to true, i.e. $\mathcal{N}^\mathcal{C} = \{|\mathcal{M}^{c_1}|, |\mathcal{M}^{c_2}|, \ldots, |\mathcal{M}^{c_n}|\}$. $Min(\mathcal{N}^\mathcal{C})$ is the smallest number in $\mathcal{N}^\mathcal{C}$ and $\mathcal{C}^{Min(\mathcal{N}^\mathcal{C})}$ is the subset of $\mathcal{C}$, i.e. $\mathcal{C}^{Min(\mathcal{N}^\mathcal{C})} = \{c_i \mid |\mathcal{M}^{c_i}| = Min(\mathcal{N}^\mathcal{C}), c_i \in \mathcal{C}\}$.

$$\Gamma_0 = \Gamma^*$$

$$\mathcal{C}_i = \{r \mid r \in R_{a,b} \ (a, b \in \Gamma_i)\}$$

$$\Gamma_{i+1} = \Gamma_i \cup \mathcal{C}_i^{Min(\mathcal{N}^{\mathcal{C}_i})}$$

If there is a resolvent with no model (i.e., $Min(\mathcal{N}^{\mathcal{C}_i}) = 0$) or the minimum number of models does not decrease (i.e., $Min(\mathcal{N}^{\mathcal{C}_{i+1}}) = Min(\mathcal{N}^{\mathcal{C}_i})$), the assumption refinement terminates and the refined assumption $\Gamma' = \mathcal{C}_i^{Min(\mathcal{N}^{\mathcal{C}_i})}$ combined with the original problem $\Gamma \cup \{\neg\varphi\}$ is passed to a theorem prover. Alternatively, if no more resolvents are generated (i.e., $\mathcal{C}_i = \varnothing$), the refined assumption is empty and the original problem is unchanged. Note that these conditions guarantee that the procedure terminates. In Fig. 2, the refined as-

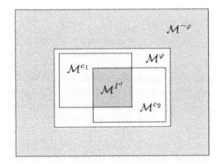

Fig. 2. Semantic diagram of the refined assumptions and the theorem

sumption clauses c_1 and c_2 are generated from Γ^*, and neither of them is true in any single model of $\{\neg\varphi\}^*$.

In summary, where Γ is a set of assumptions, a series of resolution steps between clauses in Γ derives a clause set (or a single clause) Γ'. If the clause selection for resolution is carefully constrained, Γ' does not semantically overlap with $\neg\varphi$ (i.e., $\mathcal{M}^{\Gamma'} \cap \mathcal{M}^{\neg\varphi} = \varnothing$). If in this case a resolution step between two clauses from Γ' and $\{\neg\varphi\}^*$, respectively, is possible, it will likely have the empty clause as a successor (i.e., $\Gamma' \cup \{\neg\varphi\} \vdash \square$). However, since there is no guarantee that φ follows from Γ' already, instead of substituting Γ with Γ', we have to use $\Gamma \cup \Gamma'$ as background theory. On the one hand the refined problem $\Gamma \cup \Gamma' \cup \{\neg\varphi\}$ is even bigger than the original one $\Gamma \cup \{\neg\varphi\}$, but on the other hand the search complexity is – especially when the refutation search is semantically guided – smaller. As the refined set Γ' overlaps a smaller number of models (ideally no model at all as seen in Fig. 2) with $\neg\varphi$, a semantically guided theorem prover gives heuristic preference to resolution steps between Γ' and $\neg\varphi$ rather than between Γ and $\neg\varphi$. As a result, the search for refutation in $\Gamma \cup \Gamma' \cup \{\neg\varphi\}$ takes advantage of the smaller search space of $\Gamma' \cup \{\neg\varphi\}$ with the completeness of $\Gamma \cup \{\neg\varphi\}$ still retained.

The procedure is divided into three parts, where the first is to generate the reference model set $\mathcal{M}^{\neg\varphi}$, the second to produce a refined clause set Γ', and the last to search for a refutation between $\Gamma \cup \Gamma'$ and $\neg\varphi$.

4 Example Problem

For instance, let us look at the following problem. Given the definition of set equality as having exactly the same members, set equality is symmetric.

$$\{\forall x\forall y(Q(x,y) \leftrightarrow (\forall z(P(z,x) \leftrightarrow P(z,y))))\}$$
$$\models \forall x\forall y(Q(x,y) \leftrightarrow Q(y,x))$$

To prove the consequence relation by resolution we assume the first part $\Gamma = \{\forall x\forall y(Q(x,y) \leftrightarrow (\forall z(P(z,x) \leftrightarrow P(z,y))))\}$ and negate the second part $\varphi = \forall x\forall y(Q(x,y) \leftrightarrow Q(y,x))$. By normalisation we get:

$$\Gamma^* : \quad \{\neg Q(x,y) \vee \neg P(z,x) \vee P(z,y),$$
$$\neg Q(x,y) \vee \neg P(z,y) \vee P(z,x),$$
$$P(f(x,y),x) \vee P(f(x,y),y) \vee Q(x,y),$$
$$\neg P(f(x,y),y) \vee \neg P(f(x,y),x) \vee Q(x,y)\}$$
$$\{\neg\varphi\}^* : \quad \{Q(x_1,y_1) \vee Q(y_1,x_1),$$
$$\neg Q(y_1,x_1) \vee \neg Q(x_1,y_1)\}$$

If the problem is directly tried with a conventional theorem prover like OTTER, Γ^* and $\{\varphi\}^*$ are usable set and set of support, respectively. An exhaustive refutation search is started on these clause sets. OTTER finds the empty clause after generating 138 clauses. In the following subsections, we look into the semantic goal-directed forward reasoning.

4.1 Stage 1: Generating Models

The first part of the procedure is a model generation. If we fix the cardinality to 2, FINDER selects an interpretation domain to $\mathcal{D} = \{0,1\}$ and generate 4096 models from $\{\neg\varphi\}^*$.

Models	m_1	m_2	m_3	m_4	m_5	m_6	m_7	m_8	m_9	m_{10}	$\cdots$	m_{4095}	m_{4096}
$P(0,0)$	F	F	F	F	F	F	F	F	F	F	$\cdots$	T	T
$P(0,1)$	F	F	F	F	F	F	F	F	F	F	$\cdots$	T	T
$P(1,0)$	F	F	F	F	F	F	F	F	F	F	$\cdots$	T	T
$P(1,1)$	F	F	F	F	F	F	F	F	F	F	$\cdots$	T	T
$Q(0,0)$	F	F	F	F	F	F	F	F	F	F	$\cdots$	T	T
$Q(0,1)$	T	T	T	T	T	T	T	T	T	T	$\cdots$	F	F
$Q(1,0)$	F	F	F	F	F	F	F	F	F	F	$\cdots$	T	T
$Q(1,1)$	F	F	F	F	F	F	F	F	F	F	$\cdots$	T	T
$f(0,0)$	0	0	1	1	0	0	1	1	0	0	$\cdots$	1	1
$f(0,1)$	0	0	0	0	1	1	1	1	0	0	$\cdots$	1	1
$f(1,0)$	0	0	0	0	0	0	0	0	1	1	$\cdots$	1	1
$f(1,1)$	0	0	0	0	0	0	0	0	0	0	$\cdots$	1	1
x_1	0	1	0	1	0	1	0	1	0	1	$\cdots$	0	1
y_1	1	0	1	0	1	0	1	0	1	0	$\cdots$	1	0

Typically a bigger cardinality makes the model set more informative, and models of cardinality 2 cannot be considered as representative for all finite models. However, as our experiments show, even the class of two element models often bears useful semantic information from which good heuristics for our purpose can be derived. While it is easy to use models with larger cardinality and to choose randomly a feasible set from all models, the model generation typically takes much longer for higher cardinalities. In the following we fix the domain cardinality to 2 for our experiments.

Because using the whole set of models for checking each candidate clause may be computationally expensive, we typically use only a smaller subset. In order to form a reference subset, we can either take every nth model from the original model class (the factor of n) or make a random selection. In our experiments, we adopt the first approach and the number of models is taken so that it should be in the range of $40 \leq n < 100$. One interesting feature is that the models do not provide good heuristics if the factor is d^m where d the domain cardinality and m is an integer. For instance, if the domain cardinality is 2 and the domain $\mathcal{D}$ is fixed to $\{0, 1\}$, when the factor is 4, which means that when we take every 4th model, both Skolem constants x_1 and y_1 are always interpreted as 1 and 0, respectively, in every model. For this reason, a good number for the factor is an odd prime number.

4.2   Stage 2: Generating a Refined Assumption Set

The second part of the procedure is forward refinement based on resolution. Reference models $\mathcal{M}^{\neg\varphi}$ are generated from the negated theorem $\neg\varphi$. As clauses from Γ^* are taken to resolve so that a smaller number of models in $\mathcal{M}^{\neg\varphi}$ evaluates the resolvents to true, a refined assumption set Γ' is generated after 3 steps.

Γ^*	c_1	$\neg Q(x,y) \vee \neg P(z,x) \vee P(z,y)$	
	c_2	$\neg Q(x,y) \vee \neg P(z,y) \vee P(z,x)$	
	c_3	$P(f(x,y),x) \vee P(f(x,y),y) \vee Q(x,y)$	
	c_4	$\neg P(f(x,y),y) \vee \neg P(f(x,y),x) \vee Q(x,y)$	
S_1	c_5	$\neg Q(x,y) \vee \neg P(f(y,x),y) \vee Q(y,x)$	$(c_{2.3}, c_{4.1})$
S_2	c_6	$\neg Q(x,y) \vee P(f(y,x),x) \vee Q(y,x)$	$(c_{2.2}, c_{3.1})$
S_3	c_7	$\neg Q(x,y) \vee \neg P(f(y,x),x) \vee Q(y,x)$	$(c_{1.3}, c_{4.2})$
Γ'	c_8	$\neg Q(x,y) \vee Q(y,x)$	$(c_{6.2}, c_{7.2})$

$$\Gamma' : \quad \{\neg Q(x,y) \vee Q(y,x)\}$$

4.3   Stage 3: Searching for Refutation

The last part is to make a set of clauses that contains the original assumption set Γ^*, the refined assumption set Γ' and the negated conclusion $\{\neg\varphi\}^*$, and to feed them into a theorem prover. If the theorem prover employs semantic guidance, resolution steps between clauses from Γ' and $\{\neg\varphi\}^*$ is given higher preference than those between Γ^* and $\{\neg\varphi\}^*$ or between Γ^* and Γ'. In our experiments with SCG prover, we use different model sets in the preprocessing and refutation searching stages. Models are generated from $\neg\varphi$ to guide the search for Γ' in the preprocessor and from Γ to guide the search for $\square$ in the SCG prover.

Γ^*	c_1	$\neg Q(x,y) \vee \neg P(z,x) \vee P(z,y)$	
	c_2	$\neg Q(x,y) \vee \neg P(z,y) \vee P(z,x)$	
	c_3	$P(f(x,y),x) \vee P(f(x,y),y) \vee Q(x,y)$	
	c_4	$\neg P(f(x,y),y) \vee \neg P(f(x,y),x) \vee Q(x,y)$	
Γ'	c_8	$\neg Q(x,y) \vee Q(y,x)$	
$\{\neg\varphi\}^*$	c_9	$Q(x_1,y_1) \vee Q(y_1,x_1)$	
	c_{10}	$\neg Q(y_1,x_1) \vee \neg Q(x_1,y_1)$	
S_1	c_{11}	$Q(y_1,x_1)$	$(c_{8.1}, c_{9.1})$
S_2	c_{12}	$Q(x_1,y_1)$	$(c_{8.1}, c_{9.2})$
S_3	c_{13}	$\neg Q(x_1,y_1)$	$(c_{8.2}, c_{10.1})$
S_4	c_{14}	$\square$	$(c_{12.1}, c_{13.1})$

The refutation search is much simpler with $\Gamma, \Gamma' \vdash \varphi$ than with $\Gamma \vdash \varphi$ even though additional Γ' has been added. OTTER finds an empty clause after generating only 15 clauses, which can be a great improvement over the 138 clauses to prove $\Gamma \vdash \varphi$.

5   Experiments on Pelletier Examples

We have tested our semantic goal-directed forward reasoning procedure combined with OTTER [12] and SCG [8]. Table 1 shows how many clauses OTTER generates and how many steps SCG takes, with and without the semantic goal-directed reasoning preprocessor, in order to prove each example.[1] Example 1-10 are the first ten full predicate logic problems without identity and functions (problem 35-44) from Pelletier's problem set [14]. The left most column is the number of steps that the semantic goal-directed forward reasoning preprocessor takes to produce a refined assumption set Γ'. If the initial problem is in a form that the semantic goal-directed forward reasoning cannot be applied, for instance, the problem has no assumption, or the assumption consists of only one clause where no resolution can be applied, then the procedure is not applied and labelled as "–". In this case the refined assumption set is empty, i.e. $\Gamma' = \varnothing$. The next two columns show the numbers of clauses OTTER generates to prove $\Gamma \vdash \varphi$ and $\Gamma, \Gamma' \vdash \varphi$, respectively. Finally, the right most two columns are the numbers of steps SCG takes. The proof found in step 0 means that the empty clause was found during the construction of the initial graph. When the prover

---

[1] Since SCG uses a different algorithm from OTTER, we apply different measurements – the number of clauses generated and added to the set of support in OTTER, and the number of clauses selected and added to the clause graph in SCG. In the preprocessor and SCG, we use a step to denote a resolution step which includes selecting a pair of clauses, resolving them, adding the resolvent into the clause set (or the clause graph in SCG), and updating the set (or the graph in SCG).

Table 1. Experiments on Pelletier examples

	Preprocessor	OTTER*		SCG**	
Problem	$\Gamma \rightsquigarrow \Gamma'$	$\Gamma \vdash \varphi$	$\Gamma, \Gamma' \vdash \varphi$	$\Gamma \vdash \varphi$	$\Gamma, \Gamma' \vdash \varphi$
Example 1	–	0	0	0	0
Example 2	1	11	2	7	0
Example 3	–	3	3	3	3
Example 4	–	Time out		Time out	
Example 5	–	2	2	0	0
Example 6	3	48	48	14	11
Example 7	2	2	2	2	0
Example 8	3	17	17	6	6
Example 9	3	138	15	101	6
Example 10	2	10	11	18	1

OTTER*: The number of clauses OTTER generates.
SCG**: The number of steps the semantic clause graph procedure takes.

does not produce the result in a reasonable amount of time (in our experiments 12 hours on SunE420R with four 450MHz processors), the step is rated as time out.

As we have seen in the table, the semantic goal-directed forward reasoning combined with a non-semantic prover like OTTER does not always make a big improvement. In OTTER, Γ' is not given any preference over Γ and therefore all clauses in Γ and Γ' are equally treated. Although in some examples (example 2 and 9) Γ' makes significant improvements for OTTER, more often the preprocessing does not make any difference (example 1, 3, 5, 6, 7 and 8), or even makes it worse (example 10). In those cases, the preprocessing can be considered as an additional overhead as it consumes computing resources and produces additional clause set Γ'. However, when the semantic goal-directed forward reasoning is used with a semantically guided theorem prover like SCG, it makes more stable improvements in the search for a proof. Wherever possible, preferences are given to the resolution between clauses from Γ' and $\neg\varphi$, respectively, over those between Γ and $\neg\varphi$. As seen in the table, the refined assumption set Γ' normally makes the proof search shorter in most examples.

Please note that our experiments are based on a prototype implementation and that we wanted only to explore the potential of the approach with our experiments. The current implementation is built on the Lisp extension KEIM [7] which is not very fast compared to C-implemented systems with indexing techniques, and a comparison of run time behaviour with existing provers would not be informative.

6   Conclusion and Further Work

We have described a semantic approach to goal-directed forward reasoning, showed how it reduces the search complexities by refining the problem, and presented experimental results. Our approach differs from other semantically guided approaches in that it does not search for candidate clauses likely to produce an empty clause. Instead, it firstly reduces the search space by applying resolution only between assumption clauses, and secondly the refutation is searched for. In order to obtain the refined assumption set, candidate clauses are selected in such a way that resolution is satisfied in the least number of models of the negated conclusion. The experiments with typical first order problems from Pelletier examples show that the refutation length with the semantic goal-directed forward reasoning is shorter especially when the refutation search is semantically guided.

The reference models are generated by FINDER only once at the beginning and reused during the rest of the goal-directed forward reasoning procedure, while other semantic approaches like SCOTT do not only generate models from the initial clauses but also from new ones. This is a big advantage of our approach since in general model generation is computationally more expensive than checking.

The performance of semantically guided resolution depends to a great degree on the availability of good models. Our experiments show that even with two-element models valuable heuristic information can be obtained. Whether other models are more promising or not has to be studied for different example classes. Semantic guidance seems to be a standard technique humans use when searching for proofs. Rather than generating models from scratch, they often use *typical examples* [10,9]. It remains an open question whether and to which extent this is necessary in our context. It may also be important to use infinite models as investigated by Caferra and Peltier [3].

Acknowledgement. I thank to Manfred Kerber for useful discussions on the idea and helpful comments on drafts of this paper.

References

1. M. Brown and G. Sutcliffe. PTTP+GLiDeS: Semantically guided PTTP. In D. McAllester, editor, *Proceedings of the 17th International Conference on Automated Deduction (CADE-17)*, LNAI 1831, 411–416. Springer-Verlag, 2000.
2. M. Brown and G. Sutcliffe. PTTP+GLiDeS: Using models to guide linear deductions. In Peter Baumgartner et al., editors, *Proceedings of Workshop on Model Computation – Principles, Algorithms, and Applications, CADE-17*, 42–45, 2000.
3. R. Caferra and N. Peltier. Disinference rules, model building and abduction. In E. Orłowska, editor, *Logic at Work: Essays Dedicated to the Memory of Helena Rasiowa*, 331–353. Physica-Verlag, 1999.
4. H. Chu and D.A. Plaisted. Semantically guided first-order theorem proving using hyper-linking. In A. Bundy, editor, *Proceedings of the 12th International Conference on Automated Deduction (CADE-12)*, LNAI 814, 192–206. Springer-Verlag, 1994.

5. N. Eisinger and H.J. Ohlbach. The Markgraf Karl Refutation Procedure (MKRP). In J. Siekmann, editor, *Proceedings of the 8th International Conference on Automated Deduction (CADE-8)*, LNAI 230, 681–682. Springer-Verlag, 1986.

6. R. Hasegawa, H. Fujita, and M. Koshimura. MGTP: A Model Generation Theorem Prover – its advanced features and applications. In D. Galmiche, editor, *Proceedings of International Conference TABLEAUX'97*, LNAI 1227, 1–15. Springer-Verlag, 1997.

7. X. Huang et al. KEIM: A toolkit for automated deduction. In A. Bundy, editor, *Proceedings of the 12th International Conference on Automated Deduction (CADE-12)*, LNAI 814, 807–810. Springer-Verlag, 1994.

8. M. Kerber and S. Choi. The semantic clause graph procedure. In P. Baumgartner et al., editors, *Proceedings of the CADE-17 Workshop on Model Computation – Principles, Algorithms, and Applications*, 29–37, 2000.

9. M. Kerber and E. Melis. Typical examples in reasoning. In *International Conference on Computing and Philosophy*, 1992.

10. M. Kerber, E. Melis, and J. Siekmann. Analogical reasoning with typical examples. SEKI Report SR-92-13, Fachbereich Informatik, Universität des Saarlandes, Saarbrücken, Germany, 1992.

11. R. Letz, J. Schumann, S. Bayerl, and W. Bibel. SETHEO: A High-Performance Theorem Prover. *Journal of Automated Reasoning*, 8:183–212, 1992.

12. W. McCune. *OTTER 3.0 Reference Manual and Guide*. Mathematics and Computer Science Division, Argonne National Laboratory, Argonne, Illinois, USA, 1994.

13. W. McCune. Solution of the Robbins problem. *Journal of Automated Reasoning*, 19:263–276, 1997.

14. F.J. Pelletier. Seventy-five problems for testing automatic theorem provers. *Journal of Automated Reasoning*, 2(2):191–216, 1986.

15. A. Riazanov and A. Voronkov. Vampire 1.1. In R. Goré et al., editors, *Proceedings of the International Joint Conference on Automated Reasoning*, LNAI 2083, 376–380. Springer-Verlag, 2001.

16. J. A. Robinson. A machine-oriented logic based on the resolution principle. *Journal of the Association for Computing Machinery*, 12(1):23–41, 1965.

17. J. Slaney. SCOTT: A Model-Guided Theorem Prover. In *Proceedings of the 13th International Joint Conference on Artificial Intelligence (IJCAI-93)*, pages 109–114, 1993.

18. J. Slaney. *FINDER – Finite Domain Enumerator Version 3.0 Notes and Guide*. Centre for Information Science Research, Australian National University, Canberra, Australia, July 1995.

19. J. Slaney, E. Lusk, and W. McCune. SCOTT: Semantically Constrained Otter. In A. Bundy, editor, *Proceedings of the 12th International Conference on Automated Deduction (CADE-12)*, LNAI 814, 764–768. Springer-Verlag, 1994.

20. C. Weidenbach, B. Gaede, and G. Rock. SPASS & FLOTTER, Version 0.42. In M. A. McRobbie and J. K. Slaney, editors, *Proceedings of the 13th International Conference on Automated Deduction (CADE-13)*, LNAI 1104, 141–145. Springer-Verlag, 1996.

21. L. Wos, G. A. Robinson, and D. F. Carson. Efficiency and completeness of the set of support strategy in theorem proving. *Journal of the Association for Computing Machinery*, 12(4):536–541, 1965.

Do What We Do to Find What You Want

Christo Dichev

Department of Computer Science, Winston-Salem State University
Winston-Salem, N.C. 27110, USA
dichevc@wssu.edu

Abstract. Most retrieval systems are geared towards Boolean queries or hierarchical classification based on keyword descriptors. In this paper we present a framework for domain-specific information retrieval. The proposed approach uses topic lattice generated from a collection of documents where documents are characterized by a group of users with overlapping interests. The topic lattice captures the authors' intention as it reveals the implicit structure of a document collection following the structure of informal groups of individuals expressing interests in the documents. Due to its dual nature, the lattice allows two complimentary navigations styles, which are based either on attributes or on objects. Topic lattice capturing users' interest suggests navigation methods that may be an attractive alternative to specialized domain information retrieval.

Keywords: information retrieval, web-based technology

1   Introduction

The explosion of the available information has made the problem of efficient resource discovery vital. One particular challenge is how to display and navigate large sets of interrelated documents. Browsing and searching are the two main paradigms for finding information. Both paradigms have their limitations. The problem with general search is setting up an appropriate query to find the relevant documents. This problem stems from the lexical metrics used by search engines to infer the semantics of pages from their lexical representation. Next problem is that search is sometimes hard for users who do not know how to form a search query. Frequently, people intuitively know what they are searching (new stuff) but are unable to describe the document through a list of keywords. The information retrieval problem is too big to be solved with one model or with one tool.

Recently, keyword searches have been supplemented with a drill-down categorization hierarchy, that allows users to navigate through a repository of documents by groups and dynamically to modify parts of their search. These hierarchies, however, are often manually generated and can be misleading as a particular document might fall under more than one category. An obvious disadvantage of categorization is that the user must adopt the taxonomy used by those who did the categorization in order to effectively search the repository.

Most of the documents available on the Web are intended for a particular community of users. Typically, each document addresses some area of interest and

D. Scott (Ed.): AIMSA 2002, LNAI 2443, pp. 253–263, 2002.

thus a community centered on that area. Therefore the relevance of the document depends on the match between the intention of the author and the user's current interest. Keyword matching alone is not capable to capture this intention [9]. A great deal of scientific literature available on the web is intended for example to scholars. For computer science scholars in particular, research papers are often made available on the sites of various institutions. Such examples indicate that scientific communication is increasingly taking place on the web [8]. The rapid growth of scientific information is an exciting trend, but to exploit its full potential this growth should be paired proportionally with equivalent facilities helping scholars to stay informed about what's happening. The tendency towards specialization suggests that decentralizing the search process is a more scalable approach since the search may be driven by a context including topics, queries and communities of users. The question is *what type of topic related information is practical, how to infer that information* and *how to use it* for improving search results.

Web users typically search for diverse information. Some searches are sporadic and irregular while other searches might be related to their interests and have more or less regular nature. An important question is then how to filter out these sporadic, irregular searches and how to combine regular searches into groups identifying topics of interest by observing user's searching behavior. Our approach to topic identification is based on observations of the searching behavior of large groups of users. The assumption is that a topic of interest can be determined by identifying a collection of documents that is of common interest to a sufficiently large group of users.

The purpose of this study is to present a framework for identifying and utilizing emerging ad hoc categories in information retrieval. The framework suggests a method of grouping documents into meaningful clusters, which in effect identifies topics of interest shared by certain users and a method of interacting with repository supporting such structure. The browsing approach we propose uses Formal Concept Analysis (FCA) [10]. Here FCA is used for dynamic clustering and browsing for document retrieval. It results in an organizational structure that can support searching for documents adaptable to a particular community profile. This approach enables search for similar or new documents while dynamically modifying the original search criteria.

2   Some Individuals Share Your Information Needs

Boolean search cannot naturally locate resources relevant to a specific topic. An alternative approach is to deduce the category of user queries. Situations where search is limited within a group of documents qualified by search participants as 'interesting' illustrate a *category* that is relevant to the user's information needs. The key questions are: *what type of category related information is valuable and practical at the same time, how to infer that category information, and how to use it for improving the search results*?

Our method for topic/category identification is based on observations of the searching behavior of large groups of users. The basic intuition is that a topic of interest can be determined by identifying a collection of documents (articles) that is of common interest to a sufficiently large group of users. The assumption is that if a sufficient number of users $u_1, u_2, ..., u_m$ driven by their interest are searching independently for a collection of documents $a_1, a_2, ..., a_n$, then this is an evidence that there is a topic of interest shared by all users $u_1, u_2, ..., u_m$. The collection of documents $a_1, a_2, ..., a_n$ characterizes the topic of interest associated with that group of users. While the observation on a single user who demonstrates interest in objects $a_1, a_2, ..., a_n$ is not an entirely reliable judgment, the identification of a group of users along with a collection of documents satisfying the relation *interested_in(u_i, a_j)* is a more reliable and accurate indicator of an existing topic of interest.

More conventional topical indicators of scientific literature are the place of publication (the place of presentation). These descriptors when available can support queries of the type "find similar" or "find new" documents from this topic. For example, all papers presented in the recent ECAI conferences are similar with respect to the papers qualified as AI conference papers. Yet the papers of European Conference on Artificial Intelligence - ECAI 2002 might be new for some of the AI researches. Thus a request "find new" depends on how informed on a particular topic is the individual submitting the request. For scientists the term "similar" might have several still traceable dimensions. For instance:

- Two papers are similar if both are presented at the same conference (same session);
- Two papers are similar if both are published in the same journal (same section);
- Two papers are similar if both steam from the same project.

That type of similarity suggests a browsing interaction – where user is able to scan ad hoc topics for similar or new materials. Assume that each collection of papers identified by the relation *interested_in(u_i, a_j)* is further partitioned following its publication (presentation) attributes. Assume next that user u_i is able to retrieve the collection of documents $a_1, a_2, ..., a_n$ and then able to browse the journals and conferences of interests. The place and time of publications not only provide attribute values that allow a collection $a_1, a_2, ..., a_n$ to be arranged by place and year of publication. In addition journal and conference names provide lexical material for generating meaningful name of the collection. They suggest also useful links for search for similar or new documents.

The web is changing the way that researchers access scientific literature. The amount of scientific information and the number of electronic libraries on the Internet continues to increase [8]. In a practical perspective the proposed approach for identifying a topic of interest is particularly appropriate for *specialized* search engines and electronic libraries. First, specialized search engines (electronic libraries) are used for retrieving information within specified fields. For example, "*NEC ResearchIndex*" (http://citeseer.nj.nec.com/cs) is a powerful search engine for computer science research papers. As a result, the number of users of specialized search engines is considerably smaller compared to the number of users of general-purpose search engines. Second, specialized search engines use some advanced strategies to retrieve documents. Hence the result list provides typically a good indication of the document content. Therefore, when a user clicks on one of the documents the chances to get relevant information are generally high.

The question is: *how to gather realistic document usability information over some portion of the Web (database)?* One of the most popular ways to get Web usability data is to examine the logs that are saved on servers. A server generates an entry in the log file each time it receives a request from a client. The kinds of data that it logs are: the IP address of the requester; the date and time of the request; the name of the file being requested; and the result of the request. Thus by using log files it is possible to capture rich information on visiting activities, such as who the visitors are and what they are specifically interested in and use it for user-oriented clustering in information retrieval.

The following assumptions provide a ground for the proposed framework. We assume that all users are reliably identifiable across multiple visits to a site. We assume further that if a user (saves/selects) a document it is likely that the document is relevant to the query or to the user's current information needs. Another assumption is that all relevant data of user logs are available and that from the large set of user logs we can extract a set of relations of the type: *(user_id, selected_document)*. The next step is to derive from the extracted set of relations meaningful collections of documents based on overlapping user interests, that is, to cluster the extracted data set into groups of users with matching groups of documents. The last assumption is that within each group documents can be organized according to the place and time of publication/presentation.

3   Lattices for Information Retrieval

In most FCA applications for document classification documents correspond to objects and the keywords of the document constitute attribute sets. Instead of using keywords as attributes, we use the set of users U expressing interest in a document as a characterization of that document. This enables us to explicate not evident relationship between collection of document and groups of users. In contrast to keywords this type of characterization of documents exploits implicit properties of documents. We will denote the documents (articles) in a given collection with the letter A. Individual members of this collection are denoted by a_1, a_2 etc., while subsets are written as A_1, A_2. We will denote the group of users searching the collection with the letter U. Individual users are denoted by u_1, u_2 etc., while subsets are written as U_1, U_2.

Given a set of users U, a set of documents A and a binary relation *uIa* (user u is interested in article a) we generate a classification of documents such that each class can be seen as (ad hoc) topic with respect to a group of users $U_1 \in Pow(U)$ interested in documents $A_1 \in Pow(A)$. Documents share a group of users and users share a collection of documents based on the users interest

$$A_1 = \{a \in A \mid (\forall u \in U_1) \, uIa\}$$

$$U_1 = \{u \in U \mid (\forall a \in A_1) \, uIa\},$$

Within the theory of *Formal Concept Analysis* [10] the relation between objects and their attributes is called *context (U,A,I)*. The *extent* of a concept is formed by all objects to which the concept applies and the *intent* consists of all attributes existing in those objects.

Definition. *Let $C = (U,A,I)$ be a context. $c = (U_1,A_1)$ is called a concept of C if $\alpha(A_1)=\{u \in U | (\forall a \in A_1) \ uIa\} = U_1$ and $\omega(U_1) =\{a \in A | (\forall u \in U_1) \ uIa\} = A_1$. $\pi_A(c) = A_1$ and $\pi_U(c)=U_1$ are called c's extent and intent, respectively. The set of all concepts of C is denoted by $B(C)$.*

We may think of the set of articles A_u associated with a given user $u \in U$ as represented by a bit vector. Each bit i corresponds to a possible article $a_i \in A$ and is on or off depending on whether the user u is interested in article a_i. We can generate a classification of documents such that each class can be seen as a topic (category) described by the shared user interest. Accordingly we can characterize the relation between the set of users and the set of articles in terms of *topic lattice*. To build a topic lattice we need to find the subtopic-supertopic relationship between topics. This is formalized by

$$(U_1, A_1) \leq (U_2, A_2) \leftrightarrow U_1 \subseteq U_2 \text{ or } (U_1, A_1) \leq (U_2, A_2) \leftrightarrow A_1 \supseteq A_2.$$

As a consequence, a topic uniquely relates a set of documents with a set of attributes (users): for a topic the set of documents implies the corresponding set of attributes and vice versa. Therefore a topic may be presented by its document set or attribute set only. This relationship holds in general for conceptual hierarchies: more general concepts have fewer defining attributes in their intension but more objects in their extension and vice versa. The set $C=(U,A,I)$ along with the "$\leq$" relation form a partially ordered set that can be characterized by a *concept lattice* (referred here as *topic lattice*). Each node of the topic lattice is a pair composed of a subset of articles and a subset of corresponding users. In each pair the subset of users contains just the users sharing interest to the subset of articles and similarly the subset of articles contains just the articles sharing overlapping interest from the matching subset of users. The set of pairs is ordered by the standard "set inclusion" relation applied to the set of articles and to the set of users that describe each pair. The partially ordered set can be represented by a Hasse diagram, in which an edge connects two nodes if and only if they are comparable and there is no other node - intermediate topic in the lattice, i.e. each topic is linked to its maximally specific more general topics and to its maximally general more specific topics. The ascending paths represent the subtopic-supertopic relation.

Table 1. A partial representation of the relation u_i is interested in a_j

	a_1	a_2	a_3	a_4	a_5	a_6	a_7	a_8
u_1	1	1	1	1	1	1	1	1
u_2	1	1	1	1	1	0	1	0
u_3	1	0	0	0	0	1	0	1
u_4	0	1	0	0	1	0	1	0
u_5	0	0	1	1	0	0	1	0
u_6	1	0	1	1	0	0	1	0
u_7	0	0	0	0	1	0	1	0
u_8	0	0	0	0	0	1	0	1
.	.	.	.	.	.	.	.	.

The topic lattice shows the commonalities between topics and generalization/specialization between them. The bottom topic is defined by the set of all users; the top topic is defined by all articles and the group of users (possibly none) sharing interest in them. A simple example of users and their interest to documents is presented in (Tab. 1). The corresponding lattice is presented in (Fig. 1).

4   Navigating the Topic Lattice

Different categories of users are driven by different motivations when searching for documents. Scholars typically search for new or inspiring scientific literature. In such cases keywords cannot always guide the search. In addition the term *new* depends on who is the individual and how current is she with the available literature. Novices or inexperienced researchers may also face some problems trying to get to a good starting point. Typical questions for newcomers in the field are:

Which are the most significant works in the field?
Which are the newest yet interesting papers in the field.
Which are the topics directly related to a given topic?
Which are the most active researchers in the field?

In effect general purpose search engines do not provide support for such type of questions.

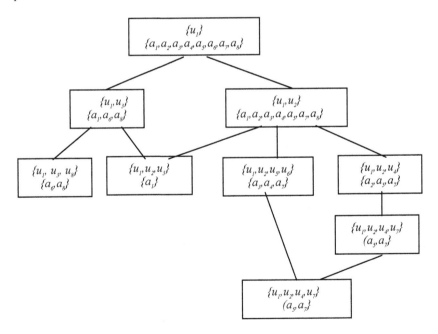

Fig. 1. A topic lattice generated from the relation represented in Table 1.

The current standard information retrieval methods are: keyword search and *hierarchical classification*. In the second method, searches are done by browsing directories organized as a hierarchy of subject categories. A hierarchical topical structure as the one described in the previous section presents some features that support browsing retrieval task: topics are indexed through their descriptors (users) and are linked based on general/specific relation. User can jump from one topic to another in the lattice; the transition to other topics is driven by the Hasse diagram. Each node in the lattice can be seen as query formed by specifying a group of users, with the retrieved documents defining the result. The lattice supports navigation from more specific to general or general to specific queries. Another characteristic is that the lattice allows gradual enlargement or refinement of a query. Following edges departing downward (upward) from a query produces refinements (enlargements) of the query with respect to a particular collection of documents.

Consider a context $C = (U,A,I)$. Each attribute $u \in U$ and object $a \in A$ has a uniquely determined defining topic. The defining topic can directly be calculated from the attribute u or article a and need not to be searched in the lattice based on the following property.

Definition. *Let $C=(U,A,I)$ be a concept lattice. The defining topic of an attribute $u \in U$ (object $a \in A$) is the greatest (smallest) topic c such that $u \in \pi_U(c)$ ($a \in \pi_A(c)$) holds.*

This suggests the following strategy for navigation. A user $u \in U$ starts her search from the greatest topic c_l such that $u \in \pi_U(c_l)$, i.e. from the greatest collection of articles interesting to u. User navigates from topic to topic in the lattice, each topic representing the current query. Gradual refinement of the query may be accomplished by successfully choosing child topics and gradual enlargement by choosing parent topics. This enables a user to control the amount of output obtained from a query. A gradual shift of the topic may be accomplished by choosing sibling topics. Thus a user u searches for documents walking through the "topical" hierarchy guided by the relevance of the topics with respect to her current interest. Decisions on the topics to be examined next are supported by their relations to the current topic c_l. If no other evidence, user can browse neighboring topics c_i when they maximize certain similarity measure with the topic c_l. A simple solution is to measure similarity based on the number of overlapping users of $c_l = (U_l, A_l)$ and $c_i = (U_i, C_i)$. Thus the browsing behavior will be guided by the magnitude $t= |U_l \cap U_i|$. We create a topic lattice using users and documents as an outer structure and scale up with other attributes into a nested structure. The nested structure is associated with the current topic of the outer structure, where the nested attributes are place of publication and year.

The defining concept property suggests also an alternative navigation strategy *guided by articles*. Assume that browsing through the topic lattice user u finds article a interesting to her and wants to see some articles similar to a, that is, articles sharing user's interest with a. Then exploiting the *defining concept property* the user u can jump to the smallest topic such that $a \in \pi_A(c)$, that is, to the minimal collection containing a, and may resume the search from this point by exploring the neighboring topics.

Our supporting conjecture for such type of navigation is that a new document a topically close to documents A_m that are interesting to a user u is also interesting with high probability. More precisely, if a user u is interested in documents A_m, then a document a interesting to her peers U_n ($a \in A_n$ such that $A_n \supseteq A_m$ ($U_n \subseteq U_m$), and $a \notin A_m$) is also relevant. Thus articles $a \in A_n$ that are *new* to the user u and relevant by our conjecture should be ranked higher with respect to the user u. Therefore in terms of the concept lattice the search domain relevant to the user $u \in U_m$ includes a subset of articles to which other members (i.e., U_k) of the group U_m have demonstrated interest. These are collections of articles A_k of the topic (U_k, A_k), such that $u \notin U_k \subseteq U_n \neq \emptyset$. This strategy supports an exploration exploiting topical structure in a collection of documents. It reflects a challenging problem related to recourse exploration: how to maintain collections of articles that are representative of the topic and may be used as a starting points for exploration.

Navigation implies notions of place, being in a place and going to another place. A notion of neighborhood helps specifying the other place, relative to the place one is currently in. Assume that a user u is in topic c_1, such that $c_p = (U_p, A_p)$ is a parent topic and $c_2 = (U_2, A_2), ..., c_k = (U_k, A_k)$ are the sibling topics, i.e. $U_i \supseteq U_p$, $i = 1, 2, ..., k$. To support user orientation while browsing we provide the following similarity measurement. Each link (c_p, c_i) from the parent topic c_p to c_i is associated with two weights W_i and w_i *absolute* and *relative* weight respectively computed according to the following formulae $W_i = |U_i|$ and $w_i = |U_i| / |U_1 + U_2 + ... + U_k|$, $i = 1, 2, ..., k$. In addition to these quantitative measures each node is associated with a name derived from the place of publication. These names serve as qualitative qualifiers of a topic relative to the other topic names.

The following is a summary of the navigation strategy derived from the above considerations. The decision for the next browsing steps are based on the articles in the current topic and on the weights (W/w) associated with the sibling nodes. User $u \in U$ starts from the greatest topic c_1 identified by her defining group $U_1 = \pi_U(c_1)$. Arriving at node (U_k, A_k) user u can either refine, enlarge the search or select a new topic from the neighborhood of the current topic. These decisions correspond to choosing a *descendant, a parent* or a *sibling* topic from the available list; any descendant topic refines the query and shrinks gradually the result to a non empty set of selected documents. The user refines the query by choosing a sequence of one or more links. As a result the number of selected documents and remaining links decreases. Correspondingly, the user enlarges the query by choosing a sequence of parent topics. In contrast, selecting a sibling topic will result in browsing a collection of articles not seen by that user but rated as interesting by some of her peers. These three types of navigations are guided by the relations between user groups such as set inclusion and set intersection as well as by topic names similarity. The next type of navigation exploits the defining topic property of an object. By selecting an article a from topic $c_i = (U_i, A_i)$, user is enable to navigate to the minimal collection containing the article a, that is to jump to the smallest topic c such that $A_k = \pi_A(c)$, $A_k \subseteq A_i$. In general traversing the hierarchy in search of documents supported by topic lattice can be viewed as sequence of browsing steps through the topics, reflecting a sequence of applications of the four navigation strategies. Once topic is selected then user can search for papers browsing the corresponding regions associated with place and time of publication.

This approach allows users to jump into a hierarchy at a meaningful starting point and quickly navigate to the most useful information. It also allows users to easily find and peruse related concepts, which is especially helpful if users are not sure what they want.

5 Topic Lattice Features

It is essential to be able to incrementally construct a topic lattice by adding new documents and users. The change of the lattice structure complies with the following assumptions. A collection of articles A_l from an existing topic (U_l, A_l) can only be expanded. This is implied by the conjecture that documents, qualified as interesting by user u do not change their status. Therefore, an expansion of the collection of articles with respect to a topic (U_l, A_l) will not impose any change of existing links. Indeed, an expansion of A_l to A'_l results in an expansion of all parent (descendent) collections A_m, A_n, such that $A_l \subseteq A_m \subseteq A_n$ i.e. from $A_l \subseteq A'_l \rightarrow A'_m \subseteq A'_n$ and therefore $(U_n, A_n) \leq (U_m, A_m) \rightarrow (U'_n, A'_n) \leq (U'_m, A'_m)$. Analogous relations hold with ancestor nodes. That is, an expansion of an existing collection of articles preserves the structure of the lattice.

Lattices are superior to tree hierarchies which can be embedded into lattices, because they have the property that for every set of elements there exists a unique lowest upper bound (join) and a unique greatest lower bound (meet). In lattice structure there are many paths to a particular topic. This facilitates recovery from bad decision made while traversing the hierarchy in search of documents. Lattice structure provides ability to deal with non-disjoint concepts.

One of the main factors in a page ranking strategy involves the location and frequency of keywords in a Web page. Another factor is link popularity - the total number of sites that link to a given page. However, present page rank algorithms typically do not take into account the current user and specifically her interests. Assume that we have partitioned users into groups associated with their topics of interest (as collections of documents). A modified ranking algorithm can be obtained by extending the present strategy with an additional factor involving the number of links to and from a topic associated with a given user. In this case the page ranking strategy takes into consideration user's interest encoded in the number and the levels of links to a topic associated with a given user. Thus, for a user $u \in U_l$, where (U_l, A_l) is a topic, the page rank of an article a depends on the linkage structure to the articles $a_i \in A_l$ representing the topic of interest of user u. We can interpret a link from article a_i to article a as a vote of article a_i for article a. Thus votes cast by article that are from the users topic weigh more heavily and help to make other pages 'more-important'. This strategy makes page-ranking *user oriented*. Such a strategy promotes pages related to users' topics of interest. From an "active users" perspective this approach enables us to recognize a community of users for which a given article is most likely to be interesting.

By incorporating navigation into a search framework based on keyword descriptors one can provide an opportunity for different modes of interaction that may be integrated on combined retrieval space. The topic lattice suggests also a partially ordering relation $(\prec)$ for ranking articles returned in response to a keyword request from a user u. Assume that c_0 is the greatest topic such tat $u \in U_0 = \pi_U(c_0)$. Then $a_1 \prec a_2$ if there exist topics c_1 and c_2, $a_1 \in \pi_A(c_1)$, $a_2 \in \pi_A(c_2)$, such that $|\pi_U(c_1) \cap U_0| < |\pi_U(c_2) \cap U_0|$, i.e. the more members of the group U_0 have expressed an interest in a given article the better. This ordering is based on the number of users that has expressed interest in a document. That implies that all articles that originate from the same topic are lumped into one rank.

At more fundamental level, the value of FCA for information retrieval is based on the assumption that when user enters a lattice at certain topic, but the document retrieved are not appropriate, then these documents will be associated with some attributes that will eventually lead you to the desired documents. This is a central but hidden assumption in proposing that a lattice browsing scheme will have advantages over hierarchical approach [6]. In a hierarchical scheme user simply go back to the top and start again. With a lattice approach user assumes that there are other features of the retrieved documents (sub-group of users) that will also occur in the document she really wants to retrieve.

6   Related Works and Conclusion

This paper has taken a step in the direction of finding an approach to a web-based information retrieval system aimed at specialized domains. In this work we propose to incorporate the community profiling with the search process. It has long been recognized in the context of information retrieval that most searches are a combination of direct and browsing retrieval and as a such, a system should provide both possibilities in an integrated and coherent interface [5]. The most challenging test of the information retrieval methods is their application to the Web. The focus of the current efforts of the Web research community is mainly on optimizing the search, assuming active users vs. passive information.

Recently there has been much interest in supporting users through collecting Web pages related to a particular topic [3, 9]. These approaches typically exploit connectivity for topic identification but not for community identification. Community identification does not play any significant roles in these methods and therefore user search experience within a community typically is ignored. Some systems do exploit the experience of Web surfers to derive clustered topical interests but the focus is on organizing surfing history in coherent topics for later use. The problem of identifying community structure was addressed in [7]. However, the approach employed for community identification is based on analysis of the Web graph structure and is not explicitly intended to support resource discovery. In collaborative filtering systems [1] items are recommended on the basis of user similarity rather than object similarity. Each target user is associated with a set of nearest neighbor users (by comparing their profiles) who act as 'recommendation partners'. In contrast, in our approach users' similarity is used to build a topical hierarchy supporting search for matching topics of interests. A derived benefit of such an approach is that it discloses some implicit relations in documents (such as author's intention) that can guide a search for matching topics of interest. Lattices are appealing as a means of representing conceptual hierarchies in information retrieval systems because of some formal lattice properties. Applied to information retrieval they represent inverse relationship between document sets and query terms. In [4] formal concept analysis is applied to capture the notion of context in information retrieval. Unlike traditional systems that use simple keyword matching, [8] is able to track and recommend topically relevant papers even when keyword based query fails. This is made possible through the use of a profile to represent user interests. Our framework is close in spirit to the application of Galois' concept lattices [2] where each document is described by exactly those terms that are attached to nodes that are above the document node. However in our approach the grouping of documents into classes is based on dynamic descriptors associated with users conducting search on a regular basis.

Domain-specific information retrieval typically depends on general search engines which make no use of user's areas of interest and require a user to look at a linear display of loosely organized search results or hand crafted specialized systems. The later systems are with a better browsing interface but are generally costly to build and maintain. In our approach *category identification* is part of *community formation* and is based on automatic identification of communities with clustered topical interests.

The particular objective of the work described here is to develop a framework supporting browsing mechanism where the search process can be accomplished within the context of a community or point of view. The framework exploits topic lattice generated from a collection of documents associated with users demonstrating interest in those documents and playing a role of descriptors. Due to its dual nature, the lattice allows two complimentary navigation styles that are based either on attributes or on objects. Topic lattice capturing users' interest suggests navigation that may be an attractive alternative to specialized domain information retrieval.

References

1. Balabanovich, M., and Shoham Y. 1997. Content-based Collaborative Recommendation. *Communications of the ACM* 40(3): 66-72.
2. Carpineto, C., and Romano, G. 1996. A Lattice Conceptual Clustering System and Its Application to Browsing Retrieval. *Machine Learning* 24: 95-122.
3. Chakrabarti, S., van den Berg, M., and Dom, B. 1999. Focused Crawling: a New Approach to Topic-specific Web Resource Discovery. In *Proceedings of the Eight International World Wide Web Conference*, Toronto, Canada, 545-562.
4. Dichev Ch, Dicheva D., Deriving Context Specific Information on the Web, *Proc. of The WebNet 2001*, Orlando, pp. 296-301.
5. Godin R., Missaoui R., April A. Experimental Comparison of Navigation in a Galois Lattice with Conventional Information Retrieval Methods. *Int. Journal of Man-Machine Studies 38(5):747-767* (1993).
6. Kim M., Compton P. A Web-based browsing mechanism based on conceptual structure. *Proc. of The 9th ICCS 2001*, California, 2001, pp 47-60.
7. Kumar, R., Raghavan, P., Rajagopalan, S., and Tomkins, A. 1999. Trawling the Web for Emerging Cyber-communities. In *Proc. of the Eight Int. World Wide Web Conference*, Toronto, 403-415.
8. Lawrence S., Giles C. L. Searching the Web: general and scientific information access IEEE Communications, 37(1):116-122, 1999.
9. Menczer F., R. Belew: Adaptive Retrieval Agents: Internalizing Local Context and Scaling up to the Web. Machine Learning Journal 39 (2/3): 203-242, 2000.
10. Wille, R. 1982. Restructuring Lattice Theory: An Approach Based on Hierarchies of Concepts. In: I. Rival (ed.): *Ordered Sets*. Reidel, Dordrecht-Boston, 445-470.

Adapting a Robust Multi-genre NE System for Automatic Content Extraction

Diana Maynard[1], Hamish Cunningham[1], Kalina Bontcheva[1], and
Marin Dimitrov[2]

[1] Dept of Computer Science, University of Sheffield
211 Portobello St, Sheffield, UK S1 4DP
{diana,hamish,kalina}@dcs.shef.ac.uk
http://nlp.shef.ac.uk
[2] Sirma AI Ltd, Ontotext Lab
38A Hristo Botev Blvd, Sofia 1000, Bulgaria
marin@sirma.bg

Abstract. Many current information extraction systems tend to be designed with particular applications and domains in mind. With the increasing need for robust language engineering tools which can handle a variety of language processing demands, we have used the GATE architecture to design MUSE - a system for named entity recognition and related tasks. In this paper, we address the issue of how this general-purpose system can be adapted for particular applications with minimal time and effort, and how the set of resources used can be adapted dynamically and automatically. We focus specifically on the challenges of the ACE (Automatic Content Extraction) entity detection and tracking task, and preliminary results show promising figures.

Keywords: information extraction, named entity recognition, robust NLP

1 Introduction

Most Information Extraction (IE) systems are designed to extract fixed types of information from documents in a specific language and domain [4,1,5]. To increase suitability for end-user applications, IE systems need to be easily customisable to new domains [17]. Driven largely by US Government initiatives such as TIPSTER [3] and MUC [18], work on IE, and in particular on named entity recognition (NE), has largely focused on narrow subdomains, such as newswires about terrorist attacks (MUC-3 and MUC-4), and reports on air vehicle launches (MUC-7). In many applications, however, the type of document and domain may be unknown, or a system may be required which will process different types of documents without the need for tuning.

Many existing IE systems have been successfully tuned to new domains and applications - either manually or semi-automatically – but there have been few advances in tackling the problem of making a single system robust enough to

D. Scott (Ed.): AIMSA 2002, LNAI 2443, pp. 264–273, 2002.

forego this need. It is well-known that the adaptation of existing systems to new domains is hindered by both ontology and rule bottlenecks. A substantial amount of knowledge is needed, and its acquisition and application are non-trivial tasks.

For systems to deal successfully with unknown or multiple types of source material, they must not only be able to cope with changes of domain, but also with changes of *genre*. By this we mean different forms of media (e.g. emails, transcribed spoken text, written text, web pages, output of OCR recognition), text type (e.g. reports, letters, books, lists), and structure (e.g. layout options). The genre of a text may therefore be influenced by a number of factors, such as author, intended audience and degree of formality. For example, less formal texts may not follow standard capitalisation, punctuation or even spelling formats. Most IE systems require manual tuning in order to deal with these different kinds of texts; however, we have developed a system which uses NE technology to detect different text types, and then automatically fires different processing resources depending on the text.

We first describe the default system in Section 2 below. We then describe in Section 3 the background for our work, namely the ACE program. We continue in Section 4 with the challenges posed by ACE, and how the system has been adapted, using the GATE technology, to overcome them. In Section 5 we discuss some aspects of evaluation in IE, and give details of preliminary results with the ACE system. Finally in Section 6 we summarise the approach used and discuss some ongoing improvements to the system.

2   The MUSE System for Named Entity Recognition

The MUSE system (MUlti-Source Entity finder) [14] has been developed within GATE, a General Architecture for Text Engineering [6,7], which is an architecture, framework and development environment for language processing research and development.

MUSE is based on ANNIE, A Nearly-New IE system, which comes as part of the standard (freely available) GATE package. Figure 1 depicts a full IE pipeline based on a LaSIE[1] backend with ANNIE shallow analysis.

The MUSE system comprises a version of ANNIE's main processing resources: tokeniser, sentence splitter, POS tagger, gazetteer, finite state transduction grammar and orthomatcher. The resources communicate via GATE's annotation API, which is a directed graph of arcs bearing arbitrary feature/value data, and nodes rooting this data into document content (in this case text).

The **tokeniser** splits text into simple tokens, such as numbers, punctuation, symbols, and words of different types (e.g. with an initial capital, all upper case, etc.). It does not need to be modified for different applications or text types.

The **sentence splitter** is a cascade of finite-state transducers which segments the text into sentences. This module is required for the tagger. Both the splitter and tagger are domain and application-independent.

---

[1] the original IE system developed within the first version of GATE

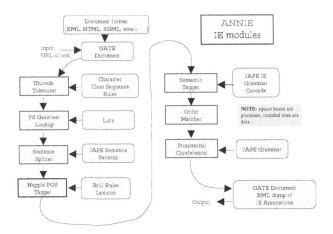

Fig. 1. ANNIE, A Nearly-New IE system

The **tagger** is a modified version of the Brill tagger, which adds a part-of-speech tag as a feature to each Token annotation. Neither the splitter nor the tagger are a mandatory part of the NE system, but the annotations they produce can be used by the semantic tagger (described below), in order to increase its power and coverage.

The **gazetteer** consists of lists such as cities, organisations, days of the week, etc. It contains some entities, but also names of useful key words, such as company designators (e.g. 'Ltd.'), titles, etc. The lists are compiled into finite state machines, which can match text tokens.

The **semantic tagger** (or JAPE transducer) consists of hand-crafted rules written in the JAPE pattern language [8], which describe patterns to match and annotations to be created. Patterns can be specified by describing a specific text string or annotation (e.g. those created by the tokeniser, gazetteer, document format analysis, etc.).

The **orthomatcher** performs co-reference, or entity tracking, by recognising relations between entities. It also has a secondary role in improving NE recognition by assigning annotations to previously unclassified names, based on relations with existing entities.

3   The ACE Program

The ACE program aims to encourage the development of robust NLP applications, by promoting faster system development from given linguistic resources, which encourages the development of general purpose retargetable systems, using a variety of methods from richly annotated corpora. It also aims to promote the design of more general purpose linguistic resources, and the development of general purpose standalone systems.

The ACE entity detection and tracking (EDT) task goes beyond existing NE tasks, in that all mentions of an entity (in the form of a name, description or pronoun) must be recognised and classified (based on reference to the same entity). The aim is to produce structured information about entities, events, and relations among them. Although, as with MUC, the texts to be used for the tasks are newswires, the scope of the task is widened by measuring results not only on standard written texts, but also on texts produced from automatic speech recognition (ASR) and optical character recognition (OCR) output. ACE focuses on the core extraction challenge however, rather than on ASR or OCR algorithms.

The ACE Program aims to create a powerful new generation of algorithms capable of extracting information accurately and robustly from human language data, and to represent that information in a form suitable for subsequent automatic analysis. Potential uses of ACE output include more precise forms of information retrieval, data mining, and the development of large knowledge bases.

3.1   The Entity Detection and Tracking (EDT) Task

The EDT task is divided into the following 5 recognition subtasks:

- entities (Person, Organization, Location, Facility and GPE[2]);
- entity attributes: type (Name, Nominal or Pronominal);
- entity mentions [optional] - entity tracking (similar to co-reference);
- mention roles [optional] - for GPEs, each mention has an optional role associated with it (Person, Organization, Location or GPE);
- mention extents [optional] - detection of the whole NP span, rather than just the head.

One of the main differences between ACE and MUC is that where MUC dealt with the *linguistic* analysis of text, ACE deals with the *semantic* analysis of text. Discussion of how the system was adapted to perform this deeper level of analysis can be found in Section 4.

3.2   Data

The ACE tasks are carried out on the following types of input data:

- Text from newswire
- (Degraded) text produced from broadcast news by ASR
- (Degraded) text produced from newspapers by OCR
- Clean versions of text produced from broadcast news
- Clean versions of text produced from newspapers

Unlike in MUC, where the texts were all related to a specific domain, the ACE news texts encompass a wide variety of domains, such as sport, politics, religion, popular culture, etc.

---

[2] Geo-Political Entity (essentially, any kind of location which has a government, such as a city or country)

3.3 Participation

The University of Sheffield team has been participating in the ACE program, and has therefore faced the challenge of adapting the core MUSE system to deal specifically with the ACE tasks. We focus here on the EDT task, since we are not currently participating in the RDC (relation detection and characterisation) task.

4 Adapting MUSE to Perform EDT

The MUSE system is designed to process multiple types of text in a robust fashion, with minimal adaptation. However, it does require some tuning in order to deal with new applications where either the guidelines for entity recognition are different, or where new tasks are involved. In this section, we describe the adaptation of the MUSE system to build the ACE system, used to perform the EDT task. We describe the two parts of the task (named entity detection and tracking) separately.

Although the two tasks are considerably different from the MUSE basic NE task, the time and effort spent tuning the system was remarkably small, because of the robust design and flexible architecture of GATE. The ACE system is just one example of this: we have also implemented similar adaptations to build the HaSIE system for IE and summarisation from company reports [15], the OldBaileyIE system for information extraction from old English court reports [2], and the Romanian NE system [12], among others.

4.1 Named Entity Detection

There are a number of features of the EDT task that have required adaptation to the original MUSE system.

1. The entity types are different. MUSE recognises the standard MUC entity types of Person, Location, Organisation, Date, Time, Money and Percent, plus the additional entity types Address (including email, phone numbers, urls, etc.) and Identifier. ACE has the first three, plus the additional types Facility (which subsumes some entities previously belonging to the MUSE types Organisation and Location), and GPE, which subsumes some, but not all, entities from the MUSE types Person, Location and Organisation). This means that on the one hand, some entities are grouped together, and on the other hand, that finer distinctions are made (for example, the division into Location and GPE).

2. A word or string does not consistently belong to an entity type in the same way that it (usually) does in MUSE; for example, in ACE "English" could be annotated as a Person or Organization, depending on the situation. Contextual information and intended meaning are very important, and world knowledge, intuition or pragmatic information may be necessary to categorise a particular occurrence of an entity correctly.

3. Entities may be used metonymously. This means that they must also be classified as such, by means of the use of roles. A metonymous mention of an entity is given a literal and an intended role. For example, in *the museum announced its new exhibit*, the entity *museum* is a facility that houses art, but in this context it is being used to describe the organisation behind the museum, and the mention should therefore be annotated as having the literal role Facility and the Intended role Organisation.
4. For some domains, such as Sport, a string may have a different entity type. For example, names of cities and countries are often used to represent team names, and should therefore be annotated as Organisations and not GPEs.

Due to the modular nature of the GATE architecture, it is relatively straightforward to adapt processing resources such as the grammar and gazetteer lists of MUSE in order to deal with the first problem. Firstly, procedural and declarative knowledge in GATE are separate, which minimises the adaptation necessary. Secondly, within the processing resources, foreground and background information are largely distinguished, so that background knowledge (such as that required for the tokenisation, name matching etc.) can remain untouched and only foreground information (that which is very specific to the domain or application) needs to be modified. For example, changes can be made to specific parts of the grammar while ensuring that the remaining parts of the grammar will be unaffected. This is of enormous benefit in reducing the time and effort spent adapting the system to a new application.

To deal with different text types, we introduced a conditional controller mechanism, which enables the user to set up the chain of processing resources according to features found in the text. A JAPE transducer is first run over the text to determine its type, by identifying salient features of the document.

The transducer adds a feature to the document indicating its domain. The conditional controller is set up so that depending on the presence or absence of certain features (e.g. a "sport" feature), a processing resource can be fired or not. In this way, we can set the controller to fire, for example, a particular sports grammar if the sports feature is present, and a regular grammar if it is not. The sports grammar annotates certain locations as Organisations, whereas the regular grammar annotates them as GPEs. The same mechanism can also be used for dealing with any kind of metonymy: if certain features are detected in the text, we can set the controller to run certain extra grammars, or to omit existing ones. The firing of other resources such as gazetteer lists or POS taggers can also be handled in the same way.

4.2   Entity Tracking

The entity tracking part of the EDT task has required the construction of some entirely new components to the MUSE system, and some further adjustments to existing parts. The main problems for the system were detection of pronominal entity mentions, coreference of proper names, and anaphora resolution.

The detection of pronouns is quite straightforward, since MUSE already contains a POS tagger which enabled us to recognise them by simply making some minor additions to the JAPE grammars.

Recognising the name mentions (i.e. finding coreference chains between proper nouns) required use of the MUSE orthomatcher, with some minor modifications to ensure that the correct entity types were considered. For example, we added new rules to match locations with their respective adjectives (e.g. France and French), and we extended the rules for Organisations so that they also took care of matches between Facilities (since Facility was not an entity type used in MUSE).

Finding the pronominal mentions (anaphora resolution) required more extensive work in the form of an entirely new module, the pronominal coreference module, which was built using the JAPE formalism. The GATE framework provided the basis for this to be designed, developed and slotted into the architecture with minimum effort. Detailed analysis of the data revealed that a few simple rules could account for the vast majority of pronominal cases. For example, 80-85% of the occurrences of [he,his,she,her] referred to the closest person of the same gender in the same sentence, or, if unavailable, the closest preceding one. In most cases, they referred back to named entities rather than nominal references. Likewise, [it,its] are handled in the same way, but with scope restriction (because there are many nominals). Currently the rules do not allow for cataphora, but occurrences of these were rare. Pronouns occurring in quoted speech are handled by a separate grammar, and require slightly more complex rules. More details of the pronominal coreference module can be found in [9].

5   Evaluation

We have evaluated the ACE system using Precision and Recall, which we calculated using the evaluation facilities developed within GATE: the AnnotationDiff tool and the Benchmarking Tool. These are particularly useful not just as a final measure of performance, but as a tool to aid system development by tracking progress and evaluating the impact of changes as they are made. The evaluation tool (AnnotationDiff) enables automated performance measurement and visualisation of the results, while the benchmarking tool enables the tracking of a system's progress and regression testing.

5.1   The AnnotationDiff Tool

Gate's AnnotationDiff tool enables two sets of annotations on a document to be compared, in order to either compare a system-annotated text with a reference (hand-annotated) text, or to compare the output of two different versions of the system (or two different systems). For each annotation type, figures are generated for precision, recall, F-measure and false positives.

5.2   Benchmarking Tool

GATE's benchmarking tool differs from the AnnotationDiff in that it enables evaluation to be carried out over a whole corpus rather than a single document. It also enables tracking of the system's performance over time. Performance statistics are output for each text in the corpus, and overall statistics for the entire corpus, in comparison with a reference corpus.

5.3   Results

The latest evaluations for the ACE system scored 82-86% precision and recall, depending on the text type (newswire scored the highest, though it also had the most substitution errors[3] (7%). For detection of pronominal mentions (anaphora resolution) the recall was low (around 40%) but precision was high (83% for broadcast news, and slightly less for the other text types). The main reason for recall being low was that we currently do not attempt to identify all types of pronouns. Detection of name mentions was also high, with the precision for newswires at 93%, and a slightly lower score for the other text types.

5.4   Other Evaluation Metrics

The most commonly used evaluation metrics in IE - precision, recall, error rate and F-measure - all stem from the IR field, and consequently so does much of the literature on this topic, e.g. [19,13,11]. Typically in IR, people want to know how many relevant documents are to be found in the top N percent of the ranking. This is reflected well by the precision metric. In IE, however, people typically want to know for each entity type how many entities have been correctly recognised and classified. In IE therefore, the proportion of entities belonging to each type has an impact on the outcome of the evaluation, in a way that the proportion of relevant documents in the collection does not in IR. Evaluation mechanisms in IE can also be affected by the notion of *relative document richness*, i.e. the relative number of entities of each type to be found in a set of documents. For this reason, error rate is sometimes preferred in the IE field, because, unlike precision, it is not dependent on relative document richness.

5.5   Cost-Based Evaluation

Using error rate instead of precision and recall means, however, that the F-measure can no longer be used. An alternative method of getting a single bottom-line number to measure performance is the cost-based metric. This appears to be becoming a favourite with the DARPA competitions, such as TDT2 [10], and is the method used in ACE. The model stems from the field of economics, where the standard model "Time Saved Times Salary" measures the use of the direct salary cost to an organisation as a measure of the value [16].

Another advantage of this type of evaluation is that it enables the evaluation to be adapted depending on the user's requirements. A cost-based model

---

[3] where an entity was correctly detected but allocated the wrong entity type

characterises the performance in terms of the cost of the errors (or the value of the correct things, depending on whether you see the glass as half-empty or half-full). For any application, the relevant cost model is applied, and expected prior target statistics are defined.

For a cost-based error model, a cost would typically be associated with a miss and a false alarm, and with each category of result (e.g. recognising Person might be more important then recognising Date correctly). Expected costs of error would typically be based on probability (using a test corpus). This makes the assumption that a suitable test corpus is available, which has the same rate of entity occurrence (or is similar in content) to the evaluation corpus. If necessary, the final score can be normalised to produce a figure between 0 and 1, where 1 is a perfect score.

The official ACE evaluations are carried out using a cost-based function based on error rate, for the reasons described above. However, since these evaluations are closed (i.e. we are not able to divulge any results other than those of our system), it is not very informative to discuss these cost-based results in isolation, since a single value means little without direct comparison, and therefore we have given our results in terms of the more widely recognised Precision and Recall.

6   Conclusions

In this paper, we have described a robust general-purpose system for NE across different kinds of text, and its adaptation for use in a specific application, the ACE EDT task. We have shown that the flexibility and open design of the GATE architecture and MUSE system enables this kind of adaptation to be carried out with minimal time and effort. Approximately 8 person weeks were spent on the development of the coreference module (which was not ACE-specific, but intended for general use within GATE); 6 person weeks were spent on the adaptation, (including those modules developed specifically for ACE), and a further 2 person weeks on familiarisation with the task and guidelines.

The conditional controller mechanism enables the system to be adapted automatically and dynamically according to the characteristics of the text being processed. Current results are promising and we aim to improve on them in the near future, with modifications to coreference and metonymy, and the use of learning mechanisms for error corrections and ambiguity resolution.

References

1. D. Appelt. An Introduction to Information Extraction. *Artificial Intelligence Communications*, 12(3):161–172, 1999.
2. K. Bontcheva, D. Maynard, H.Saggion, and H. Cunningham. Using human language technology for automatic annotation and indexing of digital library content. In *submitted to European Conference on Digital Libraries*, 2002.
3. J. Cowie, L. Guthrie, W. Jin, W. Odgen, J. Pustejowsky, R. Wanf, T. Wakao, S. Waterman, and Y. Wilks. CRL/Brandeis: The Diderot System. In *Proceedings of Tipster Text Program (Phase I)*. Morgan Kaufmann, California, 1993.

4. J. Cowie and W. Lehnert. Information Extraction. *Communications of the ACM*, 39(1):80–91, 1996.
5. H. Cunningham. Information Extraction: a User Guide (revised version). Research Memorandum CS–99–07, Department of Computer Science, University of Sheffield, May 1999.
6. H. Cunningham. GATE, a General Architecture for Text Engineering. *Computers and the Humanities*, 36:223–254, 2002.
7. H. Cunningham, D. Maynard, K. Bontcheva, and V. Tablan. GATE: A framework and graphical development environment for robust NLP tools and applications. In *Proceedings of the 40th Anniversary Meeting of the Association for Computational Linguistics*, 2002.
8. H. Cunningham, D. Maynard, K. Bontcheva, V. Tablan, and C. Ursu. *The GATE User Guide*. http://gate.ac.uk/, 2002.
9. M. Dimitrov. *A Light-weight Approach to Coreference Resolution for Named Entities in Text*. MSc Thesis, University of Sofia, Bulgaria, 2002. http://www.ontotext.com/ie/thesis-m.pdf.
10. Jonathan G. Fiscus, George Doddington, John S. Garofolo, and Alvin Martin. Nist's 1998 topic detection and tracking evaluation (tdt2). In *Proc. of the DARPA Broadcast News Workshop*, Virginia, US, 1998.
11. W.B. Frakes and R. Baeza-Yates, editors. *Information retrieval, data structures and algorithms*. Prentice Hall, New York, Englewood Cliffs, N.J., 1992.
12. O. Hamza, V. Tablan, D. Maynard, C. Ursu, H. Cunningham, and Y. Wilks. Named Entity Recognition in Romanian. Technical report, Department of Computer Science, University of Sheffield, 2002. Forthcoming.
13. C.D. Manning and H. Schütze. *Foundations of Statistical Natural Language Processing*. MIT press, Cambridge, MA, 1999. Supporting materials available at http://www.sultry.arts.usyd.edu.au/fsnlp/ .
14. D. Maynard, V. Tablan, C. Ursu, H. Cunningham, and Y. Wilks. Named Entity Recognition from Diverse Text Types. In *Recent Advances in Natural Language Processing 2001 Conference*, Tzigov Chark, Bulgaria, 2001.
15. Diana Maynard, Kalina Bontcheva, Horacio Saggion, Hamish Cunningham, and Oana Hamza. Using a text engineering framework to build an extendable and portable IE-based summarisation system. In *Proceedings of the ACL Workshop on Text Summarisation*, 2002.
16. Peter Sassone. Cost-benefit methodology for office systems. *ACM Transactions on Office Information Systems*, 5(3):273–289, 1987.
17. S. Soderland. Learning to extract text-based information from the world wide web. *Proceedings of Third International Conference on Knowledge Discovery and Data Mining (KDD-97)*, 1997.
18. Beth Sundheim, editor. *Proceedings of the Sixth Message Understanding Conference (MUC-6)*, Columbia, MD, 1995. ARPA, Morgan Kaufmann.
19. Yiming Yang. An evaluation of statistical approaches to text categorization. *Journal of Information Retrieval*, 1:67–88, 1998.

The Semantic Web: A Killer App for AI?

Carole Goble

Information Management Group
Department of Computer Science
University of Manchester
Kilburn Bulding
Oxford Road
Manchester M13 9PL
UK
carole@cs.man.ac.uk
http://img.cs.man.ac.uk

Abstract. The Semantic Web is a vision to move the Web from a place where information is processed by humans to one where processing can be automated. Currently, AI seems to be making an impact on bringing the vision to reality. To add semantics to the web requires languages for representing knowledge. To infer relationships between resources or new facts requires web-scale automated reasoning. However, there is some skepticism in the web community that AI can be made "web appropriate" and work on a web scale. I will introduce the Semantic Web concept and give a number of examples of how AI has already contributed to its development, primarily through knowledge representation languages. I will explore the reasons why the Semantic Web is a challenging environment for AI. I will suggest that this could be a killer app for AI, but we must recognize that the web is a vast and untidy place, and only a combination of approaches will yield success.

The Web as a means for publishing and disseminating information to people is unprecedented. However, to access and interpret information necessitates human intervention. So the web is a place where humans do the processing and computers do the rendering.

The vision of the Semantic Web is to evolve the web to one where information and services are understandable and useable by computers as well as humans. Automated processing of web content requires explicit machine-processable semantics associated with those web resources.

To realise this vision is in some ways mundane and in others daunting, depending on your ambition. As McBride points out [1] simple metadata and simple queries give a small but not insignificant improvement in information integration. Others have more ambitious ideas of an environment where software agents are able to dynamically discover, interrogate and interoperate resources, building and disbanding virtual problem solving environments [2], discovering new facts, and performing sophisticated tasks on behalf of humans. The key point is

D. Scott (Ed.): AIMSA 2002, LNAI 2443, pp. 274–278, 2002.
© Springer-Verlag Berlin Heidelberg 2002

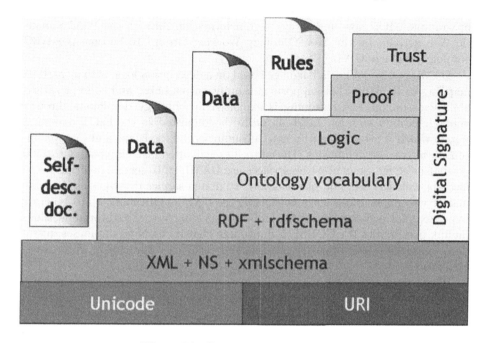

Fig. 1. The Semantic Web Layer Cake

to move from a web where semantics are embedded in hard-wired applications to one where semantics are explicit and available for automated inference.

The core technologies proposed for the Semantic Web have their roots in distributed systems, and information management, for example, the identity of resources, and the annotation of resources with metadata for subsequent querying. However, the greatest impact so far appears to have been made by AI. Ontologies will enable software agents to find the meaning of the content within web resources, and metadata attached to them by following hyperlinks to definitions of key terms. These definitions will be written using formal (logical) languages that facilitate automated reasoning.

Tim Berners-Lee's famous "layer cake" picture (seee Figure 1) puts ontologies, logic, proof and reasoning at the forefront of the Semantic Web vision. In 2001 the first Semantic Web Working Symposium was classified by Google as [Computers>Artificial Intelligence], and this year as [Science>Math>Logic and Foundations]. Similarly, semanticweb.org is classified as [Computers>Artificial Intelligence>Knowledge Representation].

Arguably the most successful example of the migration of AI techniques to the Semantic Web has been the DAML+OIL web ontology language [3]. DAML+OIL came out of various EU projects[1] and the USA DARPA DAML

---

[1] EU IST Ontoknowledge, UK EPSRC CAMELOT

programme[2]. It is now undergoing a transformation through the W3C Semantic Web activity by the Web Ontology Working Group[3] to become the W3C ontology language OWL.

DAML+OIL/OWL is a language based on a description logic with a (partial) mapping to RDF(S), that supports subsumption reasoning and concept satisfiability reasoning. The reasoning is exploited by ontology developers through ontology editors such as OilEd [4]. OilEd is connected to the FaCT reasoning engine which it uses to identify new subsumption relationships and discover inconsistent concept definitions. The editor has generated much interest, with 2500 downloads so far. Semantic web services use DAML+OIL service descriptions to discover web services, and use reasoning to match service descriptions [5,6]. Semantic web applications such as COHSE use DAML+OIL mark up to generate hypertexts for people to navigate, and use reasoning to make editorial decisions on link possibilities [7]. COHSE is unusual in that it combines databases, metadata, ontologies, and open hypermedia,and recognises the role of Web in the Semantic Web.

There are many other prospects for AI techniques. For example: semantic web services are recast as variations of agent negotiation [8], planning and rule based systems [9]; machine learning is used for emergent metadata and ontologies [10]; ontology development, evolution, merging draws upon knowledge acquisition and knowledge representation.

However, viewing the web as just an application of technologies to hand misses the point. The web was successful because it scaled, and it scaled because it challenged fundamental assumptions of the hypertext community. To bring ontologies, or any other AI technology, to the web means making similar challenges. Apart from pointing out that the web is vast, so solutions have to scale, there are other points:

- The web is *here* – we have a legacy so we will have a mixed environment where some resources are "semantic" and some are just "web". We must have a clear and achievable migration path from non- semantic to semantic;
- The web is *democratic* – all are knowledge acquisition experts and all are knowledge modellers. I believe that there will in fact be islands of quality semantic webs for communities with high quality annotation, large and good quality ontologies and sound inference, afloat in a sea of low grade and volatile metadata, ontologies of variable quality and doubtful persistence (i.e. they won't always be there). The semantics associated with a resource will migrate up and down this continuum. High end semantic web applications will be few.
- The web *grows from the bottom*. Most people wrote their first HTML by editing someone elses. Perhaps the semantic web will arise from fragments of metadata and ontologies being copied in similar way. New concepts for ontologies will be produced "just in time" by annotators.

---

[2] http://www.daml.org
[3] http://www.w3.org/2001/sw/WebOnt/

- The web is *volatile and changeable* – resources appear and disappear, resources change. Ontologies change. What if a piece of metadata is grounded on a term in an ontology that no longer exists? How do we deal with an "Error 404" for terms?
- The web is *dirty* – there is no way to ensure consistency; provenance is unknown; or whether information is trustworthy. However, tolerance of error doesn't necessarily mean one should be oblivious to it;
- The web is *heterogeneous* – no one solution or one technology will be adopted; no one ontology will prevail; no one set of metadata will apply to a resource. Agreements are difficult; mappings and translations will be commonplace. This is not a single discipline issue: databases, hypermedia, library sciences, distributed computing all have a role to play.

McBride recently said "the perception that the semantic web is concerned with artificial intelligence is not helpful to its widespread adoption in the IT industry" [1]. Why would he say that? Perhaps it is the perception that the AI community promises much but doesn't deliver. Perhaps it's a belief that AI only works small scale and where there is control, completeness and correctness. The best way to dissuade doubters is to develop some practical applications and get them out there.

In this talk I will introduce the Semantic Web concept and give a number of examples of how AI has already contributed to its development, primarily through knowledge representation languages. These examples will include DAML+OIL and applications that use DAML+OIL. I will explore the reasons why the Semantic Web is a challenging environment for AI (and any other discipline). I will suggest that this could be a killer app for AI but we must recognize that the web is a vast and untidy place, and only a combination of approaches will yield success.

References

1. Brian McBride. Four Steps Towards the Widespread Adoption of a Semantic Web. Proceedings of 1st International Semantic Web Conference (ISWC2002), Springer-Verlag LNCS 23242, June 2002, pp: 419-422.
2. Tim Berners-Lee, James Hendler, Ora Lassila. The Semantic Web. Scientific American, May 2001, pp: 29-37
3. Ian Horrocks. DAML+OIL: a reason-able web ontology language. Proceedings of Extending Database Technology (EDBT2002), Springer-Verlag LNCS Vol.2287 March 2002, pp: 2–13
4. Sean Bechhofer, Ian Horrocks, Carole Goble, Robert Stevens. OilEd: a Reasonable Ontology Editor for the Semantic Web. Proceedings of KI2001, Joint German/Austrian conference on Artificial Intelligence, September 2001 Vienna. Springer-Verlag LNAI Vol. 2174, pp: 396–408.
5. Chris Wroe, Robert Stevens, Carole Goble, Angus Roberts, Mark Greenwood. A suite of DAML+OIL Ontologies to Describe Bioinformatics Web Services and Data Submitted to Journal of Cooperative Information Systems.

6. David Trastour, Claudio Bartolini, Chris Preist. Semantic Web Support for the Business-to-Business E-Commerce Lifecycle. Proceedings The Eleventh International World Wide Web Conference (WWW2002). pp: 89-98 (2002)

7. Leslie Carr, Sean Bechhofer, Carole Goble, Wendy Hall. Conceptual Linking: Ontology-based Open Hypermedia, Proceedings Tenth World Wide Web Conference (WWW10) , Hong Kong, May 2001.

8. Terry Payne, Rahul Singh and Katia Sycara. Browsing Schedules - An Agent-Based Appoach to Navigating the Semantic Web. Proceedings of 1st International Semantic Web Conference (ISWC2002), Springer-Verlag LNCS 23242, June 2002 pp: 469-474

9. Srini Narayanan and Sheila McIraith. Simulation, Verification and Automated Composition of Web Services Proceedings of Eleventh International World Wide Web Conference (WWW2002), May 2002, pp: 77-88

10. Alexander Maedche and Steffen Staab. Ontology Learning for the Semantic Web. IEEE Intelligent Systems vol 16 no 2, 2001, pp: 72-79

Author Index

Lecture Notes in Artificial Intelligence (LNAI)

Lecture Notes in Computer Science